D1715924

Dante's Pluralism and the Islamic
Philosophy of Religion

Montante Family Library
D'Youville College

DANTE'S PLURALISM AND THE ISLAMIC PHILOSOPHY OF RELIGION

Gregory B. Stone

DANTE'S PLURALISM AND THE ISLAMIC PHILOSOPHY OF RELIGION
© Gregory B. Stone, 2006.

All rights reserved. No part of this book may be used or reproduced in any manner whatsoever without written permission except in the case of brief quotations embodied in critical articles or reviews.

First published in 2006 by
PALGRAVE MACMILLAN™
175 Fifth Avenue, New York, N.Y. 10010 and
Houndmills, Basingstoke, Hampshire, England RG21 6XS
Companies and representatives throughout the world.

PALGRAVE MACMILLAN is the global academic imprint of the Palgrave Macmillan division of St. Martin's Press, LLC and of Palgrave Macmillan Ltd. Macmillan® is a registered trademark in the United States, United Kingdom and other countries. Palgrave is a registered trademark in the European Union and other countries.

ISBN 1–4039–7130–7

Library of Congress Cataloging-in-Publication Data

Stone, Gregory B., 1961–
    Dante's pluralism and the Islamic philosophy of religion /
Gregory B. Stone.
        p. cm.
    Includes bibliographical references and index.
    ISBN 1–4039–7130–7 (alk. paper)
        1. Dante Alighieri, 1265–1321. Divina commedia—Sources.
    2. Eschatology, Islamic, in literature. I. Title.

PQ4394S76 2006
851'.1—dc22   2005049547

A catalogue record for this book is available from the British Library.

Design by Newgen Imaging Systems (P) Ltd., Chennai, India.

First edition: April 2006

10 9 8 7 6 5 4 3 2 1

Printed in the United States of America.

PQ 4394
.S 76
2006

Human perfection is achieved only in social life and this in turn is achieved only through moral virtue: thus it is necessary that humans be good, although it is not necessary that they know the truth.

Averroes

FEB 2 2007

FEB 5 2005

CONTENTS

INTRODUCTION: A *COMEDY* FOR NON-CHRISTIANS

The poem that Dante called *Comedy* was first entitled *The Divine Comedy* more than two centuries after the poet's death, on the title page of an edition printed in Venice in 1555. The adjective "divine" was added by the Venetian publisher more as a way to praise the poem's seemingly superhuman artistry than as an indicator of its content and concern. But the title *The Divine Comedy*, which we have come to mistake for the original, determines for us a certain horizon of expectations: we think that Dante must be primarily interested in disclosing the facts concerning God and divine things, that his poem in its essence involves the presentation of religious—specifically, Christian—truth.

We might do well to stop calling Dante's poem *The Divine Comedy*, if only to help hold open the question concerning its religiosity. There is no doubt but that the *Comedy* is chock-full of Christian vocabulary, biblical allusions, and Scholastic theology. But this does not mean that Dante's *aim*, the guiding orientation of his project, is necessarily Christian.

Dante is very frequently referred to as "the great Catholic poet"—as if he were the official spokesperson of the medieval Catholic Church. But we should bear in mind that that same church banned as heretical Dante's *Monarchy*, his chief book of political philosophy and the ideological blueprint of the *Comedy*. As one scholar recently has remarked: "There is an obvious irony in the reputation of Dante because in recent times he has so often been regarded as a pillar of Catholic orthodoxy. In the last decade of his life and the first decade after it no one would have thought of him that way."[1] In 1329, just a few years after Dante's death, a certain Cardinal Poujet, nephew of the pope, ordered all copies of *Monarchy* to be burned, and the title appears on the Vatican's "Index of Prohibited Books" in 1554. These efforts by the church to suppress Dante's thinking did not prevent the work from being widely circulated, although in the form of anonymous and falsely titled manuscripts that were, at times, surreptitiously hidden within other more acceptable works.[2] The fact that the first printed edition (1559) appeared in Basel, a center of Lutheranism, indicates that Dante was regarded in some circles as a "proto-Protestant" author. The Vatican's prohibition of *Monarchy* was not lifted until the late nineteenth century. But this rehabilitation of Dante's reputation in the eyes of the church had less to do with an objective reexamination of the issues than with Pope Leo XIII's strategic deployment of Dante as cultural capital useful for the promotion of neo-Scholasticism: Dante was henceforth represented by the church as having given magnificent poetic expression to the philosophy of St. Thomas Aquinas, itself honored as the measure of orthodoxy.[3] Dante's extremely virulent opposition to the church, his sympathy for various heretical movements, and his call for the radical limitation of the role allotted to "faith" in political life were conveniently ignored, since his very name could lend considerable prestige to the institutions of Catholicism. Around the turn of the century, for instance, the founder of the Dante collection at the University of Notre Dame argued that "in order for Notre Dame to achieve the greatness of European universities, it must have a great library; moreover, to become a great Catholic university, it must have the premier collection of works by and about the great Catholic Poet."[4] The notion of "Dante the Catholic" is primarily a modern invention. We should regard with a healthy dose of skepticism the idea that Dante presents, as its spokesperson, a great synthesis of the fundamental tenets of the Church—especially considering that, in the long ideological struggle between church and state that unfolded from, say, the twelfth century through the Renaissance, Dante was without question a champion—one of *the* great champions—of the state.[5]

The *Comedy* is a poem more famous than read. The average well-educated American reader knows little more about Dante than that *Inferno* offers a vivid and systematic classification of gruesome retributions. Beyond this, one might know simply that Dante's poem is "religious" or "Christian." And this latter assumption plays no small role in limiting Dante's readership. For there are undoubtedly various communities of readers who, hearing that the *Comedy* is a Christian poem (or, for some, simply hearing it called *The Divine Comedy*), will turn away from it—assuming that it might speak to Christians or to the spiritually inclined but not to others.

The more we thoroughly Christianize every aspect of the *Comedy*, the more we contribute to narrowing the scope of its appeal.[6] One way to honor Dante's poem is to show how it may speak to audiences of different faiths (or to those of no faith). This does not mean making the poem into something it is not. It means reopening the question of what it *is*.

Four Non-Christian Approaches

How do we shore up the *Comedy* against the erosion and eventual ruin of the universality of its appeal? How can we best articulate the poem's relevance for non-Christians?

In the following pages I outline four conceivable "non-Christian" approaches to the *Comedy*: aesthetic formalism; reader-oriented hermeneutics; the assertion of irony; the assertion of (Christian) humanism.

The aesthetic-formalist approach says that Christian content is there in the *Comedy* but is not what really matters. The reader-oriented hermeneutic says that Christian content *was* there (to the degree that any meaning ever is objectively there), *was* what really mattered, but is not necessarily what matters for *us*. The assertion of irony says that Christianity is not so much the poem's content as it is its "surface": the poem is religious on the literal level, as the vehicle for some other, nonreligious (e.g., political or philosophical) content. The humanist approach, reintroducing Christianity into the picture, says that the content *is* Christian—but in a way different from Christianity as normally understood.

I do not claim that this is an exhaustive list of such approaches. Together, however, these approaches adequately account for many of the non-Christian strategies for reading Dante that have been proposed in the past. My own reading of the *Comedy* in this book is, broadly speaking, a combination of the latter two.

Aesthetic Formalism

One might propose to "bracket out" the question of Dante's Christianity—to set it aside—thus insisting that the greatness of the *Comedy* is not a function of its religious content (nor, for that matter, of any of its philosophical, theological, ethical, or political content), but rather of its artistry and poetry. Fairly commonplace among Romantic-era critics, this approach is in more modern times most often associated with the Italian philosopher Benedetto Croce, who argued in *The Poetry of Dante* (1920) that "what is proper and essential in Dante's work"—what belongs to Dante and Dante alone—is not a matter of content but rather of poetic achievement.[7] Croce terms the "philosophical, ethical, and religious interpretation of Dante's work" *allotrios*—from the ancient Greek *alleon* meaning "foreign," "strange," "enemy," "alien."[8] This is in part meant to suggest that to concentrate one's attention on, for instance, Dante's religious ideas is to venture outside the proper boundaries of the work of art. While the artwork may use religious language, it does so not for the sake of religious ideas but rather for the sake of poetry. *Allotrios* also signifies "belonging to others," "someone else's." By calling the theological, philosophical, ethical, and political content of Dante's work *allotrios*, Croce indicates that Dante's ideas are not "proper to" Dante; they do not belong to him alone. Anybody could have—and many in fact did—say the things Dante said. But no one else, in saying them, created anything like Dante's poetry. What is proper to Dante is the specific and unique quality of his poetry as poetry. Dante's Christianity is among the things that, considered for their own sake and not as elements of his poetry, are "foreign" to his real achievement.

Probably the most impressive recent instance of the aesthetic-formalist approach is Teodolinda Barolini's *The Undivine Comedy: Detheologizing Dante* (1992). Barolini quite openly embraces the label "formalist"—a term that by the late 1980s had become derogatory in American literary criticism: "What is needed to get some purchase on the poem is a 'new formalism'. . . .I privilege form over content." At the same time, Barolini claims that with the brand of formalism she has in mind "form is never disengaged from content" and "form *is* the essence."[9] By this she appears to mean that the poem is "really about" its radical formal innovation and its high degree of self-consciousness concerning narrative strategies. As for the *Comedy*'s religious content, Barolini insists that it is a matter of utmost seriousness for Dante (who "views himself as one who was made a teacher by the operation of the Holy Spirit" and who "self-consciously used the means of fiction. . .in the service of a vision [i.e., a Christian vision] he believed to be true").[10] Nonetheless Barolini says surprisingly little about Dante's Christianity, in effect bracketing out religion from her reading. Barolini's Dante remains a sincere believer; what marks him off from the crowd of such believers is his extraordinary penchant and talent for writing fiction about fiction. If Barolini's book was audacious at the time of its appearance, it is not because it reveals a nontheological Dante or an "undivine" *Comedy* but because it practices—against the grain of the then-hegemonic "new historicism"—an unabashed formalism.

What Barolini means by "detheologizing" needs to be understood in a very specific context. As she says, her approach is not "antitheological."[11] Her project has little or nothing to do with questioning the actual sincerity or the extent of Dante's commitment to Christian doctrine. The "detheologizing" of her book's title refers to the somewhat vexed issue in Dante studies concerning "allegory of the poets" and "allegory of the theologians." Simply put, this is a distinction between discourse produced by humans and discourse produced by God (a "theologian," in this context, is not someone trained to employ syllogisms to solve thorny problems concerning God, angels, and man, but rather one who, as an instrument of divine revelation, transcribes the word of God). Barolini maintains that

Dante did not need to pretend to be presenting "theology" (language of divine provenance—a *logos* emanating from *theos*) in order to claim that he is offering truth. Dante was not compelled to fool us into thinking that his poem was in essence written by God, and thus he was free to reflect playfully upon its qualities as a work of human art. Dante indicates (for those readers attuned to such things) that his book is a "fabrication"—which is not to say that it is a lie. The poem's artifice does not undermine its claim to bear and propagate Christian truth. Barolini describes her book as an "attempt to analyze the textual metaphysics that makes the *Commedia*'s truth claims credible and to show how the illusion is constructed, forged, made—by a man who is precisely, after all, 'only' a *fabbro*, a maker. . .a poet."[12]

Most instances of the aesthetic-formalist approach, in bracketing off Dante's Christianity as something that is at best of secondary interest, reproduce Dante in the image of the "sincerely faithful medieval Christian"—that favorite creation of modern medievalists who, perhaps nostalgic for a great "Age of Faith," deny the very possibility of radical medieval thinking. A notion common among formalists seems to be that, since not much interesting or new can be said concerning Dante's Christianity, since the religious content of Dante's poem—some vaguely defined "Christian truth"—is stable and orthodox, the only path of interest for the literary critic is to consider the *Comedy*'s artistic beauty.

There is a certain irony in claiming both that Dante was a Christian and that what mattered to him most about his poem was its poetry, form, or aesthetic beauty. For, as a Christian, Dante has a firm conviction concerning what matters—and it is not beauty but, rather, peace:

> Hence it is clear that universal peace is the best of those things which are ordained for human happiness. That is why the message which rang out from on high to the shepherds was not wealth, nor pleasures, nor honors, not long life, nor health, nor strength, *nor beauty*, but *peace*; for the heavenly host said: "Glory to God on high [*Gloria in excelsis Deo*], and on earth peace to men of good will." And that is why the Savior of men used the greeting "Peace be with you," for it was fitting that the supreme Savior should utter the supreme salutation.[13]

We might note in passing that, according to this passage from *Monarchy*, the "best of those things which are ordained for human happiness" is not salvation but peace. Or, insofar as Christ is "the supreme Savior," the saving in question involves saving the world, not saving the individual's eternal soul. Or, perhaps more precisely, the salvation of the soul is dependent upon the salvation of the world. Marsilius of Padua, discussed below, speaks of Christ's teaching "the truth which leads to the salvation of civil life, and which is also of no little help for eternal salvation"—this truth being peace.[14]

Reader-Oriented Hermeneutics

By reader-oriented hermeneutics, I mean the notion that the significance of a text is largely a function of the way that it is understood by an audience. While Dante's contemporaries may have tended to understand the *Comedy* as a poem aiming to teach the truths of Christianity, there is nothing wrong with our using the poem in other ways—including ways that Dante could not have imagined. The *Comedy* will remain vital for a variety of audiences, the responses of whom need not be limited to restatements of the poem's original religious content. The notion that valid interpretation need not be—and cannot be—circumscribed by the author's intended meaning is by no means a modern innovation. Saint Augustine, for instance, is not at all concerned if an interpretation does not correspond to the author's intention, for the criterion by which an interpretation is judged is utility, not accuracy: "Whoever finds a lesson useful to the building of charity, even though he has not said what the author may be shown to have intended in that place, has not been deceived, nor is he lying in any way."[15]

Dante himself did imagine the basic tenets of reader-oriented hermeneutics, which he makes the subject of one of *Purgatory*'s most memorable episodes.[16] In *Purgatory* XXI, in the course of their journey up the slopes of Mount Purgatory, Dante and Virgil happen upon the Roman poet Statius. The latter's epic *Thebaid*, which describes the devastating violence of civil war in Thebes, resolved in the end by the restoration of justice and order, is a source frequently drawn upon by Dante, who shared with Statius a concern for "war and peace." Not yet knowing the identity of his new companions, Statius identifies himself as the author of the *Thebaid* and humbly acknowledges the tremendous influence and surpassing greatness of Virgil's *Aeneid*, indicating that he would willingly defer his entrance to Heaven in exchange for having had the occasion to meet Virgil in person. Soon learning that he *is* in Virgil's presence, Statius warmly expresses great gratitude to his illustrious precursor. It was thanks to Virgil's poetry, Statius says, that he became who he is. This indebtedness is not primarily a matter of poetic influence. Virgil's poetry, more than shaping Statius as a poet, shaped him as a human being. Statius recounts, in particular, two momentous events of reading that changed his life. In both cases, Statius (to paraphrase Saint Augustine) "finds a lesson useful" for his existence, even though that lesson is "not what the author may have intended."

Statius reveals that he converted to Christianity, although he kept his conversion a secret and "made a show of paganism" out of fear of the persecution suffered by Christians in Rome in the first century AD. Statius's conversion (which appears to have been a myth invented by Dante) was occasioned by his admiration for some morally upright Christians with whom he had become acquainted and, especially, by the confirmation of the truth of Christ's coming that he found in some verses of Virgil's Fourth Eclogue ("The ages are renewed; / Justice returns and the first age of man, / and a new progeny descends from Heaven").[17] Statius realizes that Virgil himself did not understand the real meaning of his own verses, that although Virgil remained "in the dark" concerning the manner in which his poetry prophesied the redemption of humankind by Christ, he nonetheless "enlightened" later generations through his premonition of Christian truth: "You were like one who goes by night / and carries the light behind him and profits not himself / but makes those wise who follow him" (*Purg.* XXII, 67–69). The value and import of Virgil's poetry, says Statius, exceed the limits of anything that could have been imagined or intended by Virgil. The locus of meaning shifts from the author's intention to the reader's reception. And we might consider that Dante means to make us aware of a certain implicit logic: if a non-Christian poet such as Virgil can have a positive "Christian" effect on posterity, then, by the same token, perhaps a Christian poet such as Dante can have a positive "non-Christian" effect upon future audiences.[18]

It is conceivable that Statius's reading of Virgil's Eclogue (his finding Christian content where the author himself may not possibly have intended it) is "correct"—for it was commonly held by medieval readers that Virgil was divinely inspired to prophesy Christ's coming. Although Statius's understanding of the Eclogue may not match Virgil's intention, it may match God's. The other momentous reading recounted by Statius, however, cannot be conceived of as "correct" (as correlating to the intention of an authority other than Statius); this other reading is truly a misreading, or one might say a positive misprision.

Statius's (secret) conversion to Christianity was preceded by and founded on a moral conversion which was the product of a reading not simply anachronistic but downright mistaken. When Virgil expresses surprise at finding Statius among those purging their avarice on the fifth terrace of Purgatory, Statius, reminding Virgil that this same terrace is also where avarice's opposite, prodigality, is purged, assures him that he did not err by hoarding money but rather by spending it too freely. Statius reformed his prodigal ways only after reading these verses in the *Aeneid*: "Quid non mortalia pectora cogis, / auri *sacra* fames?" Statius (mis)interprets these words to mean: "Why, O *blessed* hunger for gold, / do you not

govern the appetite of mortals?" (*Purg.* XXII, 40–41). His misreading is
rooted in the real ambiguity of the Latin *sacra*, which (like the French *sacré*)
can mean *either* "blessed," "holy," "sacred" *or precisely the opposite*,
"accursed," "damned." Statius thinks that Virgil meant to praise the desire
for money as a positive, healthy impulse; after reading these verses Statius
renounced his carefree spending and, in the manner of one who practices
the Golden Mean of Aristotle's ethics, developed a moderate desire to possess money. But in truth Virgil actually meant to call the desire for money
"damned" not "blessed" (the verses refer to Polymestor's murdering
for gold the youth Polydorus), and the verses ought to be translated thus:
"To what do you not drive the appetite of mortals, / O *accursèd* hunger for
gold?" Statius has clearly taken the verses out of their original context,
understanding them instead through the prism of his own existence. His
reading of the *Aeneid* was useful for his life, although not what the author
intended.

The Statius episode is fascinating not only because it seems to authorize
positive (useful) misreading—so that one might say that the *Comedy* itself
tells us that our reading need not be bound by the author's intention—but
moreover because this presentation of a reader-oriented hermeneutics is
bound up with the question of the interpretation of scripture.

Statius is the *one and only* character in the entire poem who explicitly
appears as Christ—as a figure of, or, rather, as one who is figured by,
Christ. Just prior to their meeting up with Statius, Dante and Virgil hear a
chorus of voices singing *Gloria in excelsis Deo*—those words which in the
Gospel of Luke (2.13–14) announce the birth of Christ (recall that we have
just seen those words in the passage from *Monarchy* cited above). When
they first glimpse Statius, he appears to them precisely as Christ appeared,
following the Resurrection, to two of his apostles on the road to Emmaus:

> And behold [*Ed ecco*], as Luke writes for us
> that Christ, new-risen from the sepulchral cave,
> appeared to the two who were on the way,
>
> A shade [i.e., Statius] appeared to us, and he was coming on
> behind us while we were watching the crowd.
>
> (*Purg.* XXI, 7–11)

The virtual identity of Statius and Christ is solidified by the virtual identity,
here, of Dante's words and the words of Luke: "And behold [*Et ecce*], two
of them were going that very day to a village named Emmaus. . . . And it
came to pass, while they were conversing and arguing together, that Jesus
himself also drew near and went along with them" (Luke 24.13–15). And
Statius' first words to Dante and Virgil—"O my brothers, may God give

you peace" (*Purg.* XXI, 13)—are nothing other than the words that Christ speaks, a bit later in Luke 24, to the rest of his disciples: "Peace be with you" (Luke 24.36). Recall, again, that we have seen these same words from Luke in the passage from *Monarchy* cited above: "And that is why the Savior of men used the greeting 'Peace be with you,' for it was fitting that the supreme Savior should utter the supreme salutation." Dante has clearly taken pains to present Statius, with his message of peace, as the Savior—as one whose project is to bring humankind salvation in the form of peace on earth.

What does it mean that Dante is saying that Statius is, in some sense, Christ? We can probably best respond by reversing the terms of the question: What does it mean to say that Christ is, in some sense, Statius? Statius, here in *Purgatory*, is above all else a reader, an interpreter (or, a misreader, a misinterpreter) of a prior written corpus—Virgil's poetry. Is Christ also a reader, an interpreter?

Indeed, Christ is precisely that, since the main event of the episode on the road to Emmaus (the episode around which Dante organizes *Purgatory*'s Statius episode) is *hermeneutic*—an event of interpretation: "Then, beginning with Moses and all the prophets, he [i.e., Christ] *interpreted to them the things about himself* in all the scriptures" (Luke 24.27). Just as Statius, walking with Dante and Virgil, interprets a predecessor's poetry, so Christ, walking with his two apostles, interprets the writings of a preceding tradition. And just as Statius (mis)reads verses from the *Aeneid* through the prism of his own existence, so Christ (mis?)reads the Hebrew scriptures as if they were "about himself." The question is: How far does Dante wish for us to follow the logic of this analogy? Does Christ understand that which the Jews, who were "in the dark" concerning the meaning of their own writings, could not understand? Or is Christ one who finds in Moses's writings a lesson useful for his own world, even though not what the author intended?

If Dante is a Christian, he is one who dares formulate, as a possibility, a radical conception of Christianity: that Christian truth is the product of Christ's misreading of the Hebrew tradition.

The Statius episode also amounts to Dante's implicit reflection on his own reading of the Christian tradition. Dante tends to reduce the meaning of the Gospels to one truth—universal peace on earth. But it is conceivable that the message of the Gospels is something else: peace for Christians in Heaven. Christ, after all, insistently disavows the message of peace: "Do you think that I have come to bring peace to the earth? No, I tell you, but rather division" (Luke 12.51); "Think not that I came to send peace on the earth: I came not to send peace, but a sword" (Matt. 10.34). Dante's reading of Christianity requires that he contradict Christ. We might say that Dante, like Statius, lifts the message of peace out of its context, ignoring that the "best of those things which are ordained for human happiness" is not peace on earth but rather the eternal salvation of the individual's soul. But Dante's misprision—if it is one—of the Christian tradition is in a sense perfectly "Christian," since it follows the logic of Christ's own misprision of the Hebrew tradition.

Irony

Both the formalist and the hermeneutic approach tend to accept as a given that, in its original context, for Dante and his contemporaries, the meaning of the *Comedy* was without question Christian. Formalism turns away from Dante's Christianity by maintaining that, while it is not a fact that can be doubted, it is also not a *literary* fact and thus cannot be the critic's chief concern. Reader-oriented hermeneutics can turn away from Dante's original (Christian) intention, since that intention is only one of many meaningful contexts within which his poem can be understood.

But there is no need to accept Dante's Christianity as an indubitable given. One might assert that Dante's primary rhetorical device, on the most general level, is *irony*—saying one thing but meaning another. Perhaps Dante, although he sounds very much like a Christian, is in fact something else. Are we authorized to say of Dante what Beatrice, in *Paradiso*, says of Plato: "But perhaps his meaning is other / than his words sound, and may be / of an intention not to be derided" (*Par.* IV, 55–57)? If Statius was able to persuade the world that he was a pagan when in truth he was a Christian ("for fear, I was a secret Christian, / long making show of paganism"; *Purg.* XXII, 90–91), might it be possible that Dante persuaded the world that he was a Christian when in truth he was not?

In the years 1310–11, as he was in the middle of writing the *Comedy*, Dante wrote a series of epistles encouraging Emperor Henry VII of Luxembourg to enter Italy on a mission to pacify and unify its rivaling city-states and to encourage those city-states to welcome the emperor as their legitimate ruler. The epistles are replete with messianic language that casts Henry VII in the role of Christ. Dante goes so far as to suggest that the emperor *is* Christ—saying of him, for instance: "Behold the Lamb of God, behold him who takes away the sins of the world" (Luke 1.47).[19] In statements such as these, Christian vocabulary is deployed as an apparatus for the promotion of a secular, political aim. We need to recognize that political leaders in Dante's day—rulers themselves as well as intellectuals aiming to shape ideology in some manner—used, no less so than can be witnessed today, religious language for political reasons. Not every medieval writer's invocation of the Bible is a sure indicator of "sincere belief."

We are often told that true skepticism with regard to religion was not a position really available to the Christians of Dante's time—since their Christianity was so hegemonic that they could not authentically take up a vantage point outside of it. Lucien Febvre, in *The Problem of Unbelief in the Sixteenth Century: The Religion of Rabelais* (1942), famously concluded that real atheism was quite simply impossible in Renaissance France. (And, we might add, if it was impossible then, how could it have been possible in Dante's Middle Ages?) Febvre argues that atheism was never thinkable as one's own authentically held stance but only as the outrageous and vile stance of one's political enemies. Irreligion was never more than an accusation leveled against others.

Among those accused in Dante's day was Marsilius of Padua, whose *Defensor pacis* ("The Defender of Peace") is considered the most important work of late medieval European political theory. Much like Dante, Marsilius maintains that the papacy and all related ecclesiastical institutions (the priesthood, etc.) have absolutely no legal jurisdiction over anything whatsoever. The real church is not the papacy but rather "the people," and (for Marsilius if not for Dante), it is "the people" who ought to possess full dominion over both state and church.[20] The role of the priesthood, for Marsilius and for Dante, is solely to offer instruction in doctrines concerning God and the spiritual goal of human existence; but the priesthood is in no case authorized to practice any form of coercive enforcement. For posing this general threat to the power of ecclesiastical and other elite institutions, and for various particular passages that might be construed as dangerous to the faith, Marsilius was, as Alan Gewirth remarks, long regarded as among the most subversive of heretics:

> When popes, cardinals, and writers simply concerned with preserving the social order wished to condemn heretics—Wyclif, Hus, Luther, among others—they charged them with having gotten their ideas from the "accursed Marsilius." To be a Marsilian was regarded as subversive in a way similar to that which, centuries later, attached to being a Marxist. The analogy between Marsilius and Marx is not entirely without point, in this crucial respect: both men set themselves in opposition to dominant institutions and ideas of their respective eras, and both gave expression to forces which wreaked havoc with those institutions.[21]

Among the ideas expressed in the course of *Defensor pacis* is the notion that religion is, as Gewirth puts it, "a set of fictitious beliefs devised by 'philosophers' in order to curb men's wrongdoing, through the myth of an avenging deity who punishes men in a future life for their crimes in the present life."[22] Marsilius somewhat distances himself from this position by attributing it to some ancient philosophers and by indicating that, if it is correct, it applies only to "gentile" religions and not to the true religion, Christianity. On the other hand, he does not represent skepticism concerning the afterlife as a vile outrage. Rather, the notion strikes him as a well-examined position that may in fact be a reasonable understanding of the truth of gentile religions. Marsilius has no objection to the idea that intellectuals or philosophers sometimes need to foster myths or propagate fictions—to practice irony, to say things that they do not accept as literally true. But we might add, following the spirit of Leo Strauss's *Persecution and the Art of Writing*, such irony will only work when it is not perceived as such or when it is perceived as such only by the philosophers themselves, who will do best to keep such things to themselves. As Averroes (whom we will consider several times in the course of this book) says, the philosophers' understanding of things "ought not to be expressed to the multitude."[23] And it is thus impossible to say whether Marsilius's insistence that Christianity is an exception to the rule concerning the sociopolitical origin and aim of religious discourse was his sincerely held belief or the means by which he hoped to protect himself from persecution. (As it would turn out, Marsilius's attempts to protect himself were not exactly successful, as he was forced to flee to Nuremberg following the papal condemnation of his treatise in 1326).

Now, there is some reason to suggest that Dante was a "Marsilian." This is partly because of numerous instances in which Dante's thinking is consonant with the *Defensor pacis* (which was completed in 1324, just three years after Dante's death). Consider, as one small example, the paramount concern for "peace"—which Marsilius foregrounds not only in the title of his treatise but also through the reiterative rhetoric of its introductory paragraph:

> It was for this reason [i.e., to promote "the benefits and fruits of the tranquility or peace of civil regimes"] that Christ, son of God, decreed that peace would be the sign and messenger of his rebirth, when he wanted the heavenly choir to sing: "Glory to God in the highest: and on earth peace to men of good will." For this same reason, too, he often wished peace to his disciples. Whence John: "Jesus came and stood amid his disciples and said, 'Peace be to you.'" Counseling them concerning the maintenance of peace with one another, he said, in Mark: "Have peace among you." And he taught them not only to have peace among themselves, but also to wish it to others, whence in Matthew: "When you come into the house, salute it, saying: 'Peace be to this house.'" Peace, again, was the heritage which he bequeathed to his disciples at the time of his passion and death, when he said, in the fourteenth chapter of John: "Peace I leave with you: my peace I give unto you."[24]

Marsilius opens the *Defender of Peace* by citing, among others, the same New Testament episodes concerning Christ's message of peace that Dante cites, as we have seen above, near the opening of *Monarchy* and in the Statius episode of *Purgatory*. The priority of peace—meaning peace on earth, the "peace of civil regimes"—is the fundamental premise of both thinkers. And Dante, in another gesture that might be termed "Marsilian," insists upon the centrality of peace by citing, as the *Comedy*'s very center-most verse (*Purg.* XVII, 69)—right smack in the absolute middle of the poem—Christ's saying from the Sermon on the Mount: *Beati pacifici*, "Blessed are the peacemakers."

But Dante was also connected to Marsilius in a direct, personal way. Dante is known to have lived in Verona from 1312 to 1318 and to have returned there for a time (as what we would call today a "distinguished lecturer") in 1320. Marsilius, whose life is very scantly documented, is known to have been living in Verona in 1319. In Verona, both lived in the household of and were employed by one and the same patron, that city's powerful lord, Cangrande della Scala. Given their ideological affinity and the force of their expression, given their rank as two of the most outspoken proponents of the autonomous, nonhierocratic state in the late Middle Ages, it is hard to imagine that, dwelling in the same household (perhaps—although perhaps not—at precisely the same time), they were not acquainted with each other. We can easily picture them as friends, col-leagues, comrades. Perhaps not coincidentally, it was to Cangrande that Dante dedicated the famous epistle explaining that the purpose of the *Comedy* is to guide humans to "happiness in this life."[25] In that same letter Dante indicates that, understood as allegory (which, he says, is derived from the Greek *alleon*, meaning *alienus*, "belonging to another," or *diversus*, "different"), the *Comedy*'s meaning is "different from the literal."[26] The *Comedy*'s meaning "belongs to another" order of discourse than might at first appear: as allegory, it operates through the device of irony, saying one thing while at the same time saying something "different." Dante's des-cription of his poem's allegory does not merely assert that his poem is *polysemous*, saying many things (although Dante does indeed explicitly term it that); more importantly, his account of allegory suggests that the poem's meaning is, in relation to its literal surface, *alienus* or *diversus*—something truly other than what appears. It is not so much that there are several harmonious (Christian) levels of meaning but rather that the meaningful level to some degree contradicts the literal level. There is, at the heart of the *Comedy*, something "alien" or "foreign"—something "belonging to another."

What has been said so far concerning Marsilius and Dante is meant to preface the presentation of the following passage. This is the passage in which Marsilius entertains the idea, which he ascribes to ancient philosophers, of what Gewirth calls "the socio-political basis of religion."[27] Although these words on the one hand refer to the ancients whom he mentions, it seems plausible that Marsilius is also thinking of one of his contemporaries, another "philosopher" who excelled at "painting pictures" of the afterlife, his friend Dante:

> However, besides these causes of the laying down of religious laws, causes which are believed without demonstration, the philosophers, including Hesiod, Pythagoras, and several others of the ancients, noted appropriately a quite different cause or purpose for the setting forth of divine laws or religions—a purpose which was in some sense necessary for the status of this world. This was to ensure the goodness of human acts both individual and civil, on which depend almost completely the quiet or tranquility of communities and finally the sufficient life in the present world. For although *some of the philosophers who founded such laws or religions did not accept or believe in human resurrection and that life which is called eternal*, they nevertheless feigned and persuaded others that it exists and that in it pleasures and pains are in accordance with the qualities of human deeds in this mortal life, in order that they might thereby induce in men reverence and fear of God, and a desire to flee the vices and to cultivate the virtues. For there are certain acts which the legislator cannot regulate by human law, that is, those acts which cannot be proved to be present or absent to someone, but which nevertheless cannot be concealed from God, whom the philosophers feigned to be the maker of such laws and the commander of their observance, under the threat or promise of eternal *reward* for doers of good and *punishment* for doers of evil. Hence, *they said of the variously virtuous men in this world that they were placed in the heavenly firmament*; and from this were perhaps derived the names of certain stars and constellations. These philosophers said that the souls of men who had been intemperate eaters entered the bodies of pigs, those who were intemperate in embracing and making love entered the body of goats, and so on, according to the proportions of human vices to their condemnable properties. So too the philosophers assigned various kinds of torments to wrongdoers, like perpetual thirst and hunger for intemperate Tantalus: water and fruit were to be near him, but he was unable to drink or handle these, for they were always fleeing faster than he could pursue them. *The philosophers also said that the infernal regions, the place of these torments, were deep and dark; and they painted all sorts of terrible and gloomy pictures of them.* From fear of these, men eschewed wrongdoing, were instigated to perform virtuous works of piety and mercy, and were well disposed both in themselves and toward others. As a consequence, many disputes and injuries ceased in communities. Hence too the peace or tranquility of states and the sufficient life of men for the status of the present world were preserved with less difficulty; which was the end intended by these wise men in laying down such laws and religions.[28]

The notion of painting "all sorts of terrible pictures" of the "infernal regions," of assigning "various kinds of torments to wrongdoers" according to a logic of retribution not unlike Dante's *contrapasso*, cannot but remind us (and must have reminded Marsilius) of *Inferno*. And the idea of "the variously virtuous men in this world. . .placed in the heavenly firmament" as if they were stars or constellations cannot but remind us of *Paradiso*, where Dante sees blessed souls, in the form of star-like lights, form themselves into various shapes or "constellations" according to their various virtues. Does this passage offer us a glimpse of Dante's private acknowledgement that his Christianity (to which he is commonly supposed by Dante scholars to have returned following his ultimately unsatisfying years as a "philosopher") is a rhetorical instrument in the service of a secular (philosophical) aim? Does this represent an understanding of the poem's allegory that Dante confided to Marsilius, who then discreetly (since, after all, the poet had now been deceased for a few years and could no longer be touched by persecution) divulged it to the intellectual public? We cannot say for certain. But neither can we say for certain, as so many have in recent decades, that there can be no questioning the orthodoxy of Dante's faith.[29]

In the *Epistle to Cangrande*, Dante makes it rather clear that, insofar as his poem has one primary allegorical level of meaning, that meaning is not religious but secular, not celestial but terrestrial. Depicting the fates of human souls in the afterlife is not the purpose of the poem but rather the means to achieve another purpose, the institution of justice on earth:

> And thus it should first be noted what the subject of the work is when taken according to the letter, and then what its subject is when understood allegorically. The subject of the whole work, then, taken literally, is the state of souls after death, understood in a simple sense; for the movement of the whole work turns upon this and about this. If on the other hand the work is taken allegorically, the subject is man, in the exercise of his free will, earning or becoming liable to *the rewards or punishments of justice*.[30]

The key phrase here is "the rewards and punishments of justice." For the phrase "rewards and punishments," charged with connotations, is virtually a technical term in the Arabo-Islamic and Latin Scholastic philosophical tradition. The "rewards and punishments" refer to our ultimate fates in the afterlife: the virtuous will be rewarded by eternal bliss in Paradise, the wicked punished by eternal torment in Hell. (It is in this sense that Marsilius uses the terms in the passage cited above.) As an example of the phrase, we can cite these words from the great Sunni thinker al-Ghazali (1058–1111 AD), himself an opponent (although a particularly well-informed one) of "the philosophers": "They [i.e., the philosophers] say that for bodies there is no resurrection; it is bare spirits which are rewarded and punished; and the rewards and punishments are spiritual, not bodily."[31] In general, rationalist philosophers in the Islamic tradition regarded the literal depictions of "rewards and punishments" in the Qur'an as rhetorical inducements aimed at the masses—the actual eternal life being something other than bodily pleasure and pain. Normally, this does not entail a denial of some mode of immortality. For the rationalists such as Averroes, although immortality cannot possibly involve a physical or material component, nonetheless the soul, or at least the rational part of it, can possibly be imperishable. The phrase "rewards and punishments" is a shorthand way of referring to the ordinary believer's literal (although incorrect) understanding of the afterlife as the bodily and spiritual survival of the individual in Heaven and Hell.

The term "justice" is no less charged with connotations. Although the notion of "justice" is not inherently secular (since we speak both of "divine justice" and of "human justice"), in the context of thirteenth and early fourteenth-century Western European political philosophy, "justice" *is* a secular term. Proponents of the state's autonomy from the church in temporal (political) matters argued that the proper administration of justice is extra-ecclesiastical, the task of the civil authority not the priesthood. The secular authorities represented themselves as responsible to Reason and Justice herself rather than to the claims of any particular religion. Thus, John of Paris, a Dominican friar whose political thought is akin to Dante's in several respects, states in his *On Kingly and Papal Power* (1302) that "even without Christ as ruler there is the true and perfect justice which is required for the state."[32]

But it was the Emperor Frederick II who, in the first half of the thirteenth century, most visibly secularized the notion of justice. In his *Liber augustalis*, Frederick asserts that there is an intimate kinship, indeed a virtual identity, between the Emperor ("the Roman Prince," "the Caesar") and Justice:

> Provision. . .was made for reasons of utility and necessity. . .that there concur in the selfsame person the origin as well as the protection of Justice, lest Vigor be failing Justice, and Justice, Vigor. The Caesar, therefore, must be at once the Father and the Son of Justice, her lord and her minister: Father and lord in creating Justice and protecting what has been created; and in like fashion shall he be, in her veneration, the Son of Justice and, in ministering her plenty, her minister.[33]

Against the church, which argued that the role of secular powers was the limited and secondary one of enforcing the laws and policies established by the church, Frederick argues that the secular authority (ultimately, the emperor) is both legislator and enforcer in all temporal matters. This is, in essence, Dante's position on the issue. Moreover, fundamental to Dante's political project (as we shall see below) is his support for the office of "Emperor" or "Caesar"—one who will guide the human community to peace through his commitment to justice. In *Paradiso* XVIII, in the sphere of Jupiter, a host of souls of those who have practiced justice, before taking on the shape of an eagle (the symbol of imperial Rome), arrange themselves as a series of letters that spells out, "Love justice, you who rule the earth." In Dante's mind, "justice" is, in the first instance, bound up with the notion of secular civil society.

It is surely no coincidence that the strongest claims for an entirely secular rule grounded in reason and justice came from Frederick II and his court in his native Sicily, for Frederick's Sicily was a religiously and ethnically plural culture, peopled by Muslims and Christians, and a center for cross-cultural scholarship in Arabic, Greek, and Latin. Frederick, a great champion of Islamic learning, did all he could to foster this multicultural experiment. Frederick's secular and religiously neutral political theory, besides suiting his primary aim of justifying his claim to rule as emperor over the Papal States, also offered a framework for the peaceful cohabitation of his diverse constituents. Thus Frederick in effect attempted to establish a sort of "counter-Church," dedicated to the worship not of Christ (nor even of God) but rather of justice herself:

> Frederick's *Magna Curia* [was a place] where the judges and lawyers were expected to administer Justice like priests; where the High Court sessions, staged with a punctilio comparable to Church ceremonial, were dubbed "a most holy ministry of Justice"; where the jurists and courtiers interpreted the "Cult of Justice" in terms of a *religio iuris* or of an *ecclesia imperialis* representing both a complement to and an antitype of the ecclesiastical order; where, so to speak, the robe of the law clerk was set over against the robe of the ordained cleric; where the emperor himself, "whom the Great Artificer's hand created man," was spoken of as *Sol Iustitiae*, the "Sun of Justice," which was the prophetic title of Christ.[34]

The term "justice," then, was charged with significance in Dante's day. Within a certain discursive tradition to which Dante belonged, to embrace or celebrate "justice" was to support a political order in which all juridical and coercive power would be in the hands of a secular state that would legislate, judge, and enforce without regard to religion.

The *Comedy*'s irony, according to Dante's own formulation, is this: while it is literally concerned with "rewards and punishments" in the usual sense ("the state of souls after death, understood in a simple sense"), it is allegorically concerned with *the rewards or punishments of justice*. Dante transposes or displaces "rewards and punishments" from the other world to this world, from the spiritual to the temporal, from the religious to the political plane. There is at least a hint of the notion that the picture of "rewards and punishments" as ordinarily conceived (Heaven and Hell) is a fiction and that the real "rewards and punishments" are those distributed here on earth. The poem, says Dante, is about "man, in the exercise of his free will, earning or becoming liable to the rewards or punishments of justice." Humankind has the power, by itself (without God's assistance) to "earn the rewards of justice." Our reward for being governed by justice is the peaceful social order, the ideal human community (represented in the poem as Heaven); our punishment for disregarding the guidance of justice is the community fractured by violence (represented in the poem as Hell).

If Dante and Marsilius entertain some degree of skepticism concerning the Christian afterlife as it is normally conceived, they are neither the first nor the only late medieval European intellectuals to express such thoughts. In the thirteenth century the bishop of Paris, Guillaume d'Auvergne, records the view of certain skeptics who regarded "the doctrine of survival and reward in the other world. . .as a deception used by the authorities [*imperatorum deceptio*] to keep their subjects quiet and resigned to a life of denial."[35] Among the 219 theses of the so-called Latin Averroists or Radical Aristotelians that were prohibited from being taught at the University of Paris in 1277 were these: "That happiness is had in this life and not in another" (#172); "That there are fables and falsehoods in the Christian law just as in others" (#181); "That death is the end of all terrors" (#213); "That a philosopher must not concede the resurrection to come, because it cannot be investigated by reason" (#216); "That to say that God gives happiness to one [i.e., a Christian] and not to another [i.e., a non-Christian] is devoid of reason and fictitious" (#217).[36]

But how do we know that the Averroists (among whose number Marsilius is usually reckoned, as is, to be sure, Marsilius's comrade Jean de Jandun, whom some believe to have co-authored the *Defensor pacis*[37]) really held such views? Perhaps Bishop Etienne Tempier, who issued the ban against such teachings, exaggerated their outrageousness. Were students really taught that "the Christian law impedes learning" (#180), that "simple fornication, namely that of an unmarried man with an unmarried woman, is not a sin" (#205), that "one should not confess except for the sake of appearance" (#203), that "the teachings of the theologian are based on fables" (#183) and that "the only wise men in the world are the philosophers" (#2)?

It is not, however, a matter of proving that there were genuine "free-thinkers" among the intellectuals of circa 1300 AD Western Europe and that Dante was one of them. It is not a matter of claiming that Dante was not a Christian. It is a matter of recognizing that a skeptical perspective—skeptical of the afterlife, not of God's existence—was much more available in Dante's day than we are often led to believe. We ought to hazard reading the *Comedy* from such a perspective, if only to see what might come of it. We have read Dante as if he were Thomas Aquinas, and the results have been compelling and coherent. But in the interest of fairness (especially since it is clear that, on questions of major importance, Dante is *not* Aquinas), we ought to read him as if he were a Radical Aristotelian, as if he were Averroes.

So the chief mode of the *Comedy*'s irony is political allegory. Of course this does not mean that the poem is a *roman à clef* by which Dante secretly heaps scorn on his political enemies disguised as fictional personages. (Since the poem's personages are real historical figures, not veiled "allegories," the heaping of scorn is entirely manifest.) The poem is "political allegory" in a more general sense: it appears to be concerned with the fate of individual souls in the afterlife but is in fact concerned with the *polis*, the fate of the human community in this life. It appears to be primarily theological but is primarily philosophical. It appears to be primarily religious but is primarily secular.

If the *Comedy* may appear to be religious but in fact not be especially so, it may also appear to express one religious understanding while in fact meaning to express a different religious understanding. The second chief mode in which the *Comedy* might be ironic is this: although it sounds like Christian religious discourse, it is actually some other brand of religious discourse. This view, dismissed by mainstream Dante criticism as "esotericism," has had numerous advocates dating back at least to the mid-nineteenth century. Eugène Aroux (a vitriolic debunker of Dante whose mission was to aid the papacy by unmasking the poet as one who "was through his faith and teachings, outside the communion of the Roman Church and, moreover, one of its most embittered and dangerous enemies"), in his *Dante: hérétique, révolutionnaire et socialiste* (1854), identified Dante as a closet "Oriental" who purveyed some sort of combination Templar-Cathar doctrine.[38] This tradition of "esoteric" or "hermetic" readings is alive and well, as contemporary studies have given us Dante as, among other things, a Gnostic-Cathar, a kind of Hindu, a Templar, a Kabbalist.[39] Among the most engaging of recent efforts in this vein is Adriano Lanza's *Dante all'inferno: I misteri eretici della Commedia [Dante in Hell: The 'Comedy's' Heretical Mysteries].*[40] Lanza's work offers an impressively coherent reading of Dante as a Gnostic-Cathar, vitiated only by the fact that its basic thesis—that Dante means to teach that material creation is inherently evil and that on earth we are exiled and imprisoned in the body—is utterly wrong.

The problem with most "esoteric" readings is that, rightly showing that Dante is not an "orthodox Roman Catholic," they end up representing him as a full-fledged initiate of some other spiritual system, as if Dante's project were to replace one dogma with another.

But if readings that posit that the *Comedy* is, from start to finish, canto-by-canto, hiding some systematically formulated hermetic secret are misguided, there is good reason to believe that there are some parts of the poem in which Dante is obliged to practice a sort of esotericism. Dante did *not* need to veil his political opposition to the papacy. According to the "rules of the game" by which the Inquisition was played, virtually any degree of political opposition to and criticism of the papacy was tolerated. One could not (in theory, at least) be burned for crusading against ecclesiastical corruption. Thus, Dante's disdain for the officials of the church—the *Comedy* shows numerous popes in Hell and virtually none in Heaven—was an acceptable expression of anticlerical sentiment. One could be burned, however, for promulgating false teachings on fundamental doctrines, particularly concerning matters of salvation, since doing so would harm not so much the officials of the church as it would the mass of ordinary faithful. (In practice, of course, the church did not find it difficult to assert that its chief political enemies were also promulgators of false doctrines.) If Dante practices some of the cryptic indirection of esotericism, it is when treating the question of salvation in the afterlife, which he quietly suggests (as we will see in part II) is not reserved exclusively for Christians. And if we can only glimpse Dante's thinking on salvation by reading between the lines, it is because, as Paul Alexis Ladame remarks, "he had to speak the truth while camouflaging it—for it was a question of life or death, and he did not feel like dying."[41]

Christian Humanism

The fourth and final "non-Christian" approach to the *Comedy* is to assert that it is a work in the tradition of Christian humanism. Perhaps not technically a non-Christian approach, viewing Dante as a Christian humanist can nonetheless produce readings that will readily gain the assent of non-Christians.

Christian humanism is, first, a matter of insisting on the humanity of God. It is a matter of taking the Incarnation seriously rather than glossing over it, of shifting Christianity's emphasis from the vertical trajectory of transcendence to the horizontal plane of immanence, from the celestial to the terrestrial, from the divine to the human. We might take, admittedly out of context, a line from *Purgatory* as the motto of Dante's Christianity: "O soul *still rooted in the body*, making your way toward heaven" (*Purg.*, XIV, 10). One goes to heaven not by overcoming the bodily (and not in order to do so), but rather to retrieve something that will be beneficial for its therapy. Dante's so-called pilgrimage is not a matter of escaping or seeking an alternative to material existence on earth. (This is why all presentations of Dante as a Gnostic or Cathar are mistaken.) Authentic Christianity is not primarily concerned with the afterlife but with this life. So we may have to adjust our preceding remarks concerning Dante's irony: the "allegorical" meaning which Dante says is *alienus* or *diversus* with respect to the literal Christian depiction of the fate of human souls in the afterlife—a meaning that, says Dante, concerns happiness in this life—is not necessarily non-Christian. As allegory, the *Comedy* "says something other" than Christianity as commonly conceived—but it does not necessarily say something other than Christianity.

Christian humanism is, secondly, a matter of recognizing the full moral excellence of non-Christians. It is the claim that, when it comes to their capacity to lead virtuous lives, there is absolutely no qualitative difference between Christians and non-Christians.

This aspect of Christian humanism is most often associated with Petrarch, who is frequently represented as the "father of the Renaissance" (while Dante, for his part, is represented as the summation of the Middle Ages). But when we recall that Petrarch had already achieved literary fame less than two decades after Dante's death, that as a young boy he had once met Dante, and that Dante exerted tremendous influence on his work, we realize that there is a good deal more "overlap" between these two than what the simple medieval versus Renaissance dichotomy would have us believe, and we see reason to question the idea of a definitive opposition between their worldviews. Petrarch's Christian humanism does not contradict but rather develops from his understanding of Dante.

In 1341, Petrarch was crowned Poet Laureate on the reputation of his epic *Africa*, a poem that he had not yet finished and of which only a few passages had circulated among his friends, colleagues, and patrons. Manuscript copies of one particular episode were distributed to a wider public, against Petrarch's wishes. In the episode Magone, a pagan from Carthage (modern-day Tunisia), facing death, expresses genuine repentance for his wrongdoings. Among the complaints that Petrarch's detractors directed against this episode was its anachronism: Petrarch had put in the mouth of a pagan from circa 200 BC words that could properly only have been uttered by a Christian. Petrarch responds by positing the notion of a timeless universal human morality—the idea that humans from all times and places are equally capable of virtue:

> The closer the soul is to danger the more it is enlivened and purified; thus does approaching death excite and spur the soul to virtue. And here I recall

the admirable words that I found around that time in Cicero: "In that moment [i.e., facing one's death]," he says, "one yearns most for praise, and he who has lived other than he should repents for his sins." This statement by a pagan is enough for me to refute the second charge against me— namely, that the words attributed by me to Magone seem not to be his but rather those of a Christian. And I. . .did not think that there could be born under heaven men capable of such a foolish and rash opinion, the product of a sterile and vile intellect and the sure sign of envy and ill will. In the name of God, I ask them: what is there in these verses of mine that can properly be said only by Christians, and not rather by all humans and all nations?. . .*There is not a single article of our faith, not a sacrament of the Church, not a doctrine of the Gospels, in sum, nothing whatsoever of the sort, which natural reason or innate intellect cannot inspire in the mind of a man who has reached the end of his earthly existence.* . .Even he who is not a Christian can recognize his own error and consequently feel shame and sorrow; while the reward is not equal, the repentance, however, is equal. How else could that youth in Terence's *Phormio* have said, "I know myself and my sin"?. . .And David in the Psalms: "I said, 'I will confess my transgressions to the Lord' " (and there you have confession!) "and you forgave the guilt of my sin" (and there you have the salvation of the one who confesses!). Thus although only the Christian knows to whom and how one ought to confess, nonetheless self-examination, remorse, repentance, and confession are things common to all rational beings. And if we consider their words, we find that the youth in Terence's play, recalling his illicit love and his crime, said no less than what David said in that Psalm well known to all: "For I know my transgressions, and my sin is ever before me." But of course I realize that few or none of my detractors have read these things that I have cited or any of the other philosophical say-ings of many authors, but especially Plato and Cicero, concerning the soul, God, the miseries and errors of humans, contempt for this life and desire for the other—things which, if the identity of the author were unknown, one would think had been written by Saint Ambrose or Saint Augustine.[42]

Although Petrarch gives some lip-service to the exceptionality of Christianity ("the reward is not equal" for non-Christian and Christian repentance, and "only the Christian knows to whom and how one ought to confess"), the main thrust of this passage is to emphasize the moral equivalence of pagans and Christians and the full legitimacy of pagan wisdom, even in matters con-cerning God, the soul, and life in the other world. Petrarch claims that the essential elements of confession and salvation were already in place centuries before Christ, and he implies that they have been in place always and every-where. The formal, technical apparatus administered by the church is just one particular way of organizing a universal human experience.

This is not orthodox Western Christianity. Petrarch implicitly denies that there is some point in human history (the time of the Crucifixion) after which humans are saved and before which they are fallen and damned. As Ugo Dotti remarks, Petrarch de-emphasizes Christ's role as the sine qua non for salvation:

> Of course this "Christian humanism" might be considered dangerous on the doctrinal level, insofar as it defends the idea of a perennial human morality (the idea that we can learn something useful for our salvation even from Plato and Cicero) and thus diminishes to some degree the importance of Christ's sacrifice and the doctrine of salvation.[43]
>
> Petrarch's critics, although malevolent, were not wrong in their observation, at least from a strictly orthodox point of view. Christ alone redeemed humankind through his teaching, which is the only truth, and he alone erased original sin through his sacrifice. But all of this disappears from the conceptions of Petrarch and humanism, for whom what matters most is the essence of *humanitas*. . .and, since that essence already existed before the coming of Christ, the latter is in a sense rendered insignificant. . .It seems that for Petrarch, the capacity to be emotionally moved and to repent, inherent in humans *eternally*, may suffice for salvation.[44]

It will, I hope, become clear in the present book that Petrarch learned his Christian humanism from Dante. For Dante, Christ's role is not to deliver some entirely new message, not to teach some previously unknown human ethic, not to convert or change humankind into something that it has not been in the past. Christ does not save by offering some new doctrine; rather, he ratifies and grants legitimacy to models of ethical excellence that may be found throughout human history.

At this point I should pause to remark briefly on the meaning of "diversity" as it pertains to Dante. In recent years the notion of "diversity" has been subjected to scrutiny, and it has been rejected by many as contaminated by its origins in Enlightenment universalism. The idea of "diversity" implies that, despite surface-level or accidental differences, all humans, sharing a single core essence, are deep-down the same. The problem is that we in the West have granted ourselves the authority to define that essence and, thinking that we have found it absent from a given culture, rather than questioning the definition we deny the culture's humanity. Thus "diversity" has been replaced in this time of postcolonial theory with the preferable notion of "difference"—a notion that insists that other cultures are truly (even essentially) different yet nonetheless still human.

Petrarch's humanism is clearly a thinking of "diversity" not "difference": pagans and Christians are, deep-down, the same. By and large, Dante also grounds his global ecumenicism in the thought of "diversity," viewing religious differences as superficial accidents, different ways of representing one and the same ethical truth. But we will see that Dante also conceives of a multiplicity of truths, viewing different cultures as making unique contributions to the sum total of truth.

The problem with Petrarch's Christian humanism is that it is markedly Eurocentric: for Petrarch, it is normally a matter of showing that the "ancients" (Romans and Greeks) were as wise and virtuous as any Christians. Petrarch's extension of moral perfection to non-Christians is more about validating his own project of classical philology than it is a genuine embrace of other cultures. I base this on Petrarch's crusade poem—in which he writes things about Muslims that Dante would not have countenanced. In the following stanza, for instance, Petrarch encourages the powers of Western Europe to stir up the fierce Christianized barbarians of the North so that they might slay the polytheist Muslims. Following a medieval Christian commonplace, yet nonetheless displaying remarkable ignorance, Petrarch imagines that Muslims worship a plurality of gods. And he charges that their cowardice is indicated by their preference for fighting with arrows rather than swords:

> There is a part of the world that
> always lies in ice and frozen snows,
> all distant from the path of the sun;
> there, beneath days cloudy and brief,
> is born a people naturally the enemy of peace,
> whom dying does not pain.

> If these, more devout than in the past,
> gird on their swords in their Teutonic rage,
> you will learn how much to value
> Turks, Arabs, and Chaldeans [i.e., Iraqis],
> with all those who hope in gods [i.e., all Muslims]
> on this side of the sea whose waves are blood-colored [i.e., the Red Sea]:
> a naked, cowardly, and lazy people
> who never grasp the steel
> but entrust all their blows to the wind.[45]

Petrarch appears to adopt a conventional attitude toward crusade, encouraging violence against Muslims. Dante's thinking on crusade, as elaborated in part II, is quite different: he advocates (nonphysical, discursive) violence, not against Islamic peoples but against the religious and political authorities of Western Europe. Dante does not just recognize chronological diversity (the equal capacity for moral excellence of both "ancient" and "modern" Europeans) but he recognizes geographical and cultural diversity as well (the equal capacity for moral excellence of "moderns" from all over the globe). Thus Dante includes, in the place of honor that is his Limbo, "modern" Muslims (Saladin [who, in recapturing Jerusalem from and winning a series of great victories over the Crusaders, effectively put an end to their hopes of conquest], Avicenna, Averroes) alongside such "ancients" as Plato, Aristotle, Virgil, and Aeneas. And, when considering the question of salvation, in a passage that I will examine near the end of part II, he shows particular concern for the fate of non-Christian (non-European) contemporaries such as Hindus (Asians) and Ethiopians (Africans). Dante's Christian humanism is not merely a matter of validating the classical Western past but also of acknowledging the legitimacy of the non-Western present.

Politics and Philosophy: A Brief Primer on Dante's Project for Peace

Since in the course of this book I will frequently refer to Dante's political project as formulated in *Monarchy*, it will be helpful for the reader if I offer a brief description of that project. In this section I draw freely from Etienne Gilson's and Ernst Kantorowicz's classic accounts of the treatise, both of which have stood the test of time. My aim here is primarily to give a general outline of Dante's political vision, so that the reader will be well equipped to understand any references to that vision that might appear below. But in this section I will emphasize that Dante's political project is part and parcel of his call for a philosophical framework that will promote cultural and religious pluralism in general, and, in particular, a positive dialogue with the Islamic world.

Dante's interest in peace was not, as we say, "academic." Violence in Dante's day was not something that one could ponder from a relatively safe distance. It was, rather, a inevitable fact of life in Florence, throughout most of the thirteenth century and into the fourteenth. Florence and most of the other city-states of central and northern Italy were virtually permanently at war—against each other but also internally, divided against themselves by "civil war."

Although referring to the situation in north-central Italy roughly a century before Dante's birth, Lauro Martines's description of the ubiquitous fortified towers that punctuated every cityscape can serve as an approximate metaphor for the norm of fragmentation and group–self interest that still prevailed in Dante's day and that can be loosely termed "tribalism":

> Drawing upon a strong sense of clan and consanguinity, noblemen clustered into tight-knit associations and built fortified towers so as to defend themselves to expand their rights and privileges. . .Verona, Milan, Pavia, Parma, Florence, Siena, Pisa, and other cities—all had numerous towers.

> Whether ascending to the hill city of Perugia or looking from the banks of the Arno toward Florence, the traveler came on a similar view—a nervous skyline of towers. Florence in 1180 had probably a hundred towers. . . .The mushrooming of armed family societies. . .turned neighborhoods into armed zones and delivered the streets to civil war.[46]

This image of a Florence fragmented into a hundred loci of power and perhaps dozens of rival groups—each group looking out exclusively for and violently pursuing its own interest—can represent the basic situation that prevailed throughout north-central Italy in Dante's lifetime. If, in Florence itself, there was some consolidation of power, a gradual movement in the direction of a unified locus of power in the form of "commune" government, there was nonetheless constant factional strife—most famously between Guelphs and Ghibellines throughout most the thirteenth century.[47] Dante himself, at the age of twenty-four, fought on the side of the victorious Guelphs when they defeated the Ghibellines in the Battle of Campaldino in 1289. Later, when "Ghibellinism" was for all intents and purposes a lost cause, civil war in Florence reemerged as a conflict between "White" and "Black" Guelphs. In 1302 Dante, representing the Whites, led a diplomatic mission to Rome, where he hoped to secure Pope Boniface VIII's support for a peaceful settlement of the conflict. Leaving Rome thinking the mission a success, Dante soon realized that Boniface had in truth conspired with the Blacks and Charles of Valois, brother of King Philip IV of France, to chase the Whites from Florence. As had happened several times before in a cycle of fluctuating fortunes and tit-for-tat violence, the losing party's property was confiscated and their houses were razed. Dante was sentenced to permanent exile from Florence and its environs, with the penalty of death should he return. In the remaining twenty years of his life, he never did return to Florence.

Dante's proposed solution for this violent disunity is simple (and perhaps, many would say naïve, impractical, utopian—or, worse, imperialist, "globalist"; it has even been called "fascist"[48]). But, once he had formulated the logic of this solution, based on a truth that, as he says in *Monarchy*, "no one has [ever] attempted to elucidate," he never relented in his conviction that there was no other possible answer.[49] Once he had been struck by this thought, everything that he later wrote was directly or indirectly meant to support it. The driving thought of *Monarchy*, and of the *Comedy*, is this: the necessity of the establishment of what we would call "one-world government."

The solution to disunity is obviously unity. The solution to civil war in Florence was for all of its various factions to come to think of themselves, collectively, as one polity. But a unified Florence, for Dante, would not do the trick. For everything indicates that a unified Florence would soon be warring against, say, a unified Pisa. For Dante, the inexorability of greed (cupidity, the desire to possess what belongs to others) is axiomatic. "I" am always, without exception, compelled to take what is "yours"; "we" are always, without exception, compelled to take what is "theirs." This dynamic, and the violence that is its instrument, can only stop when "I" have everything, when "we" possess all that can be possessed. A unified Tuscany would still be at war with, say, a unified Lombardy. A unified Italy would still be at war with, say, a unified France. A unified Europe would still be at war with, say, a unified Orient. There will be war until such time that there is no "us" and "them," until we all, despite our differences, are "we."

The "I" who will represent and rule over this "we" as its guide and guarantor of justice, Dante calls the "Monarch" (or, interchangeably, the "Emperor"). The Monarch will be the only one who has managed to elude the inexorable grasp of greed—and this, not by an ascetic renunciation of possessions but rather by possessing to the very limits of possibility. Having everything, the Emperor can desire nothing more, and he will thus never act out of self-interest but always for the sake of the common good. As Gilson explains:

> This *cupiditas* ("greed"), of which the She-wolf of the *Divine Comedy* is most certainly a symbol, does not at first appear in Dante as a religious and Christian notion. He borrows it from the Philosopher [i.e, Aristotle], or at any rate the Philosopher suggests it to him ("The greatest enemy of justice is greed, as Aristotle indicates in the fifth book of the *Ethica ad Nicomachum*" [*Monarchy* 1.11.11]). Eliminate greed, and there remains nothing in opposition to justice. Now it happens that the only way to procure a man free from all greed is to install in power one who, possessing all, can no longer covet anything. Such, to be exact, would be the single Monarch of Dante's dreams: a sovereign whose. . .jurisdiction is limitless. The universal Monarch exercises an authority that knows no frontiers: there is therefore no frontier for him to violate. The universal Monarch can have no feeling of greed: he therefore has feelings only of love and charity.[50]

The Emperor is not an "imperialist": he does not act for the aggrandizement of his own people or nation at the expense of others. The genealogy of the Monarchy is tricontinental: its founding hero, Aeneas, is at once African, Asian, and European (in others words, his ancestry is "global"— given that these three continents made up the totality of the inhabited world known to Dante).[51]

If the global Monarch does not represent the interests of any particular people, nation, or continent, neither does he represent any particular religion. Because the Monarchy is universal, it must necessarily be nonsectarian or religiously neutral. As Kantorowicz says:

> In order to prove that the universal Monarch was free from papal
> jurisdiction, Dante had to build up a whole sector of the world which was
> independent not only of the pope, but also of the Church and, virtually, *even
> of the Christian religion*.[52]

If Kantorowicz's basic point here—that Dante's Monarchy is not to be
conceived of as a Christian Empire—is undoubtedly correct, the phrase
"sector of the world" is perhaps misleading. For Monarchy is Monarchy
(etymologically, "one rule") precisely because it is not a "sector of" but
rather the totality of the world. What Kantorowicz means is that Dante
insisted that there is a whole aspect of human existence—a fundamental
goal of human life—that can be attained independently of any religious
guidance.

Dante's Monarchy is an all or nothing proposition: as soon as there is the
slightest exception to the Emperor's universal territorial possession and
juridical authority, as soon as there is a frontier, some other polity besides
the Empire, then, from this one chink or crack in the edifice, the whole
structure will collapse. Thus it was obligatory, in Dante's view, that the
papacy renounce its claim to possess the territories known as the Papal
States (which included a large portion of central Italy). But more importantly, the church needed to entirely renounce its claim to any and all legal
and political authority. That claim had never been so boldly asserted as it
was in 1302 by Dante's arch-enemy, Pope Boniface VIII, in his Papal Bull
Unam Sanctam: "We declare, we proclaim, we define that it is absolutely
necessary for salvation that every human creature be subject to the Roman
Pontiff."[53] Boniface means not only that every human creature must be
"spiritually" subject to the pope—must, in order to be saved, believe the
orthodox doctrines and perform the religious practices prescribed by
the church. More than that, he means that all humans must be "tempo-
rally" subject to the pope—since papal judgment is absolute and legitimately coercive and juridical concerning things both human and divine,
temporal and spiritual, political and religious. Even if humans are directly
or immediately ruled by their various kings, princes, lords, or other gov-
ernmental authorities, these authorities are themselves subordinate to the
pope, serving as the instruments through which he exercises his power and
enforces his judgments (and thus it is within his power to appoint, regulate,
and depose those authorities):

> For with truth as our witness, it belongs to spiritual power to establish the
> terrestrial power and to pass judgment if it has not been good. . . .Therefore,

if the terrestrial power err, it will be judged by the spiritual power; but if a minor spiritual power err, it will be judged by a superior spiritual power; but if the highest power of all [i.e, the pope] err, it can be judged only by God, and not by man, according to the testimony of the Apostle: "The spiritual man judgeth of all things and he himself is judged by no man" [1 Cor 2:15].[54]

Dante is utterly opposed to such claims, for several reasons, not the least being their disastrous consequences for the prospects of peace on earth. While the practicality (not to mention the wisdom or desirability) of the establishment of a universal secular monarchy may seem to us far-fetched, Dante never expresses anything but confidence that the various peoples and nations would, once they had been rightly instructed, welcome the just rule of the Emperor. By the same token, he is convinced that the world will never subject itself to the rule of the church, since not even one of the three continents acknowledges the political authority of the pope: "Not only," says Dante, "all Asians and Africans, but also the greater part of those who live in Europe" find the idea of papal authority "abhorrent."[55] Next to the general inexorable logic of greed, the primary particular cause of violence, the single greatest obstacle to both local and global peace, is the papacy. Dante's call for world peace through Monarchy is part and parcel of his call for a church completely without power and property.

Unlike the Roman pontiff, who only imagines himself a universal political authority, the Monarch would rule and represent the whole global community. As Gilson remarks:

> [Dante] for the first time set up, above the Christian ideal of a universal Church, the human ideal of a single universal temporal order with the Emperor playing the part which the Pope fills in the Church. What Dante calls the "universal community of the human race" (*universalis civilitas humani generis*) or simply "the human community" (*humana civilitas*), was bound to enter into competition with the ideal of the Church, as would a universal community ruled by a single head with another universal community likewise ruled by a single head.[56]

Dante's solution to this competition is a "dualism" or "separatism": a complete disassociation of the spheres proper to church and state, so that they are "two closed systems, which meet only in God"[57] and so that there is a "radical distinction between their goals."[58]

The Church, with no property, no legal jurisdiction, and no coercive power, was established by God solely to provide spiritual teachings conducive to the salvation of the soul. The Monarchy was established by God to guide the universal human community to peace on earth through justice. Dante insists that each of these goals is an *ultimate* goal: one is not lesser than or subordinate to the other (we consider this unusual insistence on *two ultimate goals* in more detail in part I):

> Dante distinguished between a "human" perfection and a "Christian" perfection—two profoundly different aspects of man's possible felicity, even though these two actualizations of man's potentialities were ultimately destined to support, and not to antagonize or exclude, each other. For all that, however, the sphere of *Humanitas* was, in Dante's philosophic system, so radically set apart from that of *Christianitas*, and the autonomous rights of human society. . .were so powerfully emphasized that indeed it is admissible to say that Dante has [in Gilson's words] "abruptly and utterly shattered" the concept of the undisputed unity of the temporal and the spiritual. . . .Dante did not turn *Humanitas* against *Christianitas*, but thoroughly separated the one from the other; he took the "human" out of the Christian compound and isolated it as a value in its own right—perhaps Dante's most original accomplishment in the field of political theology.[59]

The effect of Dante's insistence that the *polis* pertains to *Humanitas* not *Christianitas* is to "open up" the possibility of the reward of justice, civil happiness, felicity on earth, to peoples of all nations, cultures, and faiths. They will be guided by a monarch whose necessary qualifications for the task will include his humanity but not his Christianity; he may, but need not, be Christian.

In somewhat similar terms, John of Paris, in *On Kingly and Papal Power* (1302), separates religion and politics by arguing that the just polity is a final goal, an end in itself. As Gewirth remarks, John rebutted the claims of "political Augustinianism" by asserting that it is not essential that the perfect ruler be Christian:

> In reply to the papalists' Augustinian doctrine that moral virtues are genuine virtues only if they are Christian or religious and thus based on belief in God, so that only a Christian state is truly just, John held that "the acquired moral virtues can be perfect without the theological virtues, nor are they perfected by them except by an accidental perfection." Hence, "even without Christ as ruler there is the true and perfect justice which is required for the state, since the state is ordered to living in accordance with acquired moral virtue, to which it is accidental that it be perfected by any further virtues." Thus the relation between religion and politics, between being a Christian and being a ruler, is merely an "accidental" one. John was here maintaining in a radical manner the Christian Aristotelians' autonomy of nature and morality in relation to grace and religion; the state was sufficiently justified by the former, and hence required no "perfecting" by the latter.[60]

The religious identity of a perfect ruler (whether he be, for instance, Christian or Muslim) is an "accident," such as his being blond or dark-haired,

European or Asian. Neither a ruler nor his subjects need religion in order to acquire the perfect moral virtues that ground the ideal state.

If religion is "accidental," what is "essential" for the perfect state is justice, grounded in human law, which is grounded in ethics or moral philosophy. The Monarch, no less than the ideal pope, is a teacher—the former teaching the way to happiness in this life, the latter the way to happiness in the afterlife. Since he governs a multicultural, religiously plural global polity, the Monarch's teachings cannot be drawn from any single religious discourse. Rather, they must be drawn from the nonsectarian, religiously neutral discourse which is philosophy:

> It was, however, the major premise of the whole scheme of the *Monarchy* that Dante, inspired by Aristotle, attributed to the human community a moral-ethical goal which was "goal in itself," was para-ecclesiastical, and therefore independent of a Church which had its own goal. . . .[Dante's notion of] duality differed profoundly from the Thomistic system in which invariably the secular ends were subordinated to the spiritual. . . .Dante's monarch was not simply a man of the sword and thereby the executive arm of the papacy; his monarch was necessarily a philosophic-intellectual power in its own right. For it was the emperor's chief responsibility, by means of natural reason and moral philosophy to which legal science belonged, to guide the human mind to secular blessedness, just as the pope was charged by Providence to guide the Christian soul to supra-natural illumination.[61]

The Emperor teaches not through religion but through "natural reason and moral philosophy." His "scripture" is not the Gospels or the Qur'an but Aristotle's *Nichomachean Ethics* (a text, not incidentally, embraced with equal fervor by both Christian intellectuals and those Muslim intellectuals from whom they had learned it, and a text that provides the moral structure of Dante's Hell as well as his Purgatory).

Dante's political project in support of the state's independence from the church is thus at the same time an intellectual project in support of philosophy's independence from theology. As Gilson says, going so far as to formulate this as a "law," there is, in the tradition of political philosophy to which Dante belongs, a "necessary correlation" between these two projects:

> It may be postulated as a historically verifiable philosophical law that *the manner in which one conceives the relationship of the State to the Church, that in which one conceives the relationship of philosophy to theology and that in which one conceives the relationship of nature to grace, are necessarily correlated.*[62]

According to Gilson's law, if in *Monarchy* Dante argues for the self-sufficiency of the state (which in fact he does), he also argues for the self-sufficiency of philosophy (which in fact he does). And, again according to Gilson's law, if in the *Comedy* Dante were to argue for the subordination of philosophy to theology, he would thus at the same time be arguing for the subordination of the state to the church.

Now, the "theological" school that has dominated American Dante criticism for four decades is itself dominated by one main thought: that the poem is above all Dante's *demotion* of philosophy, a critique of its limitations, resulting in its subordination to theology, the subordination of reason to faith. According to Gilson's law, the necessary corollary would be that the *Comedy* subordinates the state to the church, the Monarch to the Pontiff. But no fair-minded reading of the poem can possibly support this view. Inscribed at the *Comedy*'s very structural center, as I will discuss in part I, is *Monarchy*'s "dualist" or "separatist" political theory—and this center anchors the poem from beginning to end, from *Inferno* I to *Paradiso* XXXIII. Either Gilson's law is wrong, or the prevailing "Christianizing" reading of the *Comedy*, with its ever-present assertion of philosophy's subordination to theology, is wrong. One of the aims of the present book is to reclaim philosophy, against theology, as the *Comedy*'s proper primary field of concern.

The obvious problem with what I have just said is this: there is no need to think that we are faced with an either/or decision; there is no need to say that the poem is either chiefly philosophical or chiefly theological. If we take Dante at his word that there are two goals, *both of which are ultimate*, then we must acknowledge that his aim was to subordinate neither philosophy to religion nor religion to philosophy. But we can still imagine, as a thought experiment, that a decision must be made. If I were absolutely forced to decide, which of the two goals do I think Dante would deem primary and which secondary? The representatives of the "theological" school of American Dante criticism do not need to be coerced—they are all too ready to make the decision, to subordinate philosophy. But there are plenty of reasons to argue that, *if* forced, we should lean in the other direction. This book is in part an attempt to gather together in a coherent fashion some of those reasons why, if we were forced, we should say that Dante would subordinate theology to philosophy. This does not mean that we must deny that the *Comedy* is religious. But, if the "tilt" *is* toward philosophy, then we will need to reconceive Dante's religion. We will need to think of his religion as religion seen through the eyes of a philosopher. We will have to become familiar with the religion of the philosophers—with the tradition of Arabo-Islamic rationalism.

In *Monarchy*, Dante often seems to speak as if global peace, the just universal human society achieved by the establishment of empire, is an end in itself. But in the beginning of the treatise he also speaks of peace as a means to another end. This "final objective" or "ultimate purpose" (*ultimus finis*), for the attainment of which global peace is a means, he describes as "the purpose of human society as a whole," as "the highest potentiality of the whole of mankind," and as "some activity specific to humanity as a whole."[63] This "purpose of human society" must be something specific to humankind, something that sets us apart from all other species of creature, something that defines our essence. This something that defines us as a species is not the bare fact of existing, for

> the [physical] elements too share in the simple fact of existence; nor is it to exist in compound form, for that is found in minerals; nor is it to exist as a living thing, for plants too share in that; nor is it to exist as a creature with sense perception, for that is also shared by the lower animals; but it is *to exist as a creature who apprehends by means of the potential intellect*: this mode of existence belongs to no creature (whether higher or lower) other than human beings. . . .It is thus clear that the highest potentiality of mankind is his intellectual potentiality or faculty.[64]

Humans, unlike other animals and all lower creatures, have the potential to *intellegere*, to "understand," to know truth. But the fact that our understanding truth is, in its initial default mode, only *potential* is what sets us apart from the higher creatures ("celestial intelligences" or "angels"), who are constantly *actually* understanding the specific truth that it is their nature to understand (namely, the truth of their own existence: "for their very being is simply the act of understanding that their own nature exists; and they are engaged in this ceaselessly, otherwise they would not be eternal"[65]). Only humans, of all creatures, can transform themselves from not (but potentially) understanding to actually understanding truth. Our purpose is to transform ourselves in this manner, to actualize this intellectual potential.

The global Monarchy is the necessary means for peace. Peace is itself the necessary means for humankind to actualize its potential intellect (to make actual its capacity to know the truth). As Gilson explains, "this is what Dante propounds as his starting-point. No universal community, no peace; no peace, no opportunity for man to develop to the highest pitch his aptitude for discovering truth or, consequently, to attain his goal. This is the fixed point, the cardinal fact to which all that Dante proves in the *Monarchy* amounts and on which it is based."[66]

Now, does the formula "No peace, no truth!" really make sense? Or is it in fact nothing more than an attractive slogan? Is it really true that we cannot know truth without (universal) peace? We can imagine a thinker somewhere, in some war-torn territory, being every bit as in touch with

truth as some leading thinker in a peaceful land. In fact, this is just what Ibn
Bajjah (Avempace), the first philosopher of the Muslim West (who wrote
in al-Andalus in the first part of the twelfth century AD), had said in his
treatise *The Regime of the Solitary*: that the philosopher who finds himself in
a corrupt and violent society ought to completely disengage from political
and practical matters; in doing so, he will be free to think, to fully actualize his potential intellect, to come to know truth. Although a peaceful
society is certainly better than a violent one, living amidst violence does
not in any way inhibit the philosopher from attaining his primary goal, the
actualization of his potential intellect—provided that he turns his back on
that society. True, it may be tremendously difficult for a philosopher
caught up in the chaos of warfare to philosophize properly—since he will
likely be first of all concerned with basic survival—but we would hardly say
that it is absolutely impossible. Yet Dante, whose arguments in *Monarchy*
are not fuzzy but rigorously logical, is positing this as an absolute: *no peace,
no truth*. To understand this formula we need to know what Dante means
by "truth."

Ibn Bajjah thinks of "actualizing the potential intellect" or "coming to
know truth" in a manner that is still commonplace today: as something that
can be performed by an individual, something that one does by oneself
alone: "When he [i.e., the philosopher as a solitary individual] achieves *the
final end*—that is, when he intellects simple essential intellects. . . .—he then
becomes one of these intellects. It would be right to call him simply
divine. . . .All these qualities can be obtained by the solitary individual in
the absence of the perfect city."[67] Ibn Bajjah thinks of the specifically
human *final end* (Dante's *ultimus finis*) as a goal that can be reached by an
individual. Truth, for Ibn Bajjah, is apparently some objective, determinate
content with which some individuals among us (although it rarely happens)
can come into conjunction.

But for Dante the *ultimus finis* of the human species is never *mine*—that
is, it is never something that "I" can accomplish alone. For Dante, the
"actualization of the potential intellect" is a collective endeavor. It is not
merely a matter of my knowing everything that I can possibly know; it is a
matter of humanity as a whole knowing everything that it can possibly
know. Dante's thinking on this issue is the polar opposite of Ibn Bajjah's.
Not only is the "actualization of the potential intellect," the coming to
know truth, not something that an individual can do, neither is it something attainable by a whole city, nor for any community smaller than the
"universal community of the human race":

> There is therefore some activity specific to humanity as a whole, for which
> the whole human race in all its vast number of individual human beings is

designed; and no single person, or household, or small community, or city, or individual kingdom can fully achieve it.[68]

Since the full actualization of humankind's potential intellect always exceeds the capacity of any particular community, culture, polity, or social group, none of these can ever claim that it "knows the truth":

> It is thus clear that the highest potentiality of mankind is his intellectual potentiality or faculty. And since that potentiality cannot be fully actualized all at once in any one individual or in any one of the particular social groupings enumerated above, there must needs be a vast number of individual people in the human race, through whom the whole of this potentiality can be actualized; just as there must be a great variety of things which can be generated so that the whole potentiality of prime matter can continuously be actualized; otherwise one would be postulating a potentiality existing separately from actualization, which is impossible. And Averroes is in agreement with this opinion in his commentary on the *De anima*.[69]

The plenitude of truth always exceeds the grasp of every individual—whether that individual be a single person or a single community. Nor can humankind's knowledge of truth be fully actualized in any single historical era. In fact the very first sentence of *Monarchy* insists that truth is constantly developing in history, such that each generation adds something unique to the totality of humankind's potential intellect ("For all men whom the Higher Nature has endowed with a love of truth, this above all seems to be a matter of concern, that just as they have been enriched by the efforts of their forebears, so they too may work for future generations, in order that posterity may be enriched by their efforts").[70] The thinkers of the present, who have built upon yet surpassed in some manner the thinkers of the past, will themselves be built upon and be surpassed in some manner by the thinkers of the future.

The analogy in the passage above between the vast number of humans necessary for the full actualization of human intellectual potential and the "great variety of things" necessary so that "the whole potentiality of prime matter can continuously be actualized" is quite suggestive. Prime matter (raw material stuff, the basic physical elements) can potentially take on a great variety of forms—rocks, ponds, fire, snowflakes, mountain ranges—to mention just a few inanimate forms in which matter can be shaped. For any manner in which prime matter *potentially can* be shaped, there must exist something in which prime matter *actually is* shaped in that manner—and thus there must be a "great variety of things" to make actual all of prime matter's potential. By analogy, a great variety of human groupings must come into existence so that all truths that *potentially can* be known by the human intellect *actually will* be known in some place or at some time. Human intellectual history, in all its multiplicity and diversity, is the necessary process by which the plentitude of human intellectual potential becomes actual. The existence of Ethiopians and Hindus, and of those Scythians (central Asian nomads) and Garamantes (blacks who dwelled in the Sahara oases of what is now southern Libya) whom Dante mentions in *Monarchy* as evidence that the peoples of different cultures need to be governed by different laws, is not superfluous.[71] This is all part of the "great variety" necessary for "the universal community of humanity" to fully actualize its potential intellect.

Dante thus regards truth as collective, historical, and multiple: truth is the sum total of all that humans can possibly know, past, present, and future, here, there, and everywhere. As Gilson says: "This total knowledge cannot be realized all at once by any individual, or even by any particular group of human beings. Only the human species taken in its entirety is entitled to lay claim to it."[72] Truth, for Dante, is the history of all truths. As Emmanuel Levinas remarked regarding "absolute truth" in the Jewish tradition: "It is as if a multiplicity of persons. . .were the condition for the plenitude of 'absolute truth', as if each person, by virtue of his own uniqueness, were able to guarantee the revelation of one unique aspect of truth, so that some of its facets would never have been revealed if certain people had been absent from mankind. . . .The multiplicity of people, each one of them indispensable, is necessary to produce all the dimensions of meaning; the multiplicity of meanings is due to the multiplicity of people."[73]

As a way of returning to the relation between truth and peace, we can look at a passage from the *Defensor pacis* in which Marsilius similarly insists on the collectivity of truth:

> Consequently, what one man alone can discover or know by himself, both in the science of civil justice and benefit and in the other sciences, is little or nothing. Moreover, what is observed by the men of one era is quite imperfect by comparison with what is observed in many eras, so that Aristotle, discussing the discovery of truth in every art and discipline, wrote as follows in the *Philosophy* [i.e., *Metaphysics*], Book II, Chapter I [993b]: "One man," that is, one discoverer of any art or discipline "contributes to it," that is, discovers about it by himself alone, "little or nothing, but by the contributions of all a great deal is accomplished." This passage is clearer in the translation from the Arabic, in which it reads as follows: "Each of them," that is, each of the discoverers of any art or discipline, "comprehends little or nothing about the truth. But when a collection is made from among all who have achieved some comprehension, what is collected will be of considerable quantity". . . .He also makes the same point in the [*Nichomachean*] *Ethics*, Book VIII, Chapter I [1155a]: "Two persons are better able to act and to

understand" (supply: than one alone). But if two, then more than two, *both simultaneously and successively*, can do more than one man alone.[74]

Truth depends upon a multiplicity of perspectives, *both simultaneously and successively*. That is, it is not just that the truths of several successive historical eras need to be collected together, but also that several truths from the present historical era need to be collected together. Truth's necessary plurality is both temporal and spatial, diachronic and synchronic, chronological and geographical. We open ourselves to the truth not only by recognizing that those who came before us may have seen, and those who will come after us may see, things that we cannot see, but also by recognizing that those who are contemporary with us, others, may see things that we cannot see.

And this is why Dante can say, "No peace, no truth!" Without peace, there can be no optimal "collection" of humankind's simultaneous and successive truths. The "activity proper to mankind considered as a whole," says Dante, "is constantly to actualize the full intellectual potential of humanity."[75] In Gilson's words, Dante is promoting "the idea, which is, moreover, a splendid one, of a unity of the human race in which the whole of humanity would at all times realize its special aim, namely to possess the entire intellectual knowledge which it is capable of assimilating" (an idea, Gilson says, that Dante owes to Averroes).[76] Now, for instance, if the Christian world is at war with the Muslim world, and if a Christian intellectual is thus prevented from knowing or disinclined to come to know some of the truths of the Islamic tradition, then such an intellectual has failed to "actualize" not only his own "full intellectual potential" but also the full intellectual potential of humanity as a whole. The ideal is for everyone everywhere continually to realize the total power of their possible intellects—to come to know all those things that they do not already know. When we are blocked by war from the truths of our enemies, the total actualization of our potential intellect is rendered impossible. Hence, "No peace, no truth!"

Certainly Dante regards peace as a good for its own sake, as an end in itself. But inasmuch as it is a means, it is a means to truth—*which is only truth when it comprehends the truths of others*, including the others who, prior to the establishment of peace, we would have called our enemies. We are not wise until we have drawn upon—to the fullest possible extent—the wisdom of those whom our predecessors have been battling against. A reading of Dante that purports to give an account of what he finds in his quest for truth is incomplete if it does not include the truths of Christendom's "other," the truths of Islam.

There is a famous (if today virtually unknown in the West) precedent for this insistence on the total actualization of our intellectual potential—an actualization that depends on an openness to the truths of others, including all other cultural traditions. I am referring to the group of Shi'ite thinkers known as the Ikhwan al-Safa ("The Brotherhood of the Pure"), who, writing in Basra (Iraq) around 1000 AD, composed the encyclopedia of knowledge known as the *Rasa'il* (*Epistles*). (I treat the Ikhwan al-Safa in more detail in part I) The *Epistles* amounts to an effort to provide a total compendium of all knowledge. The Brotherhood's methodological principle is to draw upon truth wherever it might find it, to draw from all scriptures, all creeds, all peoples, all cultures. It aims to "embrace all schools of thought and unite all branches of knowledge," and in doing so it exhibits "a total lack of hostility towards other branches of knowledge and schools of thought."[77] In fact, this absolute openness is the very substance of its "religion," as is declared in its "Creed of the Brotherhood of Purity." For the Ikhwan's creed is

> to shun no science, scorn any book, or to cling fanatically to any single creed. For our own creed encompasses all the others and comprehends all the sciences generally. This creed is the consideration of all existing things, both sensible and intelligible, from beginning to end, whether hidden or overt, manifest or obscure. . .insofar as they all derive from a single principle, a single cause, a single world, and a single Soul.[78]

The Brotherhood was not entirely unknown in the medieval West. It had its adherents in al-Andalus, including both Muslims and Jews. By the thirteenth century its doctrines had spread to Occitania (southern France). It is interesting to note that, by one account at least, Dante himself was a member of the Ikhwan al Safa.[79] Whether or not this is literally true (and I am not inclined to give it much credence), there is some truth in the *idea* of Dante as one of the Brethren of the Pure. At any rate, the Ikhwan, much like Dante, insists that humankind's attainment of its goal requires collective cooperation: "The reason why the Brethren of Purity assemble," it says, "is that each of them sees and knows that he cannot attain what he wishes concerning his well-being in this world and the attainment of success and salvation in the next world except through the cooperation of each one of them with his companion."[80]

We can add an additional clause to Gilson's law: the manner in which one conceives the relationship of the state to the church and the question of whether one embraces religious pluralism or religious intolerance are necessarily correlated. We can see this by looking at a late-medieval philosopher who, ideologically, is Dante's polar opposite—Roger Bacon (ca. 1214–92 AD). If Dante is among the great late-medieval champions of the state's plentitude of temporal power, Bacon is among the great champions of the church's: "You have," says Bacon, addressing the pope, "the Church of God in your power, and *you have the task of governing the entire world*."[81] (It is precisely this idea, that the papacy ought to govern the world, which Dante says the world, including most Europeans, find "abhorrent.") And, according to Bacon, one of the pope's chief political tasks is, in Gilson's words, "the conversion of infidel peoples and the destruction of those which cannot be converted."[82]

For Dante, as is discussed especially in part I, in the sphere of ethics (virtue, the capacity for moral excellence), all humans from all times and places are equally capable: they need only follow the natural guidance of reason. Religion is by no means the sine qua non for ethical perfection. Bacon, on the contrary, insists that human ethical perfection (how we comport ourselves toward our neighbors and toward ourselves) depends on instruction from the pope:

> Man cannot know by his own effort how to please God with the worship due Him, nor how he should stand in relation to his neighbor nor to himself, but needs the revelation of truth in these things. . . .[That] revelation must be made to one [i.e., to the pope] only. . . .He must be the mediator of God and men and vicar of God on earth, to whom is subjected the whole human race, and in whom one must believe without contradiction when it has been proved with certitude that he is such as I have just described him; and he is the lawgiver and the high priest who in spiritual and in temporal things has the plenitude of power, as a "human God," as Avicenna says in Book X of the *Metaphysics*, "whom it is permissible to adore after God."[83]

It is an indicator of Bacon's perversity as one of Europe's first major "Orientalists" (he knew Arabic philosophy and science probably better than any of his contemporaries in the West, and he was one of the first Europeans to promote the institutional study of the Arabic language) that he uses the Islamic philosopher Avicenna to support the proposition that all humans must be subject to, even worship, the pope.

In his *Opus maius*, Bacon considers the question, "Who should be proclaimed as the lawgiver and which religion should be propagated throughout the world?" After listing "the principal rites" or "major religions in this world" (of which, says Bacon, there are six: paganism, idolatry, the religion of the Tartars [i.e., Buddhism], Islam, Judaism, Christianity), and after having disposed of the claims of the nonmonotheistic religions, Bacon turns to consider the three monotheisms. He asserts that "the Christian law should be preferred," since "the teachings of the philosophers" give "noble testimonies. . .concerning the articles of the Christian faith."[84] Philosophy agrees with Christian doctrines, but not with the doctrines of Judaism and Islam:

> Philosophy, however, does not agree in this manner with the religion of the Jews and of the Saracens [i.e., Muslims], nor do the philosophers provide testimonies in their favor. Hence it is evident that, since philosophy is a preamble to religion and disposes men to it, the religion of the Christians is the only one that should be held.
>
> Moreover, the philosophers not only pave the way for the Christian religion, but destroy the two other religions; for Seneca, in the book that he composed against the religion of the Jews, shows in many ways that it is the most irrational and erroneous in that it is bound by the letter alone, in accordance with the belief of the carnal Jews who thought that it suffices for salvation. The Saracen philosophers also find fault with their own law and calculate that it will quickly come to an end. Avicenna, in Book IX of the *Metaphysics*, takes issue with Muhammad because he spoke only of corporal pleasures and not of spiritual pleasures. Albumazar [Abu Mashar], too, in Book I of the *Conjunctions*, teaches that that religion will not last longer than 693 years; and 665 years have already elapsed. . . .It is clear that the Tartars [i.e., Mongols] have nearly obliterated the entire dominion of the Saracens from the north, the east, and the west as far as Egypt and Africa, in such a way that the Caliph, who occupies the position of the Pope among them, was destroyed thirteen years ago, and Baghdad, the city of this Caliph, was captured along with an infinite multitude of Saracens.[85]

In Bacon's view, Islam is dying, breathing its last gasp. Its philosophers have turned against it, and they will no doubt find refuge in the only truly philosophical religion, Christianity. The Christian religion is rational, while the other two monotheisms are not.

Contrast this with a passage from the *Convivio* in which Dante insists on the rationality, not only of all three monotheisms, but of the religion of the Tartars and of other religions as well:

> If we look through all the books of both the philosophers and the other sages who have written on this topic, they all agree in this: that there is some part of us which is immortal. Aristotle seems to confirm this above all in his book *On the Soul*; every Stoic seems above all to confirm this; Tully [i.e., Cicero] seems to confirm this, especially in his short book *On Old Age*; every poet who has spoken according to the pagan faith seems to confirm this; every law [i.e., religious faith] confirms this—whether Jews, Saracens [i.e., Muslims], Tartars, or whoever else lives according to any principle of reason [*ragione*].[86]

For Dante, Islam, Judaism, Christianity, paganism, the religion of the Tartars, indeed every religion—all agree with the philosophers. For Bacon, philosophy is a tool, consonant with Christianity but not with other religions, by which Christendom destroys all non-Christian faiths. For Dante, philosophy is the rational content of all religions, and, as the basis for the moral guidance provided by the secular, universal state, it brings together, in common cooperation, peoples of all cultures and faiths.

This religiously neutral, nonsectarian aspect of Dante's Monarchy, meant to unite those of all religions for the sake of peace on earth, is quite plain to see. As Kantorowicz says:

> [Dante's] *humana universitas* embraced not only Christians or members of the Roman Church, but was conceived of as the world community of all men, Christians and non-Christians alike. To be "man," and not to be "Christian," was the criterion for being a member of the human community of this world, which for the sake of universal peace, justice, liberty, and concord was to be guided by the philosopher-emperor to its secular self-actualization in the terrestrial paradise. And whereas great portions of men— Jews, Mohammedans, Pagans—did not belong to the mystical body of Christ, or belonged to it only potentially, Dante's *humana civilitas* included all men: the pagan (Greek and Roman) heroes and wise men, as well as the Muslim Sultan Saladin and the Muslim philosophers Avicenna and Averroes.[87]

What has perhaps been less plain is that the *Comedy* does not retract or abrogate *Monarchy*'s basic principle of religious pluralism. The "theological" school of Dante criticism has managed to hide Dante's openness to other faiths. In this book I argue that such openness is a quality not only of *Monarchy* but of the *Comedy* as well.

Dante and Islam

If this book is in part about "Dante and Islam," it is not meant to be a study of sources or influences in the manner of, for instance, Miguel Asín Palacios's classic *La escatología musulmana en la Divina Comedia* (1919). Palacios argued that Dante's vision of the other world was massively indebted—for its structure and architecture, its imagery and details—to a variety of Islamic accounts of other world journeys. But it is not only external features and literary trappings which Dante borrowed from Islam; rather, Palacios says, the essential content of Dante's thought was itself substantially Islamic ("Dante's thought thus appears oriented in the same Arabic direction that his artistic constructions reveal to us").[88] Palacios agrees with Bruno Nardi, who had shown that

> Dante, far from being an absolute Thomist, is a rather eclectic scholar who, without following any particular master, accepts ideas and theories from all

thinkers, ancient and medieval, Christian and Islamic, to found his own personal system which occupies a middle ground between Thomism and Avicennism-Averroism, although, concerning a great number of problems, it is closer to the latter than to the former. . . .And Nardi shows how Dante's ideas, although they have some precedent in the Augustinian tradition, derive more from Arabic neo-platonic philosophy and, specifically, from the systems of al-Farabi, Avicenna, al-Ghazali, and Averroes.[89]

Palacios adds that Dante was not only indebted to Islamic philosophy, but to Islamic mysticism as well. In particular, *Paradiso* teaches "the metaphysics of light," which Dante borrowed, says Palacios, from the great Andalusia-born Sufi Ibn Arabi. And Palacios maintains that not only the *Comedy*, but also the *Convivio* and the *Vita Nuova*, are to some degree "imitations" of works by Ibn Arabi.

I give some attention to Ibn Arabi in this book (part II). But it is not an attempt to prove his direct influence on Dante. Instead it is will be a matter of general affinities, parallel paradigms—the claim that the spirit of what Ibn Arabi was aiming for is consonant with the spirit of Dante's project. While I would certainly not deny the possibility of more-or-less direct influence, my aim here has nothing to do with verifying such influence. Dante and Ibn Arabi are bound together by the fact that, deeply troubled by their witnessing persecution within communities and violence between communities of different religious identities, they responded by promoting tolerance, compassion, and respect for others (as Palacios says, Dante "proudly called himself a citizen of the world, proclaiming human brotherhood as the chief principle of political life and imbuing his poem's marvelous stanzas with a spirit of universal and eternal morality and mysticism"[90]). Ibn Arabi's response, grounded in his understanding of the Qur'an, involves an emphasis on God's divine name "the Merciful."[91] For Ibn Arabi the essence of what he calls the Muhammadan Path is its recognizing the validity of a multiplicity of differing paths. Dante is thus, by analogy at least, a "Muhammadan."

In the case of Dante's indebtedness to the Arabo-Islamic rationalist tradition, it is clear that there *is* a more-or-less direct influence at work. This is not only because such an influence was inescapable ("Considering," says Khaled Abou El Fadl, "the numerous cultural interactions and intellectual transmissions between the Muslim world and Europe, it is highly likely that every significant Western value has a measure of Muslim blood in it"[92]), but also because Dante was especially concerned with one of the main questions treated by that tradition—the question of the relation of religion and philosophy. If perhaps Dante did not directly know al-Farabi's *Principles of the Views of the Citizens of the Perfect State*, which is the *locus classicus* for the treatment of the question (and which is the centerpiece of part I of the present book), he did, through the thought of al-Farabi's greatest "disciples," Averroes and Maimonides, have a more than passing familiarity with the major issues involved. (Maimonides, the greatest philosopher in the history of Judaism, is also rightly described as an "Islamic" philosopher—not just because he wrote in Arabic but because the essence of his thought fits squarely in the tradition of Islamic rationalism.[93])

Averroes explicitly named this question, with the title of his *Decisive Treatise, Determining What the Connection is Between Religion and Philosophy* (see part II). Maimonides's *Guide of the Perplexed*, although it does not openly name the question (since Maimonides prefers to keep relatively quiet about the things that matter most) is largely concerned with determining what the connection is between religion and philosophy. (I consider some aspects of Maimonides's treatment of this question at the end of part I.) Dante, for his part, names this question with the figures of "Beatrice" and "Virgil" (according to the standard interpretation of the *Comedy*, which we will provisionally accept yet also work to overcome, "Beatrice" stands for "religion" and "Virgil" stands for "philosophy"). By organizing the *Comedy* around his journey with these two primary guides, and by compelling the reader to ask what the relation is between the two, Dante is writing his own "decisive treatise, determining what the connection is between religion and philosophy." But while Averroes had contented himself with writing *about* religious discourse, Dante does something more: he *produces* a religious discourse that contains, as one of its multiple layers of meaning, a coherent discussion about religious discourse and its relation to philosophy. As I discuss in part II, the *Comedy* is a *prophetic* text, in the specific manner in which Averroes understands the Qur'an to be prophetic ("prophetic" here does not mean foretelling the future but rather pertaining to the discourse of the religious Lawgiver).

For Averroes, the Qur'an, like any other religious revelation, aims for the establishment of a peaceful and just social order. The philosopher sees that the truth of the Qur'an is concordant with the truth of other revealed religions, and thus rather than insisting that there is only ever a single right religious path, he can say, as does Averroes, that one ought to "choose the best religion of his age, although all of them are equally true."[94] The determination that a religion is "good" (or, perhaps, "better" or "best") is not in any way related to that religion's degree of truth-content. Moreover, such a determination is historically relative: some religions are better suited to a particular historical age than others. The best religion is the one that, in a specific set of historical and material circumstances, best leads the community to peace.

The Arabo-Islamic rationalist tradition arrives at its ethical imperative, which includes the promotion of religious pluralism and a tolerance for religious diversity, by claiming that, deep-down, the truth of all religions (their philosophical content) is the same. The Islamic mysical tradition, although sometimes similarly suggesting that all religions are just different names for the same thing,[95] tends to arrive at the same ethical imperative of pluralism and tolerance in a different way—by insisting that each religion, each belief, is utterly unique, each is but a "partial" view, none is the "whole truth," and all are divinely illuminated. (The rationalist tradition thinks "diversity," while the mystical tradition thinks "difference.") This is best expressed in the remarkable writings of Islam's "Greatest Master," the *Shaykh al Akbar*, Ibn Arabi. For Ibn Arabi, the "Perfect Humans" or "Muhammadans" (whom he also calls "the People of Unveiling") are they who do not exclusively adhere to any single truth but rather recognize that all truths, even those that diverge from or contradict others, are God's "self-disclosures," manifestations of God's multifaceted reality:

> The People of Unveiling have been given an all-inclusive overview of all religions, creeds, sects, and doctrines concerning God. They are not ignorant of any of these. Adherents follow creeds, sects, conform to specific laws, and doctrines are held concerning God or something in the engendered universe. Some of these contradict, some diverge, and some are similar. In every case the Possessor of Unveiling knows from where the doctrine, the creed, or the sect is taken, and he ascribes to it a place. He offers an excuse for everyone who holds a doctrine and does not declare him in error. He does not consider the doctrine to be vain, for *God did not create the heaven and the earth and what is between them for unreality* [Qur'an 38:27] and He did not create the human being *in vain* [23:115].[96]

All humans, all cultures, all faiths, all doctrines, are *real*, and none is superfluous. As Ibn Arabi puts it: "There is absolutely no error in the cosmos." The "People of Unveiling" come to know the truth not by proclaiming the veracity of some set of truths and rejecting all others, but rather by understanding and affirming the total set of all possibilities. Truth cannot be the possession of one particular community which will deem itself to be the only real humanity. No community has been created in vain.

In a short section of *Meccan Openings* accompanied with the caption, "The goals are diverse only because of the diversity of the self-disclosures," Ibn Arabi says:

> Were God's self-disclosures one in every respect, He could have no more than a single goal. But the diversity of goals has been established, so every

specific goal must have a specific self-disclosure that is different from every other self-disclosure. For the divine Vastness demands that nothing be repeated in existence. . . .That is why effects are diverse in the cosmos.[97]

The vast multitudes of varying beliefs are not all different names for the same thing but rather different ways by which God's infinite diversity is revealed through his infinitely diverse self-disclosures. For Averroes, one and the same truth is repeated in all revealed religions. For Ibn Arabi, a given truth is never repeated twice, and every utterance, every proposition concerning God, every belief, every religious doctrine, is true. This cannot be otherwise, since all utterances or thoughts are, literally, God's word: "There is no speaker but God, and none who causes to speak but God. All that remains is the opening of the eye of understanding to God's causing to speak in respect to the fact that He only causes speech that is correct. Every speech in the cosmos derives either from wisdom or from God's decisive address. So all speech is protected from error or slipping."[98]

In a section with the caption "The self-disclosures are diverse only because of the diversity of the revealed religions," Ibn Arabi asserts the legitimacy, not only of a diversity of religions, but also of diverse interpretations *within* a specific religion:

> Each revealed religion is a path that takes to God, and these paths are diverse. Hence the self-disclosures must be diverse, just as the divine gifts are diverse. . . .Moreover, people's views of the revealed law are diverse. Each possessor of independent judgment has his own specific law that is a path to God. That is why the schools of law are diverse, even though each is revealed law, within a single revealed religion. And God has established this for us on the tongue of His messenger.[99]

Here Ibn Arabi is doing his best to promote tolerance *within* Islam, the acceptance of all of the various "schools" or sects of Islamic jurisprudence and exegesis. Similarly, as is demonstrated in part II, Dante does his best to undermine the claims of the Inquisition to determine who is and who is not a "real" Christian. Although they get there in different ways, Dante and Ibn Arabi both arrive at the thought that no one culture or interpretive community can ever claim exclusive possession of the truth, that none ever has the whole truth, and that truth is the sum total of human thinking in all its diversity.

If the primary implication for Dante of the Arabo-Islamic rationalist tradition is its promotion of religious pluralism, based on the view that the essential (philosophical) meaning of all revealed religions is identical, there is another implication of considerable, if secondary, importance for our study of Dante: the suggestion of a certain degree of skepticism concerning the immortality of the individual human soul—and thus the view of religious discourse not as "truth" but as socially useful rhetoric. We cannot properly approach Dante by pretending that he was unaware of this thought.[100]

Averroes' teachings on immortality and the afterlife can appear contradictory (since at times he seems to deny immortality while at other times he insists that the denial of immortality is heretical) but are in fact fairly coherent. The apparent ambiguity comes from the fact that Averroes always takes into account the nature of his audience. He will say things in his "esoteric" writings (those intended for a specialist audience of philosophers) that he will not say in his more "exoteric" writings (those intended for a more public audience). But he never says anything to the general public that is not, strictly speaking, consistent with what he says to his private audience of philosophers.

In his *Exposition of Religious Arguments*, which is to be reckoned as among his "exoteric" writings, Averroes unambiguously states that religion and philosophy agree that the human soul is immortal: "Now, in all religions revelation has warned that the soul is imperishable, and the philosophers have offered demonstrative proofs of that imperishability."[101] Averroes insists that there *is* indeed such a thing as "resurrection." But the real issue is not *whether* "resurrection" is, but rather *what* it is. And it is here where religion (at least in the literal representations that it offers) and reason differ, and where various religions differ from one another:

> The *reality* of resurrection is a matter about which all religions are in agreement and philosophers have offered demonstrative proofs. Religions, however, disagreed about the *mode* of this reality. In fact, they did not disagree on the mode of its existence, as much over the representations they used to symbolize this unseen state to the common people. Some religions have described it as spiritual, pertaining to souls only, while some others have described it as pertaining to bodies and souls together.[102]

When the religions are properly interpreted (as only philosophers can interpret them), they are seen to contain a "truth-content" which agrees with philosophy concerning not just the reality but also the mode of resurrection. But, since it would be socially counterproductive if religion were openly to teach the real mode of resurrection, it instead provides the general public with socially useful images or representations of the hereafter—representations that indicate the truth to philosophers but keep it safely veiled from the masses. In some religions (e.g., Christianity), the hereafter tends to be represented in more spiritual terms; in others (e.g., Islam), it tends to be represented in more corporeal terms. Since corporeal representations more easily instill desire for Heaven and fear of Hell in the common people, the latter kind of religion is more conducive to inspiring people to "seek the hereafter" (and hence to perform the actions that ensure social tranquility):

> As we stated earlier, all the different religions are in agreement that souls experience, after death, certain states of happiness and suffering; but they disagree in the manner of representing these states and in explaining the mode of their existence to mankind. It appears that the way our religion represents them is more adequate for making the majority of people understand them and rendering their souls more eager to seek what exists beyond this life. After all, the primary target of religion is the majority of people. It appears that the spiritual representation is less effective in stimulating the souls of the common people to seek what lies beyond, and the common people are less desirous and less fearful of it than they are of corporeal representations. For this reason the corporeal representation seems to be a stronger impetus for seeking the hereafter than spiritual representation.[103]

In short, Averroes, in his exoteric texts, teaches that the soul is immortal, there is an afterlife, resurrection is a reality. And, though he indicates that the afterlife understood by philosophy may be different from the afterlife represented by religion, he does not go into specifics.

Not going into specifics in his public writings is part of Averroes's effort to encourage a basic attitude of "openness" concerning such matters. For the Islamic community, he often suggests, is best unified when its fundamental dogma is kept to an absolute minimum. Provided that one does not deny life after death (which belief is the foundation of a healthy civil society), one is free, as a Muslim, to think whatever one wishes concerning that eternal life:

> The truth of the matter is that the obligation incumbent on each person is to take the position to which his speculation leads him to; provided that such speculation does not completely destroy the original principle; namely, the denial of the existence of life after death altogether. This kind of belief [i.e., that there is no afterlife] necessitates that its holder be declared an unbeliever, because the knowledge of the existence of this state of man is known to all people through religion and reason. All this is based on the immortality of the soul.[104]

The philosopher, so long as he does not "completely" deny the immortality of the soul, cannot be called an "unbeliever." But if the masses are correct in their belief that there is an afterlife, they are incorrect in their various beliefs concerning *what* it is.[105] Still, it is sufficient that the common people have incorrect beliefs concerning the afterlife, provided that they respond appropriately to revelation's call to right practice:

> But the thoughts of the general public are not moved to correct these conceptions of the resurrection, but they are moved to follow the Scriptures and practice the virtues.[106]

It is not essential, for the social good, that the whole community know the truth concerning resurrection. On the contrary, it *is* essential that they *not* know the truth, and the one who would publicly divulge the truth is to be classified a heretic.

So we will not find specifics concerning what Averroes would endorse as a "correct conception" of the resurrection by looking in a work such as *Exposition of Religious Arguments*. To find something approaching his own understanding of the matter, one needs to turn to his specialist philosophical works, such as the brief treatise, *Epistle on the Possibility of Conjunction with the Active Intellect*.

Without going into the details, we can say that, for Averroes, human immortality resides in our "conjunction with the Active Intellect." This is the ultimate point in a series of "abstractions," by which the sensible or imaginative forms (which are changeable, corrupt) are transcended by our coming to know intelligible forms (which are eternal). When we come to know the abstract or intelligible structure of the physical cosmos, then our knowledge is identical with that of the Active Intellect, whose act of knowing is in fact the cause of that cosmos. Since the object of the Active Intellect's knowing is nothing other than the Active Intellect itself, it can thus be said that in coming to know that which the Active Intellect knows, we come to know the Active Intellect itself. And since according to a basic Aristotelian principle the knowing subject, in the act of knowing, becomes identical to the known object, then in our knowing the Active Intellect we become identical with it. It is insofar as we experience this identity, this "conjunction," that we are eternal: "And if it is possible for man in the course of manifesting his perfection that he represent the existents, then this Intellect, in the mode which characterizes it, I mean, the Active Intellect, is his. *Now this is the final felicity for man and eternal life subject to neither alteration nor corruption.*"[107]

One thing that Averroes makes clear in the *Epistle* is that immortality is not an inevitable or universal attribute of the human soul. Humans do not shift from this-worldly to other-worldly existence simply because they have died, nor is dying a relevant prerequisite for our enjoying the felicity of the immortal afterlife:

> Since it has already been explained that this state, namely the felicity, by necessity belongs to man *not insofar as he dies*, but rather due to the attribute

and form by which he is immortal, what is the way to its attainment? We say that the way to attaining the Active Intellect is study and speculation.[108]

Dying does not ensure that our souls will survive eternally. Those who have not studied the proper objects to the proper degree, who have not speculated in such manner as to attain conjunction with the Active Intellect, do not ever attain the felicity of immortality. The souls of those who do not work toward the possibility of conjunction through study and speculation (and by far the majority of humans belong to their number) *are* perishable; for them there is not even the possibility of an afterlife: "Those whose life is cut off in this existence will certainly enter a never-ending state of pain, since the decree of destruction for the soul is an extremely harsh one."[109] The pain to which Averroes refers here is a metaphorical one—the pain of destruction into non-existence. But, the fact that after death the souls of non-philosophers perish into nothingness does not mean that the souls of individual philosophers will survive after death, because immortality or the afterlife, for Averroes, is not literally "life after death." Rather, it is the actualization of the soul's highest potential *in this life*: "In that all this is as we have described, it has been made clear to you that the felicity. . .*is only attainable in this life*."[110] "Heaven" or "Paradise" is not a place nor a state to which the philosopher's soul is somehow transported, after death, as a reward for having philosophized in life (as Kalman Bland puts it: "It is not that an existential break is necessary in order to gain entry into the realm of the celestial intelligences"[111]); rather, "Paradise" is a metaphor, like Plato's "Isle of the Blessed," for the "place" one reaches in life when one is deeply engaged in theoretical speculation: "Plato believed that when the great philosophers reached old age, they were relieved from governing, whereupon they retired from active life and proceeded to the 'Isle of the Blessed,' free to speculate upon that Intellect."[112] The "afterlife" refers not to a state of felicity that one will enjoy after death but rather to a felicity that one will enjoy, in life, *after* the obstacles, burdens, and obligations of "life" (the political and practical issues with which the thinker ought to be engaged) have successfully been negotiated.

The idea that there are two worlds, an inferior and a superior ("this world" and the "other world"; "Earth" and "Heaven"; "the fallen world" and "Eden"), and that our chief hope is to be saved from the former and returned to the latter, is, says Averroes, a metaphor for an epistemological distinction between "opinion" (perception of sensible forms) and "knowledge" (vision of intelligible forms). "Death" is the fall from knowledge into opinion (from the intelligible into the sensible) and "resurrection" is the reversal of this fall, the upward ascent into knowledge. The idea that we are "saved" by leaving behind our bodies is a metaphor for the psychic process of abstracting intelligible forms from corporeal ones:

> And when men, through experience, came to understand that the other psychic forms impede the noble, intelligible forms, they believed the soul's felicity arises upon separation from this body; for when it separates from it, it is *saved* from all of the sensible forms, whereupon it perfects speculation of the intelligible forms. . . .Thus, the mass of the ancients—the Empedocleans, the Pythagoreans, and the Platonists—thought that the soul was created from the outset in order to speculate upon the intelligible forms. Together with this an inclination for the sensible forms was placed in them which makes the assimilation of the sensible forms impossible, even though one were to speculate upon the intelligible forms, it is moved and speculates upon the sensible forms. . . .Now when they reviled the presence of these [sensible] forms in the body and gazed upon the intelligible form, they were saved from the world and returned to their first world. This is a true metaphor, an allusion to which is certainly found in present-day Laws which derived it from the story of Adam. . . .This matter of the state of felicity was apprehended by the ancients in antiquity, about which they gave indication with these allusions.[113]

To return to "Paradise," to enjoy eternal bliss in the "other world" of the hereafter, is to return to the felicity of epistemological perfection originally enjoyed by Adam.

We should also not fail to note that here Averroes regards the various religious Laws as different ways to represent one and the same philosophical truth. As Bland remarks:

> It is not without significance. . .that Averroes mentions the ancient, pagan philosophers—Empedocles and Pythagoras—as examples of men who have attained ultimate felicity, but not Muslims. Like the philosophers of the eighteenth-century enlightenment, who saw man's reason as sufficient in itself for the attainment of man's ultimate perfection irrespective of his religious identity, the validity of Averroes's position finally rested on the fact that philosophers in every epoch and in every place could attain immortality without the need for divine revelation.[114]

It is this notion of the universality of philosophical truth, a truth which all of the various religions, properly interpreted, are seen to represent more or less adequately, which permits Averroes to say that the philosopher ought to "choose the best religion of his age, although all of them are equally true."

We can view the skeptical implications of the Averroist tradition by seeing how they became explicit near the end of that tradition, in the teachings of the famous Aristotelian-Averroist professor Pietro Pomponazzi (1462–1525), who fascinated a generation of students, hundreds of whom at a time would crowd to hear his lectures at the University of Bologna in the first quarter of the sixteenth century. I need to emphasize that Pomponazzi's Averroes is not exactly the real Averroes (and I will note a few differences shortly). But still, Pomponazzi's essential point—that the surface or literal level of scripture does not teach the truth—is indeed accurately attributed to Averroes.

Pomponazzi was a "naturalist" or materialist who taught that the human soul, as the "form" of the body, can only exist in tandem with the body. Since no "form" can exist without its "matter," then the death of the body is at the same time the death of the soul. (Pomponazzi took care to insist that, while this is the only conclusion that can be reached by "reason" or "philosophy," faith on the contrary leads us to believe that the soul *is* immortal; and he claimed, of course, to be a good faithful Christian.) According to philosophy, then, religious discourse concerning human immortality is beneficial, in that it provides a foundation (albeit a fictional or illusory one) for ethics, but it is not true. Pomponazzi, for his part, teaches that ethics is self-grounding: virtue is its own reward, and we do not need fictions concerning the "rewards and punishments" of the afterlife in order to act virtuously.

In one of his lecture courses, as he was commenting on Averroes's commentary of Aristotle, "lingering," as Gilberto Sacerdoti says, "with obvious pleasure over certain passages from Averroes that were potentially threatening to the faith," Pomponazzi told his students the following:

> As Aristotle says, it is impossible to live without laws, and it is clear that by "laws" he means "religious laws." Now, in instituting these necessary laws, the religious Lawgiver must speak in a manner different than does the philosopher. Moreover, his aim is that the masses act well, and thus in the discourses contained in his "laws" he does not care about the truth, because he knows that come what may a large portion of humanity, just like animals, will not let themselves be guided by the truth of reason, but only by sensual appetite. Consequently, to induce the community to behave well the Lawgivers say, for example, "you will go to Hell," and thus in their laws they do as the nanny who, to educate the child, makes him or her believe numerous fables and other trifles. In thus manner the "laws" are instituted so that men may be brought back to peace.[115]

In the following year's lecture course, Pomponazzi told his students that for Averroes, religious discourse is, in literary terms, a kind of "apologue." The "apologue" is a Renaissance narrative genre closely related to the fable—the difference being that in the fable the interest of the story tends to prevail over the interest of the moral while in the apologue the interest of the moral prevails over the interest of the story. In Pomponazzi's definition, the apologue involves a certain relation of truth and fiction: at first sight we take a fable for fiction but in the end we grant that it is truth; religion (being an apologue), on the contrary, we first take for truth but in the end recognize as fiction. According to Averroes, says Pomponazzi:

> The discourses contained in the diverse "sects" of Christ, Moses, and Muhammad are, properly speaking, "apologues" meant to correct the souls of the citizens. An "apologue" is constituted by something fictional, but under a veil of truth [aliquod fictum, sed sub velamento veritatis]. But this type of fictive speech. . .is necessary, because without custom, laws, and discipline men would be wild animals. And since the very first men were especially similar to wild animals, the art of poetry was invented to distance them from vice and to lead them to virtue. Then came rhetoric, which does not at all speak of things as they are but rather persuades. But the philosophers alone are the ones who speak the pure truth. Poetry, rhetoric, and philosophy are thus all meant for the instruction of humankind, and Averroes, in his commentary on the Poetics, says that the laws [leges] are similar to poetry, and they do not speak the truth—in fact, "poets sing marvelous things but not things to be believed." But they do it to lead men to act well and to instruct them. And he says that the story of Abraham, who was willing to sacrifice his son according to God's command, is not true; and that the Bible says this in order to lead men to rectitude.[116]

Averroes himself does not really teach that religion is not truth or that only philosophers speak the truth. He does indeed distinguish between three discursive modes (rhetorical, dialectical, philosophical, with only the latter conveying the truth—see below, part II), but he asserts that religious discourse itself employs all three discursive modes. That is, while for Pomponazzi the distinction between religion and philosophy is the distinction between fiction and truth, for Averroes religion is itself philosophical, since when properly interpreted by philosophers it will be seen to agree with the truths of philosophy. For Averroes, the truth of religion is in its philosophy, not in its poetry or rhetoric—which means that religion is not entirely distinct from but rather in a certain sense is philosophy and truth. And Averroes says that, in the final analysis, religion is superior to philosophy, since while the philosopher can state the truth, he can rarely ever induce or persuade the people to act virtuously. Still, Pomponazzi is right in the sense that Averroes does maintain that religious scriptures do not work by getting the masses to know truth but rather by inducing them, through fiction and rhetoric, to act well.

We will come to see that Dante, too, "devalues" truth, in this particular sense: for Dante, neither the Comedy nor Christianity are meant primarily to deliver truth to the people. Dante's poem does not aim above all else to convey the truth. Its moment of highest truth-content, Dante's vision of God at the very end, does not so much disclose God to us as it keeps Him veiled, forever hidden behind multiple layers of metaphor. The *Comedy* does not aim to teach us the truth concerning God.

Muhammad

A sure stumbling-block to any project such as mine is the notorious fact of Dante's condemning Muhammad, as one of the "sowers of discord" in the ninth pouch of the eighth circle of Hell. The imagery of the passage is particularly repulsive, as Muhammad is portrayed with his torso split wide open and his organs hanging out, the result of a wound inflicted on him by a devil, who repeatedly takes his sword to cleave the bodies of Muhammad and the other "sowers of scandal and schism." Among these others is Muhammad's cousin, Ali, whose face is split open from forehead to chin:

> His [i.e., Muhammad's] entrails were hanging between his legs,
> and the vitals could be seen and the foul sack
> that makes shit of what is swallowed.
>
> While I was absorbed in gazing on him,
> he looked at me and with his hands pulled open his breast,
> saying, "Now see how I rend myself,
>
> See how mangled is Muhammad!
> In front of me goes Ali weeping,
> cleft in the face from chin to forelock.
>
> And all the others whom you see here
> were sowers of scandal and schism
> in their lifetime, and therefore thus are cleft."
>
> (*Inf.* XXVIII, 25–36)

We can easily understand why Dante is reputed to be a vehement enemy of Islam and why some Western Muslims have objected to the teaching of the *Comedy* to students in their communities. One can only imagine the degree of outcry that would arise among some Christians in the United States if one of the great Islamic authors had depicted Christ in such fashion.

The problem of Muhammad's presence deep in Hell cannot be evaded. It calls for a thoughtful response that acknowledges that Muslims are right to take offense (and even utterly to reject Dante), yet which nonetheless asserts that the notion of Dante as an enemy of Islam is an oversimplification. This is difficult to do without falling into a rhetoric of apologetics, and it is a task beyond the scope of this book. But, at the risk of trying to defend the indefensible, I will suggest a few reasons why this infamous passage does not invalidate the general point of this book.

My argument is not that Dante was particularly familiar with the Qur'an, nor that he would have identified himself as a follower of Muhammad. Rather, I am saying that the "philosophy of religion" that is one of the fundamental components of the *Comedy*—a discourse aiming to promote tolerance for religious and cultural diversity—was in large part a legacy of the Arabo-Islamic philosophical tradition. If and when Dante fails, even abjectly, to live up to the ethical values of that discourse, that failure does not nullify the presence in the *Comedy* of a formulation of religious pluralism that may rightly be called Islamic.

One needs to consider Dante's logic in condemning Muhammad and Ali to Hell, as well as his understanding—in fact, a complete misunderstanding—of the historical origins of Islam. Dante did not view Muhammad as one who augmented or extended the community of monotheists but rather as one who divided into two an already wholly monotheistic community. For medieval European legend had fabricated a false biography, according to which Muhammad was a Christian apostate, a cardinal who, for his personal aggrandizement, had broken off from the community of Christendom and started his own Church.[117] Muhammad's sin, for Dante, is *schism*—the division of the community into parts. As Aquinas says, "schism takes its name from being a scission of minds, and schism is opposed to unity. Wherefore the sin of schism is one that is directly and essentially opposed to unity." We have seen above that dividing the community is, for Dante, the gravest of political errors. Muhammad and Ali (whose followers inaugurated Shi'ism, hence, one might say, dividing themselves off from the community of Muslims who would later be known as Sunni) embody, for Dante, violent division (the marks of which they bear literally on their bodies) rather than peaceful unity.

What Dante did not know and probably could not have known is that in fact Muhammad's political project was not one of division but rather of unification. His message succeeded by promising to transform an Arabian peninsula fragmented by tribal violence and by the emergence of class conflict into a unified and peaceful polity, the "abode of peace" (*dar al-salam*). If there ever was a precedent for Dante's political project in *Monarchy* (the attainment of world peace through a framework of unity that would permit diversity while serving to curb partisan greed), it is Muhammad's political project as revealed in the suras of the Qur'an.

Dante's condemnation of Muhammad to Hell does not amount to a claim that Muhammad, as a person, is evil. Nor does it in any way tell us that Muslims, being foreigners or alien to Christendom, are evil. Nor does it in any way mean that Islamic belief is evil. I will briefly explain each of these points.

Brunetto Latini was a thirteenth-century Florentine civil servant and man of letters whom Dante, in the *Comedy*, treats with great reverence, indicating that he loves him even more dearly than he loves his own father. By weaving numerous allusions to Brunetto's poem *Trésor* into the *Comedy*'s first canto, Dante honors Brunetto as perhaps his most important immediate precursor, his role model as the politically engaged vernacular poet. Dante treats Brunetto with nothing but honor, respect, and love. Nonetheless Brunetto is condemned to the third ring of the seventh circle of Hell, along with others guilty of "violence against nature." He is obviously not in Hell as an object of Dante's hatred. Nor does his presence there mean that Dante has somehow come to regard him as an evil person. Rather, Brunetto is in Hell for a certain failure in his political vision: his Guelph ideology that championed the autonomous city-state was a formidable obstacle to the establishment of Dante's Global Monarchy. Brunetto's "violence against nature" is his unnatural delimitation of the boundaries of the polity (which, for Dante, ought to be cosmopolitan— i.e., without any boundaries whatsoever). Brunetto is condemned to Hell not because Dante felt for him some emotion of hatred but rather because of the uncompromising logic of Dante's political vision.[118]

My point in mentioning Brunetto here is simple. To be condemned to Dante's Hell is not necessarily to be marked as evil nor to be characterized as the object of Dante's scorn. More than anything else, it means that the political implications of one's thoughts or deeds are the object of Dante's critique (thus Brutus and Cassius, for opposing Caesar—the Emperor—are at the very bottom of Hell, perpetually munched in Satan's mouth). Dante's condemning Muhammad for reasons of political theory and practice is not different in kind from any number of other such condemnations in *Inferno*. It is by no means a sign of a particularly intense hatred for the person Muhammad.

There is nothing in *Inferno* XXVIII to suggest that Muhammad's sin as a "sower of schism" is rooted in the generally sinful nature of Arabs as a group or Muslims as a group. Unlike Petrarch's crusade poem (cited above), which does assign a collective malignity to the Orient as a whole (Muslims are, says Petrarch, "a naked, cowardly, and lazy people"), Dante condemns Muhammad and Ali as individuals, not as emblematic representatives of a certain collectivity. More precisely, insofar as they are representative, they do not represent any ethnic or religious group but rather an erroneous political alternative (division into sectors) to the undivided community.

If Muhammad is not condemned for his ethnicity, neither is he condemned for his religious beliefs. It is significant that Dante represents Muhammad as a schismatic, not a heretic. Heresy is when someone within the community insists on holding and promulgating a false belief. Schism is when someone of true belief insists on dividing the community.

As Aquinas remarks, heretics are necessarily also schismatics (because their false doctrines are divisive), but schismatics (because they hold true beliefs) are not heretics.[119] Schismatics lack "charity" (the love that binds together the peaceful community) but they do not lack faith (that is, there is nothing wrong, doctrinally, with their religion). Dante surely knew that in presenting Muhammad as a schismatic he was not calling into question the truth of Muhammad's faith.

What Dante did not know is that the essence of his political vision—which involves overcoming the boundaries that divide communities against each other, yet without assimilating diversity into a single hegemonic identity—is truly consonant with the essence of Muhammad's.

Summary of Contents

Part I, "Virgil's Happiness (Dante, Al-Farabi, Philosophy)," shows Dante's secularism and humanism, and it locates both of these values (that humankind's this-worldly aim is equivalent or indeed prior to its other-worldly aim, and that all human cultures in their own ways have access to the same virtue and ethical excellence) in the political philosophy of al-Farabi, founder of the Islamic rationalist tradition. We will see that, following al-Farabi, Dante views religion primarily as an imaginary, particular representation of the universal principles of practical philosophy. Reading *Purgatory* and *Paradiso* will show us that Dante reduces to a minimum the importance of theory (knowledge of truth) for practice. True knowledge of God, the science of the divine—knowing, for instance, that God is Three-and-One or God-and-Man—is entirely superfluous to the construction of the perfect political state.

Part II, "The Right Path (Dante's Universalism)," shows that Dante's ecumenical attitude pertains not only to citizenship in the perfect political state on earth but also to the afterlife. In other words, Dante suggests that salvation in Heaven is not reserved solely for Christians. (Here we should bear in mind that, although Dante may in fact be skeptical of the afterlife as it is normally conceived, he is also aware of the strategic ethical implications produced by different ways of speaking about the afterlife.) Part II draws upon a variety of writings in both the Christian and Islamic traditions (the Gospels, the Qur'an, Ibn Arabi, etc.), including certain radical or heretical Christian writings (the Spiritual Franciscans, Catharism, etc.), to emphasize that the notion of "universal salvation" (the idea that all virtuous humans—or in some cases all humans period—are destined to be "saved") was widely circulated in Dante's time and was highly appealing to those who were threatened by the Church of Rome's insistence that it alone held the keys to salvation.

Parts I and II, then, present a coherent sequence: a demonstration of Dante's religious pluralism, first in matters concerning this life on earth, secondly in matters concerning the other life in heaven. The book's division into two parts thus corresponds to Dante's distinction between humankind's two ultimate goals.

Averroes figures prominently in both parts I and II, since his thinking on the relation between religion and philosophy is a model for several facets of Dante's pragmatic understanding of religion.

By showing that the *Comedy* does not enact Dante's turning from philosophy to religion, but rather bears the message of the Arabo-Islamic "philosophy of religion," this book offers an alternative to the theological approach that has dominated interpretations of the poem for the past half century. At the same time we will come to see the Islamic roots of Dante's pluralism.

PART I

VIRGIL'S HAPPINESS (DANTE, AL-FARABI, PHILOSOPHY)

It is possible that excellent nations and excellent cities exist whose religions differ, although they all have as their goal one and the same felicity and the very same aims.

Al-Farabi

In the *Comedy*'s opening episode, Dante finds himself wandering, for "the straight way was lost," in a dark wood at the foot of a mountain. His hopes are momentarily brightened when the sun appears and illuminates the slopes of the peak. Apparently his aim is to ascend to the mountaintop. As he begins the journey upward, three fierce beasts force him to head back down to the valley where he had started. It is then that he encounters Virgil, who has been sent to guide him. But rather than continuing the route directly up the slope that he had been attempting, a route that Virgil terms "the short way up the fair mountain" (*Inf.* II, 120), instead Dante will need to follow Virgil along a much longer alternate course: "You must go by another way. . .if you would escape from this wild place" (I, 91–93). We soon learn that this other way demands a *descent* rather than an ascent. Dante and Virgil, if they are ever to reach the summit, must first journey *downward* into the bowels of the earth.

In finding and following Virgil, Dante regains his orientation on the *diritta via*, the straight way. His initial error was to assume that the straight way was simply the direct and immediate assault on the summit. Instead the right path turns out to be one that leads for the time being down and away from the mountaintop, even if only as a means eventually to arrive there. And his error was compounded by the fact the he was undertaking the climb alone, unguided. So the *Comedy*'s opening episode poses this question: why is success in the appointed journey predicated upon traveling *downward with company* rather than upward and alone?

In a forceful interpretation that has become a classic of American Dante criticism, John Freccero formulates a compelling response to this question.[1] His starting point is the thesis that the *Comedy* is Dante's "conversion" away from the intellectual path that he had taken in the *Convivio*.[2] The earlier book, which Dante abandoned unfinished after he began his masterpiece, places a great deal of trust in the power of philosophy, and *philosophy alone*, to grant humans the knowledge that they need to attain felicity. The *Convivio* seems motivated by the idea that the aim of human existence is knowledge of truth, and that reason or philosophy is the means by which such knowledge is gained. The summit that Dante sets out to conquer at the opening of *Inferno*, which Virgil calls "the delectable mountain, the source and cause of every happiness" (I, 77–78), is in Freccero's view an allegory for "Truth." Dante's error was his believing that there is a "short-cut" to Truth, that the human mind, by drawing solely on its own resources, can acquire the knowledge requisite for happiness. His aborted journey figures the fact that the way to Truth mapped out in the *Convivio* (Aristotelian philosophy) is a dead-end.

Freccero sees Dante's failed first ascent (the first sixty lines of *Inferno*) as a purely intellectual and self-reliant attempt to save oneself. What Dante does not yet know, until he comes upon Virgil, is that one's own mental resources can never be sufficient for the attainment of felicity. In giving himself over to Virgil's guidance, Dante takes the first step in becoming a "new" Dante— one who has come to learn that there is no unguided journey to Truth, that human reason, in and of itself, can never lead us to the heights of happiness. Freccero sees Dante's coming to rely on something outside himself as an event modeled on Augustine's conversion. For Augustine only "sees the Light" after he commits himself to relying on God—not on the powers of his own intellect—as his "guide" and "helper."[3]

The *Comedy*'s opening scene, in Freccero's reading, amounts to an admission that humans need guidance in their quest for knowledge, truth, and felicity. Philosophy (the power of the human mind alone) must be supplemented—indeed directed and informed by—theology (the power of God's word). Dante's turning from solitary traveler to one who is guided by another is, for Freccero, an allegory for his conversion from philosophy to theology. Virgil himself represents nothing less than "God's guidance," so that in turning to Virgil Dante is in some sense already turning to God: "God's guidance, represented dramatically in the poem by the pilgrim's three guides [Virgil, Beatrice, St. Bernard], transforms philosophical presumption into Christian confession."[4] Overall, according to Freccero, the *Comedy* bears witness to Dante's new willingness to be guided by scripture, to accept the authority of faith, to place his trust in revelation rather than in reason, in religion rather than philosophy.[5]

If Freccero thus explains why Dante must rely on a "guide" and "helper," he at the same time explains the journey's downward orientation.

Dante's intellectual attitude prior to his composing the *Comedy* was marked above all by "philosophical pride," an excessive self-confidence that the author of the *Convivio* shared with the masters of classical philosophy:

> The ancients saw no need for a guide on such a journey. Plotinus explicitly says that one requires self-confidence to reach the goal, rather than a guide. This self-confidence was precisely what Augustine interpreted as philosophical pride, the element that in his view vitiated all such attempts.[6]

The remedy for pride is humility, and Dante must overcome his philosophical pride by humbling himself if he is ever eventually to scale the summit. The requisite humility is embodied in the *Comedy*'s opening scene by the *downward* trajectory of Dante's journey. Dante must first abase himself, in the mode of delivering himself over to Virgil's authority (God's guidance), before he will be enabled to climb. This self-abasement is figured in the poem as the movement toward the earth (one might bear in mind that the word "humility" is derived from the Latin *humus*, "earth") rather than toward the heavens.

In sum, for Freccero the fact that Dante must make a *downward journey* in the *company of a guide* is to be explained thus: Dante must humble himself by admitting the the insufficiency of philosophy without revelation, the deficiency of reason without faith.

We presently consider an alternative understanding of the issues posed by the *Comedy*'s opening movement. The questions remain the same: Why does Dante, having set his sights upward toward a delectable mountaintop, turn instead to a journey downward through the bowels of the earth? Why can he not chart his own solitary course? Why does the *Comedy* commend, as the authentic *diritta via*, the long, indirect way rather than the direct short-cut?

The Two Cities

It is Virgil himself who poses the question shortly after first meeting Dante:

> But you, why do you return to so much woe?
> Why do you not climb the delectable mountain,
> the source and cause of every happiness?
> (Inf. I, 76–78)

Virgil, as he will soon reveal, knows that *he himself* cannot climb the ultimate height. He will not serve as the guide for the ultimate ascent; he can lead Dante to the base camp, but he cannot help him summit the peak:

> And to these [i.e, the blessed souls in Heaven] if you would then ascend,
> there shall be a soul worthier than I to guide you;
> with her I shall leave you at my departing.

For the Emperor who reigns there above
wills not that I come into His city
because I was rebellious to His Law.

In all parts is His empire, in that part is His kingdom,
there is His city and His lofty seat.
Oh, happy he whom He elects thereto!

(I, 121–129)

Virgil poses his question in the manner of one who knows that he cannot ascend to Heaven asking another who *can* why he does not do so without delay. He is saying to Dante: "You, unlike me, can go up there. Why don't you, who are capable, try now to make the ascent?"

The most significant event in the opening episode is Dante's refusal of this tempting prospect. He represents himself as resisting the urge to "go directly to Heaven." His first heroic gesture is to renounce the appeal of transcendence, to opt instead for the downward orientation of immanence.

The metaphorical language that Virgil uses to speak of Heaven is significant: it is figured as a *city*, a *kingdom*. Virgil is asking Dante: "Why do you defer taking up your rightful citizenship in God's City? Why do you not enter the lofty eternal kingdom?"

There can be no doubt that the operative text informing the allegory of the first canto (and, more specifically, informing Virgil's representation of Heaven as a "city" and "kingdom") is Augustine's *City of God*. Faced with the temptation of narrating a solitary journey to the City of God, Dante narrates instead a journey, in solidarity with fellow humanity, through the City of Man. The overall thrust of the *Comedy*'s opening scene is its opting squarely to face the difficulties of the earthly *polis* rather than to escape to the Kingdom of God. Dante's turn to Virgil is not, as Freccero would have us believe, a turn to theology, to the divine; it is rather the turn to the earthly, to concern for the fate of the human polity.

For Augustine, human society—its political history, its basic enduring tendencies, its recurring patterns and configurations of values—is fundamentally corrupt. The leaders of the earthly *polis* (the City of Man) are driven by the will to dominate others and by love of self. Political life on earth is vitiated by violence, warfare, interminable conflict: "The earthly city is generally divided against itself by litigation, by wars, by battles, by pursuit of victories that bring death with them or at best are doomed to death."[7] Occasional periods of peace are doomed to pass, and virtuous human polities are eventually doomed to fail. Augustine thus counsels humans to place their hopes not in transitory human communities but rather in the one everlasting community, the heavenly City of God. Humans who hope to gain citizenship in the City of God should be, here on earth, politically "disengaged," since earthly politics distracts and contaminates the soul, leading to perdition rather than salvation.

Augustine reads the story of Cain and Abel as an allegory for the respective values of political "engagement" (Cain) and "disengagement" (Abel). For Augustine, Cain's crime was not so much his murder of his brother as it was his political engagement, his *founding a city* (or, more precisely, Cain's violence against his brother and his political actions are two sides of the same coin):

> Scripture tells us that Cain founded a city, whereas Abel, as a pilgrim, did not found one. For the City of the saints is up above, although it produces citizens here below, and in their persons the City is on pilgrimage until the time of its kingdom comes. At that time it will assemble all those citizens as they rise again in their bodies; and then they will be given the promised kingdom, where with their Prince, "the king of ages," they will reign, world without end.[8]

To place one's hopes and efforts in the City of Man, as did Cain, is to follow the way that leads only to perdition. The descendants of Abel, for their part, do not belong to any terrestrial polity. On earth they are not citizens but rather "pilgrims," passing through without being distracted or detained by the false lure of the earthly *polis*. The only regime in which they trust and of which they are citizens is the kingdom to come in the afterlife, the kingdom of God.

But the *Comedy* is thoroughly informed by Dante's hope for and trust in an earthly regime, a terrestrial polity, the Monarchy. In following Virgil, who emphasizes from the outset that he cannot be a citizen of the heavenly city, of the kingdom of God, Dante exhibits the decidedly non-Augustinian thrust of his thinking. And if Abel is merely a pilgrim on earth before assuming his true status as a citizen in heaven, Dante's trajectory is precisely the reverse: he is a pilgrim in the afterlife, a pilgrim in heaven, before assuming his role as a politically engaged citizen of *this* world—one whose engagement consists in writing the *Comedy*. Dante's Heaven, the City of God that Virgil mentions in *Inferno* I and that Dante visits in *Paradiso*, is not so much an end in itself as it is a means, an exemplar, an ideal model meant to aid in founding a city (in fact, for Dante, a global empire) on earth, the City of Man.[9]

In a recent book the title of which, rendered in English, is *The "Divine Comedy" and the City of Man*, Ugo Dotti insists that the *Comedy* is, from beginning to end, primarily concerned with the *this*-worldly rather than with the afterlife. Dante's chief significance in the history of ideas is his eminence as a pivot in the turn from a medieval Augustinian mentality of transcendence to a Renaissance/modern mentality of immanence. To read the *Comedy* as a manual meant to train individual humans to gain eternal salvation in the afterlife is to see it through precisely the Augustinian lens that Dante was working to replace:

> [For Augustine] the Heavenly City, *and this alone*, will be the homeland of those redeemed from the sin of Cain, the first citizen of the *civitas terrena*. Can one really say this concerning Dante's *Comedy*? Can one really maintain that the purpose of the poem is to cause people to devote themselves to and to worship the true God, after which they will be granted the prize awaiting them in the realm of the saints? Can one really say. . .that the city of Cain contemplated by the poet from the heights of heaven is, after being condemned, then forgotten once and for all and reduced to oblivion in an act of mystical transcendence? The answer. . .can only be negative. . . .If Augustine's magnificent *City of God* prepared the advent of the Middle Ages, Dante's poem. . .constituted the foundation of that "immanent utopia" that human society is still struggling to achieve.[10]

In Augustine's vision of history, there is no place for a just earthly society in the future. Augustine does not hold out any hope for social or political *progress*: life on earth will, until the end of time, be more or less as bad as it is currently. The *Comedy* marks a profound shift away from Augustine's pessimism in the direction of a progressive, even utopian, optimism. The poem is more concerned with working toward a just human social order than it is with providing information on how individual humans might gain eternal beatitude.

We should add that Dante was by no means working alone to bring about the end of the Augustinian Middle Ages. His was an especially forceful and a magnificently artistic expression of a general late medieval revaluation of life on earth. Now political life was no longer to be shunned, evaded, or escaped, but rather to be improved, perfected. There was hope for a future in which the human will and the human civil order would *not* be hopelessly corrupt. In this light, to opt for the "short way up the fair mountain" (with the understanding that at its summit is the heavenly City of God) is to abdicate the human responsibility to reform the City of Man. Dante with the guidance of Virgil must, like Cain, "found a city." Yet this founding must redeem Cain's sin: its very principle will be bringing to an end man's violence against his brother. If Augustine is resigned to the inevitability of violence in human society ("and even peace is a doubtful good"[11]—doubtful because never lasting), Dante dares to imagine world peace. At the very center of the *Comedy*, in the central verse (the 69th of 139) of the central canto (the 17th of 33) of the poem's central canticle (the 2nd of 3), Dante cites (as the 4th—the central—of the 7 beatitudes that punctuate the journey up Mt. Purgatory), the following: *Beati pacifici*, "Blessed are the peacemakers." *Peace on earth* is quite literally Dante's central—in some sense his one and only—concern.

Some of the most dynamic and progressive formulations of late medieval "secularism" (meaning by that term not a non-religious or religiously neutral attitude but rather one that concentrates its attention on the *saeculum*, the "world") unfolded within the Christian tradition. The Christianity that nourished Dante did not counsel *contemptus mundi*. Perhaps the most significant religious influence on Dante was the discourse of the Spiritual Franciscans (whom I treat at length in part II); their foremost figure, Pier Olivi, was a teacher at Santa Croce, one of the Florentine cathedral schools that Dante attended in his youth.[12] Dante learned from Olivi to challenge Augustine's philosophy of history, according to which, since the unfolding of the various ages of human history was already complete—sealed with the birth of Christ—there could be no further essential amelioration in the quality of human society.

Augustine taught that there are seven ages or periods of history, which correlate with and are figured by the seven days of Creation recounted at the beginning of Genesis. The seven ages are identified with key inaugural figures of Biblical history: first, from Adam to Noah; second, from Noah to Abraham; etc. The sixth age begins with the birth of Christ and lasts until the end of time, the Last Judgment. The seventh age, beginning with the Last Judgment but never ending and symbolized by the seventh day of Creation (the day of rest), is qualitatively different from the others: it is not strictly speaking an age or period, since it is the eternal afterlife, beyond time and the world. The details concerning these various periods are not important for our present purposes; what matters is to recognize that for Augustine there has been no significant historical development—no major paradigm shift—since the time of Christ. And indeed there will be no such development or shift in the future: the only thing yet to happen is the end of the world, the passing away once and for all of human life on earth. Since the birth of Christ, humans have been living in the sixth age, the last truly historical age and the final age of the world.[13] If the world is now a vale of woe, a scene of violence and warfare directed by leaders driven by the will to dominate and the love of self, such will more or less be the case until the end of time. *Christ's birth had no real positive political consequences here on earth.* Although it inspired individuals to live and act in accordance with charity, it did not reform human polities as such.

The Spiritual Franciscans were indebted to the radically novel conception of history of the twelfth-century Calabrian abbot Joachim of Fiore, according to which the current age of Christ is—*contra* Augustine—*not* the final stage of human history. Instead the age of Christ will, prior to the Last Judgment, give way to a new age *within* history and in *this* world, the age of the Spirit. Olivi, who resists teaching, as did some Spirituals, that the new age would be "post-Christian," identifies this age of the Spirit with the Second Coming of Christ. But what is distinctive in Olivi's vision is that this Second Coming does not herald the Last Judgment, the end of the world and of time. Those truly ultimate historical events are deferred to a distant future, the moment of Christ's Third Coming. Instead of marking the end of time and the world, the Second Coming will inaugurate an era of universal peace and justice *here on earth*— which for Olivi is characterized above all by the absence of "private property," by the common shared possession by all humans of all material goods and resources. As Sergio Cristaldi remarks:

> The Franciscan master [i.e., Olivi] is not primarily interested in an eschatology concerning heavenly reality, nor even in a vision of the end of the unfolding of history. Before the final conflagration he situates a new era which, not yet the "beyond" with its absolute perfection, is also no longer the present state of things; it is, rather, a qualitative progress to be counted on happening in the future. This notion was the legacy of Joachim of Fiore: the Calabrian abbot had been the first to defer the Last Judgment into the distant future, predicting, in a way that had not been done before, that there would be a different sort of crisis in the near future, and teaching that the inevitable crumbling of present reality would be the passing of *a* world not *the* world. On the ashes of the present order would rise a higher and more perfect order, free from encumbrances and contradictions, pervaded with the tranquil and ardent energy of the Spirit. Thus Joachim transformed the expectation of the end into the expectation of a new era *within history*, contesting the notion that the completion of history had already happened, and forcefully re-launching messianic hope. . . .Already exemplified during the course of the First Coming, [Christ's] mode of life was at that time only adopted by a small number of his early followers; but in the messianic future to come, it is destined to become universal practice. . . .The totality of humankind will put into practice harmoniously and without exception the undivided communion of goods that traditionally had been postponed to the otherworldly afterlife.[14]

Dante and Olivi share the notion that the chief immediate object of human concern ought to be the reformation of political life on earth, not the formation of individual souls who will be worthy of eternal life in heaven. Like the discourse of the Spirituals, the *Comedy* is replete with messianic prophecy, with apocalyptic language announcing, not the final conflagration that will end human history, but rather the advent of a new historical era. Dante, who tells us that the "current" year 1300 AD is smack in the middle of human history (and not near the end, as Augustine would have had us think), foresees the passing of *a* world not the end of *the* world.[15] As David Burr remarks, the Spirituals imagined a historical "scenario that was apocalyptic without being notably eschatological. . . .In Olivi's case, the end of the world was rendered uninteresting by the fact that he projected a dawning third age of around seven hundred or eight hundred years. [The Inquisitor] Bernard Gui tells us that some Beguins expected it to last one hundred years—which is fewer than eight hundred, but certainly long enough to relieve eschatological tension."[16] Dante far outdoes both Olivi and the Beguins in this regard, for in *Paradiso* Adam informs us that the world, now 6500 years old, will last another 6500 years. For Dante, as the *Comedy*'s first two words indicate, we are now *nel mezzo*, "in the middle" of time and history—and hence our most urgent concern is the here-and-now rather than Last Things. The *Comedy* is thoroughly apocalyptic without being eschatological: it announces and works to effect an imminent and profound shift in the status of life on earth. The *Comedy* aims to help create a new world; it does not dwell upon the ultimately ephemeral nature of creation, nor does it teach humans to renounce or transcend the world as something unsatisfying because transitory, and it is in this sense essentially "secular."

But how can we say that Dante may have cared more about life in this world than the afterlife and Last Things? Is this not just an imposition of our own modern secularism on a poem that is, as we are so often told, profoundly and sincerely "Christian"?

We can reply, first, that it is Dante himself, in the *Epistle to Cangrande*, who tells us that the poem is concerned above all with *this life*. In that treatise, meant to serve as an introduction to the reading of *Paradiso* as well as the *Comedy* as whole, Dante succinctly formulates the very purpose of his poem:

> But, without going into details, it can be briefly stated that the aim of the whole [i.e., the *Comedy*] as of the part [i.e., *Paradiso*] is to remove *those living in this life* from the state of misery and lead them to the state of happiness [removere *viventes in hac vita* de statu miseriae et perducere ad statum felicitatis].[17]

This formulation leaves a certain room for ambiguity. It could perhaps be taken to suggest that, since "this life" is one of misery, the *Comedy* aims to lead humans to the "state of happiness" in the afterlife, the eternal life of the blessed. Happiness is to be found in heaven not on earth. But in *Monarchy* Dante says that humankind has two ultimate goals, one of which being "happiness in this life."[18] So we cannot say that for Dante the "state of happiness" can simply be equated with eternal life in heaven. Indeed,

Dante does *not* say that the aim is to lead those living in this life from misery to happiness by removing them *from* this life. Rather, the change from misery to happiness is one that will occur *in this life* (*in hac vita*). This is another instance in which Dante's optimism concerning human potential runs counter to Augustine's pessimism, for Augustine asserts in the *City of God* that "life will only be truly happy when it is eternal."[19] The purpose of the *Comedy*, including the part of the poem, *Paradiso*, that presents a vision of Heaven, is to bring about happiness on earth. As Franco Ferruci remarks, "The *Comedy* displays *the eternal as a figure for the terrestrial world*, and not vice-versa. . . .The divine world, even at the moment when it is most highly celebrated, turns out to be a magnificent metaphor for human hope."[20]

We can reply, second, that placing paramount value on the happiness of human life on earth is perfectly compatible with "Christian" truth. The renewed secularism of Dante and the Spirituals is an innovation with respect to Augustine's Christianity, but it is not necessarily an innovation with respect to what we might see as the authentic, primitive meaning of Christ. For the key fact of Christianity, the Incarnation, is the bringing-down-to-earth of God. It is the relocation of the kingdom of God, from being remote, alien, otherworldly, to being right here, at hand, present as the human community on earth: John the Baptist proclaims that "the kingdom of God is at hand" (Mark 1.15), and Christ says that "the kingdom of God is among you" (Luke 17.21). As Thomas Sheehan tells us, Christ's message directed humans to cast aside their hopes for otherworldly salvation and instead to concentrate their efforts on practicing justice, charity, and mercy toward others:

> Henceforth, according to the prophet from Galilee, the Father was not to be found in a distant heaven, but was entirely identified with the cause of men and women. Jesus' doctrine of the kingdom meant that God had become incarnate: He had poured himself out, had disappeared into mankind and could be found nowhere else but there. . . .The doctrine of the kingdom meant that henceforth and forever God was present only in and as one's neighbor. Jesus dissolved the fanciful speculations of apocalyptic eschatology into the call to justice and charity.
>
> Jesus' message. . .marked the death of religion and religion's God and heralded the beginning of the postreligious experience: the abdication of "God" in favor of his hidden presence among human beings. The Book of Revelation, written toward the end of the first century of Christianity, captured this idea dramatically and concretely, albeit apocalyptically, in a vision of the end of time: "Then I saw a new heaven and a new earth, for the first heaven and the first earth had passed away, and the sea was no more. And *I saw the holy city, new Jerusalem, coming down out of heaven from God,*

prepared as a bride for her husband. And I heard a great voice from the throne saying: 'Behold, the dwelling of God is with men and women. He will dwell with them, and they shall be his people, and God himself will be with them'." [Rev. 21.1–3; emphasis added][21]

In John's vision, the City of God descends, comes down to earth out of heaven. Augustine's Christianity teaches us to train ourselves to ascend from earth to heaven. But Augustine thus reverses the orientation of primitive Christianity, which announces the downward movement of the kingdom of God to earth rather than the upward movement of humans to the kingdom of God. According to the fiction of the *Comedy*, instigating this downward movement from heaven to earth is precisely Dante's task as his poem comes to a close: he will return to earth and write the *Comedy*, thus bringing the holy city down out of heaven to the human community. The aim of the *Comedy* is to make incarnate, in this life, here on earth, the exemplary polity that Dante has beheld in heaven. As Dotti says, Dante's journey to heaven is not a matter of his "mystical ascent or an itinerary of the soul to God" but rather is a matter of his retrieving a "paradigm on which to model earthly historical reality."[22] So we see that the two cities are in a sense one and the same—the City of God being the future con-figuration, *within* human history, of the City of Man.

The Common Good

If the earthward orientation of the journey with Virgil indicates that Dante's Christianity is not characterized by a world-denying impulse toward tran-scendence, the fact that it is a journey *with* Virgil indicates that neither is his Christianity the brand that places the highest value on individual salvation. The "wrong way," the way that Dante pursues in the poem's first sixty verses, is the solitary way; in joining up with Virgil, Dante is put back on the *diritta via*, the right way, the path of solidarity with others.

When Dante first encounters Virgil, the latter immediately introduces himself not so much as an individual but rather as one whose identity is bound up with his membership in ever-larger communal groupings—self, family, city, region, empire:

When I saw him in that vast desert,
I cried to him, "Have pity on me
whatever you are, shade or living man!"

"No, not a living man, though once I was,"
he answered me, "and my parents were Lombards,
both Mantuans by birth.

I was born *sub Julio*, although late,
and I lived at Rome under the good Augustus
in the time of the false and lying gods.

I was a poet, and I sung of that just
son of Anchises who came from Troy,
after proud Illium was burned."

(*Inf.* I, 64–75)

There is a palpable shift from the "vast desert" of solitude in which Dante
has been wandering to the "civilization" of Virgil, in which the one who
says "I" at the same time emphasizes the importance of his links to parents,
place, and rulers. The hero of Virgil's poem is himself identified as one who
occupies a position in a family and a polity: he is not named Aeneas, but
instead as "son of Anchises who came from Troy."

As Elaine Pagels points out, the Christianity of late antiquity developed a
marked preference for virginity and celibacy. This was not simply motivated
by an ascetic urge to elevate the spirit over the flesh. Rather it was meant to
liberate the Christian individual from the social obligations represented, in the
first instance, by family ties. The Christian was no longer advised to regard
himself as a "father" or a "son." But opting out of family life was not an end
itself: it was the first step in opting out of one's identity as a *citizen* whose value
would be measured by his contributing to the welfare of the state:

> Christian renunciation, of which celibacy is the paradigm, offered freedom—
> freedom, in particular, from entanglement in Roman society. . . .Most
> Roman citizens would probably have agreed with Aristotle that "a human
> being is a political animal," that the measure of one's worth was what one
> contributed to the "common good" or to the business of the state, as
> defined by men of influence and power. . . .Jesus' message attacked such
> assumptions. "What profit is it for a man if he gains the whole world, but
> loses his own soul?" Jesus asks in Matthew [Matt. 16.26]. Jesus himself, as
> we have seen, belonged to the tradition of Jewish people who for many
> centuries had lived as groups of outsiders, often not citizens, within the
> pagan empires of the Persians, Egyptians, Greeks, and Romans. These out-
> siders apparently rejected the view that human value depends upon one's
> contribution to the state and originated instead the idea that developed
> much later in the West as the "absolute value of the individual." The idea
> that each individual has intrinsic, God-given value and is of infinite worth
> quite apart from any social contribution—an idea most pagans would have
> rejected as absurd—persists today as the ethical basis of western law and
> politics.[23]

Let us note, first, that Dante explicitly aligns himself with the side in
this debate that Pagels characterizes as Aristotelian and pagan: asked by

Charles Martel in *Paradiso* VIII, "Would it be worse for man on earth if he were not a citizen?," Dante replies, "Yes, and here I ask for no proof"—as if it is axiomatic that citizenship is an essential aspect of human nature (*Par.* VIII, 115–117). If Pagels' representation of Christian celibacy as a mode of "dropping out" from the entanglements of political life is a valid characterization of a major current in Christianity, this is not the current that fed Dante's Christianity. For Dante was reared and educated in a Christian tradition that placed the highest possible emphasis on citizenship, on the "common good" and "the business of the state." We shall see that Dante, influenced by his teachers in Florence, would perhaps have re-written Matthew as follows: "What profit is it for a man if he gain his own soul, but the whole world loses?" *Dante does not go to heaven to save himself.* Having gone there, he returns to save the world—not by converting humanity into a collection of politically disengaged individuals who turn their eyes heavenward, but by saving the world politically, as a state.

There is, however, solid scriptural authority for understanding Christianity as an imperative to renounce the entanglements of family and state. Although Christ tells his followers, "Honor your father and mother" (Mark 10.19), he and his audience both know that this is one of the Ten Commandments, part of the Old Law that Christ's message will supercede. More specifically *Christian* is a redefinition of the meaning of "family": it no longer designates those who are related by blood, but rather those individuals who choose to ally themselves, spiritually, as Christians. Christ sets the example for the rejection of biological family with the disrespect that he shows to his own closest relatives:

> Then his mother and his brothers came; and standing outside, they sent to him and called him. A crowd was sitting around him; and they said to him, "Your mother and your brothers and sisters are outside, asking for you." And he replied, "Who are my mother and my brothers?" And looking at those who sat around him, he said, "Here are my mother and my brothers! Whoever does the will of God is my brother and sister and mother." (Mark 3.31–35)

There is certainly a socially and politically positive aspect to this redefinition of "family," for it encourages people to form new notions of community that overcome the limitations of tribalism and ethnocentric nationalism. As Pagels indicates, the "western idea of democratic society owes much to that early Christian vision of a new society—a society no longer formed by the natural bonds of family, tribe, or nation but by the voluntary choice of its members."[24] On the other hand, one might say that this new family, even if its members come together as a community of noncitizens on earth as they await the promise of future citizenship in heaven, does not give rise to peace on earth but rather to violent disunity and division. This is the terrible dark side of Christ's message:

> "Do you think that I have come to bring peace to the earth? No, I tell you, but rather division. For henceforth there will be five in one house divided, three against two, and two against three. The father will be divided against the son, and the son against the father: the mother against the daughter, and the daughter against the mother: the mother-in-law against her daughter-in-law, and the daughter-in-law against her mother-in-law." (Luke 12.51–53)

When Christ enters Jerusalem, his followers do not chant "Peace on earth!" but rather "Peace in heaven!" (Luke 19.38). The brand of Christianity that encourages individuals to renounce family and polity has lost hope in the possibility of peace on earth, and it does not dare imagine that peace might ever be universal. It accepts the inevitability of and even bears some responsibility—in sanctioning the division of families and households—for violence on earth. The only peace to be counted on is peace in heaven, and to gain that peace one must risk tearing apart the very fabric of the human community on earth. One must risk dividing the earthly human community for the sake of undivided communion with the saints in heaven. The new family of Christians, hoping to save itself, must set itself apart from the larger community, must divide itself from the rest of humankind.

For Dante, *division* in any form is entirely incompatible with peace. This is why he champions the undivided global polity—Empire or Monarchy—as the sine qua non for peace on earth. This is why he cannot tolerate the existence of a papal state that would opt out of membership in the global polity. And this is why he would not endorse the brand of Christianity that, hoping for peace in heaven, encourages individuals to withdraw from, set themselves apart from the community as a whole. To leave one's own family, to evade one's responsibilities as a citizen in the service of the state, is from Dante's point of view an egoism motivated by self-preservation rather than concern for others. Dante's journey to God is not that of a mystic but rather that of a prophet: as Antonio Piromalli remarks, Dante's vision "does not conclude with egoistic beatitude" but rather its goal is the renewal of all humankind.[25]

One of the *Comedy*'s basic elements is the parallel that it establishes between Dante and Aeneas (Dante, as a latter-day Aeneas, is destined to work toward the foundation of the global Empire). At the poem's opening Dante, wandering alone in the "vast desert," finds himself in the very situation that faced Aeneas during the conflagration that burned Troy, as we see in this passage from the *Aeneid*:

> I look'd about, but *found myself alone,*
> *Deserted* at my need! My friends were gone.
> Some spent with toil, some with despair oppress'd,
> Leap'd headlong from the heights; the flames consum'd the rest.
> Thus, *wand'ring in my way, without a guide....*[26]

Momentarily alone, Aeneas soon finds his family—father, wife, and son—about to be engulfed by the flames that are consuming the city. On several occasions his father begs that Aeneas leave him behind, so that at the very least Aeneas himself might escape from Troy. But Aeneas flatly refuses to save himself if it means that his father must perish. Eventually Anchises consents to be carried from the flames, as Aeneas flees Troy, not in solitary fashion, but in solidarity with his family:

> Haste, my dear father, ('t is no time to wait,)
> And load my shoulders with a willing freight.
> Whate'er befalls, your life shall be my care;
> *One death, or one deliv'rance, we will share.*
> My hand shall lead our little son; and you,
> My faithful consort, shall our steps pursue.[27]

Aeneas will either die or survive along with his father, wife, and son, but he will not abandon them for the sake of his own salvation. The *Comedy*'s reference to the burning of Troy, in the context of Virgil's situating his identity in a network of allegiance to family and state, stands as an early indication that Dante is not particularly interested in teaching individuals to save their own skins (and souls). The decision to go down with Virgil amounts to a renunciation of salvation, if salvation must mean leaving in a shambles the world beneath the delectable mountain.

We can compare the *Comedy*'s opening with a positive emphasis on family and civil society with Augustine's negative views of the same. For even when offering lip-service to the necessity of the "social," Augustine cannot refrain from bad-mouthing wives, children, and city life:

> The philosophers hold the view that the life of the wise man should be social; and in this we support them...heartily....And yet, who would be capable of listing the number and the gravity of the ills which abound in human society amid the distresses of our mortal condition? Who would be competent to assess them? Our philosophers should listen to a character in one of their own comedies, voicing a sentiment with which all mankind agrees: "*I married a wife; and misery I found!/Children were born, and they*

increased my cares" [these are lines from a play by the Roman author Terence]. . . .If, then, safety is not to be found in the home, the common refuge from the evils that befall mankind, what shall we say of the city? The larger the city, the more is its forum filled with civil lawsuits and criminal trials, even if that city be at peace, free from alarm or—what is more frequent—the bloodshed, of sedition and civil war.[28]

Augustine has lost all hope in civil society as a possible source of human happiness. Our only resort is to renounce the City of Man in favor of the City of God.

We can now sum up the lesson of Dante's encounter with Virgil in *Inferno* I. What initially appears as "the right way," the immediate solitary ascent to the summit of the delectable mountain, is soon revealed to be "the wrong way." But we are not obliged to see these ways, in the manner of Freccero and many others, as the "wrong way" of pagan philosophy and the "right way" of Christian theology. Rather, these are, for Dante, two ways of conceiving Christianity itself: he characterizes as "wrong" a Christianity fixated on heaven and the individual's hopes for getting there and as "right" a Christianity concerned above all with the common good of the earthly community. But the choice between two ways is not necessarily a choice between two *Christian* ways, for the distinction between secular solidarity and solitary transcendence "cuts across" the distinction between pagan and Christian, philosophy and theology. Just as there can be community-oriented and secular theology, so can there be philosophy that promotes the individual's elevation above the entanglements of historical and material life. Both the pagan Virgil and the Christian Dante follow one and the same way of immanence and fellowship. Dante's Christianity is closer to Virgil's paganism than it is to the brand of Christianity that he is attempting to overcome.[29] He follows Virgil, but does so as a Christian; Virgil, as a pagan, leads Dante along a way compatible with Dante's brand of Christianity.

Remigio de' Girolami

If the Christian thinking of late antiquity and the early Middle Ages tended to counsel the individual's withdrawal from politics, this tendency was reversed in late medieval Scholasticism, which by and large accepted Aristotle's assertion that humans are by their very nature "political animals." The Scholastic commitment to "the common good" developed from the study of Aristotle's *Nichomachean Ethics*; the following passage from that text was the basis for the various Scholastic treatments of the issue:

For even if the good is the same for a single man and for a state, that of the state seems at all events something greater and more complete both to attain

and to preserve; for though it is worth while to attain the good merely
for one man, it is finer and more godlike to attain it for a nation or for
city-states.[30]

Aristotle's claim that providing for the political happiness of an entire
community is "more godlike" than providing for one's own individual
happiness appealed to thirteenth-century Christian thinkers, who saw this
as evidence for the presence of a theological vision in Aristotle's philosophy.
Humans most come into their own as the "image of God," the *imitatio dei*,
insofar as they most fully dedicate themselves toward the common welfare
of their communities.

The most direct influence upon Dante's concern for "the common
good" was the Dominican friar Remigio de' Girolami, who composed his
treatise *De Bono Communi* ("On the Common Good") in 1302–1303, in
the years just prior to Dante's beginning the *Comedy*. A Florentine who
studied philosophy at the University of Paris is the 1260s, Remigio
returned to his native city, where he taught at the cathedral school at Santa
Maria Novella from 1273–1319. Dante, who tells us in the *Convivio* that in
his youth he followed "the disputations of the philosophers" at the
cathedral schools of Florence, surely came to possess a more than passing
familiarity with Remigio's teachings.

Remigio's fundamental premise is that the good of the whole is always
greater than the good of the part. Hence he asserts that it is "beyond
doubt" that the common good should be preferred to the individual good.
And, since man is by nature a political animal, those who withdraw from
the *polis* cannot rightly be called human: "If someone is not a citizen, he is
not a human being" (*si non est civis, non est homo*).[31] For Remigio, humans
simply do not exist in isolation from their political communities:
"If Florence were destroyed, he, who was a Florentine citizen, no longer
can be called a Florentine. . . .And if he is no longer a citizen, he no longer
is a man, because man by his nature is a civic animal."[32] And because an
individual's humanity is bound up with the fate of his community, self-
sacrifice for the common good is the highest ethical principle: a citizen
"should be willing to go to Hell rather than see his commune there, if this
could be done without offending God."[33] Remigio considers a certain
contempt for one's own salvation to be an essential component of authentic Christianity, and on this point he cites no less an authority than St. Paul:
"I could wish that I myself were cursed and cut off from Christ for the sake
of my brothers" [Romans 9.1–4].[34] Among the several "individualist" theses that Remigio *refutes* is this one: "That an individual must prefer that the
community, even the whole world, should be damned than that he should
be damned and not the community."[35] In following Virgil to Hell rather
than ascending alone to the delectable mountaintop, Dante is *risking* his

own salvation, daring to tread among those who are damned. But it is Virgil himself who, even more than Dante, achieves Paul's Christian desire, for he exemplifies the striving for the common good by one who will apparently remain forever "cursed and cut off from Christ."

Following the example set by Ernst Kantorowicz in his classic treatment of medieval political theory, *The King's Two Bodies*, modern commentators have tended to view Remigio as an extremist devoted to an ideology of "radical corporatism," according to which the good of the state is an absolute value which always takes priority over, and hence effaces or dissolves the value of, the good of the individual. For Kantorowicz, Remigio's doctrine is a "monstrosity," a "pure collectivism" that "all but smothered the value of individual perfection."[36] The passion behind Kantorowicz's denunciation of Remigio is rooted in the scholar's own life history: a politically conservative German Jew who fled Nazi Germany for America in the 1930s, he was ardently opposed to both Hitler's National Socialism and Soviet Communism. Kantorowicz, while recognizing that Dante's political thought owes some debt to Remigio, presents the latter as a fanatical ideologue whose course the moderate Dante could not possibly follow to its limit. Kantorowicz's Remigio is dangerous insofar as his thinking harbors the seeds of both "nationalism" and "communism." He is "nationalist" in his hyper-patriotic love for his own city of Florence (when Kantorowicz accuses Remigio of advocating "the eternal death of the soul, that is, the jeopardy of individual salvation and celestial beatitude, for the sake of the temporal *fatherland*," it is not difficult to see that he is using Remigio as a screen upon which to project his disdain for Nazism). He is "communist" in the "illicit extremes" to which he carries his view that "there was perfection only in the community, in the Whole."[37]

In a recent thorough study of the issue of "the common good" in late medieval philosophy, M.S. Kempshall has called into question Kantorowicz's portrait of Remigio as a dangerous extremist. Kantorowicz presents a Remigio for whom Florence is the only "whole," indeed the only thing, that truly matters—a Remigio whose motto is *pro patria mori*, death (including the death of one's soul) for the sake of the noble fatherland. While it is true that, as Kempshall says, Remigio assembles a "litany of exempla (classical, biblical, historical, and contemporary)...in order to demonstrate the obligation of every citizen to sacrifice property, limbs, family, even life itself, for the good of the community," in fact Remigio's motivation is not a delusional, "nationalist" fixation on the unsurpassable greatness of Florence.[38]

Remigio's teaching concerning the good of one's "commune" is a nuanced one, for he reminds us that we are part of several "wholes" (communities) and that what may appear a "whole" from one perspective may itself be a "part" from another perspective. The scope of Remigio's concern is larger than simple Florentine patriotism, and one's proper "commune" is not merely equivalent to one's own city-state. As Kempshall says, Remigio "uses *commune, communitas*, and *civitas* as terms which can describe all of the various 'communities' of which every individual is a member, be it the city, the province, the church, the kingdom, the human species, *the world*, Creation, and even God."[39] Remigio's theory is flexible in the sense that it allows us to shift our allegiance when a new perspective opens up a broader notion of the "whole" to which we belong. Embracing the "common good" does not mean, as Kantorowicz maintains in branding Remigio's doctrine "nationalist," embracing one's own community against all other communities; rather, it means always taking the broadest, most inclusive approach to the common welfare. If I emphasize "world" here, it is to indicate that Dante learned from Remigio to view the "common good" from the perspective of what is good for the *world as a whole*; for Dante, overvaluing one's own city or nation—not regarding it as a part of the global whole—is a failure to adhere to the ethical principle demanded by the notion of the "common good."

Remigio, contrary to his image as a hyper-patriot who overly esteems his own homeland, certainly does not glorify Florence or indulge in jingoistic proclamations of its greatness. Quite to the contrary, he severely rebukes his city with a rhetorical stridency (and a love of linguistic play) rather like Dante's:

> What pleasure can a Florentine citizen possibly derive in seeing the sad and wholly woeful condition of his city? In fact the plazas are dis-placed, the houses un-housed, the families fragmented, relatives are un-related, pleasures are dis-pleasures, the games have been played and lost, the worthies appear un-worthy, such as the potentates and captains who have left the city. . ., the vineyards cut, the palaces destroyed, and there is no longer farm or estate in which one can live or where one can go without fear or trembling. In fact the flower is de-flowered and the fragrance of its fame has been transformed into the horrible stench of infamy, according to the prophetic insight implicit in the name given the city in the vernacular language of its citizens: they do not call it "Fiorenza," as do foreigners, but rather "Firenze." The French, in fact, when passing by dung [*fimus*] or other fetid matter, say "Fi, Fi" and hold their noses, as if to say "What a fetor!" And thus *Florentia* has been changed to *Flerentia* ["City of Weeping"]. Thus every citizen, out of the natural love that he has for Florence, ought naturally to cry.[40]

Florence is not a fragrant flower (*fiore*) but a stinking cesspool, a fact that its citizens unconsciously anticipated by changing the commencement of its name from "Fio" to "Fi" (an exclamation of disgust that we might approximate with "phew"). In Remigio's view, it is foreigners who overestimate Florence's worth, while its own citizens more properly name it a pile of dung.

While presenting a general theory of the common good, Remigio's *De Bono Communi* was at the same time meant as a remedy for the ills of a specific historical situation—the division into rival factions that had torn apart Remigio's (and Dante's) Florence. Like Dante, he aimed to heal the fragmented polity by teaching its citizens to think first of common good rather than self-interest. As Kempshall says, Remigio's "political ideas were formed against a background of public controversy in which familial feuding, class conflict, party violence, and competition for office were increasingly regarded as evils endemic to civic life. . . .In 1302–1303, when Remigio composed *De Bono Communi* in order to urge his fellow citizens to demonstrate their love for the common good, this was more than just a scholastic commonplace. It was Remigio's direct response to the expulsion of the 'White' Guelf faction."[41] Dante was himself among the "White" Guelfs who in 1302 had been exiled by the "Blacks," as part of the continual tit-for-tat in which each faction acted for its own good and to harm the other. Dante would certainly have welcomed *De Bono Communi* as precisely the sort of discourse needed for the salvation of Florence.

If Remigio is clearly not a "nationalist," neither does his teaching amount to—as Kantorowicz says it does—a pernicious "anti-individualism." For Remigio does not view dedication to the "common good" as necessitating an either/or choice between the good of the state and the good of the individual. If it is true that, in absolute terms, the good city is better than the good individual—"the city possesses a greater abundance of intellectual, moral, and theological virtue than one citizen (since a city contains a greater number of virtuous individuals)"—this does not mean that the good city does not include good individuals *as* individuals.[42] In other words, it is only within the framework of the virtuous city that virtuous individuals become fully virtuous: the good city depends upon and produces good individuals. "According to Remigio, the good of the whole is a greater good in itself as well as a greater good for the part. . . .The individual citizen can become more virtuous by existing in a community than he can by living in isolation."[43] The "common good" is a good for the whole as well as for all of its parts: "The individual should show greater love for the common good because the individual is a part within the whole, because the good of the part depends for its existence on the good of the whole, and because the good of the individual is included within the good of the whole."[44] Thus Dante's initial decision—whether to ascend alone to the delectable mountaintop or to follow Virgil through Hell—is not a choice between his own individual good and the common good.

Rather, it is in pursuing the common good of Virgil's way that Dante also comes to pursue what is good for himself as an individual: to save himself while ignoring the world would amount to vice rather than virtue.

Casella's Song

Not long after his arrival on the shores of Mt. Purgatory, Dante meets his old friend Casella, a Florentine musician who was apparently fond of setting to music the words of some of Dante's lyric poems. Wearied by the strenuous effort of his journey thus far, Dante asks Casella if he would help refresh his soul by singing one of those songs as he used to do:

> And I, "If a new law does not take from you
> memory or practice of the songs of love
> which used to quiet me in all my longings,
>
> May it please you therewith to comfort [*consolare*]
> my soul somewhat, which coming hither
> with its body is so wearied."
>
> "*Love that discourses in my mind*,"
> he then began so sweetly
> that the sweetness of it still within me sounds.
> (*Purg.* II, 106–114)

Dante here inserts the performance of one of his own lyric poems into the *Comedy*'s narrative. Critics agree that his purpose is not so much to glorify as it is to condemn his earlier poem. But what are the grounds for this condemnation? What is wrong with Casella's song—that is, with Dante's poem, the one that begins "*Love that discourses in my mind*"?

Dante and Virgil are not the sole audience for Casella's performance. They are presently in the company of a whole group of souls newly arrived on the shore of Mt. Purgatory. Casella himself is a member of that group of more than a hundred souls, who all came together in a single boat. As their boat was nearing the shore, they could be heard singing in unison a psalm from the Bible, the one that begins "*In exitu Israel de Aegypto*":

> At the stern stood the celestial steersman,
> such that blessedness seemed to be inscribed upon him;
> and within sat more than a hundred spirits.
>
> "*In exitu Israel de Aegypto*"
> all of them were singing together with one voice
> with the rest of that psalm as it is written.
> (*Purg.* II, 43–48)

Soon after the souls disembark, having joined up with Dante and Virgil, they are treated to the performance of Dante's love song. All are delighted by the music, carried away into an attentive reverie, when suddenly they are brusquely interrupted by the stern old Cato, guardian of the shore of Mt. Purgatory. Cato berates the assembled listeners, accusing them of negligence and by implication denouncing the song and its performance as something of no or little worth. The chagrined crowd, including Dante and Virgil, hasten to make amends by immediately commencing their journey up the mountain.

The episode, juxtaposing the psalm *In exitu Israel de Aegypto* and the love song *Love that discourses in my mind*, seems constructed in such manner that the psalm is sanctioned while the song is interdicted. But why is the psalm but not the song acceptable?

The simplest reply is that at stake here is the difference between "profane" and "religious" verse. Since Dante is now in the "Christian" realm of Purgatory, he must learn to reject his early secular verse.[45] His writing must now draw upon scripture rather than upon the worldly tradition of courtly love. Since he is now in a higher realm, he must overcome his attraction to earthly things. Teodolinda Barolini views the condemnation of Casella's song in the context of a "theologizing of courtly *topoi* along Augustinian lines": in Purgatory, Dante will gain "the ability to relinquish even the best and most beautiful of earthly things—such as. . . Casella's song."[46] However beautiful its melody may be, *Love that discourses in my mind* is devoid of Christian content, perhaps even altogether devoid of serious meaning. Amilcare Iannucci maintains that the purgatorial souls are "drawn to [Casella's song] and lulled by it primarily because of its sonorous beauty, and not the words of the text"; hence the song is "inappropriate because it is the wrong song and has no moral charge, neither in its words nor its tune."[47] In sum, there is a rather large contingent of critics who claim that Dante condemns his own earlier verse as at best vain, perhaps sinful—on the grounds that it is not religious.

This approach ignores the fact that *Purgatory* is—in ways that are discussed below—the most insistently secular and "non-Christian" of the *Comedy*'s three canticles. It is hard to attribute to the pagan Cato some special fondness for biblical verse. One of the main lessons to be drawn from the ascent up Mt. Purgatory is the essential "equality" of religious and nonreligious ethics. Why, then, would the canticle begin by privileging religious over nonreligious literary discourse?

Freccero offers a more subtle understanding of the deficiency of Casella's song. He does not accept at face value that *Love that discourses in my mind* can be characterized as simply a love song. In fact it is one of the poems for which Dante, in the *Convivio*, supplies an extended commentary. There Dante tells us that those who may have taken such poems for love songs in the conventional sense have not properly understood his meaning. The lady for whom he appears to be singing is not really a lady: rather she is a personification of philosophy, Lady Philosophy. As Freccero points out, when Dante asks Casella to "comfort" his soul by singing one of Dante's old songs, the Italian verb translated "comfort" is *consolare*.[48] The informed reader recognizes here an allusion to Boethius's *Consolation of Philosophy*, a work that takes the form of a dialogue between Boethius and Lady Philosophy. Dante, then, is asking Casella to offer him the consolation of philosophy—and, says Freccero, it is this inclination toward philosophy that is the first thing that must be purged on the shores of Mt. Purgatory. *Purgatory* opens, then, with a repetition of *Inferno*'s primal scene: once again, a pagan figure functions to direct Dante away from philosophy toward theology: "In the *Purgatorio*. . .the goal is *supernatural* happiness, for which *philosophy is definitely not sufficient*. Just as Boethius's *Philosophia* had cast out the Muses of secular poetry, she in turn is 'cast out' in Dante's text by Cato's rebuke."[49]

Although Freccero's reading is blessed with a certain convincing coherence, it is based on an extremely questionable understanding of the goal of Purgatory. As is discussed below, the goal of Purgatory is *not* supernatural happiness but *natural* happiness (Mt. Purgatory is, after all, part of the natural world; it is in Dante's poem a real place, right here on earth— albeit on the other side of the globe), for which *philosophy is in fact definitely sufficient*. In the case of *Inferno* I, Freccero obliges us to regard Virgil as an allegorical figure for "God's guidance"; his reading relies upon the counter-intuitive notion of a theologized Virgil. And, similarly, in the case of *Purgatory* he turns Cato into a theologian. But, as shall become clear, the single most important fact about Cato is precisely that he is *not* a theologian.

Thus we need to revisit the juxtaposition of *In exitu Israel de Aegypto* and *Love that discourses in my mind*. If the distinction between the psalm and the song is neither that between "profane" and "religious" nor that between "philosophy" and "theology," then what is it?

We can gain insight into the difference between the psalm and the song by momentarily setting aside any consideration of their "content"—that is, by approaching them solely in terms of the nature and circumstances of their performance.

In exitu Israel de Aegypto is a choral performance: "all of them were singing together with one voice." The entire community of more than a hundred souls gathered together in the boat participates in the singing of the psalm. The voice of the song is "one" (*una*) yet at the same time many. There is a striking emphasis on the collective subjectivity of this group: not only when they are singing, but even when they speak directly to Dante and Virgil, their language is represented as the voice of a subject that is at the same time both plural and singular:

> The crowd which remained there seemed
> strange to the place, gazing about
> like he [colui] who tries [assaggia] new things.
>
> The sun was shooting forth the day
> on all sides and with his deft arrows
> had chased Capricorn from mid-heaven,
>
> When the new people [gente] raised its face [la fronte]
> towards us, saying to us, "If you know,
> show us the way up the mountain."
>
> (Purg. II, 52–60)

There is something grammatically strange in these lines: the crowd (a plurality) gazes about "like *he* (a singular subject) who *tries* (third-person singular verb) new things." Charles Singleton "corrects" Dante's grammar by translating the phrase as "like *those* (a plural subject) who *try* (third-person plural verb) new things." Equally strange is the grammatical "barbarism" of the phrase "the new people raised its face"—as if this crowd of more than a hundred persons shares one and the same face. Again, Singleton is compelled to correct Dante, translating the phrase as "the new people raised their faces," thus turning the crowd back into a collection of distinctly discernable individuals. But this is a betrayal of Dante's purpose, which was to represent this group as a plural-singular subject, a subject to which the distinction between "he" and "they," between "I" and "we," does not pertain.[50] Dante aims here to endow the community as a whole with the indivisible subjectivity that is normally reserved solely for a single human. Posing the question concerning the way up the mountain, they do not rely on a "spokesperson"; although it may violate verisimilitude, they all simultaneously say the same thing. They speak as an entire undivided *gente*, with the communal voice of a whole people, a nation.

If the performance of *In exitu Israel de Aegypto* is assigned to a chorus who sing, speak, and act collectively, *Love that discourses in my mind* is on the contrary represented as the virtuoso performance by an individual "star," Casella. The transition from the performance of the psalm to the performance of the song is marked by Casella's separating himself from the rest of the community in which, up to this point, his individual subjectivity has been submerged:

> I saw one [una] of them [lor] draw forward
> to embrace me, with such great affection
> that he moved me to do the same.
>
> (Purg. II, 76–78)

This is no longer the *una* of those who "were singing together with one [*una*] voice." This is now the *una* of individualism, of the one who divides himself off from the rest of the community.

As we turn from the song's performance to its content, we find confirmation of our suspicion that the song is condemned for its excessive individualism. For one might say that *Love that discourses in my mind* is "all about *me*." The song's first stanza, for instance, is notable for its repetition of "me" and "my":

Amor che ne la mente *mi* ragiona
de la *mia* donna disiosamente,
move cose di lei *meco* sovente,
Che lo 'intellect sovr'esse disvia.
Lo suo parlar sì dolcemente sona,
che l'anima ch'ascolta e che lo sente
dice: «Oh *me* lassa! ch'*io* non son possente
di dir quel ch'odo de la donna *mia*!»[51]

(Love which, with fervent desire, in the mind,
Discourses with *me* concerning *my* lady,
Often raises with *me* things about her
Of which the intellect cannot keep track.
His speech so sweetly sounds,
That the soul which listens to and hears it
Says: "Oh woe is *me*! for *I* have not the power
To say what I hear about *my* lady!")

This stanza offers a particularly heightened example of the concern with "self" that is characteristic of lyric poetry in the courtly tradition—a tradition nicely summed up here by the "*Oh me lassa!*" ("Oh woe is me!"). Although the song purports to represent a dialogue between Love and the poet, what transpires is in fact an internal monologue: the poet's mind is turned inward on itself.

We find a striking difference when we compare the individualist subjectivity of *Love that discourses in the mind* with the ambiguous plural-singular subject of *In exitu Israel de Aegypto*. As we can see from the psalm's opening verses, the voice of the self, of the "I," is absent from this discourse:

When Israel went out from
        Egypt,
The house of Jacob from a
        People of strange language,
Judah became his sanctuary,
    Israel his dominion.
            (Ps. 113 [114])

Not only is there no "I" or "me" in the psalm, but the third-person subject, "Israel," both is and is not an individual. "Israel" is the name that God gives to Jacob in Genesis. But "Israel" also names the whole community of Jacob's descendants, the "house of Jacob," the nation of Israel. It is these descendants of Jacob who "went out from Egypt"—Jacob himself having already died before the exodus. So the psalm's first line employs the name of a single individual, "Israel" (Jacob), to signify an entire *gente*: the subject has the appearance of individuality but is in fact a collective one. Moreover, "Israel" also functions to name the place that is this people's destination. The psalm, especially when read in contrast with Casella's song, indicates the merging of the individual's fate with the fate of the community: the identity of the "he" is inextricably bound up with the identity of the "they." Israel (Jacob) survives as Israel (the nation and the place).

It is fitting that it should be none other than Cato who should put an end to the performance of Casella's song. For in Dante's day Cato had come to signify the very concern for the "common good" that the performance of *Love that discourses in my mind* seems to vitiate. As Ronald Martinez remarks, "renewed interest in Roman history had made of Cato an exemplum for medieval defenses of the *bonum commune*. . . .Cato represents the virtuous citizen that Dante's empire was meant to fashion: one who lived not for himself but for his fellow citizens and all the world."[52] John A. Scott, who offers a rich discussion of Cato in his invaluable book *Dante's Political Purgatory*, also informs us of the link that Dante must have forged between Cato and Remigio's notion of the "common good":

> Dante regarded. . .the suicide. . .of Cato. . .as an act of supreme self-sacrifice on behalf of the *res publica*; and, as we learn at the beginning of *Monarchia* [2.5]: "Whoever purposes the good of the commonwealth, purposes the goal of right." It is therefore interesting to discover that. . .we find a similar attitude in a passage of the *De Bono Communi*, written by Remigio de' Girolami: "One reads of innumerable heroic Romans that frequently exposed themselves to death for the state, in other words for the common good, for they cared more for the good of the commonwealth than for their own. . . .Thus Cato killed himself, as some believe, because the dominion of Rome had fallen to Julius Caesar and he believed that the state was in great peril."[53]

We can now fully understand why it is Cato, emblematic of those who care "more for the good of the commonwealth than for their own," who stands in judgment over the relative merits of the song and the psalm. Cato does not scorn non-Christian music; rather, he scorns self-centered individualism.

In sum, *Love that discourses in my mind* and *In exitu Israel de Aegypto* are indeed juxtaposed in such manner that we are meant to see the distinction between them as heralding a transition from the infernal to the purgatorial. But what is at stake in *Purgatory* II is neither a distinction between "profane" (non-Christian) and religious (Christian) literary discourse nor a distinction between philosophy and theology. Cato opposes Casella's song not because is it insufficiently Christian but rather because its exclusive concern for the self distracts from the psalm's concern for the welfare of the state. The transition from Hell to Purgatory (a transition for which Cato serves as the symbolic "threshold") is not the transition from a "non-Christian" to a "Christian" space; instead it is the transition from a world characterized by fragmentation and selfish individualism to one characterized by community and collectivism.[54]

Cato, Nature, the Earthly Paradise

Purgatory, opening with an insistence on the "common good," thus places up front a message that is not particularly "Christian." Nor, on the other hand, is this message to be conceived of as "non-Christian." Rather, the striving for the "common good" is an impulse that, ideally, motivates all humans, regardless of any religious concerns.

Indeed, in *Monarchy* this very notion of the common good serves as the example of the sort of knowledge that all rational human beings will arrive at *naturally*, without need of any assistance from scripture or revelation:

> For there are some judgments of God which human reason can arrive at by its own unaided efforts, such as this: that a man should sacrifice himself for his country; for if the part should put itself at risk for the sake of the whole, then since man is part of his community, as Aristotle says in the *Politics*, then a man should sacrifice himself for his country, as a lesser good for a greater. And so Aristotle says in the *Ethics*: "though it is worthwhile to attain the good merely for one man, it is finer and more godlike to attain it for a people or a community."[55]

The truth that Cato exemplifies at the outset of *Purgatory* is a truth that was fully known to Aristotle and which can be fully known to all those who pursue the path of philosophical reason. Such truths—those that humans can arrive at by their "own unaided efforts"—were in the Middle Ages termed "natural." They were distinguished from "supernatural" truths, those which cannot be attained by reason alone but which instead can only be granted by revelation or divine grace. Truths that are "natural" are culturally universal: people from all times and places, of all religions and races, are born with the potential to grasp them.

Purgatory, then, opens with a lesson (concerning the primacy of the collective whole over the individual part) that can be grasped by people of all faiths and by reason alone, without faith. We do not, and Cato did not, need to read the Bible to learn this lesson (we will see near the end of part I that Cato is precisely he who does not need a god to tell him how to act virtuously). It is a truth accessible to all peoples, in all times and places. As this book reveals, this "equal access" for Christians and non-Christians alike is an essential aspect of the allegorical significance of Dante's journey to the summit of Mt. Purgatory.

When Cato is first introduced, near the beginning of *Purgatory* I, he is already strongly associated with the notion of "natural" (as distinct from "theological" or "Christian") virtue. The canto opens with Dante and Virgil having just finished their journey up from the depths of Hell, in the center of the earth, back to the earth's surface. They find themselves now on the shore of Mt. Purgatory, in the southern hemisphere. Dante turns his attention to the South Pole, and he sees in the sky a certain "four stars":

> I turned to the right and gave heed
> to the other pole, and saw *four stars*
> never before seen save by the first people.
> (*Purg.* I, 22–4)

Turning his attention toward the North Pole, Dante now sees Cato for the first time, and Cato's face is illuminated by the light shining from these four stars:

> His beard was long and streaked with white,
> like his locks of which a double tress
> fell upon his breast.

> The rays of the *four holy lights*
> so adorned his face with brightness
> that I saw him as if the sun were before him.
> (*Purg.* I, 34–39)

Cato's significance as a key element of *Purgatory*'s allegory is distilled in this image of the four stars that illuminate his face. Commentators agree that the four stars represent the "four cardinal virtues"—which in the thirteenth and fourteenth centuries were said to be the primary subject of a late classical collection of moral aphorisms, read by every schoolboy as a sort of Latin primer, known as the *Distichs of Cato*.[56]

The four "cardinal" (or, "moral") virtues (traditionally said to be prudence, temperance, justice, and fortitude—although the specific enumeration need not concern us here) are those "natural" moral qualities that are shared in common by all virtuous humans. They are the roots of the good actions of any human being. The notion of the four cardinal virtues accounts for the undeniable goodness of humans in all cultures, regardless of religion. A Christian, a Jew, a Muslim, a pagan such as Cato, even an atheist may well possess the four cardinal virtues.

All humans are naturally born with the faculties requisite for the development of the four cardinal virtues. Some humans, through the grace of God, are also granted possession of the three theological virtues—faith, hope, and charity (love). If the four cardinal virtues "come naturally" to human reason, the three theological virtues, on the other hand, can only be had through grace or revelation. As Aquinas asserts, humans who possess only the four cardinal virtues are able to "act well" within the framework of life on earth; they will not be able, however, to enjoy the "supernatural happiness" of those who will be saved in the afterlife—a happiness which depends upon their possessing the three theological virtues, which can only be known "by Divine revelation, contained in Holy Writ."[57]

A bit later in *Purgatory*, Virgil (who like Cato embodies the concept of the virtuous non-Christian), discussing his status as a resident of Limbo, makes an implicit reference to his possessing the four cardinal virtues while explicitly acknowledging that he does not possess the three theological virtues:

> There I abide with those who were not
> clothed with the three holy [i.e., theological] virtues, and without
> sin knew the others [i.e., the cardinal virtues] and followed all of them.
> (*Purg.* VII, 34–36)

Virgil and his fellow residents of Limbo (pagans such as Homer, Aeneas, Socrates and Plato, and Muslims such as Saladin, Avicenna, and Averroes), knowing and following the four cardinal virtues, are every bit as sinless, as morally pure, as are the most virtuous Christians. And so is that virtuous Hindu whom Dante imagines in *Paradiso*, all of whose "wishes and acts are good. . . ./without sin in life or speech," (*Par.* XIX, 73–75), although he lives "on the bank of the Indus" where "none is there to speak, / or read or write of Christ" (70–72). Dante never once suggests that the moral practice of such non-Christians, *as citizens of the human community*, might have been improved had they been Christians. They are all illuminated by the four cardinal virtues.

The locus for Dante's treatment of the three theological virtues is Paradise, a place presumably off-limits to virtuous non-Christians (I say "presumably" because, near the end of part II, I question whether this is in fact the case). Preparatory to his beatific vision of God, Dante must first pass an "exam" indicating his possession of the theological virtues—faith, hope, and charity (*Paradiso*, cantos XXIV–XXVI).

By assigning the four cardinal ("moral") virtues to Purgatory and the three theological virtues to Paradise, Dante thus appears to divide the *Comedy*'s latter two canticles into a natural (philosophical) and a supernatural (theological) domain. (Later in part I we will question the adequacy of this distinction between a "philosophical" *Purgatory* and a "theological" *Paradiso*; for the time being, however, we will provisionally accept it.) He disassociates the summit that can be attained by natural moral virtue from the summit that can be attained only by grace, by revelation and theology. He establishes *two goals*: one that may be attained by peoples of all cultures, regardless of their faiths, and one that may be attained only by that portion of humanity blessed with Christian revelation.

Dante's insistence that one can acquire the "cardinal" or "moral" virtues entirely without Christianity aligns him with John of Paris, who just a few years previously, in his *On Kingly and Papal Power* (1302), had said more or less the same thing. As Kempshall says, paraphrasing John's position: "Perfect justice *can* exist in a political community, even a pagan community, which is not subject to Christ or to His vicar [i.e., the pope]; moral [i.e., "cardinal"] virtues *can* be acquired perfectly without their theological counterparts. . . .John of Paris realized that, if Aristotle's life of virtue was to be cited as the goal of the temporal ruler without thereby subjecting the king to the church, then moral virtue would have to be released from its necessary connection with grace. . . .There *can* be true and perfect justice where Christ is not the ruler, namely where the kingdom is ordered towards the life of acquired moral virtue [i.e., the 'cardinal' virtues]."[58]

By placing the purgatorial souls in Cato's charge, by presenting Cato in the light of the four cardinal ("moral") virtues, and by employing Cato as a moral instructor whose lesson (the primacy of the community over the self) is, in Dante's mind, the very epitome of those things that "human reason can arrive at by its own unaided efforts," Dante makes it clear from the beginning that *Purgatory* offers something of concern to everyone, Christians and non-Christians alike. The *Comedy*'s central canticle opens under the aegis of this ecumenical understanding of human virtue. Cato's role as guardian of Purgatory means that one need not be Christian to be welcome as a participant in the project of the purgatorial community.

Purgatory's initial movement is not, as Freccero argues in his interpretation of Casella's song, the purgation of natural reason and the exposition of philosophy's insufficiency. Rather, it is a movement that endorses humankind's innate potential to act in accordance with rationality in a manner sufficient for the purgatorial goal. In *Purgatory* "philosophy" (by which is signified the moral and rational faculties common to humans of all cultures and faiths) is not "cast out" (to use Freccero's phrase) but rather truly comes into its own.

That theology, religion, faith, are not essential components of the purgatorial project does not mean that they are necessarily absent. Rather, it means that their presence is not a *prerequisite* for the attainment of the goal. On the *literal* level, of course, Christianity is omnipresent in *Purgatory*—the very idea of an intermediate realm of judgment, between Hell and Heaven, being a specifically Christian contribution to the imagery of eschatology. But to say that Purgatory (the place) is Christian does not oblige us to say that the meaning or purpose of *Purgatory* (the poem) is Christian. Nor, in saying that religion is inessential to the primary aim toward which Dante works in the second canticle (which happens to be the same as the primary aim of the *Comedy* as a whole and of Dante's life as a whole), are we saying that Christianity is not itself fit and sufficient for the accomplishment of that aim. The purgatorial aim may be achieved by Christians *as* Christians (they do not need to be philosophers to reach the summit of Mt. Purgatory). But the summit does not exclude—rather it invites and indeed relies upon—the presence and participation of non-Christians *as* non-Christians. Reason and revelation, philosophy and religion, are parallel ways of accomplishing the purgatorial project.

What precisely is the aim, the goal of the purgatorial project? It is *literally* the Earthly Paradise (the Garden of Eden), which is situated at the summit of Mt. Purgatory and toward which all purgatorial souls are advancing. But the Earthly Paradise functions as a figure, an allegory for the just and peaceful human society, the ideal undivided global community that Dante calls "Monarchy" or "Empire." The purgatorial journey is not an effort to transcend earthly things; it is a journey *toward* the earth—the earth as it once was and as Dante hopes it will again be in the future, a place of undisturbed peace. As Enzo Girardi remarks, "it is clear that *Purgatory* is. . .the canticle of the earth and of living on earth in a state of freedom."[59] And, as Scott tells us, the Earthly Paradise at the summit of Mt. Purgatory represents "the happiness attainable through Justice and the teachings of philosophy."[60]

We can present this understanding of *Purgatory*'s allegory with a great deal of confidence because it is firmly grounded in Dante's *Monarchy*. According to the theological approach to Dante, the *Comedy* represents a single linear progression—from Hell through Purgatory to Heaven— toward the goal of the beatific vision of God. Purgatory is thus seen as a place of transition in which Christians souls are "passing through." The Earthly Paradise is not a goal in itself but rather a "way station" where Christians linger for a while on their journey to Paradise. Humankind has a single authentic goal, a single mode of happiness—that which is "supernatural." Heaven is the ultimate goal—and since the notion of "ultimate goal" necessarily entails that the goal is singular, then the summit of Mt. Purgatory, even if it may be called a goal, can at best be a lesser or intermediate one.

But in *Monarchy* Dante insists that the earthly goal is not to be conceived as a lesser or merely intermediate one. Rather, the goal of "natural" happiness—felicity here on earth—is every bit as *ultimate* as is the goal of "supernatural" happiness, since human nature is uniquely *dual*, a combination of a terrestrial and a celestial essence:

> Thus if man is a kind of link between corruptible and incorruptible things, since every such link shares something of the nature of the extremes it unites, man must necessarily have something of both natures. And since every nature is ordered toward its own ultimate goal, it follows that *man's goal is twofold*: so that, he alone among all created beings is ordered to *two ultimate goals*, one of them being his goal as a corruptible being, the other his goal as an incorruptible being.[61]

Dante's ascribing "ultimate" status to the goal of natural happiness is a remarkable novelty with respect to the mainstream tradition of Christian Scholasticism. Aquinas, for example, also recognizes that human nature is composite, such that on the one hand we share something in common with "God and the angels" while on the other hand we share something in common with the "other animals." But for Aquinas the two modes of happiness corresponding to these two aspects of our nature and their corresponding modes of happiness (speculation, contemplation, or *theoria*—the happiness of God and the angels; action or *praxis*—the happiness of animals) are by no means both ultimate goals; rather, the primacy of *theoria* as our "last end" means that *praxis* can at best yield "imperfect happiness," the happiness of those who have not really achieved their goal:

> Therefore the last and perfect happiness, which we await in the life to come, consists entirely in contemplation. But imperfect happiness, such as can be had here, consists first and principally, in an operation of the practical intellect directing human actions and passions, as stated in *Nichomachean Ethics* 10. 7–8.[62]

Aquinas does not deny that there can be human happiness here on earth. But he does deny that such happiness—which is the happiness of the practical rather than the speculative intellect, of *praxis* rather than *theoria*—can be anything more than a secondary goal. As Etienne Gilson insists, Dante's notion of humankind's "two ultimate goals" is a major departure from Aquinas's position.[63] And, as we shall see below, this elevation of earthly happiness to a goal the status of which equals (or even excels) the goal of happiness in the afterlife is a legacy of the Arabo-Islamic philosophical tradition founded by al-Farabi in Baghdad in the tenth century AD.

Dante's insistence that the two goals are *both* ultimate is manifest in his revising a commonplace figure for the relation between man's spiritual (theoretical) and political (practical) life. Proponents of hierocratic ideology, according to which the powers of the state are subordinate to and dependent upon the powers of the church, were fond of comparing the two powers to the moon and the sun. In *Monarchy*, Dante outlines the hierocratic use of the analogy, the validity of which he does *not* accept:

> Firstly they say, basing themselves on Genesis, that God created "two great lights"—a greater light and a lesser light—so that the one might rule the day and the other rule the night; these they took in an allegorical sense to mean the two powers, i.e., the spiritual and the temporal. They then go on to argue that, just as the moon, which is the lesser light, has no light except that which it receives from the sun, in the same way the temporal power has no authority except that which it receives from the spiritual power.[64]

Dante spends the rest of this chapter of *Monarchy* refuting the logic of this analogy. But if in *Monarchy* Dante is content to question the conclusions that hierocratic ideologues draw from the analogy of moon and sun, in the *Comedy* he rejects the very premise of the analogy. There he envisions a new analogy, *a relation between equals*, figured now not as the relation between moon and sun but as the relation between *two suns*:

> Rome, which made the world good,
> used to have *two suns*, which made visible both
> *the one road and the other*, that *of the world and of God.*
> (*Purg.* XVI, 103–108)

We should note that these words from the speech of Marco Lombard are situated very near the center of the *Comedy*, coming at the end of the 50th of the poem's 100 cantos. So this message—that humankind has *two goals* that are essentially equal—is central to the message of the *Comedy* as a whole. (One might suggest that the poem's central message is not "Thou shalt be Christian!" but rather "Thou shalt be more pagan!") There are *two roads*—the road of the world and the road of God—each with its own light, each equally "great" (both are *suns*), neither subordinate to the other.

Dante could have said, if he had wanted to, that there is one road—the way to God—and that the moon of philosophy (Virgil) guides us part of the way along that road, until the sun of theology (Beatrice) rises to illuminate the final stages of the journey toward the one ultimate destination.

This is in fact how the poem is normally read by the "theological" school of Dante criticism that has dominated American Dante scholarship in recent decades. (This school betrays Dante by turning him into Aquinas.) But what he wanted to say is that there are *two* goals, that those goals are to be equally valued, and that each goal has its own proper source of guidance and illumination. Virgil is not a moon but is a sun; indeed Dante addresses him precisely as such in *Inferno* XI: "O sun that heal every troubled vision" (91). Philosophy is the one sun, the source of illumination when we are seeking happiness in the way of the world. (Happiness in the way of the world is thus rendered independent from religion and made attainable by peoples of all religions.) Theology is the other sun, the source of illumination when we are seeking happiness in the way of God. Taken together, the passage from *Monarchy* concerning our two ultimate goals and the passage from the *Comedy* concerning the two roads show that Dante was working hard to resist the subordination of practical (political, natural) to theoretical (contemplative, supernatural) happiness that is evident in the teachings of Aquinas, for whom there is a single road and a single ultimate goal.

For earthly happiness we do not need illumination from theology. A passage from the conclusion of *Monarchy* sheds a great deal of light on the point of *Purgatory*'s allegory, which is to assert that the construction of a just and peaceful human society (the Earthly Paradise) does not in any way depend upon religious enlightenment:

> Ineffable providence has thus set before us *two goals* to aim at: i.e., *happiness in this life*, which consists in the exercise of *our own powers* and is figured in the *earthly paradise*; and happiness in the eternal life, which consists in the enjoyment of the vision of God (to which our own powers cannot raise us except with the help of God's light) and which is signified by the heavenly paradise. Now these two kinds of happiness must be reached by different means, as representing different ends. For *we attain the first through the teachings of philosophy*, provided that we follow them putting into practice the moral and intellectual virtues [e.g., *the four cardinal virtues*]; whereas we attain the second through spiritual teachings which transcend human reason, provided that we follow them putting into practice *the theological virtues*, i.e., faith, hope, and charity. These ends and the means to attain them have been shown to us on the one hand by human reason, which *has been entirely revealed by the philosophers*, and on the other hand by the Holy Spirit, who through the prophets and sacred writers, through Jesus Christ the son of God, coeternal with him, and through his disciples, has revealed to us the transcendent truth we cannot do without.[65]

Here Dante speaks of "happiness in this life" as being "figured in the earthly paradise"—indicating to us that *Purgatory*'s Earthly Paradise is to be read precisely as a "figure," an allegory for the terrestrial felicity that we can achieve through "our own powers," which need not be assisted by theology. To achieve the goal of the just and peaceful undivided human society, humans do not require religious revelation, since the means to that end have been "entirely revealed to us by the philosophers." If for the second goal, the "enjoyment of the vision of God," humans cannot do without the "transcendent truth" revealed by scripture, for the first goal of happiness on earth we *can* entirely dispense with such truth.

Christianity thus has no *necessary* role to play in the political reform that is at the center of Dante's mission. In a sense, religion is irrelevant to the *Comedy*'s central project. But we must emphasize that this does not mean that Christianity will not, cannot, or ought not play a role in the formation of the Earthly Paradise, the just and peaceful global community. Rather it means that, strictly speaking, religion is not needed. But as we shall see below, religion contributes to the "philosophical" goal of happiness on earth insofar as it functions, for some people and some cultures, as an "image" or representation of philosophical truth.

Dante needed to say that religion is inessential to humankind's natural goal of happiness on earth because he wanted to insist that the global Monarchy, which would include all the nations and cultures of the world, would not be a *Christian* Monarchy. Dante knew that the various peoples of the world, even if they would perhaps one day consent to give up their political autonomy for the sake of the common global good, would never consent to give up their religions. (The church's claim to have ruling authority in the political sphere, Dante says, is an idea found "abhorrent" by "not only all Asians and Africans, but also the greater part of those who live in Europe."[66]) The global Monarchy is not culturally imperialistic; it does not aim to make over all nations in the image of the one ruler's nation (and that is why the Monarch is himself "above" or removed from nationhood). In *Monarchy*, Dante outlines a plan according to which particular cultures retain their particularity while submitting themselves, for the sake of global peace (itself the condition for their own happiness), to a "common law" administered by the Monarch and founded on the universal philosophical truths (e.g., the good of the whole is greater than the good of the part) that are relevant to all humans:

> For nations, kingdoms, and cities have characteristics of their own, which need to be governed by *different laws*; for *law* is a rule which governs life. Thus the Scythians, who live beyond the seventh zone and are exposed to nights and days of very unequal length, and who endure an almost unbearable intensity of cold, need to have one set of laws, while the Garamantes require different laws, since they live in the equatorial zone and have days

and nights of equal length, and because of the excessive heat of the air cannot bear to cover themselves with clothes. . . .Mankind is to be ruled by [the Monarch] in those matters which are common to all men and of relevance to all, and is to be guided toward peace by a common law.[67]

Dante's insistence that the diverse peoples of the global Monarchy would retain their "different laws" could not but suggest to Dante's contemporaries that they might also retain their different religions. For the word "law"—which Dante here defines as "a rule which governs life"—was in Dante's age a synonym for the word "religion." Marsilius of Padua, for instance, says: "In this sense of the term law [lex] all religions [sectae], such as that of Muhammad or of the Persians, are called laws in whole or in part."[68] In fact, just a sentence or two following this passage Dante uses the word "law" in this religious sense ("Moses himself writes in the law that. . ."). And it was a commonplace of the Islamic and Jewish philosophical tradition to which Dante was partly indebted that the diversity of religious laws was among those diverse locally specific phenomena rooted in natural environmental differences such as climate.[69]

The "common law" that will guide mankind toward peace is the law of philosophy, not any one religious law. Dante does not envision the future new age as the Christianization of the globe. If Dante sees himself as a "missionary" to the whole world, his mission is not a religious but rather a political one.

It is true that there is something "divine" or "sacred" about the Monarchy: God wills that the Monarch rule the earth, and the Monarch's legitimacy and authority derive directly from God. But if God wills and institutes the Monarchy, He does not will that it be a *Christian* Monarchy. The idea of a *Christian* Monarchy would fatally undermine the Monarchy's very purpose—for it is an idea that would further divide the peoples of the earth rather than unite them. The philosophical "earthly paradise" does not overthrow or replace the various religions already in place. It allows various peoples to pursue their various religious paths—which for many of these peoples function as a kind of philosophy—while clearly displaying the fact that no single religious path is a prerequisite for the terrestrial felicity of human society.

Religion and Imagination

Precisely in the center of *Purgatory*—in the seventeenth of the canticle's thirty-three cantos—Virgil enlightens Dante concerning the rational structure of "vice" or what we might call "the bad" (if we hesitate to use the terms "sin" and "evil," it is because these have religious connotations which are notably absent from Virgil's discourse). As Virgil presents his teaching, he and Dante are located on the fourth of Purgatory's seven terraces; that is to say, they are right in the middle of Purgatory. If Virgil's account of the rational order that underlies "every action deserving punishment" (*Purg*. XVII, 105) is thus at the structural center of *Purgatory*, it is because that order functions as the philosophical "core"—the deep structure—upon which the Christian imagination has erected its doctrine of the Seven Deadly Sins.[70] Virgil teaches the bare-bones, abstract universal schema of "the bad," stripped of all adornment, imagery, contingent circumstance, and particular elaboration.

Virgil begins with an exposition of some general principles, before turning to a more specific enumeration of the structure of vice. He indicates that love is the motive force of every good and bad action. Love is itself of two types, "either natural or of the mind." By "natural love" is meant something akin to animal instinct—the desires that we share with all terrestrial creatures for such things as nourishment, shelter, self-preservation, reproduction. When we follow these natural instincts, our actions in this sphere are "always without error." But humans are also motivated by desires above and beyond those of animal instinct; it is in this sphere concerning desires "of the mind" that our actions are qualified as good and bad. We love badly either by desiring bad things or by desiring good things either too much or too little:

> He began: "Neither Creator nor creature,
> my son, was ever without love,
> either natural or of the mind, and this you know.
>
> The natural is always without error;
> but the other may err either through a bad object,
> or through too much or too little vigor.
>
> While it is directed on the primary good,
> and on secondary goods observes right measure,
> it cannot be the cause of ill pleasure.
>
> But when it is turned to the bad, or speeds
> to good with more zeal or with less than it ought,
> against the creator works his creature.
>
> Hence you can comprehend that love must
> be the seed in you of every virtue
> and of every action deserving punishment."
>   (*Purg*. XVII, 91–105)

Setting aside consideration of the doctrine presented here, we note the abstract, philosophical style of this discourse—a style more universal than particular. After he has finished part of his lesson, Virgil is referred to as a "doctor" (i.e., professor of philosophy) whose discourse is an act of "reasoning": "The lofty doctor [*dottore*] had made an end of his reasoning [*ragionamento*]" (XVIII, 1–2). Twice during the episode Dante calls Virgil his *maestro*—the Italian for *magister*, a title assigned to the professor of philosophy (XVII, 81; XVIII, 10). And Virgil explicitly associates his speech with "reason" in a famous stanza, the implications of which we shall consider later in part I: "As far as reason sees here / I can tell you; beyond that wait / only for Beatrice, for it is a matter of faith" (XVIII, 46–48). Dante clearly means for us to perceive that what we are given here, in the very center of *Purgatory*, is a lesson in rational philosophy: we are invited to witness Dante at "school."

As Virgil continues, he explains the rationale that distinguishes Mt. Purgatory's seven terraces. On the lower three terraces are purged the vices of those who love "the bad," those whose desire inclines toward the wrong things. On the central terrace (where Virgil and Dante presently find themselves) is purged the vice of those who apprehend "the good" but who do not strive sufficiently to gain it. On the upper three terraces are purged the vices of those who love "secondary goods" (things that are good in themselves but which are lesser than "the good" which will make them happy) in an excessive manner. Virgil further explains that the three modes in which we may love "the bad" are all subsumed under the category "wishing harm to our neighbor," and we recognize that these three modes correspond to the Christian sins of pride, envy, and wrath. We also recognize that the vice of loving "the good" yet doing so in a "lukewarm" manner corresponds to the Christian sin of sloth. As for the three modes of excessive love for "secondary goods," Virgil—in the manner of a good *magister* encouraging his pupil to begin to reason for himself—assigns to Dante the task of recognizing the distinctions between them; as *Purgatory* continues we will come to see that these lesser goods are money, food, and sex, and the vices of loving these good things too much correspond, respectively, to the Christian sins of avarice, gluttony, and lust:

> Another good there is which does not make man happy,
> it is not happiness, it is not the good essence,
> the fruit and root of every good.
>
> The love which abandons itself too much to that
> is wept for above in three circles,
> but how it is rationally distinguished [*si ragiona*] as threefold
>
> I do not say, that you may search it out for yourself.
> (*Purg.* XVII, 134–139)

Virgil understands as the rational structure of vice that which Christianity represents through the rhetorical device of the seven deadly sins. In the

sphere of ethics or morality, reason and religion stand as two systems that
are parallel and in accord. Christianity uses imagery to exhort the mass of
believers to conform to the good ethical practice that an intellectual elite—
such persons as Virgil and his student Dante—can come to understand
philosophically. In this sphere, revelation does not surpass reason but rather
serves as its representation.

Virgil's philosophical discourse is almost entirely lacking in imagery. But
Mt. Purgatory and its seven terraces are marked as strikingly "imaged"
terrain. Indeed *Purgatory*, in which the most memorable and prominent
figures whom Dante and Virgil encounter are artists of one sort or another,
musicians, painters, poets (such as Casella, Oderisi, Sordello, Statius,
Arnaut Daniel, to name just a few), is rightly regarded as the canticle in
which Dante emphasizes the artistic imagination. The most general reason
for this emphasis is that Purgatory (the place) is itself a work of art—an
imaginative, particular, or poetic representation grounded upon the
abstract, universal, rational structure of ethics. Purgatory is a religious
image of philosophical truth.

This emphasis on "imagination" is made clear as soon as Virgil and
Dante set foot on the first terrace of Purgatory proper. There Dante is
amazed by the sculpted walls of the cliff at his side, the artistry of which
(attributed to God) is so great that it almost literally brings to life the scenes
depicted:

> Nor yet had we moved our feet on it
> when I perceived that the encircling bank,
> which, being vertical, lacked means of ascent,
>
> was of pure white marble, and was adorned
> with such carvings that not only Polycletus
> but Nature herself would there be put to shame.
> (*Purg.* X, 28–33)

The walls of this terrace—the terrace where the sin of pride is purged—are
covered with sculpted scenes representing three exemplary figures of
Pride's opposite, the virtue of humility. The first of these "images [*imagini*]
of humilities so great" (X, 98)" is the Virgin Mary's humble reply to the
Angel Gabriel following the Annunciation of the Incarnation ("Behold the
handmaid of the Lord [*Ecce ancilla Dei*]; be it done to me according to thy
word"; Luke 1.38):

> The angel who came to earth with the decree of peace,
> wept for since many a year,
> which opened Heaven from its long ban,

before us there appeared so vividly
graven in gentle mien
that it seemed not a silent image [*imagine*]:

one would have sworn that he was saying "*Ave*"!
For there she was imaged [*imaginata*] who
turned the key to open the supreme love,

and these words were imprinted in her attitude:
"*Ecce ancilla Dei*," as expressly
as a figure is stamped on wax.

(*Purg.* X, 34–45)

Dante then sees, "carved in the same marble" (X, 55), a scene from the life of David, who was not ashamed to dance and mingle with his people (to the dismay of his embarrassed wife) following his success in returning the Ark of the Covenant to Jerusalem. The third example of "visible speech" (X, 95) that is "there storied" (X, 73) comes from the life of the Roman Emperor Trajan, who, in the urgency and hubbub of departing with his army for an important battle, allowed himself to be persuaded by a poor widow to pause to render her justice in the matter of her son's murder.

Taken together, these three "images of humilities" amount to an ecumenical display of the virtue of humility—a virtue taught by stories from the Old Testament, the Gospels, and the legends of Roman history and exemplified by the actions of a Jew (David), a Christian (Mary), and a pagan (Trajan). Christians and non-Christians share a common faculty for one and the same virtue, although that virtue is "imaged" differently in different traditions.

In his recent book *Le due mani di Dio*, Franco Ferruci speaks of a *convivenza purgatoriale*. This phrase, which we can translate loosely as "purgatorial fellowship," is meant to indicate that *Purgatory* promotes the peaceful co-existence of different religions. For Ferruci, the religions in question are "paganism" and "Christianity" (his approach is diachronic, emphasizing the moral equivalence, in Dante's view, of humans before and after the birth of Christ): "Purgatory, the canticle of friendship, holds in store various surprises concerning the compatibility of the two religions."[71] Commenting on Dante's words in *Convivio* concerning Cato ("And what earthly human is more worthy of signifying God than Cato? Certainly no one" [*Conv.* 4.28]), Ferrucci remarks that, in "one of the most surprising cultural conjunctions that has ever been witnessed. . .a pagan hero is chosen as the human example of the greatest possible similitude to the Christian God."[72] The essential point of *Purgatory* is its Christian humanism, the assertion that Christ did not add some previously unknown dimension to human virtue but rather granted his seal of approval to already existing models of moral excellence:

> If paganism has expressed such an exalted ethic in its greatest representatives [e.g., Cato], it is clear that the breath of divine truth is already present in humans before the descent [i.e., the Incarnation] of Christ; whose essential duty, for Dante, will be that of affirming such a presence and *legitimating* it in so far as He is Himself divine.[73]

Christ does not revise or reform non-Christian ethical paradigms; rather, with his divine authority, he ratifies them. The images sculpted by God on the terrace of pride suggest that God produced pagan myths and legends for pagans just as he produced Biblical history for Jews and Christians: "The Judeo-Christian heritage and the classical-pagan heritage are commemorated together by the hand of the great Divine Artist. . . .God cites pagan history and myth with the same ease as Christian history and narrative, as if there were no important difference between the two."[74] Contrary to the claim made by those who condemn Casella's song for being "non-Christian," God himself shows that there is no difference in the moral content of "Christian" and "non-Christian" art.

The sculpted walls of the terrace of pride establish a precedent that will be followed in each of the remaining six terraces of Purgatory: when Dante ascends to a higher terrace, he will first be greeted with a kind of "visible speech," with imaginative representations of the virtue opposed to the vice purged on that particular terrace. In each case a rendition of a Gospel story concerning the life of Mary is "balanced" with a rendition from ancient Roman or Greek legend or myth. Using a carefully crafted pattern of symmetrical structural repetition, Dante punctuates each terrace all the way up to the Earthly Paradise with both Christian and non-Christian *exempla* of virtue, as if to indicate that the way to summit the mountain is not reserved exclusively for Christians.

On reaching the terrace of envy Dante hears the voices of flying spirits who call out images of love (envy's opposite), one drawn from the Gospels and one from Greek myth:

> The first voice that passed flying
> called out loudly, "*Vinum non habent*,"
> and passed on behind us repeating it;
>
> and before it had become wholly inaudible
> through distance, another passed, crying,
> "I am Orestes," and also did not stay.
> <div align="right">(<i>Purg.</i> XIII, 28–33)</div>

Love (in the sense here of generosity) is exemplified by Mary's concern for the guests at the wedding of Cana ("They have no wine!"; John 2.3) and by Orestes's refusal to let his friend Pylades assume his identity in order to save Orestes's life. Although the flying spirits who present these scenes are "heard, but not seen" (XIII, 25–26), their discourse amounts to another mode of "visible speech": they use concrete, narrative imagery to depict in particular terms the virtue that Virgil understands rationally and abstractly.

On reaching the terrace of wrath Dante has an "ecstatic vision" in which he witnesses two stories of gentleness (wrath's opposite): Mary's mild rebuke to the young Jesus after he had wandered away from home for a few days and the Athenian Pisistratus' refusal to punish a young man who had approached his daughter and kissed her in public (XV, 85–105).

On reaching the terrace of sloth, Dante hears two souls shouting images of haste, and in this case it is Mary and Julius Caesar who function as the twin representations of sloth's opposite:

> "Mary ran with haste to the hill country,"
> and "Caesar, to subdue Lerida,
> thrust at Marseilles and then ran on to Spain."
> (*Purg.* XVIII, 100–102)

The concise (indeed hasty) economy of this stanza heightens our perception of the symmetry between the Christian and non-Christian figures of virtue.

On reaching the terrace of avarice, Dante hears a companion spirit narrate episodes from the lives of Mary and the Roman hero Fabricius, both of whom chose lives of virtuous poverty (XX, 19–27).

On reaching the terrace of gluttony he hears a voice from within some leaves praise the moderate appetites of Mary, the women of ancient Rome, and Daniel:

> Then it said, "Mary thought more
> how the wedding-feast might be honorable and complete
> than of her own mouth;
>
> and the Roman women of old were content
> with water for their drink; and Daniel
> despised food and gained wisdom."
> (*Purg.* XXII, 142–147)

In this case the role of non-Christian exemplar of virtue is shared by the pagan Roman women and the Jew Daniel.

And on reaching Purgatory's uppermost terrace, where the lustful are purged, Dante hears a group of singers proclaim the exemplary chastity of

Mary (who indicates her virginity to the angel Gabriel with the words "I do not know man") and the pagan goddess Diana:

> After the end which is made to that hymn,
> they cried aloud, "*Virum non cognosco*,"
> then softly began the hymn again.

> when it was finished, they further cried,
> "Diana kept to the woods and chased Helice forth,
> who had felt the poison of Venus."
>
> (*Purg.* XXV, 127–132)

Somewhere in the course of our reading, as we follow Dante and Virgil up the terraces of Mt. Purgatory, we come to expect that, shortly after reaching a new terrace, will we come across an image representing a Gospel story concerning the life of Mary followed immediately by one representing a story concerning a virtuous figure from pagan antiquity. The reiterated reference to Mary is a strategic device that calls our attention to the paired *exempla*, a sort of "landmark" that helps us get our bearings: in each case the reference to her Christian virtue tells us that a reference to a virtuous non-Christian will shortly follow. In every case, and with a perfect symmetry, an episode from the Gospels is balanced with an episode from pagan antiquity, and both exemplify—represent through imagery—the virtue that Virgil understands abstractly, as part of a rational system of philosophic ethics. Christians can follow Mary, pagans can follow their heroes and gods, as guides to the Earthly Paradise. And Dante can follow philosophy.

In the sphere of ethics, Gospel stories function for Christians in the same way that Old Testament narratives function for Jews and myths function for ancient Greeks and Romans. The Bible—both the Old and New Testaments—are characterized as "imaginary." But this does not mean that they are illusions or somehow devoid of truth. It means that the Bible includes imaginative depictions that, like the stories of pagan myth and history, serve as lessons in moral practice that direct people in the ways of virtue. Whether or not such images are "true stories" (and perhaps Dante would have said that the stories about Mary represent events which really did happen while those about Diana do not), in either case they have a true effect. The truth of an image is not measured so much by its correspondence to pre-existing reality but by its capacity to shape the response of its beholders. This is in fact how Dante conceives the "truth" of such obviously "untrue" images as those fantastical sculpted figures that one sometimes finds wedged between the wall and ceiling of a medieval building:

> As for corbel to support a ceiling or roof,
> sometimes a figure is seen to join
> the knees to the breast—

which, not true, true distress makes
arise in the one who sees it. . . .
                    (*Purg.* X, 130–134)

Whether or not a sculpted image is "true" (an accurate depiction of historical reality), the "truth" that matters is located in the effect which arises in those who come under its sway. Thus Dante can suggest that—in terms of the truth that matters for ethical practice—the Gospels and pagan myth are "equally true," even if those things imaged in the Gospels truly happened while those things imaged in myth did not.

Dante's concern with the "imaginative" faculty comes to the forefront in Canto XVII. Here on the terrace of wrath Dante "imagines" three exemplary figures of the vice. First, he imagines Procne, who killed her own son and fed him to her husband Tereus as revenge for the latter's raping her sister—and who afterward metamorphosed into a nightingale. Next, he imagines Haman, prime minister for the Persian king Ahasuerus, who having felt insulted when the Jew Mordecai did not bow down to him, persuaded Ahasuerus to order the death of all Jews in the Persian Empire—but who was himself executed after Esther, wife of Ahasuerus and cousin of Mordecai, intervened in favor of the Jews. Third, he imagines Amata, who hanged herself in anger, mistakenly thinking that Turnus, whom her daughter Lavinia was engaged to marry, had been killed in battle and that Lavinia would thus marry Aeneas, whom she opposed:

Of her impious deed who changed her form
into the bird that most delights to sing,
the impress appeared in my imagination [*l'imagine*],

and at this my mind was so restrained
within itself, that from outside came naught
that was then received by it.

Then rained down within the high fantasy
one crucified, scornful and fierce in his mien,
and thus was he dying.

Round about him were the great Ahasuerus,
Esther his wife and the just Mordecai,
who was in speech and in deed so blameless.

And when this imagination [*imagine*]
burst of itself, like a bubble
for which the water fails beneath which it was made,

there rose in my vision a maiden,
weeping sorely, and she was saying, "O Queen,
why through anger have you willed to be naught?

You have killed yourself in order not to lose Lavinia:
now you have lost me! I am she who mourns,
mother, at yours, before another's ruin."

As sleep is broken, when on a sudden
new light strikes on the closed eyes,
and being broken, quivers before it wholly dies away,

so my imagining [*l'imaginar*] fell down from me
as soon as a light, brighter far than that to which
we are accustomed, smote on my face.

(*Purg.* XVII, 19–45)

Each of these three *exempla* is explicitly designated an *imagine*, indicating
that Dante's aim here is to treat the essence of "imagination." Part of the
point is to strengthen our sense that all of the narrative episodes depicted
on the seven terraces that lead up to the Earthly Paradise—whether
sculpted, envisioned, sung, or otherwise voiced—belong to the genus
"image." We are reminded of the three scenes engraved on the rock walls
of Purgatory's first terrace (the Annunciation, David's dancing with his
people, Trajan's pausing from the rush of war to render justice for a poor
widow), which were collectively referred to as "images [*imagini*] of
humility." In particular, we are reminded of the Annunciation scene,
which was twice in the space of three lines characterized as an "image"
("It seemed not a silent image [*imagine*] / One would have sworn that he
was saying '*Ave*'! / For there she was imaged [*imaginata*]"). Clearly Dante
is guiding us to think of Gospel narrative as "imaginary"—in a sense that
is discussed below. Scripture is presented as a mode of imagination.

In order to gain insight into Dante's understanding of religion, then, we
need to consider further his understanding of "imagination." We will come
to see that the issue of religion and imagination was a major concern of the
tradition of medieval rationalist philosophy—a tradition founded in
Baghdad by the Arabic philosopher al-Farabi. Al-Farabi presents a positive
view of religious revelation as "imaginary"—which does not mean that
religion is delusion or error, but rather that it is a representation in sensible
imagery of "intelligibles," things known by philosophers without imagery.

Just before Dante imagines these three images of wrath, near the
beginning of Canto XVII, he delivers an apostrophe to imagination itself,
in a passage that both confirms the importance of this issue and helps us
formulate his theory of imagination:

O imagination [*imaginativa*], that do sometimes so
snatch us from outward things that we give no heed,
though a thousand trumpets sound around us,

Who moves you if the sense affords you naught?
a light moves you which takes form in heaven,
of itself or by a will that downward guides it.
(*Purg.* XVII, 13–18)

Imagination is a faculty of vision that does not commence with the "outward things" of sense experience. Or, more precisely, imagination operates in two ways: it spiritualizes corporeal things by memorizing them, and it corporealizes spiritual things by giving them virtual physicality. But in cases where imagination is not operating by representing external physical reality, this does not mean that it is error, folly, or madness. Images of the sort that are deployed in *Purgatory* have their source in a light from above (the Active Intellect). Imagination is enlightened, illuminated by a higher truth. Images are not devoid of truth but rather directly emanate from the realm of truth.

Recall that this is the same canto—the *Comedy*'s central one, the seventeenth of *Purgatory*'s thirty-three cantos—in which Dante, by giving us Virgil's philosophical explanation of the "intelligible," underlying structure of Purgatory, emphasizes the centrality of reason. This canto begins with a lengthy insistence on imagination and ends with an extended lesson in philosophy. Dante thus places imagination and philosophy right in the center of the *Comedy*. Imagination and reason are wedded together as both central, two aspects of the same. The "imaginary" is not the untrue or the irrational; it is, rather, informed by the light of rationality.

The relation between imagination and philosophy is not a marginal issue; rather, it is literally central to the poem. The central canto of *Purgatory* dramatizes this relation, as it plots a trajectory from imagination to reason, from religious and mythical depiction to philosophical understanding: in the beginning of the canto Dante sees images but not the higher light from which they move; by the end of the canto he has begun to see their source more directly.

Canto XVII's opening few stanzas condense in miniature the movement of the canto as a whole—which is figured as a movement from a "misty" to a gradually more lucid perception of the light:

Recall, reader, if ever in the mountains
a mist has caught you, through which you could not
see except as moles do through the skin,

how, when the moist vapors begin
to dissipate, the sphere of the sun
enters feebly through them,

and your imagination [*imagine*] will quickly
come to see how, at first, I saw the sun
again, which was now at its setting.

So, matching mine to the trusty steps
of my master [*maestro*], I came forth from such a fog
to the rays which were already dead on the low shores.
                                    (*Purg.* XVII, 1–12)

Dante's emergence, following in his *maestro*'s footsteps, from the fog to the
light prefigures his transition from one who sees images to one who, learning from the "sun" that is Virgil, comes to understand their rational
source—his transition from non-philosopher to philosopher. Stylistically,
Canto XVII itself mimics the transition from imagination to reason, from
poetry to philosophy: it begins poetically, full of imagery (mountains,
moles, and mist) which Dante explicitly refers to as such (calling upon the
reader to use his or her *imagine*), and it ends with the mathematical abstrac-
tion of Virgil's prosaic philosophy lesson ("But how it is rationally distinguished [*si ragiona*] as threefold/I do not say, that you may search it out for
yourself"; lines 138–139).

That the sun pertaining to Purgatory is, of the "two suns" that guide us,
the sun of philosophy not theology is apparent in these lines from Canto
XIII, where it is quite clear that Virgil's road (the road to the Earthly
Paradise) is illuminated by the sun of reason:

Then he [i.e., Virgil] set his eyes fixedly on the sun,
made of his right side a center for his movement,
and brought round his left.

"O sweet light, by trust in which
I enter on this new road, do you guide us,"
he said, "with the guidance that is needful in this place.

You warm the world, you shed the light upon it;
if other reason [*ragione*] urge not to the contrary,
your beams must ever be our guide."
                                    (*Purg.* XIII, 13–21)

In the last of these stanzas Virgil is invoking the basic principle of
Aristotelian logic, the law of noncontradiction. A logically deduced proposition shall be counted as valid so long as it does not contradict another
already affirmed rational truth (that is, so long as what is known to be true
does not "urge to the contrary"). The basic tool of philosophical reasoning,
the law of non-contradiction, is invoked here as a way of telling us that the
light in question, the light that Virgil follows, the light that, according to
Dante's theory of the imagination, is the source of religious and mythical
imagery, is the light of reason. It is this light which is the "guidance that is
needful" *here*, "in this place," in Purgatory, the "ultimate goal" of which is

terrestrial happiness. Other guidance—theological guidance—may be needful to lead humans to their other destination, to achieve their other "ultimate goal." But *here* there is no need for that other sun.

The relation between imagination and reason is at the same time the relation between religion and reason—for *Purgatory* plainly tells us that religious narrative, along with myth and legend, is among the modes of the "imaginary." The images by which religious scriptures teach have as their source the light of philosophical reason.

So the center of *Purgatory*, the center of the *Comedy* itself, presents a "philosophy of religion" that is in almost every aspect (but for one of great importance that is discussed below) identical to that offered by the Arabo-Islamic rationalist tradition from al-Farabi near the beginning of the tenth century AD to Averroes near the end of the twelfth. One of the primary motifs of this tradition is its view of religious revelation as the imaginative depiction of philosophical truth. Religious imagery functions as a kind of philosophy for those who are nonphilosophers. Its images are good and useful vehicles for the delivery of truths that philosophers, for their part, can know philosophically. As al-Farabi remarks in his *Book of Religion*: "Virtuous religion is similar to philosophy. . . .The practical things in religion are those whose universals are in practical philosophy."[75] Virgil *knows* (in the mode of "knowledge" that is practical wisdom—discussed further below) the universal principles (the abstract "intelligibles") of practical philosophy (ethics). Christian and Jewish scriptures, and pagan writings, present *images* of the abstract principles of practical philosophy—principles that, while universal, can be depicted in various particular ways, in various religions, for various peoples. And we should note that in the *Convivio* Dante affirms the "rationality" of various other religious laws (faiths), insisting that they are in accord with the "principle of reason."[76]

Purgatory's openness to non-Christians and its striking insistence on the issue of imagination are two sides of the same coin: there are different, culturally specific, ways to imagine one and the same set of universal truths—which for Dante, are those truths which direct humankind to the ultimate happiness of a peaceful, undivided, and just society.

In his *Principles of the Views of the Citizens of the Perfect State*, al-Farabi aims to direct humankind toward happiness, which for him means, in the first instance, political happiness. The perfect state ("city" or "regime") is that which is oriented toward true happiness. Political happiness is predicated upon knowledge of those actions, goals and ways of life that make a city truly happy. Imperfect cities have incorrect opinions concerning the ultimate happiness of the *polis*: they mistakenly believe that such happiness is to be identified, for instance, with honor, domination, wealth, sensual pleasure, individual freedom, etc. It is the philosopher who knows what makes for the city's true felicity, and thus the perfect city is ruled by the philosopher. But not everyone is a philosopher (to the contrary, very few have the requisite acumen, inclination, and training). So the philosopher—in his role as prophet or religious lawgiver—presents knowledge leading to political happiness in symbolic or imaginative form, i.e., as religion.

The citizenry attains a kind of knowledge through images. But different sets and sorts of images are appropriate for the peoples of different communities. Speaking of "the things in common which all the people of the excellent city ought to know," al-Farabi says:

> The philosophers in the city are those who know these things through strict demonstrations and their own insight; those who are close to the philosophers know them as they really are through the insight of the philosophers, following them, assenting to their views and trusting them. But others know them by imitation, because neither nature nor habit has provided their minds with the gift to understand them as they are. . . .Now, these things are reproduced by imitation for each nation and for the people of each city through those symbols which are best known to them. But what is best known often varies among nations, either most of it or part of it. Hence these things are expressed for each nation in symbols other than those used for another nation. Therefore *it is possible that excellent nations and excellent cities exist whose religions differ*, although they all have as their goal one and the same felicity and the very same aims.[77]
>
> It is possible to imitate these things for each group and each nation, using matters that are different in each case. Consequently, *there may be a number of virtuous nations and virtuous cities whose religions are different, even though they all pursue the very same kind of happiness.* For religion is but the impression of these things or the impressions of their *images*, imprinted in the soul.[78]

Just as *Purgatory*'s imaged terraces compel us to see the Christian Gospels, the Hebrew scriptures, and pagan myths as specific, alternate ways that different peoples arrive at the same goal, the path to which is known by philosophy (Virgil), so al-Farabi validates religious diversity on the grounds that each religion is a culturally appropriate image of philosophical truth. Religion for al-Farabi is in its essence *imaged* rationality:

> Most men accept such principles as are accepted and followed, and are magnified and considered majestic, in the form of *images*, not cognitions. Now the ones who follow after happiness as they cognize it and accept the principles as they cognize them, are the wise men. And the ones in whose souls these things are found in the form of *images*, and who accept them and follow after them as such, are the believers.[79]
>
> Now, these things are philosophy when they are in the soul of the legislator. They are religion when they are in the souls of the multitude. For when the legislator knows these things, they are evident to him by sure

insight, whereas what is established in the souls of the multitude is through an *image* and a persuasive argument. . . .The *images* and persuasive arguments are intended for others, whereas, so far as he is concerned, these things are certain. They are a religion for others, whereas, so far as he is concerned, they are philosophy.[80]

Dante's Virgil is al-Farabi's philosopher-ruler, guiding humankind to the formation of the perfect state (the Earthly Paradise). Dante, as an apprentice to Virgil, is like "those who are close to the philosophers," knowing things "as they really are through the insight of the philosophers, following them, assenting to their views and trusting them." The Jews, Christians, and pagans (the implied audiences for whom Purgatory's images were originally intended) who have been moved to practice the cardinal virtues by heeding the lessons of the imagery provided by their religious traditions are like the "multitude" for whom the truths of practical philosophy are not cognized but "established through an image."

Philosophy amounts to knowledge of the "common law" that underlies the diverse virtuous religious traditions. Philosophy can thus, better than any one particular religion—serve as the foundation for empire, for the undivided global polity. For the teachings of philosophy will be met with universal assent, each nation recognizing its own religious tradition as an image of those teachings. Virgil can lead Dante (and humankind) to the Earthly Paradise because he can bring the diverse religious communities together, teaching as he does the core practical truths that they share in common. As Dante says quite unambiguously in *Monarchy*, we achieve happiness in this life (a happiness figured by the Earthly Paradise) through the teachings of philosophy. But *Purgatory* enriches this statement by indicating that the teachings of philosophy are available to the multitudes in the form of religious imagination. To present religion as imagination is, following al-Farabi, to admit the possibility that "there may be a number of virtuous nations and virtuous cities whose religions are different."

But why did Dante use Virgil, not Aristotle, to signify philosophy's guiding humankind to felicity? Perhaps because, as al-Farabi asserts in *The Attainment of Happiness*, the true philosopher himself must be a poet as well:

If the philosopher who has acquired the theoretical virtues does not have the capacity for bringing them about in all others according to their capacities, then what he has acquired from it has no validity. . . .He cannot bring them about in all others according to their capacities except by a faculty that enables him to excel in persuasion and in representing things through images.[81]

Similarly, in *The Perfect State*, al-Farabi insists that the philosopher-ruler must excel in leading his people to felicity by rousing their imaginations:

> He [i.e., the philosopher] is the man who knows every action by which felicity can be reached. This is the first condition for being a ruler. Moreover, he should be a good orator and be able to rouse other people's *imagination* by well chosen words. He should be able to lead people well along the right path to felicity and to the actions by which felicity is reached.[82]

Virgil, as philosopher, knows things philosophically. But he excels Aristotle because he is not just a philosopher but rather is a philosopher-poet, one who is able to direct the multitudes through the use of imagery—through the *Aeneid*, for instance. Similarly, Averroes argues in *The Incoherence of the Incoherence* that prophetic discourse, while containing the same truth-content as purely philosophical discourse, is in fact superior to philosophy, since the prophet is *both* philosopher and prophet, while the same cannot be said about the philosopher: "Philosophy has always existed among the adepts of revelation, i.e., the prophets, peace be upon them. Thus, the soundest proposition in this regard is that every prophet is a philosopher, but not every philosopher is a prophet."[83] Dante aspires to be not only a philosopher, but rather the true philosopher—namely, the philosopher-poet-prophet. If he did not aim to educate the "multitude" (which cannot be done through the rational abstractions of philosophy but only through the imaged discourse of poetry), he would be a defective philosopher. Dante's turning to Virgil is not only turning to the common good and to natural, terrestrial happiness; it is turning to poetry/prophecy as the act that completes philosophy. Dante had tried to philosophize in *Convivio*, but had gone about it the wrong way. If the *Comedy* indeed "corrects" the *Convivio*, it does so not by rejecting philosophy in favor of theology but by providing the "imaginative" discourse (the graphic depictions of rewards and punishments in Heaven and Hell, for example) that the earlier work lacks. And the *Comedy*, which is in a sense the "image" of *Monarchy*, provides for the multitudes an imaged representation of those things that *Monarchy* teaches philosophically.

A passage from al-Farabi's *Attainment of Happiness* sums up his position on the harmony of reason, religion, and imagination: "In everything of which philosophy gives an account based on intellectual perception or conception, religion gives an account based on imagination."[84] This is almost precisely what we learn from *Purgatory*, especially in its central canto (XVII), which displays religious imagination's derivation from the light or "sun" of reason. *Purgatory* manifests Dante's assent to this tradition of Islamic rationalism.[85]

I say "almost," however, because Dante can only follow al-Farabi so far. Notice that al-Farabi says that *everything* of which philosophy gives an account is given a corresponding account in religious imagination. Dante agrees that *everything in the sphere of ethics* (everything pertaining to happiness on earth, everything that is a matter of practical wisdom) is intellectually known by philosophy and imagined by religion. But there is another side of religious discourse, for religion (more specifically, Christianity) presents some things that cannot be characterized as grounded in or derived from reason. These other things pertain to the human "vision of God" which is salvation or happiness in the afterlife. Human reason will never come to give an account of the Christian God, since that God violates the basic principle of philosophy, the law of non-contradiction. Thus humans need another "sun," the sun of theology—a sun that illuminates God for some humans but that adds nothing to the project of political happiness here on earth, a project in which all humans of all nations and faiths are called to participate.

Averroes on Imagination and Practice

We have seen that Virgil understands philosophically that which the multitudes come to know through images. Now, according to Averroes, the sort of knowledge that can be provided through images is *practical*, not theoretical, wisdom. It would follow, then, that Virgil's philosophy pertains to *praxis*, not to *theoria*. This is indeed what is revealed as part I unfolds. At this point it will be helpful to look very briefly at Averroes's insistence on the link between imagination and the philosophy of *praxis*.

It is sufficient for this purpose that we cite a portion of Roger Arnaldez's account of Averroes's commentary on Aristotle's *De anima*, where Averroes discusses "the practical rational faculty":

> Averroes begins by speaking of the "practical faculty." It is, he says, the easiest to study, and it does not pose a great deal of problems. *It is common to all humans; no one lacks it.* Humans are only distinguished, in terms of the practical faculty, by "more" and "less." The "speculative" [i.e., theoretical] faculty, in contrast, seems to be entirely divine: *it only exists in some humans. . . .* Unlike speculative [theoretical] intelligibles, which are an end in themselves, practical intelligibles aim to command the action that takes place in the world of sense-perception and imagination. . . . In humans, images are the moving force of the practical rational faculty. *Practical intelligibles are thus always linked with images*, which permits reasonable action to take place in the world of perceptions and experience.
>
> Thus the "practical intelligibles" are not to be thought of as eternal truths that can be the objects contemplated by speculative [theoretical] knowledge;

rather, they can be "generated" and are "corruptible," and they only appear to humans in concrete situations. . . .Averroes concludes: "If these practical intelligibles existed without the imaginative soul, their existence would be vain and useless."

Thanks to this [practical rational] faculty, humans love and hate, live in society and form bonds of friendship. It is the source of the moral virtues, *"because the existence of these virtues is nothing more than that of the images by which we are moved to practice virtuous deeds."*[86]

For Averroes, imagination and practical philosophy are mutually interdependent. If *Purgatory* shows Virgil as the philosopher of the imagination (in the sense that he understands the intelligibles of those ethical imperatives that are presented to the people in images), then it is also showing him as the philosopher of *praxis*, of the practical not the speculative (theoretical) intellect.

Virgil's brand of philosophy pertains to all humans, since no one is lacking the practical rational faculty (although some have "more" and others "less"). It is only in matters pertaining to the speculative (theoretical) intellect that we can posit a real ontological distinction between some humans and others, between some who are, so to speak, relatively "blessed" and others who are not—for Averroes teaches that the capacity for theoretical philosophy is a divine gift given to few humans. As we shall see, this "narrowing-down" or "selection"—in which a relatively small "elite" are marked as relatively "divine" because of their capacity for "theory," is signified in the *Comedy*'s scheme by the threshold between *Purgatory* and *Paradiso*, the difference between Virgil and Beatrice. Virgil's "Oh, happy he whom He elects thereto!" (*Inf.* I, 129) alludes to Averroes's doctrine of "salvation": the happy few are they whom God has endowed, not only with Virgil's practical rational faculty, but also with Beatrice's theoretical rational faculty.[87]

Al-Farabi and Dante

Al-Farabi (ca. 870 AD–ca. 950 AD), known in the classical Islamic philosophical tradition as the "Second Teacher" (second only to Aristotle himself) may rightly be considered the founder of Islamic philosophy, and he remained among its greatest and most influential figures throughout the Middle Ages. Prior to al-Farabi there had certainly been many Islamic scholars and thinkers who employed the tools of Greek rationalism; but they had done so as theologians, using logic to dispute and support positions that were already accepted as dogma. But for al-Farabi Greek philosophy was much more than a tool or instrument, of alien origin, that one might use to defend an already held theological opinion. Rather than seeing philosophy as a means to prove revelation (and hence as something subservient to revelation), he regards revelation as being in the service of philosophy. Al-Farabi urges adherents of revealed religions to study philosophy not just to learn methods of argument with which to defend their religious doctrine, nor merely to learn about philosophy's inadequacy, but to become enlightened concerning their religion's deepest wisdom, which is equivalent to the practical wisdom of classical political philosophy. For al-Farabi, philosophy is not something alien to Islam, not something "imported" from the outside which must necessarily distort Islam's essence. He indicates philosophy's status as "domestic" or "native" to the Islamic world by tracing its origins, not to Greece, but to Iraq: "It is said that this science existed anciently among the Chaldeans, who are the people of al-Iraq, subsequently reaching the people of Egypt, from there transmitted to the Greeks, where it remained until it was transmitted to the Syrians, and then to the Arabs."[88] Thus al-Farabi, who did a good deal of his philosophizing as a resident of Baghdad, saw himself as working to restore philosophical understanding to the people of its native soil. For the spirit of Greek philosophy (which lies in its political teachings) is not alien to the spirit of Islam (which lies in its political teachings). But it is fairly clear that for al-Farabi religion is, in the final analysis, secondary to philosophy: it depends upon philosophy and follows after it in time. Al-Farabi originates for the monotheistic traditions the notion of a philosophical religion—a notion embraced by two later Arabic writers, both from al-Andalus, who also profoundly influenced the Christian West—the Muslim Averroes and the Jew Maimonides.

Al-Farabi is the master of medieval political philosophy. This does not so much mean that he treats "political science" as one among the several suitable topics for philosophical discussion. Rather, he presents philosophy itself as primarily concerned with politics. For philosophy's aim is the "attainment of happiness"—not the happiness of the isolated sage but the happiness of the perfect political regime.

Recall that the *Comedy's* opening canto dramatizes Dante's confusion concerning la *diritta via*, "the straight way," the right path. He had thought that the right way is to rise above the rest of the world, to embark upon a solitary journey of transcendence. He had thought that happiness is to be found above human society. But his encounter with Virgil reorients him to the genuine right path, the way toward political happiness in solidarity with the rest of humankind. He is redirected to pursue that path that leads to the common good, the reformation of the City of Man, the "perfect state."

Similarly, al-Farabi characterizes as "missing the right path" those who would by-pass the attainment of earthly happiness (the perfect state) in favor of supernatural transcendence: "The city which misses *the right path* ('the erring city') is the city which aims at felicity *after this life*."[89] This "erring city" is, according to al-Farabi's typology, distinguished from the "perfect city" (the city that aims for felicity *in this life* and knows that true earthly felicity is the just and peaceful polity), from the "ignorant city" (the city that aims for earthly felicity but mistakenly believes that such felicity is found in honor, wealth, domination, pleasure, freedom, etc.), from the "wicked city" (which knows precisely what the perfect city knows but whose people act in a manner indistinguishable from the people of the ignorant city), and from the "city which has deliberately changed" (the city which once shared the views and actions of the perfect city but now holds different views and performs different actions).[90] For al-Farabi, "missing the right path" is a metaphor for a specific kind of political imperfection: it is renouncing the task of political reform on earth in favor of salvation is heaven. Al-Farabi expands upon this point later in *The Perfect State*, in a section entitled "Views of the Cities which Miss the Right Path":

> Others believed that there is a felicity and a perfection which man reaches after his death and in the life-to-come, and there are true virtues and truly excellent actions by which felicity after death will be attained. . . .Therefore they thought it right to assume that the natural existents as observed in this state have another existence different from the existence observed today [i.e. in our earthly life] and that this existence which they have today is unnatural for them, indeed contrary to the existence which is natural for them, and that one ought voluntarily to direct one's aim and action towards bringing this existence to an end so that the other existence which is the natural perfection emerges; because this our present existence is the obstacle on man's road to perfection: once it is brought to an end, perfection will emerge. . . . Hence some people held that the connection of the soul with the body is not natural for man and that the real man is the soul and that the connection of the body with man impairs the soul and changes its actions, that vices arise in the soul only because the body is connected with it, and that its perfection and its excellence consists in its release from the body, that in its state of felicity it is in no need of a body, and that also for attaining felicity it can dispense with the body as well as with the exterior goods such as wealth, neighbors, friends, and fellow-citizens, and that only man's corporeal existence calls for associations in the city and other exterior goods. Therefore they held that this corporeal existence should be cast off altogether.[91]

Al-Farabi refers to these and other views which similarly deny the goodness of humankind's material and civic nature—which deny the value and perfectibility of our natural life on earth—as "pernicious views of the Ancients. . .from which religions have been derived in many of the cities which miss the right path."[92]

Given that the Qur'an designates Islam as "the straight way" or "the right path" ("Show us the straight way, / The way of those on whom Thou hast bestowed Thy Grace, those whose (portion) is not wrath, and who go not astray" [1.6–7]; "Most surely you show the way to the right path" [42.52]), we can see that al-Farabi is characterizing the world-denying impulse, the impulse to solitary supernatural transcendence, as un-Islamic. Those who think that the straight way, the right path, demands their escape from and elevation above the earthly *polis* are among "the erring cities," of whom one can say that "a kind of happiness that is not true happiness is established for, and represented to, them; and actions and opinions are prescribed for them by none of which true happiness can be attained."[93] As Richard Walzer comments, al-Farabi shows particular disdain for those who counsel contempt for the world:

> The "erring" state is rebuked as strongly as that ignorant state which makes power and conquest its guiding principles. . . .The attack on the "erring state". . .is almost as violent, and al-Farabi's usual detachment for once does not prevail. It is true that the rulers of the "criminal" ["wicked"] and "changed" states are also stigmatized as downright wicked, and their fate in the afterlife will be miserable. But the first ruler of the "erring state," i.e., its founder, is blamed in much harsher terms. He is called an imposter and a misleading and deceiving crook who set out to make people believe that he had succeeded in attaining a genuine "revelation," presumably of the philosophic type. The main gist of this message of falsehood is that it recommends a forced escape from this world by placing felicity exclusively in the world to come.[94]

Dante's erring in *Inferno* I is the wandering of one searching for the path that would elevate him above and thus enable him to escape the earthly *polis*. In the *Comedy*'s opening scene he is tempted to fall for an erroneous conception of the *diritta via*—a false orientation that might be characterized as "un-Christian" insofar as it is "gnostic" or "dualist."[95] Had he continued his ascent, had he failed to accept Virgil's invitation to follow *his* path, he would have—like the citizens of al-Farabi's "erring city"—"missed the right path," the path of "associations in the city" with "neighbors, friends, and fellow-citizens."

Al-Farabi's Heaven

We can see why the twelfth-century Andalusian philosopher Ibn Bajjah (Avempace) would have felt compelled to defend al-Farabi against the charge that he claimed "that there is no afterlife and no existence other than sensible existence and that the only happiness is political happiness."[96]

Such a thought appears to have accompanied the tradition of medieval Islamic philosophy as one of its possible implications, if we can properly judge by one of the 219 "Averroist" theses banned from the University of Paris in 1277: "That happiness is had in this life and not in another."[97]

But the claim that al-Farabi denied the reality of the afterlife is debatable—not least because in both *The Perfect State* and *The Political Regime* he offers an explicit account of the afterlife, formulating a notion of heaven that bears some striking similarities to the heaven of Dante's *Paradiso.*

For al-Farabi, the fate of one's soul after death is dependent upon its attaining philosophical knowledge (whether directly or through imaginary representations) on earth, and the attainment of such knowledge is itself primarily determined by the character of the "city" to which one belongs. Since not all humans are guided in such manner that they become rational, not all human souls are eternal. The souls of the citizens of the "erring," "ignorant," and "changed" cities do not survive the death of the body: "These are the men who perish and proceed to nothingness, in the same way as cattle, beasts of prey and vipers."[98] The souls of the rulers and citizens of the "wicked" city survive after death in a state of eternal misery, as do the souls of the rulers (but not the citizens) of the "erring," "ignorant," and "changed" cities, since such rulers are by their very actions to be counted among the citizens of the "wicked" city: "As to the people of the cities which have gone astray: the man who led them astray and turned them away from felicity. . .is himself one of the people of the wicked cities; therefore he alone but not the people of his city will be wretched. But the others will perish and ultimately dissolve."[99] Only the souls of the rulers and citizens of the "perfect" ("excellent") city will survive after death in a state of eternal felicity. For al-Farabi, citizenship in the perfect *polis* on earth is not an alternative to individual salvation in heaven, nor is it an accidental quality that some, but not others, of those who will be "saved" might happen to enjoy. Rather, such citizenship is the very prerequisite for eternal bliss. The notion of "individual salvation" (or, damnation) does not have a place in al-Farabi's scheme: it is whole cities, along with all of their citizens, that are saved, damned, or perish into nothingness. The perfection of the earthly political state is the very basis for, the sine qua non of, eternal bliss—an idea to which Dante subscribes in the introduction of *Monarchy.* We can see more clearly why Dante *had* to follow Virgil: there is no felicity that is not grounded, in the first instance, on political felicity.

Dante follows al-Farabi by conceiving of the eternally wretched or blissful souls in the afterlife as inhabitants of "cities," so that, from a certain perspective, we can see that it is not so much individuals but rather the "wicked city" (of which, for Dante, Florence is the paradigm) that is damned to Hell and the "perfect city" (of which, for Dante, the Monarchy is the paradigm) that is saved in Heaven. Or, as Joan Ferrante has shown, Dante's Hell is a metaphor for the corrupt, divided city and his Paradise a metaphor for the just, peaceful, undivided global Empire.[100] Indeed the "gate of the city" through which Dante and Virgil pass in *Inferno* III names Hell precisely as a city—*la città dolente* ("the woeful city"). And Hell proper (Lower Hell), which Dante and Virgil, after some struggle, eventually enter in *Inferno* IX, is itself a walled yet divided city, the City of Dis ("Now, my son," says Virgil, "the city that is named Dis draws near,/with its grave citizens, with its great garrison"; *Inf.* VIII, 67–69). And if Hell is the "wicked city," Heaven is "the perfect state"—a peaceful imperial polity of global extent: when Beatrice and Dante come to behold all the souls of Heaven assembled together, she exclaims, "See our city, how wide is its circuit" (*Par.* XXX, 130), and Dante's final guide to the vision of God, St. Bernard, refers to Heaven as "this most just and pious empire" (*Par.* XXXII, 117).

There is no doubt that Dante holds ordinary individuals responsible for their wickedness; but, like al-Farabi, he holds their leaders even more responsible—because the polity plays such a role in forming, shaping, and directing individuals. As Walzer comments concerning al-Farabi's view of the moral responsibility of the multitudes:

> The citizens of the "erring" and "changing" states are not deemed responsible for their wrong actions, and hence, like the citizens of the ignorant states, are neither rewarded nor punished in the after-life, but disappear into non-existence. In other words, al-Farabi seems to be convinced that the ordinary man is born to be dependent on his superiors and is simply the product of the reigning political principle.[101]

Similarly, the ordinary human is by and large absent from the *Comedy*, a fact to which Cacciaguida calls our attention in *Paradiso* (XVII, 134), indicating that Dante's poem will primarily be an attack against the "loftiest summits" (the ruling secular and ecclesiastical aristocracy), against those whom we can term the rich and famous. For Dante, just as for al-Farabi, the burden of blame for an individual's following illusory rather than genuine goods, false rather than true happiness, lies squarely on the shoulders of the political leaders. One's virtues and vices are shaped by one's city.

We might note that, just as al-Farabi maintains that a large category of human souls (the citizens of those cities that are "in-between," neither "wicked" nor "perfect") will perish after the death of their bodies, and hence will know neither misery nor felicity in the afterlife, so the *Comedy* tells us that a vast multitude of human souls ("a long train/of people that I should never have believed/that death had undone [*disfatta*] so many";

Inf. III, 55–57)—apparently *the majority of humankind*—will end up, after death, in a sense "nowhere." If these people are technically in Hell, they are barely spoken of and are assigned no real place in its structure. "Mercy and Justice disdain them" (III, 50) means that they end up neither in Heaven (where God rewards through his mercy) nor in Hell (where God punishes through his justice). These people, neither "good" nor "evil" (neither "perfect" nor "wicked"), "displeasing to God and to his enemies" (III, 63), are stung by flies while worms feed on their blood—details that suggest the physical decomposition which may spell the ultimate fate not only of their bodies but also of their souls. Although Dante does not say, as al-Farabi does, that the souls of these "in-between" people perish, this is perhaps implied: they are said to be "un-made" (*disfatta*) by death (III, 57). Unnamed, their ultimate fate is a kind of nothingness. The *Comedy*, then, is not what it is normally taken to be: it does not represent the fate of "our" souls in the afterlife, since it indicates that "we"—most of us, the vast majority of ordinary humans—end up nowhere and are undone by death.

The notion that one's virtues and vices are shaped by one's city, is indeed one of the *Comedy*'s "central" doctrines: it is the gist of the speech delivered in the 50th of the poem's 100 cantos by Marco Lombard, a figure whom Dante appears to have invented to function as his "double" and to give voice to his own teachings. There Dante asks Marco Lombard to explain why the world is so wicked:

> The world is indeed as utterly deserted
> by every virtue as you declare to me,
> and pregnant and overspread with iniquity,
>
> but I beg you to point out to me the cause.
> (*Purg.* XVI, 58–61)

The premise of Marco's reply is that the human soul, at birth, is a *tabula rasa*, knowing nothing, moved solely by an instinctive drive toward happiness. But since the soul does not naturally know true happiness, it is likely to settle for the false happiness of a lesser good. Hence humans need to be guided toward true happiness by their leaders, by lawgivers who will govern in accord with their vision of the "true city" (thus we see that the idea of the excellent city—al-Farabi's primary concern—is at the very heart of the *Comedy*):

> From His hands, who fondly loves it
> before it exists, comes forth after the fashion
> of a child that sports, now weeping, now laughing,

The simple little soul, which knows nothing,
save that, proceeding from a glad maker,
it turns eagerly to what delights it.

First it tastes the savor of a trifling good;
there it is beguiled and runs after it,
if guide or curb bend not its love.

Wherefore it was needful to impose law as a bridle,
it was needful to have a ruler who could discern
at least the tower of the *true city*.

(*Purg.* XVI, 85–96)

Humans are not naturally wicked or corrupt. If humans have indeed become corrupt, it is because they have not been rightly guided by their rulers:

Well you can see that ill-guidance
is the cause that has made the world wicked,
and *not nature that is corrupt in you*.

Rome, which made the world good,
used to have two suns, which made visible both
the one road and the other, that of the world and of God.

(*Purg.* XVI, 103–105)

Humans—more precisely, bad human rulers—have *made* the world wicked by failing to govern by the light of philosophy. But though the world is thoroughly wicked, there is great cause for optimism: humans themselves, by re-instituting the rule of philosophy (or, at least rule by one who, if not himself a card-carrying philosopher, might discern philosophy's basic outlines—"a ruler who could discern/at least the tower of the true city"), have the power to make the world good again. The world is not, by nature or by cosmic or divine decree, hopelessly evil. Marco Lombard teaches that humans, having made their own history, have the power to change it, the freedom to perfect themselves by founding the perfect regime, the "true city," the city governed by the principles of philosophical ethics.

What is perhaps most striking in Marco Lombard's teaching is that he plainly and unambiguously rejects one of the most fundamental tenets of Catholicism—the doctrine of "original sin."[102] With manifest fondness for "the simple little soul," Marco Lombard insists upon our "original innocence." For he denies that humans are naturally corrupt, instead blaming our wrongdoings not on a corrupt nature that we all inherit from Adam but on bad government. According to the doctrine of original sin, humans, without God's grace, cannot help but tend toward wickedness. But Marco Lombard teaches that in fact humans *can* help it, they *are* free to act virtuously, and that to do so they need rely not on God's grace but rather on philosophically sound lawgivers.

The notion of freedom is in fact central to the *Comedy*, and it is *literally* so as part of the poem's structure. I am referring to the fact discovered by Singleton a few decades ago: that Dante intentionally "frames" the poem's center, in perfectly symmetrical fashion, with two instances of the phrase "free will."[103] Singleton noticed that these two instances of *libero arbitrio* ("free will") are balanced, with mathematical precision, around the poem's central canto, *Purgatory* XVII: the first appears precisely twenty-five stanzas before *Purgatory* XVII's first verse, and the second precisely twenty-five stanzas after *Purgatory* XVII's last verse (and in both instances *libero arbitrio* appears in the middle verse of its stanza).

Thus Dante has taken pains to inscribe "free will" into the very heart of his poem's structure, as if to say that at the core of the *Comedy* is an insistence on human freedom. (Recall, as we saw in the Introduction, that in the *Epistle to Cangrande* Dante says that his poem, allegorically, concerns "man, in the exercise of his *free will*, earning or becoming liable to the rewards or punishments of justice.") But this does not mean primarily that Dante aims to make a formal contribution to the traditional question of "free will vs. determinism." Rather, his insistence on freedom goes hand-in-hand with Marco Lombard's denial of "original sin." ("Free will" is above all the *freedom from sin*; as Augustine says, "the first free will is the ability to avoid sin."[104]) According to the doctrine of original sin, because of Adam's iniquity humans are *not free* to act virtuously; rather, the human will is forevermore impaired, unless it be healed by God's grace. In practice, this grace is normally made available only to members of those communities which have been granted divine revelation—that is, the Bible. But "free will," for Dante and Marco Lombard, means that human societies, *at all times and in all places, before and after Christ*, are *free to act virtuously*, and the key to attaining this freedom is to place the governance of the community in the hands of those who are guided by the teachings of philosophical ethics. To teach that non-Christians, living without God's grace, cannot live fully just lives and thus cannot come to construct the "perfect city," is to teach that the greater portion of humankind lacks "free will." It is to teach that, without God's help, we *must* be bad. If pagans, for instance, had been dependent for their virtue on a grace that was never or at most only rarely granted them, then they would not have been free. By insisting on humankind's universal freedom, Dante aims to liberate us from the pernicious pessimism fostered by the doctrine of original sin—a doctrine which Dante recognizes as providing a convenient excuse for the continuing corruption of the earthly *polis*. The doctrine of free will, on the other hand, insists that the power to reform and indeed perfect the *polis* is entirely in our own hands. Free will, for Dante, means *freedom from original sin*. It means that human societies—even those which have not been granted revealed truth—are free to reform themselves. If Dante here follows Augustine in conceiving of freedom as freedom from sin (as Augustine says, "because human nature sinned when it had the power to sin it is set free by a more abundant gift of grace so that it may be brought to that condition of liberty in which it is incapable of sin"[105]), he also once again displays his distance from Augustine: for the latter, very near the conclusion of the *City of God*, characterizes free will as pertaining exclusively to the afterlife: "In the Heavenly City, then, there will be freedom of will."[106] For Augustine, humans on earth, since Adam, are never free from sin and hence never enjoy "free will." But Dante dares imagine, as one of his poem's central affirmations, the possibility of freedom of will—freedom from original sin— down here in the earthly City of Man, the "true city," the perfect state. This freedom from original sin is our capacity to *redeem ourselves* without having to depend upon divine grace—a capacity shared in common by *every* human community. Central to the *Comedy* is a project of liberation: non-Christian communities are liberated from the accusation that, living without God's grace and without the benefit of revelation, they must necessarily sin.

Like the blessed souls in Dante's Heaven, the felicitous of al-Farabi's afterlife inhabit an immaterial polity that is *corporate* and *graded*. By "corporate" I mean that souls are grouped together in the afterlife with those who practiced a similar "art," occupation, or vocation on earth—so that the afterlife is in a sense divided into various "guilds." By "graded" I mean that these groups are ranked in a hierarchy, some "higher" and others "lower," some enjoying more and others less pleasure in the afterlife. For al-Farabi, this hierarchy of heavenly pleasure is a matter of the proximity to pure philosophical knowledge of the knowledge given by the various "arts." The philosopher-prophet-lawgiver attains more knowledge in life than does the street-sweeper, and hence he enjoys greater pleasure in the afterlife, since one's rank in heaven is determined by the clarity and completeness of one's vision of truth. The importance of one's role in the earthly *polis* determines the intensity of one's pleasure in the afterlife:

> It is evident that the kinds of happiness attained by the citizens of the city differ in quantity and quality as a result of the difference in the perfections they acquire through political activities. Accordingly, the pleasures they attain [in the afterlife] vary in excellence.[107]

Groups or "guilds" of like-functioning or "kindred" citizens assume in heaven the same political/social ranks they occupied on earth— philosophers enjoying eternal bliss with other philosophers, administrators with other administrators, warriors with other warriors, street-sweepers with other street-sweepers. When one generation of those who perform a particular political function (e.g, lawgiving, jurisprudence, oratory, pharmacology, cloth-making, dancing, etc.) passes away, it joins the souls of the past generations that have performed that same function. And as the size of each group in the afterlife continually increases as generations of its kindred citizens continue to pass away, so the bliss felt by each individual member of the group continually increases—since the larger the group, the greater the pleasure of each member:

> As one group of them passes away, and their bodies are destroyed, their souls have achieved salvation and happiness, and they are succeeded by other men who assume their positions in the city and perform their actions, the souls of the latter will also achieve salvation. As their bodies are destroyed, they join the rank of the former group that had passed away, they will be together with them in the way that incorporeal things are together, and the kindred souls within each group will be in a state of union with one another. The more the kindred separate souls increase in number and unite with one another, the greater the pleasure felt by each soul; and the more they are joined by those who come after them, the greater the pleasure felt by each of the latter through their encounter with the former as well as the pleasure felt by the former through their union with the latter. For each soul will then be intellecting, in addition to itself, many other souls that are of the same kind; and it will be intellecting more souls as the ones that had passed away are joined by the ones succeeding them. Hence the pleasure felt by the very ancient ones will continue to increase indefinitely. Such is the state of every group of them.[108]

Dante's paradise is similar to al-Farabi's afterlife in obvious ways. The blessed of *Paradiso* are represented as "guilds" or groups of like-functioning souls: scholars and intellectuals are grouped together in the sphere of the Sun; holy warriors in the sphere of Mars; etc. And, as in al-Farabi's afterlife, the groups of blessed in Dante's Paradise are ranked in a hierarchy, so that some groups attain more and others less felicity and pleasure:

> Then it was clear to me how everywhere
> in Heaven is Paradise, even if the grace
> of the Supreme Good does not rain down there in one same measure.
> (Par. III, 88–90)

If the souls of Dante's Heaven experience ever-increasing joy, this increase in joy is not a matter of an individual soul's elevating itself into a higher celestial rank by "switching" to a higher grade of Heaven (only the journeying Dante, whose presence in Heaven is exceptional, is able to experience that sort of increase in joy). Rather, it involves the continual increase of a given group's joy as it welcomes more and more like-functioning individual souls into its ranks. Thus, when Dante reaches the sphere of Venus and beholds the circle of lights that are the souls of the loving, the size and joy of that group—who take Dante for one of their own—increases: "I saw it increase in size and brightness, / through the new joy that was added/to its bright-ness when I spoke" (*Par.* VIII, 46–48). When Dante enters the sphere of Mercury, the group of those souls who have been politically active in the pursuit of honor and fame, taking Dante for one of their own, greets him as a new member whose presence shall augment the group's bliss: " 'Lo, one who shall increase our loves!' / And, as each came up to us/the shade was seen full of joy" (*Par.* V, 105–107).

The hierarchy of Dante's Heaven, like that of al-Farabi's, reflects the hierarchy of "arts" and diverse positive modes of human existence on earth. The diversity of the heavenly ranks ("diverse voices make sweet music,/so diverse ranks in our life/render sweet harmony among the wheels"; *Par.* VI, 124–126) is directly rooted in the diversity of roles per-formed by the citizens of the earthly polity ("men below live/in diverse ways for diverse duties"; *Par.* VIII, 118–119).

For both Dante and al-Farabi, then, Heaven is an image of the perfect state on earth. Heaven is not an *alternative* to earthly politics (as it is for Augustine); rather, it is the exemplary model of earthly political perfection.

Al-Farabi's Heaven is a hierarchy of greater and lesser *vision*: at the top is he who *sees* most clearly and comprehensively, at the bottom those who see least. The highest rank in Heaven is reserved for the philosopher-poet-lawgiver, who sees truth clearly and completely; above all he sees the truth of the oneness of the First Cause (God). His students and followers in philosophy see truth slightly less clearly, and their rank in Heaven is accordingly slightly lower. Those who administer his laws see truth in a slightly lesser fashion than his followers in philosophy, and their rank is slightly lower. This hierarchy of vision descends, through the various lev-els of civic function, all the way down to the street-sweeper, who "sees" only through images, and even then only in a limited fashion.

Dante's Heaven is similarly a hierarchy of greater and lesser vision. Beatrice teaches Dante that each of the celestial spheres is presided over by a different kind of "Intelligence" or angelic rank, that these Intelligences are arranged in a hierarchy that corresponds to the intensity and plentitude of their vision of truth, and that the scale of vision measures blessedness in paradise:

And you should know that all have delight
in the measure of the depth to which their sight
penetrates the Truth in which every intellect finds rest;

from which it may be seen that the state
of blessedness is founded on the act of vision,
not on that which loves, which follows after;

and the merit, to which grace and good will give birth,
is the measure of their vision;
thus from grade to grade the progression goes.

(Par. XXVII, 106–114)

The "highest" point in Heaven, the summit of Dante's journey in the *Comedy*'s final canto, is the point of most perfect vision—the locus (or non-locus, since it takes place in the nonspatial place which is the immaterial Empyrean) of Dante's direct vision of God ("I united / my gaze with the Infinite Goodness"; *Par.* XXXIII, 80–81). If for al-Farabi this summit of vision is reserved for the philosopher-poet-prophet, in *Paradiso* this rank of highest distinction is reserved for. . .Dante himself! In assuming the highest rank in the celestial *polis*, Dante assumes the role reserved, in al-Farabi's scheme, for the philosopher-poet-prophet.

Dante and al-Farabi also share a similar view of the dimensions and extent of the ideal earthly *polis*. Both go far beyond Aristotle, who does not consider the possibility of a polity larger than the individual city-state, by envisioning the truly perfect state as necessarily global and multinational. For al-Farabi, there can be three kinds of perfect regime—the city, the nation, and the union of all nations:

> There are three kinds of perfect society, great, medium, and small. The great one is *the union of all societies in the inhabitable world*; the medium one the union of one nation in one part of the inhabitable world; the small one the union of the people of a city in the territory of any nation whatsoever.[109]
>
> [The philosopher-poet-lawgiver] is the sovereign over whom no other being has any sovereignty whatsoever: he is the Imam; he is the first sovereign of the excellent city, he is the sovereign of the excellent nation, and the sovereign of the universal state (the *oikumene*).[110]
>
> The excellent universal state will arise only when all the nations in it co-operate for the purpose of reaching felicity.[111]

If al-Farabi, unlike Dante (for whom the only legitimate polity is the universal state, the *oikumene*, the union of all societies in the inhabitable world), admits the possibility of perfect cities and nations, he nonetheless considers the virtuous multinational state to be more perfect than the virtuous nation and the virtuous city: "The absolutely perfect human societies are divided into nations."[112] To be "absolutely perfect," the polity must be multinational. This is because the range of possible modes of excellence offered by a combination of nations (each of which is linguistically and culturally unique) is greater than that offered by a single nation alone.[113]

Recall that the governance of Dante's Monarchy combines a "common law" that applies to all nations ("Mankind is to be ruled by [the Monarch] in those matters which are common to all men and of relevance to all, and is to be guided toward peace by a common law") with locally specific laws that take into account the unique difference of each nation ("For nations, kingdoms, and cities have characteristics of their own, which need to be governed by different laws; for law is a rule which governs life"). Similarly, al-Farabi maintains that, because of the historicity of the definition of "man," which is different in different times and places, the "excellent universal state" must govern through a combination of "universals" and "particulars":

> The states and accidents in [the idea "man"] are at one time different from the ones it has at another time, after or before. The same is the case with respect to different places. The accidents and states it has when existing in one country are different from the ones it has in another.[114]
>
> One should draw a distinction between the similitudes [i.e., images] that ought to be presented to every nation, and in which all nations and all the citizens of every nation should share, and the ones that ought to be presented to a particular nation and not to another, to a particular city and not to another, or to a particular group among the citizens of a city and not to another.[115]
>
> Therefore [the supreme ruler] has to secure certain groups of men or certain individuals who are to be instructed in what causes the happiness of particular nations, who will preserve what can form the character of a particular nation alone, and who will learn the persuasive methods that should be employed in forming the character of that nation.[116]

Neither al-Farabi nor Dante envisions the ideal multinational state as one that would operate by cultural or religious imperialism. They do not advocate forced conversion to a single paradigm, but rather the preservation of difference within a framework of peaceful coexistence.

Theory, Practice, Religion

But, despite all these affinities between Dante and al-Farabi, *there is one crucial difference*. Understanding this difference—which concerns the status of "theoretical" and "practical" truths in religious discourse—will help us greatly enrich our understanding of the *Comedy*. More particularly, it will help us retrieve an alternate approach to the *Comedy*'s most fundamental allegory—that revolving around the distinction between "Virgil" and "Beatrice."

Al-Farabi maintains that political excellence is twofold, depending on both "views and actions." The citizens of the *polis* need both to possess knowledge of truth (even if some do so only indirectly through the images) and to perform the right deeds. This emphasis on the twofold aspect of philosophy is manifest in al-Farabi's frequent reiteration of the phrase "views and actions":

> The city which has deliberately changed is a city whose *views and actions* were previously the *views and actions* of the people of the excellent city, but they have changed and *different views* have taken their place, and its actions have turned into *different actions*.[117]

In short, for al-Farabi the citizens of the perfect state need both "theoretical" and "practical" knowledge—that is, knowledge of right "views" (theory) and of right "actions" (practice).

The essential difference between the objects of "theory" and the objects of "practice" is that the former are "real" and the latter "artificial." For "theory" concerns those things that *are what they are* entirely independent of human activity, while "practice" concerns those things that humans themselves make or do. An object of "theory" is something that, as al-Farabi succinctly puts it, "we are not able to do when we know it," while an object of "practice" is conversely something that we are able to do. Theoretical knowledge concerns things "whose existence and constitution owe nothing at all to human artifice":

> The name "knowledge" applies to many things. However, the knowledge that is a virtue of *the theoretical part* is for the soul to attain certainty about the existence of *beings whose existence and constitution owe nothing at all to human artifice*.[118]

If theoretical knowledge concerns things that we are not able to make or do, practical knowledge concerns the sphere of human activity:

> *Practical intellect* is the faculty by which a human being—through much experience in matters and by long observation of sense-perceptible things—attains premises by which he is able to seize upon what he ought to prefer or avoid with respect to each one of the matters we are to do.[119]

The theoretical intellect knows those things that stand on their own entirely apart from human beings, while the practical intellect knows those things that are intimately bound up with human existence.

What sorts of things does al-Farabi have in mind when speaking of the objects of "theory"? Included among those "things in common which all of the people of the excellent city ought to know" and which are clearly to be reckoned as "theoretical" in al-Farabi's sense of the term are such things as "the immaterial existents [i.e., intelligences or angels] and their specific qualities and the order and rank of each of them"; "the celestial substances [i.e., the stars and planets] and the qualities of each of them"; and "the natural bodies which are beneath them, and how they come to be and pass away."[120] All such things are what they are without input from human activity or artifice, which plays no role in producing, constituting, or altering them. Although such things may have an effect upon us, we do not have an effect upon them. These are things that we can come to *know* but that we can never *make or do* (we cannot, for instance, make planets or angels—although modern technology has perhaps enabled us to craft "natural bodies" and to have impact upon the cosmos in ways that al-Farabi could not have foreseen). In general, theory treats "the way things really are," the reality of the physical and immaterial cosmos, including the reality of the human body and its faculties (for "the generation of man and how the faculties of the soul come to be" is next in al-Farabi's enumeration of those things that the citizens ought to know, and these matters of human biology and psychobiology are to be classified as matters for the theoretical not the practical intellect). In short, "theory" in al-Farabi's sense is more or less synonymous with "science" (although we must bear in mind the domain of medieval science is broader than that of modern science, since the Middle Ages posited the existence of immaterial not just material entities).

But the paradigmatic and ultimate object of "theory" is God, for the theoretical obligation of the citizens of the excellent city is "in the first place to know the First Cause [i.e., God] and all its qualities."[121] God is the highest of those beings "whose existence and constitution owe nothing at all to human artifice," that reality which is what it is in complete independence of human activity. God is God outside of all human practice and regardless of whether humans ever come into existence.

If God [the First Cause] is the ultimate object of the theoretical intellect, then the ultimate object of the practical intellect is the perfect political state. The practical intellect deals with the domain of "ethics" rather than "science"—the sphere of things that are impacted by human will, choice, desire, and practices. Among those "practical" things that the citizens ought to know are: "the first ruler [i.e., the philosopher-poet-lawgiver] and how 'revelation' is brought about; then the rulers who have taken his place when he is not available at a given time; then the excellent city and its people and the felicity which their souls ultimately reach, and the cities contrary to it and the condition to which their souls are reduced after death, some of them to wretchedness and the others to nothingness; and the excellent nations and the nations contrary to them."[122] The perfect state only ever comes into existence, and only becomes what it is, as a result of human activity.

God and the perfect state are, respectively, the ultimate objects of "theoretical" and "practical" philosophy. When we know the perfect state we are potentially able to "make" or "do" it. Of course it goes without saying that when we know God we are by no means empowered to "make" or "do" him. Thus, then, we see that the essential difference between the "theoretical" and the "practical" lies in our capacity to bring about change in (or to bring into existence) the object of our knowledge.

Now, recall that for al-Farabi religious discourse provides images of philosophical truths. Since philosophical truths are of two primary kinds—theoretical and practical—religious images are themselves of two primary kinds: some are imaginative representations of "the way things really are" (things independent of human activity such as the First Cause, the intellects, and the celestial bodies), while others are imaginative representations of things that we ought to make or do (things such as the perfect state). Religion provides knowledge of both "science" and "ethics," albeit in the lesser or "subordinate" mode of imaginative discourse:

> Thus, virtuous religion is similar to philosophy. Just as philosophy is partly theoretical and partly practical, so it is with religion: the calculative theoretical part is what a human being is not able to do when he knows it, whereas the practical part is what a human being is able to do when he knows it. The practical things in religion are those whose universals are in practical philosophy. . . .Therefore, all virtuous laws [i.e., religious commandments] are subordinate to the universals of practical philosophy. The theoretical opinions that are in religion have their demonstrative proofs in theoretical philosophy and are taken in religion without demonstrative proofs. Therefore, the two parts of which religion consists [i.e., theoretical and practical religious discourse] are subordinate to philosophy.[123]
>
> Once the images representing the theoretical things demonstrated in the theoretical sciences are produced in the souls of the multitude and they are made to assent to their images, and once the practical things (together with the conditions of the possibility of their existence), take hold of their souls, and dominate them so they are unable to resolve to do anything else, then the theoretical things and the practical things are realized. Now these things are philosophy when they are in the soul of the legislator. They are religion when they are in the soul of the multitude.[124]

For al-Farabi, the philosopher first knows, in an abstract universal way (in the case of practical intelligibles) and through demonstrative proof (in the case of theoretical ones), all the requisite theoretical and practical things, including the highest and ultimate ones—respectively, the First Cause (God) and the perfect state. Then, in his capacity as prophet or lawgiver, the philosopher represents these things, in an imaged and more particular form, and without rational demonstration but rather through various devices of rhetorical persuasion, to the multitudes. In the case where the philosopher establishes the "absolutely perfect," multinational state, he will provide a multiplicity of culturally specific religions, each representing the same universal set of theoretical and practical things, but in a particular way befitting a particular people. Each particular people will, in its own way, know through its particular religious imagery *both* theory and practice— *both* the things that we ought to do *and* the way (nonhuman and nonartificial) things really are. Each religion will provide its people with an adequate (if imaged) and appropriate representation of that highest being "whose existence and constitution owes nothing at all to human artifice" and which the philosopher knows as the First Cause.

As Richard Walzer shows in his commentary on *The Perfect State*, al-Farabi's view of religion was deeply influenced by discussions of the topic in Stoic and other later Greek philosophy. In particular, al-Farabi ascribed to the view that each religion is a sort of "language": just as different languages all name one and the same set of universal things, so do different religions name the same set of universals. Walzer cites, as an example of the sort of Greek thinking with which al-Farabi was familiar in Arabic translation, a passage from the *Corpus Hermeticum*:

> Reason (*logos*) and speech (*phone*) are very different. Reason is common to all men, but speech differs from nation to nation. But humanity is nonetheless one, and in the same way reason is one, but is translated into different languages, and one discovers that it is the same in Egypt and Persia and Greece.[125]

Al-Farabi, as Walzer says, "finds no difficulty in comparing the origin of languages and the origin of religions, laws, and customs, and goes so far as to identify the [religious] lawgiver (*nomothetes*) and the 'giver of language' (*onomatothetes*)." And Walzer continues by offering further examples of the later Greek understanding on religion which shaped al-Farabi's thinking:

> The various religious groups differ just as languages vary, although they all reproduce, in symbolic form, one and the same metaphysical truth which is well known to philosophers and teachers of natural theology all over the world—wherever it may have first sprung into existence. This idea was worked out especially by Stoic thinkers and was accepted, though not without variations, by most of the later Greek philosophers. It is well known, for

instance, from that Stoic demonstration of the existence of God which is based on the consensus of all nations: they all pray and offer sacrifices and build temples since they all agree that divine beings exist, although they describe the godhead in different terms and disagree about its nature. Three passages taken more or less at random from late Greek authors may illustrate the specific turn which this idea takes in al-Farabi's mind. Plutarch, *De Iside et Osiride*, emphasizes the difference in quality by which the different religious symbolic representations of truth are characterized: "In the same way as sun and moon and heaven and earth and sea are common to all, but called differently by different people, so, although one divine mind orders the universe and one providence governs it, there are different honors and different names according to law and custom. . . ." The same attitude appears, for instance, at the end of the second century in Celsus' attack against the Christians: the Christians have no right to claim a unique position for their god: "The goatherds and shepherds thought that there was one god called the Most High, or Adonai, or the Heavenly One, or Sabaoth, or however they like to call this word." "Not even their doctrine of heaven is their own but, to omit all other instances, was also held long ago by the Persians, as Herodotus shows in one place. . . .I think, therefore, that it makes no difference whether we call Zeus the most High or Zen or Adonai, or Sabaoth, or Amoun like the Egyptians, or Papaeus like the Scythians."[126]

For al-Farabi, each religion is its own culture's way of saying the same things—both theoretical and practical—that are said by the religions of other cultures.

Al-Farabi thus views Islam as one of many religious "languages" which differ from each other in "speech" (*phone*) but not in rational content (*logos*). Muhammad provided an Arabic "speech" to name for Muslims the universal truths of philosophical *logos*. That which the philosophers know as the First Cause is named "Allah" in the Qur'an. When the Qur'an speaks of the "Spirit of Holiness" or the "Angel of Revelation," it is naming that which the philosophers know as the Active Intellect. "Darkness" and "Light" refer to the philosophical notions, respectively, of matter and form. The Islamic "Imam," for al-Farabi, signifies the Platonic philosopher-king. That which Islam terms *wahy* ("revelation") means, as Walzer says, "the highest human knowledge which only the metaphysician is able to attain."[127]

Dante agrees with al-Farabi that religion is partly theoretical and partly practical. He agrees that the practical (ethical) part of each particular religion is an imaged similitude of universal practical philosophy. But he *disagrees* concerning the *theoretical* part of the Christian religion. The "God" of Christian revelation cannot be taken as a signifier for philosophy's highest and paradigmatic object of theory (the First Cause). For the philosopher knows, through demonstrative proof, that the First Cause is absolutely unitary, absolutely one. But, according to the "theory" provided by Christian religious discourse, God is three-in-one. The philosopher knows, through demonstrative proof, that man is man (not God) and God is God (not man). But the highest object of Christian "theory," the object that Dante sees at the highest point of his journey at the very end of the *Comedy*, is God-man. The "theory" provided by Christianity violates the basic philosophical principle of noncontradiction, and thus, unlike Islamic "theory" as al-Farabi understands it, it is not subordinate to, not an imaged representation of, the truth of theoretical philosophy. From Dante's point of view, not all religions offer equivalent and interchangeable images of God. Many religions, including Islam, name God in a way that is a fitting image for the First Cause conceived as an absolutely unitary One. But to call God, for instance, "the Heavenly One," is from a Christian perspective to use a misleading and inadequate image: pure monotheism fails to name God properly. Christian "speech" about God is irrational, illogical—it does not provide an image grounded in universal reason (*logos*).

Al-Farabi insists that the citizens of the perfect state need to have both the right views and the right practices. He seems to suggest that they need to know "science" in order to ground their "ethics." Hence *The Perfect State* begins with a lengthy theory of the cosmos before finally turning to matters of practical philosophy. The *Comedy* reverses this order, showing first the construction of the perfect state (*Purgatory*'s Earthly Paradise), then offering, almost as an afterthought, the "theory" of the cosmos.

The citizens of Dante's Global Monarchy have the right practices; they may have the right views about some things—such as, "what are the right practices?"—and they may in addition have the right views about some of the lesser theoretical things, matters of natural science such as human biology (treated by Statius in *Purgatory* XXV). But this citizenry, which includes the peoples of all nations and religions, does not *need* to have the right view about the ultimate object of theoretical knowledge: God. *The citizens of Dante's perfect state are liberated from the burden of having to know, for the purposes of practical and political excellence, God.* We do not need "theory" (complete knowledge of extra-human reality) in order to ground our human practice.

For Dante, the Christian religion—like all virtuous religions—provides imaginative representations of practical philosophical truths; but its highest and ultimate theoretical content—its vision of God—is *not* an image of a truth that can be known philosophically. Whereas al-Farabi maintains that there is a holistic harmony between Islam and philosophy, Dante's *Paradiso* ultimately displays the division between philosophical and Christian theory. Dante distinguishes between the knowledge that the citizens need for the construction of the perfect state (a practical philosophical knowledge imaged in all religions) and the politically and ethically superfluous knowledge provided by Christian revelation (a theoretical knowledge imaged only in the Christian religion). "Virgil" and "Beatrice" are the names for this distinction—the distinction between a "practical wisdom" common to all religions and a "theoretical wisdom" unique to Christianity. All religions tell us, in their particular ways, what we ought to "make" or "do" (the perfect state). Only Christianity (but we shall challenge this Christian "exceptionality," both at the end of part I and in part II) tells us the truth about the highest of those "beings whose existence and constitution owe nothing at all to human artifice." But such "science" of the divine Being is not a prerequisite for, and thus is essentially irrelevant to, the human project of "making" the excellent political regime.

Virgil and Beatrice: Reason and Faith, or Practice and Theory?

Since the time of the earliest commentaries on the *Comedy* in the fourteenth century to the present day, there has been a general consensus concerning the terms of the *Comedy*'s basic allegory: "Virgil" stands for "reason" (philosophy) and "Beatrice" stands for "faith" (theology). "Virgil" signifies that which the human mind can acquire "naturally" (without the aid of religious revelation), while "Beatrice" signifies that which can only be acquired "supernaturally" (through divine grace and Christian revelation). Virgil's words to Dante in *Purgatory* apparently provide irrefutable textual support for this view: "As far as reason sees here / I can tell you; beyond that wait / only for Beatrice, for it is a matter of faith" (*Purg.* XVIII, 46–48).

It would be foolish for us to assert that this understanding of the poem's basic allegory—an understanding grounded in the text, sanctioned by centuries of exegetical tradition, and demonstrated by the sound philological efforts of innumerable scholars—is "wrong." Dante clearly intended for the Virgil/Beatrice distinction to function, *for some readers*, as an allegory for a distinction between philosophy and religion. But Dante also clearly intended to write a "prophetic" text (one that gains the assent of *all* readers by offering to each level of audience a suitable level of meaning; I describe "prophetic" discourse in more detail below, part II, in my remarks on Averroes). Dante crafted his poem in such manner that religiously-oriented readers would find it religious and philosophically-oriented readers would find it philosophical. Dante knew that there would be some readers who would be comforted by thinking of the *Comedy* as a "journey to Beatrice," an enactment of Dante's return to religious faith. But he also wrote for those who would see the poem as a "journey with Virgil," a testament to the sufficiency of philosophy in the realm of *praxis*. It is for the latter audience that he intended the Virgil/Beatrice distinction to function as an allegory for the distinction, *within* philosophy, between practice and theory.

Let us for the sake of argument momentarily "bracket out" our objections to understanding the Virgil/Beatrice distinction as another name for the reason/faith distinction; let us pretend for a moment that we are at ease with this understanding of the poem's basic allegory.

The question, then, is what does this allegory *mean*? What is Dante's point in writing of a journey on which he is guided first by Reason and then by Faith? More particularly, what has this allegory signified in the exegetical tradition in which we are now embedded, American Dante criticism of the past few decades?

The founding principle that anchors much of this criticism is the premise that, in the final analysis, the *Comedy* is a critique of, and indeed against, philosophy. The operative assumption is that Dante left off writing the *Convivio* because it was too philosophical—in which case his turning to the *Comedy* is his "conversion" to theology. The poem's leaving Virgil behind at a certain point—prior to crossing the threshold into the realm of those who are saved—dramatizes Dante's loss of confidence in the power of natural reason. These critics read Virgil as a "tragic" figure, routinely characterizing him as deficient, inadequate, impotent, as if Dante exploits Virgil's fate as a way of saying to the would-be philosopher, *Thou shalt be Christian*! The whole poem becomes an imperative to convert from a "secular" to a "religious" stance. The *Comedy*'s message becomes, *Philosophy killeth, but Religion giveth life*.

Amilcare Iannucci, who penned the entry called "Philosophy" for the recent *Dante Encyclopedia*, repeats the gist of this current orthodoxy:

> Dante's philosophers, though representative of value, do not represent the truest value, because their words are not imbued with the word of God. . . . It is because of this *great deficiency* [emphasis added] of theirs that Dante in the *Commedia* revisits his earlier flirtation with the *donna gentile* of philosophy of the *Convivio*. Now everything is focused on following the true path, and anything that diverges from that true path is seen as error.[128]

In Iannucci's presentation of Freccero's interpretation, the issues are reduced to an elemental starkness: the "true path" = Christian theology and the "false path" = philosophy. Although philosophy may be said to have some value, it is ultimately a dead-end because it cannot lead to felicity, ultimate happiness.

The problem with the interpretation that denigrates Virgil is that it views the poem's trajectory as mapping out a single straight linear path of progress to a single destination (Heaven or God). Since these critics do not acknowledge what Dante so clearly insists upon—that there are *two roads, two suns, two destinations*—they are obliged to see Virgil as a tragic failure rather than a comic success. Yet Dante tells us that there are *two* paths—not one "true" and one "false," but both of them true paths. Virgil's path leads to a different goal than Beatrice's, and he is guided to the goal by a different source of illumination. But he *does* get there; he does not fail, and his way is not error. Virgil is fully adequate to the task. He reaches his destination. Illuminated by the sun of philosophy, Virgil leads Dante along the true path to its finish, the Earthly Paradise, where, in what is perhaps the poem's greatest scene of comic triumph, he crowns Dante philosopher-king. Virgil, and Dante with him, attains felicity, a happiness that Dante himself calls nothing less than *ultimate*. How can the attainment of ultimate happiness be deemed a tragedy?

So, even if we acknowledge that "Virgil" is reason and "Beatrice" is faith, the significance of this basic allegory is *not* that the latter always trumps the former. It is, rather, the autonomy of reason, its sufficiency and adequacy in the political sphere of human existence. For the flip-side of Virgil's not leading Dante to the Heavenly Paradise is Beatrice's not leading him to the Earthly Paradise.

The *Comedy* is like a triptych (an art-form that had recently come to prominence in Dante's Florence), with a left side-panel (*Inferno*), a central panel (*Purgatory*), and a right side-panel (*Paradiso*). Although it has become customary for Dante exegetes to emphasize the right-side panel as the bearer of highest significance, this is not necessarily consonant with Dante's intention. Is Dante trying to say that you must be Christian to be saved (or, less literally, that felicity depends upon the theoretical vision of truth—a vision that can be had only through Christian revelation)? If we emphasize *Paradiso*, we might be led to say that—in which case we will see Virgil as a tragic figure. But if we emphasize the central panel, *Purgatory* (for the central panel of a triptych is indeed meant to be its most important), then Virgil's fate will appear comic: Virgil can, on the strength of his own powers, guide us to the just ideal society on earth. *Christianity, indeed religious faith itself, is irrelevant to this goal.*

The assertion that the Virgil/Beatrice distinction is an allegory for the reason/faith distinction can be "saved" by recognizing that Dante's point in constructing the *Comedy* around this distinction is not to denigrate one of its terms and celebrate the other, but rather to insist that each has its own legitimate sphere of concern. Both Virgil and Beatrice lead Dante to a Paradise; neither can serve as chief guide in the other's domain. Beatrice is not necessary (although for some people and some cultures she may be useful) for humankind's practical goal, the attainment of happiness in the perfect political state. Virgil, for his part, cannot lead us to a theoretical vision of a fundamentally nonrational God. So, the reason/faith approach to the *Comedy*'s basic allegory can be affirmed by understanding that allegory as part and parcel of Dante's fundamental political tenet: that there needs to be a "division of labor" between State and Church.

But if Virgil does not need Beatrice, on the contrary it is clear that Beatrice does need Virgil. The world must be reformed politically, and without the divisive interference of religion, if religion is itself to be set back on the right track. It is axiomatic for Dante that theoretical happiness can only be attained by those whose practical affairs are in order. In the first paragraph of the *Convivio*, for instance, Dante maintains that the mass of humanity is deprived of the "ultimate happiness" which is (theoretical) "knowledge" because of sundry "handicaps" in their material existence: physical and mental impairments; souls trained in vice rather than virtue; lack of the requisite leisure due to the pressing affairs of everyday life; and the relative lack of educational opportunity that prevails in some parts of the world. The happiness of theory can only be attained by those humans fortunate to thrive in the right set of material circumstances. Dante reiterates this thought near the opening of *Monarchy*, where he insists that humankind's leisure or rest—that is, universal peace—is the necessary prerequisite, the sine qua non, for the full development of humankind's theoretical knowledge:

> Now it has been sufficiently explained that the activity proper to mankind considered as a whole is constantly to actualize the full intellectual potential of humanity, primarily through thought and secondarily through action (as a function and extension of thought). And since what holds true for the part is true for the whole, and an individual human being "grows perfect in judgment and wisdom when he sits at rest," it is apparent that mankind most freely and readily attends to this activity—an activity which is almost divine, as we read in the psalm: "Thou hast made him a little lower than the angels"—in the calm or tranquility of peace. Hence it is clear that universal peace is the best of those things which are ordained for human happiness. . . .From the arguments developed so far, it is clear what is the better, indeed the best, way of enabling mankind to engage in the activity proper to humanity; and consequently we see the most direct means of achieving the goal to which all our human actions are directed as to their final end. That means is universal peace, which is to be taken as the first principle for the arguments which follow.[129]

Here Dante speaks of humankind as having a goal, a final end—namely, "thought." That "thought" is here conceived of primarily as "theory" is indicated by the fact that it is said to "grow perfect" only when we "sit at rest" (as we shall see below, the "activity" of theory is non-activity, the leisure of speculation). "Rest" (peace) *is not the product of theory but rather its starting-point.* Universal peace, then, is the necessary material condition, the indispensable means, by which humankind readies itself for reaching its intellectual goal of theoretical thought.

Beatrice, understood now as the full deployment of our (theoretical) intellectual potential—the perfect "judgment and wisdom" that we might achieve when we "sit at rest"—can only show herself *after* Virgil has done his work. We must first construct the perfect global state, first come to dwell in the Earthy Paradise, before we can take flight for the paradise of theory. Knowledge of things nonhuman depends upon the prior human activity of crafting the perfect *polis*. Virgil *must* succeed, *must* attain his goal, before Beatrice can ever be deployed. Virgil's fate *must* be a comic one— for without Virgil's brand of happiness there can be no happiness with Beatrice. The *Comedy* does not display Virgil's "great deficiency" and "inadequacy" but rather his *indispensability*, his status as a sine qua non. As Gilson says, for Dante, "ethics and politics, though mere concomitants of contemplation, are its *essential* concomitants."[130] (I believe that Gilson was mistaken to say "mere" here, since, as we have seen and will continue to see, and as Gilson himself remarks elsewhere, Dante aims to overcome the graded hierarchy that sets theory above practice. Still, Gilson's main point is correct: "no peace, no truth!") The poem does not counsel us to renounce Virgil (or to say, with Hollander, "Poor Virgil!"[131]) but rather to hail him as the only way that we can come to join her company. The notion of a "tragic" Virgil, the notion that grounds the predominant trend of late twentieth-century American Dante exegesis, is founded on a flawed understanding of the poem's basic allegory. The *Comedy* is not the *Comedy* without a "comic" Virgil.

Let us emphasize that, according to this passage from *Monarchy*, the message of Christ, world peace, is delivered so that humankind might be at leisure constantly and *freely* to develop its intellectual potential. Christ's message does not provide the readymade *contents* for our intellects to contemplate; rather, it offers a prescription for bringing about the *conditions* under which we might freely employ our intellects. Christ offers ethics rather than science. But the ethics that he offers is not a uniquely Christian one.

Our remarks have already indicated that reducing the *Comedy*'s basic allegory to the reason/faith distinction does not do justice to the richness of Dante's conception. In our effort to "save" these allegorical terms, we were compelled to adjust them: Virgil appears as the terrain of political happiness (universal peace and justice) which must be prepared before Beatrice, "thought" or humankind's complete scientific intellectual potential, can "grow perfect." If Beatrice guides Dante in that Paradise that awaits us in the "afterlife," it is because she represents those intellectual attainments in the field of "theory" that can only flourish *after "life"*—after the practical affairs of material or political existence—has been properly arranged and rendered conducive to thought. This may seem like a punning invention on our part, but in fact this is precisely one of the understandings of the "afterlife" that was formulated by Averroes, who posits in his *Epistle on the Possibility of Conjunction with the Active Intellect* that the "afterlife" is the "blessed" life of science that one is free to pursue after having successfully negotiated one's duties in the realm of "governing": "Plato believed that when the great philosophers reached old age, they were relieved from governing, whereupon they retired from active life and proceeded to the 'Isle of the Blessed,' free to speculate upon that Intellect."[132] If Virgil's felicity is clearly "governing," Beatrice's is to dwell and speculate in the "Isle of the Blessed."

Perhaps the most compelling reason to resist the notion that Virgil = reason and Beatrice = faith is that her characteristic discourse has very little to do with disclosing the tenets of faith and a great deal to do with disclosing the facts of science. The objects of the two fundamental doctrines of Christian faith—the Trinity and the Incarnation—are only ever revealed to Dante at the end of the poem, well after he has left Beatrice behind and after he has similarly left behind his subsequent guide, St. Bernard. Why, then, do we not more often hear of the great deficiency and inadequacy of Beatrice? Why do we not hear that the poem is structured to show the limitations of theology?

If there is something dubious about the notion that Beatrice is faith, it is even more dubious to disassociate her from philosophy.[133] We cannot read very far into *Paradiso* before coming to see that the rigor of Beatrice's philosophizing makes Virgil appear, by contrast, a purveyor of *belles-lettres*. Aristotelian rationalism is by no means reserved for Virgil, since Beatrice is, if anything, a greater master of Aristotle's philosophy than is Virgil. To see this one need only read *Paradiso* II, where Beatrice delivers what is probably the *Comedy*'s most expert and analytical scientific demonstration—a lengthy and difficult discussion of the cause of the dark spots on the moon, replete with references to Arabic natural science. Dante's first major move in *Paradiso* is to present Beatrice, not as religious or informed by faith, but as a past-master of Arabo-Aristotelian theoretical and cosmological science. If she appears even more rational than Virgil, it is because the objects of her philosophizing are theoretical, not practical ones.

Critics have been puzzled by Dante's beginning *Paradiso* with such an apparently tangential digression. Why does he risk losing the audience's interest right from the start of the third canticle? Why do we need to know so much about the physical makeup of the moon and the optics of its reflected light (Beatrice even provides detailed instructions that one might follow to carry out an empirical experiment to prove her optical theory)? The answer is that Dante needed to establish, from the start of the canticle, that the objects of thought proper to Paradise are *theoretical* objects: the moon is paradigmatic of those beings "whose existence and constitution owe nothing at all to human artifice."

One of the first things Dante says about *Paradiso* is that it is inessential— that the multitude of readers will be better off not reading it:

> O you that are in your little bark,
> eager to hear, following behind
> my ship that singing makes her way,
>
> turn back to see again your shores.
> Do not commit yourselves to the open sea,
> for, if you lost me, you would perhaps remain astray
> (Par. II, 1–6)

Attempting to follow *Paradiso* will, for most readers, cause more harm than good: failing to understand or to accept the truths of theory, many will come to question the truths of right practice and will thus go "astray." *Paradiso* may be safely studied only by an "other few," an intellectual elite:

> You other few who lifted up your neck
> at times for the bread of angels,
> on which one here subsists but never becomes sated,
>
> You may indeed commit your vessel
> to the deep brine, holding to my furrow
> ahead of the water that turns smooth again.
> (Par. II, 10–15)

(We should note that "the bread of angels" is an expression that Dante uses in the *Convivio* to name "philosophy".) Since Dante knows that most readers cannot follow *Paradiso* to the end without danger of losing their way, does this mean that the *Comedy*, aspiring to be a matter of import for all humans, is bound to be a failure? It would only be a failure if, to derive their ultimate benefit from the poem, all readers necessarily must follow him to the end. It would only be a failure if *Paradiso* were conceived as the treasure-house of absolutely vital truths that all humans simply must come to know. But this would be an intolerable contradiction: Dante saying, on the one hand, that for our good all of us simply must come to know the truths revealed in *Paradiso*; and Dante saying, on the other hand, that the multitude can never grasp those truths and would be better off not trying. In fact *Paradiso* does not offer truths that all humans must know. If Dante can urge the greater part of his audience to ignore *Paradiso*, this is because the greater part of humanity can blissfully ignore theory: we do not need theory (a vision of the way things—beings not made or done by man— really are) to ground our right practice. The multitude of readers will derive their ultimate benefit from the poem's middle—*Purgatory*'s ideal of fashioning the Earthly Paradise through right practice grounded in the principle of the common good.

In his *Decisive Treatise on the Harmony of Religion and Philosophy*, Averroes maintains that religion has two facets, theory and practice: "We say: the purpose of the Law is to teach true science and right practice."[134] But if a religious law teaches both "true science" (theory) and right practice, it does not do so for all people. For the "true science" taught by, for instance, the Qur'an, is nothing other than Aristotelian theoretical philosophy, and it is meant to be understood only by a small intellectual elite—the philosophers. The multitude of Muslims do not need the Qur'an's "true science," and it is best for the intellectual elite to keep quiet about it, to discourage average humans from attempting to grapple with it, and instead to encourage them to concentrate their efforts on following—as the philosophers themselves are no less obliged to do—Islamic teachings in the domain of right practice. (For a more detailed treatment of Averroes's distinction between an audience comprised of the "multitude" and a much smaller audience comprised of the "elite," see below, part II.) Recall that, as mentioned above, Averroes says that *all* humans have the practical rational faculty while only a few have the "divine" speculative (theoretical) faculty. Dante's distinction between the audience who ought to read *Inferno* and *Purgatory*—all of us— and the much smaller audience of intellectuals whom he encourages to read *Paradiso* is consonant with Averroes's view of the two facets of prophetic discourse: the *Comedy*'s first two canticles primarily treat "right practice" (which concerns all humans) while its third canticle primarily treats "true science" or "theory" (which concerns only an intellectual elite).[135]

Thus *Paradiso* is a "surplus": it is not essential reading for all humans but optional reading for a few. It is surplus because it treats objects of "science"—things that we need not know or see in order to ground our "ethics." If Christianity excels non-Christian religious laws in the highest reaches of "theory" by disclosing a vision of God as He really is (as, that is, the Trinity and the Incarnation), this "divine science" may be a most excellent source of bliss for a happy few, but it is by no means a prerequisite for humankind's right practice in the perfect global state. Universal peace does not demand that we all know that God is a Trinity and an Incarnation.

It is not a coincidence that the three main categories of "beings whose existence and constitution owe nothing at all to human artifice" that Dante comes to behold in Paradise—the planets and stars; the immaterial intelligences or angels; and God—are precisely the three highest ranking categories of theoretical objects enumerated by al-Farabi in *The Perfect State*. For *Paradiso* is not so much where faith (theology) surpasses reason (philosophy), but where Dante treats, through a combination of philosophy and theology, objects of theory rather than principles of right practice. Beatrice guides in the realm of theory (*Paradiso*), whether the objects of theory happen to be disclosed in philosophy (as is the moon in *Paradiso* II, a passage based on Aristotelian science) or in theology (as is the hierarchy of angelic intelligences in *Paradiso* XXVIII, a passage based on the theologian Pseudo-Dionysius the Areopagite's *De caelesti hierarchia*). Virgil guides in the realm of "practice" (*Purgatory*), whether its principles happen to be known philosophically or imagined theologically. The *Comedy* is not arranged to show that Virgil has an inadequate vision of theoretical objects; it is arranged, rather, to show that for him such objects are not matters of prime concern.

Leah, Rachel, Matelda, Beatrice

Is our revised understanding of the *Comedy*'s basic allegory ("Virgil" = practice; "Beatrice" = theory) grounded in the text? Indeed there is ample evidence to support this reading, both in passages that are somewhat subtle and others that are absolutely explicit. Let us turn first to an instance of the somewhat subtle.

There is an odd passage in *Purgatory*—a tangential digression resembling, in the seemingly irrelevant excess of its hyper-scientific discourse, Beatrice's treatment of the dark spots of the moon in *Paradiso* II. I am referring to Statius's disquisition, in *Purgatory* XXV, on human sexual reproduction and the manner in which the nascent human animal comes to possess an immortal soul having the faculties of intellect and will. Statius explains in great detail the production of sperm in the male, the insemination of the female, the formation of the embryo, its development into a fetus and an organism possessing first an animal soul, then, with God's act of "in-spiriting" more-than-animal powers into the body of each human animal, a human soul. What is all this doing here? Statius could easily have answered Dante's question—why do the shades in Purgatory appear to have corporeal qualities?—by skipping all this preliminary and extraneous material.

An explanation lies in the fact that the matter treated in Statius' digression is one of the categories of "theory" enumerated by al-Farabi in *The Perfect State*: "The generation of man and how the faculties of the soul come to be and how the Active Intellect sheds light on them so that the first intelligibles and will and 'choice' can arise."[136] The "generation of man" (human sexual reproduction), "how the faculties of soul come to be," and how the soul becomes *human* (capable of intellecting and willing) are *precisely* the topics of Statius' digression. These matters are "theoretical" because, although they certainly involve human beings, they are not the outcome of human artifice but rather are fully determined by nature and/or God: the facts of human physiology and psychology (in the medieval sense, "science of the soul") are not man-made, not within our control; and although they involves processes of development and change, the overall process is itself ahistorical, always and everywhere the same. These topics are matters of science not ethics.

From our perspective, what matters most about Statius's presentation of the theoretical science of human generation and psychology is not the theory itself, nor that such a theory finds a place in the *Comedy* (which, assuming that al-Farabi's *Perfect State* does provide a sort of schematic blueprint for the matters treated in Dante's poem, is just what we would expect), but rather the fact that this presentation is *out of its proper place*. Indeed Statius acknowledges that this sort of theoretical talk belongs in *Paradiso* rather than *Purgatory*, and he apologizes to Virgil for introducing theory into the *Comedy* prematurely:

> "If I explain to him [i.e., to Dante] the eternal view [*la veduta etterna*],"
> replied Statius, "where you [i.e., Virgil] are present,
> let my excuse be that I cannot deny you."
>
> (*Purg.* XXV, 31–33)

Statius makes it clear that he is about to violate the poem's protocol by using the discourse of Beatrice in the presence of Virgil, by offering something—namely, *la veduta etterna* ("the eternal view")—that is outside Virgil's proper field of concern. This kind of discourse, involving a *view* [*theoria*], the vision of eternal, ahistorical realities, of things not subject to human control, rightly belongs in *Paradiso*. But what kind of discourse is it? It is neither faith nor theology, but Aristotelian natural science and psychology. Statius's speech is out of place, not so much because it may be said to contain some elements of a *Christian* theory of the soul, but rather because its object is *theoretical*.[137] Statius's violation of the poem's protocol is *not* that he speaks in *Purgatory* with insight that can only be granted by the Christian religion (and which thus should appear only in *Paradiso*), but that he speaks there of matters that have no relevance to human practice: he offers science there where it is not wanted or needed. This violation of the poem's arrangement is the exception which proves the rule: the distinction between Virgil and Beatrice is not that between philosophy and faith (nor between non-Christian and Christian) but rather between practical and theoretical philosophy.

But there is much more explicit evidence that the poem's basic allegory is constructed on the distinction between theory and practice. In *Purgatory* XXVII, Dante literally dreams this distinction, as he sees in a dream the two sisters from Genesis, Leah and Rachel:

> I seemed to see in a dream a lady young and beautiful
> going through a meadow *gathering flowers*
> and, *singing*, she was saying,
>
> "Whoso asks my name, let him know that I am Leah,
> and I go moving my fair hands around
> to make myself a garland.
>
> To please me at the glass I adorn me here,
> but my sister Rachel never leaves
> her mirror and sits all day.
>
> She is fain to behold [*veder*] her fair eyes,
> as I am to deck me with my hands:
> *she with seeing* [*lo vedere*], *I with doing* [*l'ovrare*] am satisfied."
> (*Purg.* XXVII, 97–108)

In the medieval exegetical tradition, Leah was taken to signify the active life (*praxis*) while Rachel was taken to signify the contemplative life (*theoria*). In Dante's dream, Rachel "speculates" (gazes into a mirror, a *speculum*) as Leah works: Rachel is associated with disengaged "vision" (*lo vedere*), Leah with the "making" or "doing" which is "working" (*l'ovrare*).

Now, if Dante dreams the practice/theory distinction in the figures of Leah and Rachel, this fact alone tells us nothing about the distinction between Purgatory (Virgil) and Paradise (Beatrice). But this dream, like the two others that Dante dreams in *Purgatory*, operates in part by foreshadowing events that will occur and characters that will appear later in the poem. Shortly after dreaming of Leah and Rachel (of practice and theory), Dante begins to explore the place to which Virgil has guided him, the summit of Mt. Purgatory, the Earthly Paradise, the garden of Eden. In a wood near a stream Dante sees a fair lady (named Matelda, as we will later learn) *singing* and *gathering flowers*:

> And there appeared to me there, as appears
> of a sudden a thing that for wonder
> drives away every other thought,

A lady all alone, who went
singing and *culling flower from flower*,
with which all her path was painted.
                    (*Purg.* XXVIII, 37–42)

The striking verbal similarity of the verses that describe the activity of Leah
and Matelda (the former is *cogliendo fiori e cantando* [XXVII, 99], "gathering
flowers and singing"; the latter is *cantando e scegliendo fior da fiore* [XXVIII,
41], "singing and culling flower from flower") tells us without question
that Dante's dreaming of Leah was a premonition of his encountering
Matelda in the Earthly Paradise. And, since Leah signifies doing rather than
seeing, craftsmanship rather than speculation, practice rather than theory, it
is clear that Matelda too embodies, at the summit of Purgatory, the principle of *praxis*.

Matelda herself provides some further evidence that she functions as an
allegorical personification of practice. For she tells Dante and Virgil that
they will come to understand her identity by considering some verses from
Psalm 92:

"You are newcomers," she began,
"and perhaps, why I am smiling in this place
chosen for nest of the human race

some doubt holds you wondering;
but the psalm *Delectasti* gives light
that may dispel the cloud from your minds."
                    (*Purg.* XXVIII, 76–81)

As Singleton insists, the particular verses to which Matelda refers are these:

Because Thou didst delight me, Lord, in Thy work [*factura*];
And in the works [*operibus*] of Thy hands I will rejoice.
How praiseworthy are Thy works [*opera*], O Lord.[138]

Matelda's glossing her own significance as "works" (*opera*) recalls Leah's
glossing herself as "working"/"doing" (*ovrare*).

The Earthly Paradise (garden of Eden), the "ultimate goal" of the purgatorial journey, is home to a fair lady who personifies "working." This is
not the "working" of mere labor (labor is, in fact, the penalty suffered with
exile from Eden) but the "working" that is "working on" some object.
This is craft, artisanship—an activity that produces, shapes, or otherwise has
some effect upon its object. Matelda signifies this *praxis* and its distinction
from a "seeing"/"knowing" (*theoria*) that does not itself produce, shape, or
have some effect upon its object. Virgil, whose means to guide humans to

the Earthly Paradise is personified in Matelda, masters the sort of knowledge that enables humans to "work on" themselves, to produce and shape the ideal human society. This knowledge is "practical philosophy"—above all ethics and politics.

If the Leah of Dante's dream foreshadows and signifies Matelda, the Rachel of Dante's dream foreshadows and signifies Beatrice. By analogy, Leah is to Rachel as Matelda is to Beatrice. If Leah and Matelda are *praxis* and Rachel is *theoria*, then Beatrice is *theoria*. This identification of Beatrice and Rachel is affirmed in *Paradiso*, as St. Bernard, pointing out to Dante the seating arrangement of the blessed in God's celestial court, emphasizes the affinity between Rachel and Beatrice ("in the order which the third seats make, sits *Rachel with Beatrice*, as you see"; *Par.* XXXII, 7–9). And in *Inferno* II Beatrice tells Virgil that, in Paradise, she "sat with ancient Rachel" (102). If the province of Virgil's mastery is the practical philosophy of ethics and politics, the province of Beatrice's mastery is the theoretical philosophy of physics and metaphysics.

The Primacy of Practice

From the perspective of medieval philosophy in the Arabo-Aristotelian tradition, *theoria* is immortal salvation and vice versa. The "afterlife" is nothing other than the act of theoretical speculation. One achieves immortality, hence "saving" the rational soul, when one achieves the theoretical vision of reality. As one modern scholar says: "Medieval philosophers regarded the study of God's created world a theoretical activity whose reward was the immortality of the rational soul, or the intellect."[139] Thus, reading the *Comedy* from a philosophical rather than theological perspective does not mean that we must deny what it is so very obvious—that Beatrice "saves" Dante. Yet, at the same time, to acknowledge that Beatrice is for Dante the way to immortality does not require us to say, as Freccero and his followers say, that Dante ultimately renounces philosophy as inadequate. For salvation simply *is* philosophy's theoretical vision.

But this point—that Dante remains an adherent of the school of those who equate the eternal afterlife with theoretical vision—loses some of its importance when we remember that such things as immortality, salvation, and the afterlife are not among Dante's highest priorities. Or, to put this in philosophical rather than theological language, Dante is less interested in physics and metaphysics (theory) than he is in ethics and politics (practice).

But how do we know that for Dante the field of concerns represented in *Purgatory* rivals or even outranks that represented in *Paradiso*? Why do we feel confident in claiming that Dante thinks it more urgent for us to attain to Virgil's happiness than Beatrice's? On what grounds do we elevate practice over theory, statecraft over speculation, ethics over metaphysics?

We can take a strong hint from Book II of the *Convivio*, where, in ordering all the sciences by rank through an analogy with the ordered rank of the spheres of the Cosmos, Dante places ethics in the position corresponding to the *Primum Mobile*—the highest of all ranks:

> And likewise, if moral philosophy [i.e., ethics] ceased to be, the other sciences would for a while be eclipsed, there would be no survival of felicity, nor would life hold any happiness, and these sciences would have been formulated and discovered of old in vain. Whence it is very clear that this heaven [i.e., the *Primum Mobile*] is connected with moral philosophy.[140]

In the *Convivio*, Dante ranks ethics higher than metaphysics. As Gilson remarks, this is a tremendous departure from the usual Aristotelian position on this issue, as represented above all by Aquinas:

> The thesis which Dante here maintains is quite extraordinary for the Middle Ages. Taken literally, it amounts to the maintenance of the primacy of ethics over metaphysics, a doctrine which at any rate could not claim the authority of Aristotle and perhaps still less that of St. Thomas Aquinas. It is impossible to doubt that to these two philosophers the supreme, chief and architectonic science is metaphysics, a theoretical, purely speculative science, which knows only the ultimate cause of everything, that is to say what is best in the whole of nature, the cause of causes: God. St. Thomas is as steadfast on this point as is Dante in the inverse sense.[141]

Ranking Beatrice higher than Virgil (as does the "theological" school of Dante criticism) is in accord with the intention of St. Thomas Aquinas. It is *not*, however, in accord with Dante's intention.

We know this because Dante himself tells us so. In the *Epistle to Cangrande*, Dante tells us unequivocally that his poem is wholly determined by the primacy of practical over theoretical philosophy:

> The branch of philosophy which determines the procedure of the work as a whole [i.e., the *Comedy*] and in this part [i.e., *Paradiso*] is moral philosophy, or ethics, inasmuch as the whole and this part have been conceived for the sake of practical results, not for the sake of speculation. So even if some parts or passages are treated in the manner of speculative philosophy, this is not for the sake of theory, but for a practical purpose, following that principle which the Philosopher [i.e., Aristotle] advances in the second book of the *Metaphysics*, that "practical men sometimes speculate about things in their particular and temporal relations."[142]

The possibilities that we are raising—that Dante is more concerned with the *Comedy*'s central than with its final canticle; that *Purgatory* rivals or even outranks *Paradiso*; that theoretical cosmology is not an end in itself but rather is meant to serve practical ethics; that Dante might think it more important for us to attain Leah's happiness rather than Rachel's, Virgil's rather than Beatrice's—are all strongly supported by Dante's own clear insistence on the priority of *praxis* to *theoria*. For here he tells us that *Paradiso* is not meant as an authentic fulfillment of the human need for a speculative, theoretical vision—a vision of the way non-artificial things, such as God, really are—but rather that such a vision is offered as a strategic means of guiding and shaping human practice. At any rate, there can be no question but that Dante here describes himself, borrowing a phrase from Aristotle, as a "practical man." The *Comedy* presents Beatrice's "eternal view" *for the sake of* Virgil's temporal activity, religion *for the sake of* politics, God's heavenly empire *for the sake of* the terrestrial one. The *Comedy* does not aim to reveal "the truth" to us; it aims to alter and shape our action.[143]

A passage from near the beginning of *Monarchy* offers further evidence that the priority of practice to theory is a fundamental given in Dante's thinking, at the same time showing that Dante was thoroughly familiar with the understanding of the distinction between *theoria* and *praxis* that we have proposed as the foundation of the poem's basic philosophical allegory. The difference between objects of theory and objects of practice, says Dante (drawing upon an Aristotelian distinction that was introduced to the West through the Arabo-Islamic philosophical tradition—through al-Farabi, as we have seen, but also through Averroes), is that the former are "outside human control" and the latter "within our control":

> And since this present treatise in a kind of inquiry, we must at the outset investigate the principle whose truth provides a firm foundation for later propositions. For it must be noted that there are certain things (such as mathematics, the sciences and divinity) which are *outside human control, and about which we can only theorize, but which we cannot affect by our actions*; and then there are certain things which are *within our control*, where we can not only theorize but also act, and *in these action is not for the sake of theory, but theorizing is for the sake of taking action*, since in these the objective is to take action. Now since our present subject is political, indeed is the source and starting-point of just forms of government, and everything in the political sphere comes under human control, it is clear that the present subject is not directed primarily towards theoretical understanding but towards action.[144]

In *Monarchy*'s second chapter Dante says that, since his treatise is a kind of philosophical inquiry, there must from the outset be established a "principle whose truth provides a firm foundation for later propositions." A bit later he speaks of this "first principle" as "an agreed point of reference to which anything which had to be proved might be referred back, as to a self-evident truth."[145] In the latter passage he identifies this "firm foundation," this "first principle": it is "universal peace." Dante's view of philosophizing here is entirely pragmatic: the desired ethical-social situation (universal peace) is *its own foundation*. Right practice provides its own proof, without having to rely upon the support of theoretical knowledge, without needing an underpinning of right science concerning the way things really are. We do not decide upon our practical aim after having attained a theoretical vision; rather, we start with our notion of the right practical aims and then, to the extent that we do theorize, our theory functions to serve our practical purposes. Ethics need not be founded on knowledge, theory, science—not even knowledge of divinity is a prerequisite for moral philosophy. Virgil does not need Beatrice.

In the *Comedy*, Beatrice is assigned the task of teaching Dante some of those things that are, in Dante's words, "outside human control." Virgil is assigned the task of teaching Dante things that are, in Dante's words, "within our control." Both kinds of teaching are philosophy. Beatrice does not surpass, transcend, or overcome philosophy. Her teaching is one of the kinds of philosophy: specifically, science; more generally, theory. But Dante's fundamental impulse is to subordinate that kind of philosophy to the other kind of philosophy, to subordinate Beatrice to Virgil.

Ulysses and Cato: Science and Ethics

Paradiso appears to tell us that true science of God, real knowledge of the highest object of theory, cannot be given by reason but only by revelation—and in fact only by *Christian* revelation. But the *Comedy* as a whole is designed to tell us that such true science is superfluous to virtuous practice. This pragmatic view of ethics is perhaps best revealed by our considering the fates of two pagan heroes whom Dante surely means for us to compare—Ulysses and Cato.

In *Inferno* XXVI Dante invents a remarkable "sequel" to Homer's *Odyssey*. In the eighth pouch of the eighth circle of Hell (a place reserved for the punishment of fraudulent counselors), Dante encounters Ulysses, whose soul appears in the form of a tongue-shaped flame. Ulysses recounts to Dante what he did following those events narrated by Homer's poem. Having returned home to Ithaca after years of warfare and wandering and having been reunited with his family and his faithful wife Penelope, he soon became restless for more adventure:

> Neither fondness for my son, nor reverence
> for my aged father, nor the due love
> which would have made Penelope glad,

could conquer in me the longing
that I had to gain experience [*divenir. . .esperto*] of the world,
and of human vice [*li vizî*] and worth [*valore*].

                                        (*Inf.* XXVI, 94–99)

With his most loyal comrades, who were now "old and slow" (106), Ulysses sailed to the far reaches of the Western Mediterranean, to the limits of the known world, the pillars of Hercules at the Strait of Gibraltar. (According to medieval lore, this was the "point of no return" beyond which no ship could voyage with any hope of safe return.) Then, using his considerable rhetorical skill, Ulysses persuaded his elderly companions to dare pass beyond those limits, to venture far into the Atlantic Ocean and southward for the sake of discovering what is there in the uninhabited regions of the world:

> "O brothers," I said, "who through a hundred thousand
> dangers have reached the west,
> to this so brief vigil
>
> Of our senses that remains to us,
> choose not to deny experience [*l'esperïenza*],
> following the sun, of the world without people [*mondo sanza gente*].
>
> Consider your origin:
> you were not made to live as brutes,
> but to pursue virtue and knowledge [*virtute e canoscenza*]."
>
> With this little speech I made
> my companions so keen for the voyage
> that then I could hardly have turned them back.
>
>   (XXVI, 112–123)

Nearing the South Pole after having been at sea for some five months, Ulysses and his men were gladdened to perceive in the distance the outline of an extraordinarily high mountain (which, although Ulysses himself did not know it as such, is Mount Purgatory—the only land in the Southern Hemisphere, according to the geography of the *Comedy*). As they approached the mountain, however, their ship was engulfed in a whirlpool, and they drowned at sea.

Dante's Ulysses has fascinated a good number of critics, many of whom share the sense that he is not just another of the poem's "characters" but rather a figure of high importance to the overall significance of the *Comedy*.[146] Some have seen Ulysses (despite his being among the damned in Hell) as a positive hero, one whom Dante cannot help but admire and celebrate. Such readers cheer Ulysses' unquenchable thirst to know the unknown; he appears as one who, despite tremendous danger, dares, for the sake of knowledge [*canoscenza*], to move beyond the limits of conventional thinking set by established authorities (the limits that are represented here by the pillars of Hercules). Ulysses is thus a prototype of the modern empirical scientist, one whose science is founded on "experience" rather than "authority" (indeed the language of "experience," with connotations of "expertise" and "experimental," is a noticeable feature of Ulysses' narrative). Others, taking the episode somewhat more literally, celebrate Ulysses' for his sense of adventure; he appears as a prototype of the New World discoverer, a Christopher Columbus *avant la lettre*. Another camp of critics, regarding as a "romantic" error the notion that Dante might secretly admire the denizens of Hell, argues that we ought not to praise Ulysses but rather to blame him for his sin. But what exactly is that sin? Perhaps it is just what the topography of Hell tells us that it is: the use of fraudulent counsel (in which case his act of sin is the "little speech" by which he persuades his crew of old men to undertake a challenge for which they are by no means fit). Or perhaps he compounds the vice of deceitful rhetoric with other vices. He lacks, for instance, filial piety and familial devotion, in which case he is the antitype of Aeneas, who is presented in *Inferno*'s first canto precisely as one who does *not* desert his father, son, and wife (and whom Ulysses mentions by name in the verse that immediately precedes his admission that he could not be swayed to stay home by "fondness for my son, nor piety / for my aged father, nor the due love / which would have made Penelope glad"; XXVI, 94–96). Often Ulysses is seen as marred by immoderate *curiositas*: in his longing for encyclopedic knowledge he ignores what is truly important—human fellowship. Or perhaps Ulysses' greatest sin is his intellectual hubris: as a kind of Icarus (a link established by his characterizing his voyage as a "mad flight"), Ulysses fails to recognize that there are limits to human knowledge. Others see Ulysses neither as an unqualified hero or sinner but rather as a complex figure for Dante himself: the episode appears as Dante's way of registering trepidation concerning his own "mad flight," his own audacious project in undertaking the *Comedy*.[147]

For our purposes, what is most significant about the Ulysses episode is a function of its "extent": it reaches both back and forward in the poem, to two of the *Comedy*'s most important episodes—the opening scene of *Inferno* and, especially, the opening scene of *Purgatory*. At the very opening of the poem Dante has just escaped perishing in "dangerous waters" (*Inf.* I, 24), having somehow negotiated the "passage / that never left anyone alive" (I, 26–27), and he finds himself at the foot of a high mountain. Like Ulysses, Dante faces death at sea in sight of a high mountain; unlike Ulysses, Dante manages to survive.[148] But if the landscape (and seascape) of *Inferno* I, which is perhaps more symbolic than real, strongly resembles the

seascape (and landscape) where Ulysses perishes in a shipwreck, this relationship of symbolic resemblance becomes, when we compare the Ulysses
episode with *Purgatory*'s opening scene, one of not merely symbolic but
rather of actual geographical identity: Ulysses dies somewhere off the coast
of Mount Purgatory. This death of a pagan hero must be considered in
relation to the survival of another pagan hero, one whose task is to patrol
that very coast—Cato. Ulysses is the pagan who glimpsed Mount
Purgatory but perished before reaching its shores; Cato is the pagan who
did successfully negotiate the passage to Mount Purgatory, who not only
reached its shores but presides there as its guardian. Ulysses' vice, then, is
best revealed through its comparison with Cato's virtue.[149]

"Virtue" is indeed the operative word in the comparison of Ulysses' failure with Cato's success. When we recall that Cato is essentially synonymous
with "virtue" (ethics, morality) and that the work known as the *Distichs of
Cato* was said to teach the "cardinal virtues," we can begin to understand a
deep sense in which Ulysses' "little speech" to his elderly companions
amounts to "fraudulent counsel." What is fraudulent is his feigned interest
in ethics. Twice in this episode he insists that his intellectual quest has a
twofold aim: he says that he seeks expertise in both "nature" (physics) and
in "vice and virtue" (ethics). He tells Dante that his voyage was motivated
by his desire to "become expert" (*divenir. . .esperto*) in "the world" (i.e., the
natural world) "*and* in human vices and worth" (i.e, right and wrong). This
in essence repeats what he had told his comrades in his "little speech": that
the goal of their journey is "experience" (*l'esperïenza*) of the "world without
people" (i.e., the purely physical world, the world insofar as it may be considered an object of theory); that they are seeking "virtue *and* knowledge"
(*virtute e canoscenza*—i.e., both ethics and science).

We know that Ulysses is *feigning* concern for moral philosophy
because of the plain absurdity of the notion of ethics in a "world without
people." For "human vices and worth" do not pertain in the *mondo sanza
gente*, in places devoid of humanity. Ulysses is a physicist (a theorist, one
who seeks knowledge of the extra-human) who gives lip-service to the
importance of ethics. His pretense of interest in virtue cannot be taken
seriously, since virtue is located in human communities, in those groupings—
such as father, son, and wife—that Ulysses can so easily, and without
virtue, desert. If it is true that Ulysses keeps with him until the end a
community of comrades, it is clear that he does not care for the good of
this community but rather feigns solidarity, using the community as the
necessary instrument for the implementation of his own solitary will.
Ulysses is indeed the antitype of both Aeneas (*Inferno* I) and Cato
(*Purgatory* I), both of whom, as we have seen above, embody the priority
of the common good.

Or (and it is this possibility that will prove most helpful for us), we might consider that Ulysses' desire for wisdom concerning virtue is genuine, but he is mistaken about where to seek it. Ulysses subordinates ethics to physics, practice to theory, thinking thereby to find a firm physical or theoretical basis upon which to ground human practice. Ulysses is akin to those who—to use the terms that I have been developing here—would value Beatrice over Virgil, *Paradiso* over *Purgatory*, the theoretical vision of God over the practical establishment of the just human community on earth, individual salvation in the beyond over the common good in the here-and-now. Ulysses thinks that we need to get to a vantage point *outside* human practice, that we need to go to the "world without people," to find the sort of certain knowledge that can provide a sure foundation for morality. He thinks that we need to have theory (knowledge of non- or extra-human reality) before we can have right practice. He needs, to satisfy his sense that only where there is knowledge (*canoscenza*) can there be virtue, something *external* to human communities, something that can only be found somewhere else, "there," beyond the pillars of Hercules—we can call it "God" or "Science." Ulysses is one of those who think that humans can "become expert" (*divenir. . .esperto*) in right and wrong, that there can be "expertise" in ethics, that there ought to be "morality experts" to whom we can turn for guidance. His sin—and the cause of his "fall"—is his presumption that there can be theoretical knowledge in the sphere of virtue (*virtute e canoscenza*).

We have already considered Cato in some detail. But there is one more crucial facet to the figure of Cato. Dante was familiar with Cato above all through Lucan's historical epic *The Civil War* (*Pharsalia*), a poem that ranks among the most important of the *Comedy*'s classical sources. One of *The Civil War*'s most memorable episodes involves Cato and the question of Virtue. Cato and his comrades, having marched to the southern extremes of the Libyan desert, find themselves in the environs of Africa's only temple, site of one of Jupiter's—the highest deity's—oracular seats. Cato's men urge him to take advantage of this tremendous occasion to obtain a share in God's knowledge of things. One of Cato's officers, Labienus, begs him to seek divine insight, not only concerning their present predicament and future outcome, but also into the very essence of virtue and goodness:

> "Chance," said [Labienus], "and the hazard of our march have put in our way the word of this mighty god [i.e., Jupiter] and his divine wisdom. . . .I cannot believe that Heaven would reveal mysteries and proclaim truth to any man more than to the pure and holy Cato. . . .And now behold! power is given you to speak with Jupiter; ask then concerning the end of Caesar the

abhorred, and search into the future condition of our country: will the people be allowed to enjoy their laws and liberties, or has the civil war been fought in vain? Fill your breast with the god's utterance; a lover of austere virtue, *you should at least ask what Virtue is* and demand to see Goodness in her visible shape."[150]

Cato's reply is a remarkable manifesto of the self-sufficiency of humankind's ethical faculty: he refuses to consult the oracle, insisting instead that he already knows, without having to seek external confirmation, what he ought to do. Cato refuses to conceive of ethical truth as something located outside, remote from, or beyond human existence; he does not need to find metaphysical comfort for his practical choices; he does not look for external (extra-human) constraints to provide a moral foundation; in sum, he does not need to "ask the expert":

> Cato, inspired by the god whom he bore hidden in his heart, poured forth from his breast an answer worthy of the oracle itself: "What question do you bid me ask, Labienus? Whether I would rather fall in battle, a free man, than witness a tyranny? Whether violence can ever hurt the good, or Fortune threatens in vain when Virtue is her antagonist? Whether the noble purpose is enough, and virtue becomes no more virtuous by its success? I can answer these questions, and the oracle will never fix the truth deeper in my heart. . . .*The gods have no need to speak*; for the Creator told us once for all at our birth whatever we are permitted to know. Did he choose these barren sands, that a few might hear his voice? Did he bury truth in this desert? Has he any dwelling-place save earth and sea, the air of heaven and virtuous hearts? *Why seek we further for deities?* All that we see is God; every motion we make is God also. Men who doubt and are ever uncertain of future events—let them cry out for prophets: I draw my assurance from no oracle but from the sureness of death. The timid and the brave must fall alike; the god has said this, and it is enough." With these words he departed from the altar, preserving the credit of the temple, and left Ammon [i.e., Jupiter], untested by him [*non exploratum*], for the nations to worship.[151]

Precisely contrary to Ulysses, Cato is not driven by the urge to "explore." If he resembles Ulysses in making a southward journey to the far-flung margins of the world, he is not there as one in search of knowledge in the sphere of ethics. Cato insists that he always already bears ethical insight with him wherever he may be, and he quite easily resists the temptation to pretend that his ethical choices are legitimate because sanctioned by a "higher authority," by the oracle of God or Science. Cato is morally self-sufficient: he sees no need for a prophet, a divine voice, a revelation.

In placing Mount Purgatory under Cato's stewardship, Dante indicates that *Purgatory*, far from being a "Christian" canticle (except on a superficial or literal level), is instead meant to display the possibility of ethics without scientific knowledge, morality without (our having knowledge of) God, right practice without true theory. The difference between Ulysses and Cato is that the former seems to think, while the latter certainly does not, that we need theoretical knowledge (a vision of the "world without people"—e.g., physics, metaphysics, theology) as a foundation for virtuous human action. And Dante's "damning" Ulysses while "saving" Cato tells us that theoretical science is superfluous to practical ethical know-how.

Maimonides and the Fall into Ethics

Ulysses confuses what the *Comedy* tells us to hold distinct: ethics and science (*virtute e canoscenza*). This confusion—when the ethicist thinks that we ought to be able to express the "immutable laws" governing human moral practice with just the same certainty by which the physicist can express the immutable laws governing the theoretical objects of natural science—is regarded by the great twelfth-century Jewish philosopher Maimonides (1135–1204 AD) as the real meaning presented in Genesis's myth of the original sin of Adam and Eve. Maimonides, a native of al-Andalus, wrote his magnum opus *The Guide of the Perplexed* in Arabic. It is a work that aims to carry on—and to extend to the exegesis of the Hebrew scriptures—the Islamic tradition of Aristotelian philosophy epitomized by al-Farabi and by Maimonides's Andalusian contemporary, Averroes; and it is one of the primary conduits by which the essence of this tradition was eventually disseminated in Europe.[152] As Shlomo Pines says concerning Maimonides' allegiance to al-Farabi: "It is clear that Maimonides was persuaded that the approach and the methods and style of exposition and formulation adopted by al-Farabi in all matters impinging upon, or connected with, the sphere of organized religion constituted the most notable and authoritative of the responses made by philosophers to the challenge, the danger, and perhaps the opportunity presented by allegiance to a monotheistic religion. In other words, he felt that al-Farabi had shown what attitude a philosopher ought to take in these latter times."[153]

Before turning to Maimonides' rather astonishing exegesis of what Genesis terms "knowing good and evil" (Gen. 3.5), let us recall al-Farabi's remarks concerning the definition of "knowledge" in the strict sense. While recognizing that "knowledge" is an "equivocal" name, al-Farabi says that "knowledge" in the most worthy sense of the name must be theoretical (its object must not be a product of human doing or making) and must have for its object something that is unchanging:

> The name "knowledge" applies to many things. However, the knowledge that is a virtue of the theoretical part is for the soul to attain certainty about

the existence of the beings whose existence and constitution owe nothing at
all to human artifice.[154]

Knowledge in truth is what is accurate and certain for all time, not for
some particular time but not some other, nor existing at one moment and
possibly becoming nonexistent afterwards. . . .Therefore, the Ancients did
not set down as knowledge the perception of what can possibly change from
condition to condition, such as our knowing that this human being is sitting
now. For it is possible for him to change and come to be standing after he
was sitting. Rather, they set down as knowledge the certainty about the existence of a thing that cannot possibly change, such as three being an odd
number. For the oddness of three does not change. That is because three
does not become even at some point nor four odd. So if this [i.e., our knowing that this human being is sitting now] is called knowledge or certainty, it
is done so metaphorically.[155]

Notice that al-Farabi denies that "knowledge" in the strict sense pertains to
what one might call "the human condition." To the extent that humans
produce and perform their own existences, those existences cannot be the
proper objects of "knowledge."

In Genesis God, having created Adam and placed him as caretaker in the
Garden of Eden, tells him that he may partake of the fruit of every tree
other than *the tree of the knowledge of good and evil*: "You may freely eat of
every tree of the garden; but of the tree of the knowledge of good and evil
you shall not eat, for in the day that you eat of it you shall die" (Gen.
2.16–17). God then decides to provide for Adam "a helper and a partner,"
and so he takes one of Adam's ribs and makes it into a woman. In their
primeval dwelling, Adam and Eve go about unclothed: "And the man and
his wife were both naked and were not ashamed" (Gen. 2.25). Some time
later the serpent persuades Eve that God is deceiving her and Adam; he
persuades her that eating the fruit will bring not death but rather God-like
knowledge of good and evil (i.e., right and wrong, ethics) and that God is
in truth jealously hoarding such knowledge:

> But the serpent said to the woman, "You will not die; for God knows
> that when you eat of it your eyes will be opened, and you will be like
> God [*Elohim*], knowing good and evil." So when the woman saw that
> the tree was good for food, and that it was a delight to the eyes, and
> that the tree was to be desired to make one wise, she took of its fruit
> and ate; and she also gave some to her husband, who was with her, and
> he ate. Then the eyes of both were opened, and they knew that they
> were naked; and they sewed fig leaves together and made loincloths for
> themselves. (Gen. 3.4–7)

God punishes Adam and Eve, apparently for presuming to share his
privileged knowledge of good and evil (they now *know*, for instance, that

their nakedness is wrong), by expelling them from the Garden of Eden and condemning them to a variety of hardships.

In *The Guide of the Perplexed*, Maimonides brings to light the problematic weakness, if not (from his point of view) downright absurdity, of the usual understanding of the myth of the Tree of the Knowledge of Good and Evil. He attributes the critique of this myth to a certain learned "objector," and he answers this critique not by defending the ordinary understanding of the myth but rather by offering his own highly idiosyncratic interpretation. But before presenting the objector's critique and his response to it, Maimonides prefaces all this by glossing one of the Hebrew words that will be important for what follows—*Elohim*:

> Years ago a learned man propounded as a challenge to me a curious objection. It behooves us now to consider this objection and our reply invalidating it. However, before mentioning this objection and its invalidation, I shall make the following statement. Every Hebrew knew that the term *Elohim* is equivocal, designating the deity, the angels, and the rulers governing the cities. Onqelos the Proselyte, peace be on him, has made it clear, and his clarification is correct, that in the dictum of Scripture, *And ye shall be as Elohim, knowing good and evil*, the last sense is intended. For he has translated: *And ye shall be as rulers*.[156]

As Maimonides indicates here, *Elohim* has a plurality of meanings: it can mean "God" ("the Lord"); or, "angels"; or, "human rulers" ("lords"). To understand the serpent's claim—"you will be like *Elohim*, knowing good and evil"—we must first decide which sense of the word *Elohim* is correct in this context. For Maimonides the only possible correct sense of *Elohim* in Gen. 3.5 is "human rulers." We must forget what we have always been taught, that the serpent tells Eve, "You will be like God [*Elohim*], knowing good and evil"; in fact he tells her, "You will be like the rulers governing the cities, knowing good and evil." Maimonides cannot allow this *Elohim* to mean "God" because, as we shall see presently, there can be no *knowledge* (in the strict sense) in the sphere of ethics. We cannot speak of God's *knowing* right and wrong; nor can we speak of the human discernment of right and wrong as *knowing* except—as al-Farabi says—metaphorically. God's knowledge, which is knowledge in the strict sense (its objects are theoretical and eternal), cannot have for its objects good and evil, right and wrong (ethics), since these latter, being products of human artifice and marked by historicity, cannot possibly be the objects of knowledge in the strict sense. If good and evil are ever "known," they are only "known" in a metaphorical way, not in the manner of God's certain knowledge.

Maimonides then presents the objector's critique of the myth of the Fall. The gist of the objection is that the story represents humans as originally *unknowing* and then, following upon their act of disobedience, *knowing*. Humans appear to have "fallen" from ignorance into knowledge—a strange notion of a "fall," since it is clearly instead an "ascent." God must have a perverse sense of justice if he punishes the disobedient by rewarding them, making them better than they were before:

> This is what the objector said: It is manifest from the clear sense of the bib-lical text that the primary purpose with regard to man was that he should be, as the other animals are, devoid of intellect, of thought, and of the capacity to distinguish between good and evil. However, when he disobeyed, his dis-obedience procured him as its necessary consequence the great perfection peculiar to man, namely, his being endowed with the capacity that exists in us to make this distinction. . . .Now it is a thing to be wondered at that man's punishment for his disobedience should consist in his being granted a perfection that he did not possess before, namely, the intellect. This is like the story told by somebody that a certain man from among the people dis-obeyed and committed great crimes, and in consequence was made to undergo a metamorphosis, becoming a star in heaven.[157]

The objector takes the myth to mean that humans were only first endowed with "intellect" after the Fall; moreover, he regards ethical discernment as the highest perfection of the human intellect. Maimonides will deny both of these claims.

In reply, Maimonides insists that Adam was, before the Fall, fully endowed with a perfect human intellect, that his faculty of *knowledge* (in the strict sense) was at its ultimate perfection prior to his tasting the forbidden fruit of the Tree of Knowledge of Good and Evil. Maimonides asserts, con-trary to the objector, that Adam was *more* knowledgeable, *more* "intellec-tual," before the Fall than after, so that the outcome of the Fall was indeed a decrease rather than an increase in human knowledge:

> For the intellect that God made overflow unto man and that is the latter's ultimate perfection, was that which Adam had been provided with before he disobeyed. It was because of this that it was said of him that he was created *in the image of God and in His likeness.*[158]

From the moment of his creation until the Fall, Adam possesses a God-like intellect, a capacity for theoretical knowledge.

Before the Fall, there was no such thing as ethics. Within the limitations imposed by his being human not divine, Adam possessed perfect theoreti-cal knowledge, and he was thus able to proclaim with certainty the truth or falsity of propositions concerning objects of theory (e.g., he knew that it is true that the earth is spherical not flat). Adam knew the true and the false, but he had no knowledge—for there can be no such knowledge—of the right and the wrong:

> Through the intellect one distinguishes between truth and falsehood, and that was found in Adam in its perfection and integrity. Fine and bad [i.e., right and wrong; good and evil], on the other hand, belong to the things generally accepted as known [endoxa], not to those cognized by the intellect For one does not say: it is fine [i.e., right, good] that heaven is spherical, and it is bad [i.e., wrong, evil] that the earth is flat; rather, one says true and false with regard to these assertions.[159]

Before the Fall, Adam was pure intellectual cognition. He was fully occupied with *theoria*. All objects of his thinking were such that can be known with certainty (i.e., were theoretical and eternal). He did not consider "things generally accepted as known"—things that, since they can possibly differ according to circumstance, time, and place, are historically relative and hence cannot be "known" in the strict sense. In an utterly anti-Platonic manner, Maimonides teaches the radical and absolute separation of the true and the good:

> Now man in virtue of his intellect knows *truth* from *falsehood*; and this holds good for all intelligible things. Accordingly when man was in his most perfect and excellent state [i.e, Adam before the Fall], in accordance with his inborn disposition and possessed of his intellectual cognitions—because of which it is said of him: *Thou hast made him but little lower than Elohim* [i.e., God]—he had no faculty that was engaged in any way in the consideration of generally accepted things [endoxa], and he did not apprehend them. So among these generally accepted things even that which is most manifestly bad, namely, uncovering the genitals, was not bad according to him, and he did not apprehend that it was bad.[160]

Theoretical knowledge has nothing to do with passing ethical judgments, since the good and the evil can never be *known* in the strict sense. God does not know that humans' uncovering their genitals is bad. Before the Fall, Adam knew, for instance, that heaven and earth are spherical. But he did not know that nakedness is wrong, because the wrongness of nakedness is not eternal and extra-human but rather a historical product of human artifice (the first act of human *praxis*—sewing loincloths from fig leaves—is virtually coeval with the first ethical judgment). The wrongness of nakedness is not absolute but rather "generally accepted." It is a matter for the faculty that considers *endoxa*, not theoretical truth.

Endoxa are conventional beliefs or norms that are a matter of community consensus. In the words of a modern scholar: "The *endoxa* are the remarkable opinions of a community, that is to say those propositions that are in the common opinion (i.e. in the *doxa*), and thus are generally accepted, reliable and credited within a community. Aristotle in his *Topics* defines the *endoxa* as those opinions which are shared by everyone, or by most people, or by the experts of a given community, and, if this is the case, by all of them, or by most of them or by the most famous and highly regarded (*Topics* I 100b)."[161] Matters of convention grounded in community consensus cannot be the object of knowledge, since they will vary in different communities. Recall Dante's remarks, cited above, in which he says that nakedness is wrong for the Scythians but is not wrong for the Garamantes; right and wrong on this issue is a matter for *endoxa* and can vary from community to community. Abstracted from reference to a certain community, in some "world without people" such as that imagined by Ulysses, one cannot *know* that nakedness is wrong, since nakedness is wrong only sometimes and for some peoples. Similarly, we cannot *know* that suicide is wrong, since, as Seneca says, "that same death which in Cato is a glorious thing immediately becomes shameful and dishonorable in Brutus."[162] If Dante condemns "the suicides" to the seventh circle of Hell, he does not put *all* of them there: for while suicide may be wrong for a Christian, it is not for a Roman Stoic such as Cato. Ulysses' demise is bound up with his unwillingness to embrace the historical relativity of ethics, a relativity exemplified above all by Cato's suicide.

For Maimonides, Adam's punishment for his disobedience was his loss of exclusively theoretical knowledge:

> However, when he disobeyed and inclined toward his desires of the imagination and the pleasures of his corporeal senses. . .he was punished by being deprived of that intellectual apprehension [i.e, *theoria*, knowledge]. He therefore disobeyed the commandment that was imposed upon him on account of his intellect and, becoming endowed with the faculty of apprehending generally accepted things [*endoxa*], he became absorbed in judging things to be bad or fine [i.e., evil or good; wrong or right]. Then he knew how great his loss was, what he had been deprived of, and upon what a state he had entered.[163]

The Fall, for Maimonides, is a descent from knowledge into ethics, from *theoria* into *praxis*, from science (physics, metaphysics) into morality. As Marvin Fox says, Adam's "first loss then is clearly abandonment of the pure life of the intellect and absorption in conventions, modes of behavior that are generally accepted. It is the shift from a life of metaphysical speculation to a life of concern with the ethical. The realm of ethics is not a realm of true knowledge. It is not concerned with truth and falsehood, but only with generally held opinions."[164]

The Guide of the Perplexed is a notoriously complicated text.[165] Fortunately for us, our aim here is not to understand why Maimonides characterizes the beginnings of ethical discourse as a "decline" or "fall"—why he aims, as Fox remarks, "to show that acquiring a concern with the realm of moral judgment is not an advancement for man but a mark of tragic deterioration."[166] Rather our aim is limited to considering, in relation to the *Comedy*, a few facets of Maimonides' denial of the possibility of "knowing good and evil."

First, we should recognize that Maimonides' exegesis of the Fall amounts to a fairly radical avowal of the contingency of all human moral systems, codes, and laws—or, at the very least, an insistence that ethics cannot be grounded in reason. As Fox says:

> Maimonides holds that reason itself provides no grounds for ethical principles. Reason tells us nothing about good and bad. . .; moral rules are at best principles generally held to be correct. They are the conventions of individual societies which in the course of social history turn into fixed laws. Such laws are, in Maimonides view, nothing more than well-established and officially authorized conventions. There is about them an element of the arbitrary, an element of individual taste that never approaches the certainty of rational principles.[167]

The ground for ethical judgment is not extra-human reason but rather the moral community itself: the morality of a community is self-grounding. Morality does not depend upon God or science, upon a knowledge sought-after in and retrieved from the "world without people."

Inferno and *Purgatory* (the two canticles which Dante recommends to most readers, whom he advises to ignore *Paradiso*, which is suitable only for an intellectual elite) recount a moral progress for which "knowing God" is irrelevant. Dante's ethical perfection is accomplished by his following the guidance of those who do not know God (Cato, Virgil, Aristotle). *Virtue is not a matter of knowledge of the divine.* It is thus that Virgil, when Dante first encounters him in *Inferno* I, can speak of "the *good* Augustus" who lived "in the time of the *false* and lying gods" (*Inf.* I, 71–72). Like Maimonides, Virgil (in his very first speech in the *Comedy*) distinguishes between the human capacity for *good and evil* and the human capacity to know *the false and the true*. Augustus could not tell the true from the false, and thus he was led by an erroneous religion to hold incorrect views concerning divine reality. Yet (as the exemplary Emperor whose reign Dante aims to restore) he was nonetheless perfectly wise in matters of right and wrong. Augustus' imperfect knowledge of reality, grounded in his theoretically imperfect religion, has no bearing on the perfection of his practical wisdom.

Maimonides, as an Aristotelian, aims to help us overcome the old Platonic error according to which, since virtue is knowable (in the strict sense), our obligation as ethical subjects is to gain knowledge. As Fox explains:

> For Plato. . .good and evil are knowable in the same way as we know any other truths. The school of Aristotle, on the other hand, taught that there is a distinction between the theoretical and the practical sciences. The former derive from first principles that are known intuitively to be true, and they yield conclusions whose certainty is demonstrated. The latter are established, as Aristotle puts it, by *nomos* not *physis*—that is, they are derived from convention or humanly instituted law, rather than from principles of reason or the fixed order of nature. . . .Maimonides allies himself with the Aristotelian camp, but takes an even stronger stand on the fundamental issues than most Aristotelians. He denies categorically that we can know moral distinctions by way of the intellect. The reason is that the intellect is concerned only with truth and falsehood.[168]

Dante's Ulysses is a Platonist, foundering on the mistaken notion that there can be a science of ethics, that we can pursue, as one and the same project, *virtute e canoscenza*. On the level of its philosophical allegory, the *Comedy* is, as a whole, Aristotelian in the strong manner of Maimonides: it "denies categorically that we can know moral distinctions [*praxis*] by way of the intellect [*theoria*]." That is why Beatrice only enters the scene after Dante has come to enjoy the full perfection of Virgil's happiness.

On the level of the poem's religious allegory (aimed at the mass of ordinary readers), Virgil is "reason" pure and simple and Beatrice is "faith." But on the level of its philosophical allegory, the distinction is not between reason and something other than reason but rather between two modes of reason: Virgil is practical, Beatrice theoretical reason. The former does not depend for its perfection upon the latter. As Aristotle formulates it in *Nichomachean Ethics*, practical wisdom is a kind of reason that is not knowledge:

> Thus in general the man who is capable of deliberating has practical wisdom. Now no one deliberates about things that cannot be otherwise nor about things that it is impossible for him to do. Therefore, since knowledge involves demonstration, but there is no demonstration of things whose first principles can be otherwise (for all such things might actually be otherwise), and since it is impossible to deliberate about things that are of necessity, *practical wisdom cannot be knowledge*. . ., because that which is done is capable of being otherwise. . . .[Practical wisdom] is a true and reasoned state of capacity to act with regard to the things that are good or bad for man.[169]

And, near the beginning of the *Nichomachean Ethics*, Aristotle informs us that "we learn this part of philosophy [i.e., ethics] not with the purpose of gaining knowledge but of becoming better."[170] Dante follows Virgil (ethics/politics[171]) with the purpose of becoming better. Having accomplished this aim, he then journeys with Beatrice (physics and metaphysics) for the purpose of gaining knowledge. But the knowledge that Beatrice passes along to him does not make him better. Truth, whether Christian (the truth of the Trinity and the Incarnation—*Paradiso* XXXIII) or otherwise (the truth of the moon's dark spots—*Paradiso* II), has no bearing upon virtue. A Christian Virgil would in no way surpass the pagan Virgil in "the capacity to act with regard to the things that are good or bad for man."

For Maimonides, Genesis 3.5 ought to be read as meaning, "You will be like human rulers [*Elohim*], knowing good and evil." But there can be no such thing as "knowing good and evil." Why, then, would scripture speak of political leaders as "knowing good and evil"? Since God surely knows that there can be no knowing good and evil, the phrase "knowing good and evil" can only be the product of human error: it can only be humans who erroneously believe in such knowledge. The Fall is the moment after which humans delude themselves into thinking that there can be knowledge of ethics. The Fall is the point after which humans tend to believe that they must know true and false in order to discern right and wrong. The *Comedy* as a whole is meant to help us overcome that error. We do not need to see God as he truly is (the Trinity and the Incarnation) to make the perfect human society; we do not need Beatrice; we do not need Christian truth. The "rulers governing the cities," the lords (*Elohim*) of the earth, do not need to be guided, in determining good and evil, by true and certain knowledge concerning the Lord.

Adam and Solomon

In *Paradiso* X, in the sphere of the Sun, twelve flashing lights dance in a circle around Dante and Beatrice; at one point they pause as one of the lights—the soul of Thomas Aquinas—introduces himself and all the rest. They are all intellectuals or "wise men" of one sort or another: primarily philosophers and theologians, (Aquinas, Albertus Magnus, Peter Lombard, Dionysius the Areopagite, Boethius, Richard of St. Victor, Siger of Brabant), but also a jurist (Gratian), historians (Orosius, Bede), an encyclopedist (Isidore of Seville), and, in one case, a "ruler" (Solomon).

Of these twelve intellectuals, one—Solomon—stands out as different from the others. He is the only one who was not a Christian. His life predated the birth of Christ by nearly a millennium, while the eleven others all lived in the Christian era, most several centuries if not more than a millennium after Christ.

The singling out of Solomon (whose name is derived from shalom, "peace"—Dante's most fundamental concern) for special consideration is not something that we have undertaken arbitrarily. Rather, this singling out is first performed by Dante's Aquinas in *Paradiso* X. For there Aquinas tells Dante that Solomon in effect outshines all the others, that, although he is fifth in order of introduction, for his wisdom Solomon ranks first among the twelve:

> The fifth light [i.e., Solomon], which is the most beautiful among us,
> breathes with such love that all the world
> there below thirsts to know [*saper*] tidings of it.
>
> Within it is the lofty mind to which was given
> wisdom [*saver*] so deep that, if the truth be true [*se 'l vero è vero*],
> there never rose a second of such full vision [*veder*].
>
> (*Par.* X, 109–114)

Aquinas appears to assert that Solomon is the greatest of all intellectuals in human history, that this non-Christian attained a plentitude of wisdom that has never before or since been matched. And this wisdom appears to be a matter of *vision* ["there never rose a second of such full *vision*"], a matter of *theoria*—an impression reinforced by the noticeable vocabulary of "truth" (*vero*) and "knowledge" (*saper, saver*) in the surrounding verses. It seems that Aquinas is ranking Solomon as the greatest theorist of all time.

Dante, for good reason, struggles to accept this. For the next few cantos he remains perplexed by the notion that Solomon was the unsurpassed master of theoretical wisdom. Aquinas, who, like the rest of the blessed in Paradise, enjoys the ability to perceive Dante's unvoiced thoughts, offers to resolve Dante's doubt:

> You are perplexed, and you wish my words
> made clearer, in plain and explicit language
> leveled to your understanding. . .
>
> . . .where I said, 'there never rose a second';
> And here is need that one distinguish well.
> (*Par.* XI, 22–24; 26–27)

Two cantos later, after resolving some other of Dante's doubts, Aquinas distinguishes between two kinds of wisdom—a distinction without which Dante had been unable to understand Aquinas's celebration of Solomon. For Dante had thought that Aquinas ranked Solomon as the unsurpassed master of theoretical wisdom, when in fact he ranked him as the unsurpassed master of practical wisdom.

Before clarifying this distinction, Aquinas first reiterates the gist of Dante's perplexity. Dante believes, says Aquinas, that only two—Adam and Christ—have ever been fully "enlightened," and thus it cannot be the case that none have ever matched Solomon in wisdom:

> You believe that into the breast from which the rib
> was drawn to form her beautiful cheek
> whose palate costs dear all the world [i.e., into Adam],
>
> and into that which, pierced by the lance,
> both before and after made such satisfaction,
> that it turns the scale against all fault [i.e., into Christ],
>
> whatever of light it is allowed human nature
> to have was all infused by that Power
> which made the one and the other;
>
> and therefore you wonder at what I said above,
> when I declared that the excellence which is enclosed
> in the fifth light [i.e., Solomon] never had a second.
>
> (Par. XIII, 37–48)

Aquinas verifies that Dante's premise—no human intellects have ever matched those of Adam and Christ—is correct. He gives a somewhat lengthy scientific account of the manner in which the Divine Intellect, emanating down through the nine spheres of the cosmos, comes to be "stamped" on the "wax" which is the physical materiality of mortal creatures. The product of this process is always to some degree "defective," owing to the variations in the configurations of the heavens and to imperfections in nature's craftsmanship and in the material itself. But twice in history this process worked perfectly—in the creation of Adam and in the Immaculate Conception. Adam and Christ, alone among humans (for Aquinas is considering Christ in his aspect as a fully human being), have possessed perfect human intellects, enjoying the "clear vision" which is theoretical perfection:

> If the wax were exactly worked,
> and the heavens were at the height of their power,
> the light of the whole seal would be apparent.
>
> But nature always gives it defectively,
> working like the artist who in the
> practice of his art has a hand that trembles.
>
> Yet, if the fervent Love disposes and imprints
> the clear vision [chiara vista] of the primal Power,
> complete perfection [perfezion] is there acquired.
>
> Thus was the dust once made fit
> for the full perfection of a living creature [i.e., Adam];
> thus was the Virgin made to be with child [i.e., Christ];

so that I approve your opinion
that human nature never was,
nor shall be, what it was in those two persons.

(Par. XIII, 73–87)

The Adam of Dante's Aquinas is very much akin to the Adam of Maimonides: at his origin, he is in full possession of the highest knowledge; he sees with the clear vision of his intellect the highest object of theory—i.e., the primal power, God. (Maimonides speaks of "the intellect that God made overflow unto man [i.e., unto Adam] and that is the latter's *ultimate perfection*.")

If Adam and Christ, alone of all humans, possessed complete theoretical perfection, "the clear vision of the primal Power," a plentitude of vision that has never and never will be matched by any other human, then how could Aquinas possibly say that Solomon, "was given/wisdom [*saver*] so deep that, if the truth be true,/there never rose a second of such full vision [*veder*]"?

Aquinas's explanation justifying his praise of Solomon involves in part a lesson in hermeneutics. He tells Dante that, before one can venture to understand a difficult discourse such as his, one must be sure to read as carefully as possible, for otherwise one will be as one who "fishes for the truth and has not the art" (*Par.* XIII, 123). An essential preliminary in the art of reading is "distinguishing well"—that is, determining which words may have equivocal senses, which of those senses is intended in a given context, and which words ought to be emphasized. (This reminds us of Maimonides's reading of Genesis, which he begins by distinguishing between equivocal meanings of *Elohim* and which also involves distinguishing between "knowing" in the strict sense and "knowing" in an equivocal, metaphorical sense—as in the phrase "knowing good and evil.") If Solomon was indeed unmatched by any humans in history for the depth of his "wisdom," "knowledge," and "vision," this is because each of these terms is equivocal: there are two kinds of "wisdom," two kinds of "knowledge," two kinds of "vision." There is the "wisdom," "knowledge," and "vision" of *theoria*—and it is *this* which Adam and Christ possessed to its full perfection, unmatched by any others in human history. But there is also the "wisdom," "knowledge," and "vision" of *praxis*—and it is in *this* that Solomon has been unmatched in human history. Solomon, as Aquinas pointedly remarks, "was a king": he was the unparalleled master of that knowledge pertaining to, as Maimonides would say, "the rulers governing the cities, the *elohim*"—namely, ethics and politics. Thus Solomon did not care to know about the celestial intelligences ("the number of the mover/spirits here above"), nor about problems concerning logical necessity, nor about whether there can be a motion independent of any cause (*si est dare primum motum esse*), nor about geometry. Solomon's "wisdom," "knowledge," and "vision," which is called "prudence" (Aristotle's *phronesis*, "practical wisdom"), entirely sufficient for the task of governing, is also entirely independent from "theory." Solomon did not need to know the "true and the false"; he only needed wisdom in judging concerning "the good and the bad." As Aquinas explains:

> I have not so spoken that you cannot
> plainly see that *he was a king*, who asked for *wisdom*,
> in order that he might be a worthy [*sufficiente*] king;
>
> *Not to know* the number of the mover
> spirits here above, nor if *necesse*
> with a contingent ever made *necesse*;
>
> Nor *si est dare primum motum esse*;
> nor if in a semicircle a triangle can be
> so constructed that it shall have no right angle.
>
> Wherefore, if you note this along with what I said,
> *kingly prudence* [*prudenza*] is that peerless vision [*vedere*]
> on which the arrow of my intention strikes.
>
> And if to 'rose' you turn your discerning eyes,
> you will see it has respect only
> to kings—who are many and the good are rare.
>
> Take my words with this distinction,
> and they can stand thus with what you believe
> of the first father [i.e., Adam] and of our Beloved [i.e., Christ].
>
> (*Par.* XIII, 94–111)

Solomon is unmatched in his "prudence," which is the medieval term for Aristotle's *phronesis*, "practical wisdom." Solomon's "knowledge" pertains to objects of *praxis*, not to objects of *theoria*.[172]

Aquinas's distinction between the "wisdom" of Adam and Christ and the "wisdom" of Solomon is based on Aristotle's distinction between "wisdom" pure and simple ("knowledge" in the strict sense) and "practical wisdom." In the strict sense, "wisdom is knowledge, combined with comprehension, of the things that are highest by nature."[173] But "wisdom" in the strict sense, which concerns things extra-human and extra-historical, is in fact quite useless for our lives: "This is why we say Anaxagoras, Thales, and men like them have wisdom but not practical wisdom, when we see them ignorant of what is to their advantage, and why we say that they know things that are remarkable, admirable, difficult, and divine, but useless; viz. because it is not human goods that they seek."[174]

The other essential text that Dante's Aquinas is drawing on here is the episode in 1 Kings where the Lord appears to Solomon in a dream and tells him that he may have anything he wishes. Solomon, addressing God, asks only for "an understanding mind to govern your people, able to discern between good and evil" (1 Kings 3.9). Solomon asks to be (as Maimonides would say) one of the *elohim*, one of the lords "knowing good and evil." God is more than willing to grant Solomon his wish:

> God said to him, "Because you have asked this, and have not asked for yourself long life or riches, or for the life of your enemies, but have asked for yourself understanding to discern what is right, I now do according to your word. Indeed I give you a wise and discerning mind; no one like you has been before you and no one like you shall arise after you." (1 Kings 3.11–12)

(This last phrase is of course the basis for Aquinas's assertion that "there never rose a second" to match Solomon.) Because of Solomon's demonstration of moral excellence in asking to be a just ruler rather than to satisfy personal desires (for health, wealth, revenge), God not only gives Solomon a mind able to discern between good and evil but he also promises him those things for which he did not ask—wealth, honor, and a long, healthy life.

Dante's Aquinas revises this story in a small but very significant way: Solomon is to be admired not because he eschewed riches, longevity, and power in favor of the ability to govern justly, but rather because he eschewed perfection in *theoria* for perfection in *praxis*: rather than to ask God for "wisdom" in the strict sense ("knowledge of the things that are highest by nature"), he asked instead for "practical wisdom" ("knowledge of good and evil"). Solomon, willingly renouncing "theory" or "wisdom" in the strict sense, expressly limiting himself to excellence in discerning what is best in the realm of human actions, does not long for the "science" of an Adam or a Christ. He does not need to know the true and false, only the right and wrong (and this, of course, can only be "known" in an equivocal, metaphorical sense). He asks, not for knowledge of extra-human realities such as the stars, the celestial intelligences, and God, but for wisdom in the sphere of ethics. He wishes to be like Virgil, not like Beatrice.

The real Thomas Aquinas taught that, while practical wisdom (prudence) is a good, it is a lesser good than theoretical wisdom, without which one is to some degree imperfect. There is a graded hierarchy: while we should aim for, we should not limit ourselves to, *phronesis*, for until we attain the higher goal of *theoria* we have not reached our final perfection and hence we have not attained happiness. Thus the fourteenth-century philosopher John Buridan can assert that "the true metaphysician is a good and perfect man without qualification, while the prudent man, who is also a good man, does not achieve the same completion and perfection as the metaphysician."[175] In *Paradiso* Dante appears to have turned Aquinas into a spokesperson for Dante's own non-Thomist "dualism" or "separatism," according to which there are two distinct human perfections, so that the perfectly good ruler is just as perfect (although in a different way as suits a different goal) as is the perfectly knowledgeable metaphysician. (If Adam and Christ are perfect in their way, so Solomon is perfect in his way; he does not need to perfect himself further by becoming Christ-like.) As Gilson says, "the special achievement of Dante's thought is to have eliminated the hierarchical gradations essential to Thomism and replaced them merely with a system of equal authorities."[176] The practical is not to be ranked below the theoretical, since peace on earth is a goal not to be ranked below salvation. And it is of course one of the ironies of *Paradiso* that Dante attributes this revised Thomism to none other than Aquinas himself!

Adam and Christ have unmatched (theoretical) wisdom concerning "things that cannot be otherwise" and "things which have not an end." Solomon has unmatched (practical) wisdom concerning "the best for man of things attainable by action." No one has ever been a better scientist than Adam and Christ. No one has ever been a better ruler than Solomon, who does not need science of the divine, "the clear vision of the primal Power." Even here in *Paradiso* Dante is reiterating the essential gist of *Purgatory*: the wisest king in human history did not know the truth, did not know Christ and did not have Christ's knowledge of God. As John of Paris says: "Even without Christ as ruler there is the true and perfect justice which is required for the state."[177] Christianity is entirely "accidental to" (non-essential for) "the best for man of things attainable by action"—namely, the Monarchy or perfect state.

Maimonides, Dante, and the Transitional Historicity of the Law

Situated rather safely and randomly in his *The Guide of the Perplexed* is a chapter (III, 32) in which Maimonides does nothing less than call into question the truth (but not the goodness) of the Mosaic Law. The chapter begins by calling our attention to "the deity's wily graciousness and wisdom" in designing things according to a plan of "gradual successions." For instance, Maimonides points out (drawing on a medical treatise by Galen), the physiology of the brain exhibits a steady transition from soft to moderately solid to solid parts: "The brain is an example of the gradation. . .: for its front part is soft, very soft indeed, whereas its posterior part is more solid. The spinal marrow is even more solid and becomes more and more solid as it stretches on."[178] Another example of "gradual successions" is the transition in the food of mammals, from the very soft to the gradually more and more solid:

> Similarly the deity made a wily and gracious arrangement with regard to all the individuals of the living beings that suck. For when born, such individuals are extremely soft and cannot feed on dry food. Accordingly breasts were prepared for them so that they should produce milk with a view to their receiving humid food, which is similar to the composition of their bodies, until their limbs gradually and little by little become dry and solid.[179]

Both of these examples drawn from natural science are analogies meant to signify that human history—including the history of religious revelation—is itself designed as a series of "gradual successions." When God deems that it is time for a change in the Law, he does not bring about an abrupt switch or a total break (since the people would not be prepared for such an extreme change); rather, he works step-by-step, through a steady series of palatable transitions:

> Many things in our Law are due to something similar to this very governance on the part of Him who governs, may He be glorified and exalted. For a sudden transition from one opposite to another is impossible. And therefore man, according to his nature, is not capable of abandoning suddenly all to which he was accustomed. . . .Therefore God sent *Moses our Master* to make out of us *a kingdom of priests and a holy nation* [Exod. 19.6]. . .so that we should devote ourselves to His worship.[180]

Maimonides is asserting what we might call *the transitional historicity of religious Laws*. The Mosaic Law is not the end-point, not the ultimate disclosure of "truth"; rather, it is a transitional phase between a past and a future historical phase (which are themselves transitional). As Sacerdoti says: "Nor can the process inaugurated by the philosopher-prophet Moses be considered to have reached an end once and for all, since the sacrificial laws necessary for his time may no longer be necessary in the time of the philosopher Moses ben Maimon [i.e., Maimonides], and they may be even less necessary in the future. If Moses meant to 'purify' his people's idea of God, the purification may and indeed should continue."[181]

More specifically, prior to the revelation of the Mosaic Law, humankind, who were then in their "infantile" stage, were generally speaking idolaters, following the rites led by their priests, including animal sacrifice and worshipping idols at temples. They saw themselves as serving various lords—for instance, the stars:

> At that time the way of life generally accepted and customary in the whole world and the universal service upon which we were brought up consisted

in offering various species of living beings in the temples in which images
were set up, in worshipping the latter, and in burning incense before them—
the pious ones and the ascetics being at that time, as we have explained, the
people who were devoted to the service of the temples consecrated to
the stars.[182]

In managing the transition from polytheistic idolatry to pure monotheism,
God offered to the people, as a transitional (one might say "adolescent")
stage, the Mosaic Law. It retained many of the ritual trappings of idolatry
(temples, altars, sacrifices, a priesthood)—the only real difference being that
worship was now directed to God rather than to the gods:

> Therefore He, may He be exalted, suffered the above-mentioned kinds of
> worship [i.e., the "idolatrous" elements of the Mosaic Law] to remain, but
> transferred them from created or imaginary things to His own name, may He
> be exalted, commanding us to practice them with regard to Him, may He be
> exalted. Thus He commanded us to build a temple for Him: *And let them
> make Me a Sanctuary* [Exod. 25.8]; to have an altar for His name: *An altar of
> earth thou shalt make unto Me* [Exod. 20.24]; to have the sacrifice offered up
> to Him: *When any man of you bringeth an offering unto the Lord* [Lev. 1.2]; to
> bow down in worship before Him; and to burn incense before Him. And
> He forbade the performance of any of these actions with a view to someone
> else: *He that sacrificeth unto the gods shall be utterly destroyed, and so on* [Exod.
> 22.19]; *For thou shalt bow down to no other god.* [Exod. 34.14][183]

The Mosaic Law is still thoroughly permeated with idolatry. If it is not the
"liquid food" of polytheism, it is however "soft food," not yet the "dry,
solid food" of the Law of humankind's maturity. The relation between the
Mosaic Law and the Polytheist Law that preceded it is *not* a relation of
"truth" and "falsity." Rather, at a certain time in history, the Mosaic Law
becomes generally accepted as "good" and Polytheist Law generally
accepted as "bad." The institution of the Mosaic Law is part of a historical
transition from one ethos to another. If it appears "good" for a time, the
time will come that it itself will appear "bad."

Maimonides gives us a pretty clear indication that he thinks that, in
his own day and age, humans are generally still somewhere between
adolescence and full maturity. His contemporaries are not yet ready for the
revelation of what would, in Maimonides's view, amount to the True Law
(the law of philosophy):

> For one could not then conceive the acceptance of [such a Law], consider-
> ing the nature of man, which always likes that to which it is accustomed. At
> that time this would have been similar to the appearance of a prophet in
> these times who, calling upon people to worship God, would say: "God has

given you a Law forbidding you to pray to Him, to fast, to call upon Him
for help in misfortune. Your worship should consist solely in meditation
without any works at all."[184]

Maimonides suggests that in his own view, religion should consist in nothing other than "meditation" (i.e., contemplation, thinking, philosophy).
The stunning, perhaps shocking point of the chapter is this: if idolatry was
"baby-food," then the Mosaic Law was, as it were, "a kid's meal," a merely
transitional menu offered to those not yet ready for the full-grown, mature
adult repast which is the religion of the philosophers. (Maimonides knows
that this will shock his audience, which he represents in the person of a certain young pupil, a possible apprentice in philosophy: "I know that on
thinking about this at first your soul will necessarily have a feeling of repugnance toward this notion and will feel aggrieved because of it."[185]) The
"ultimate" religion, the religion of the future, is a religion of thinking and
nothing else—no priests, no rites, no sacrifice, no service, no prayer, no
hoped for rewards. As Sacerdoti says, Maimonides is trying to "gradually
train the reader who is potentially a philosopher to practice that philosophical contemplation which for Maimonides is the only form of worship
worthy of one who has been fully divested of humanity's infantile habits
and imaginary beliefs."[186] But Maimonides knows that the people of his era
are not ready to accept a religion with neither commandments nor rites and
whose adherents neither worship nor pray to God: as Sacerdoti remarks, "a
prophet who in the twelfth century would have tried to convince his people that 'worship should consist solely in meditation' would not have had
any success, according to Maimonides, because the brain of the people was
still too 'soft' to pass from the liquid food of religion to the solid food of
philosophy."[187]

If for Maimonides, the religion of the people will gradually become
more and more solid until, sometime in the perhaps distant future, it will
become philosophy, this does not mean that there will ultimately be a disclosure of "truth" in the sense of true knowledge of God. Rather, the end-
point of the history of revelation will be when we come to know that we
cannot have such knowledge—since for Maimonides, God is absolutely
unknowable. Maimonides, says Shlomo Pinès, "maintains the absolute
impossibility of our having the slightest knowledge of God."[188] The religion of the philosophers is a "negative theology"; it is our recognition that,
as Maimonides insists in the *Guide*, we cannot know God:

God, may He be exalted, cannot be apprehended by the intellects,
and. . .none but He Himself can apprehend what He is, and. . .apprehension
of Him consists in the inability to attain the ultimate term in apprehending

Him. Thus all the philosophers say: We are dazzled by His beauty, and He is hidden from us because of the intensity with which He becomes manifest, just as the sun is hidden to eyes that are too weak to apprehend it. . . .The most apt phrase concerning this subject is the dictum occurring in Psalms, *Silence is to praise thee* [Ps. 65.2] which interpreted signifies: silence with regard to You is praise.[189]

Solomon, peace be on him, has rightly directed us with regard to this subject, in words that should be sufficient for us, when he said: *For God is in heaven and thou upon the earth; therefore let thy words be few.* [Eccles. 5.1][190]

Philosophy teaches us that it is best for us not to speak about what God is. It teaches us to limit ourselves to physics and ethics, since all metaphysical speculation is in vain. It teaches us to limit ourselves, as Solomon advised, to talking about the earth.[191]

Dante's vision of God in the final canto of the *Comedy* might be looked at from this perspective. Again and again Dante prefaces his account of this vision by saying that his words are not in the slightest bit adequate to speak of what he saw. And just before telling what he saw, Dante says that the description that follows will be "infantile," no better than the speech of one who nourishes on "liquid food":

Now will my speech fall more short,
even in that which I remember, than that of an *infant*,
who *still bathes his tongue at the breast*.
(*Par.* XXXIII, 106–108)

Dante describes himself here as, to use Maimonides' phrase, one of "the living beings that suck." He is *infans*, "without speech," "mute"—which means that his speech concerning God will amount to silence.

The description that follows is first, of the Trinity, and secondly, of the Incarnation. Is Dante thus saying that the two chief doctrines of Christianity are analogous to "liquid food," which, as readers of Maimonides know, means that these doctrines may well be "good" (in a certain historical time and place) but not "true"? Is Dante's statement of the "mutation" of God's appearance, which altered in time as Dante himself changed ("But through my sight. . ./. . .one sole appearance, /even as I changed [*mutandom'io*], was altering itself to me"; *Par.* XXXIII, 112–14) meant to indicate the transitional historicity of revelation, which alters its content in accordance with the development of human history?

To answer these questions would require a much more extensive treatment than I am prepared to offer in this book. My point for drawing on this aspect of Maimonides here at the end of part I is more simple. Maimonides, in writing the *Guide*, did not serve dry, solid food, but rather something "moderately soft," or perhaps "moderately solid." It is possible to take passages from the *Guide* and put them together so that Maimonides appears as a perfectly pious and observant Jew; or, it is possible to make Maimonides appear, as we have done, as one fully committed to the non-religious religion of the philosophers. The point is that Maimonides purposefully mixed both of these together (in a way that makes his writing notoriously contradictory), so that his work would operate as God does, by fostering a "gradual succession" rather than an abrupt break.

The same can be said of the "double discourse" of the *Comedy*—a poem that can be read both theologically *and* philosophically. But this strategy is itself evidence that the poem is philosophical, since it is a strategy recommended by the Arabo-Islamic philosophical tradition. If Dante is a philosopher who writes as a religious lawgiver, it is because, in his assessment, the people of his time and place are not yet ready to live without their religious Law. If God Himself, as Maimonides says, can give the Mosiac Law "as if this were a ruse invented for our benefit," then Dante can surely do the same with his vision of Hell, Purgatory, and Heaven.[192] We should bear this in mind as we turn, in part II, to the question of salvation—a question concerning which it is possible to present Dante's view as both perfectly orthodox and as radically non-Christian.

PART II

THE RIGHT PATH (DANTE'S UNIVERSALISM)

> All things walk on the Straight Path of their Lord and, in this sense, they do not incur the divine Wrath nor are they astray.
>
> Ibn Arabi

In the opening verses of the *Comedy*, Dante writes memorably of *la diritta via*, "the straight way," the right path. A few verses later he speaks of *la verace via*, "the true way."

> In the middle of the journey of our life,
> I came to myself in a dark wood,
> for *the straight way* [*la diritta via*] was lost. . . .
>
> I cannot really say how I entered there,
> so full of sleep was I at the point
> when I abandoned *the true way* [*la verace via*].
> (*Inf.* I, 1–3; 10–12)

What is this *via*, this *way, straight and true*, which Dante claims once to have abandoned and lost—the recovery of which will apparently be the matter treated in his poem?

The Christian tradition readily provides an answer, with the words of Christ himself: "I am the way [*ego sum via*], and the truth, and the life. No one comes to the Father except through me" (John 14.6). Indeed, what could be more obvious than that the "straight and true way," the right path that Dante abandoned, lost and regained and which his poem above all else exhorts us to find, is the path of Christianity? It seems beyond doubt that the *Comedy* is primarily an imperative call to humankind: *Thou shalt be Christian!*

If this is so, then the *Comedy* might be construed as a threat to ways other than the Christian way, a denial of ways such as Islam, which from the beginning presents itself as the straight way. The Qur'an's first sura recites a prayer to God: "Show us the straight way, / The way of those on whom Thou hast bestowed Thy Grace, those whose (portion) is not wrath, and who go not astray" (1.6–7). In Sura 42 God says to Muhammad: "Most surely you show the way to the right path" (42.52).

Dante's *Comedy* and the Qur'an both open with the claim that the way to be mapped out is the straight way, the right path. Yet does this mean that each simply proclaims its own religious path as the single right way?

Dante tells us that he had lost and then found the straight way. The Qur'an tells us that Islam is the straight way. Can there be, on the question concerning the identity of the right path, any common ground between a Christian *Comedy* and the Islamic holy book? Or must we acknowledge that Dante and Islam are necessarily adversarial participants caught in a polemical clash of ways?

The Qur'an and Religious Pluralism

In the case of Islam, an answer presents itself: a plurality and diversity of ways is divinely ordained, for the Qur'an teaches that each and every human community, in every historical era, has been blessed with a truthful prophet: "To each nation we have given a prophet" (10.47). Muhammad does not offer a radically new revelation, a heretofore unheard of message (Qur'an 46.9: "Say: 'I am not an innovation among the messengers'."). What is new is not the truth that Muhammad brings but rather the insistence that all peoples have always been brought the truth. Truth has been revealed to each community, throughout human history, in a way that is appropriate for the specific historical situations of each. Truth is not a special gift bestowed upon an elect nation, nor is it only first revealed at a certain midpoint of human history, following ages during which humankind was doomed to struggle in the dark. Rather, the Quranic teaching is that all human communities, everywhere and always, have been "reminded" by their prophets of what they ought already to know: to do good and avoid doing wrong—epitomized in the early Meccan revelations as charity to widows and orphans. Since each and every human community has been blessed with its own truthful prophet, the Qur'an encourages each people to embrace the truth (which amounts to the practice of "good works") that is already there in its own tradition.

The Qu'ran's most notable ecumenical verse tells us that *each* divinely revealed way is, in its own way, a right way:

> For every one of you [*li-kull-in*: "unto each"] We have ordained a law and a way. Had God pleased, He could have made you one community: but it is His wish to prove you by that which He has bestowed upon you. Vie (as in

a race) with one another in good works, for to God you shall all return and He will explain for you your differences. (5.48)

God does not merely tolerate, but rather he actively orchestrates and maintains religious and cultural differences. He does not wish for diversity to be overcome, here on earth, by the conversion of difference into identity. God has intentionally created human ethnic, racial, national, and gender differences, not so that some groups would thus be marked as superior to others, but so that each would get to know others ("superiority" thus belongs not to groups but to individuals; it is a matter of one's awareness of God and an honor that can be bestowed on individuals from any of the different groupings): "O humanity! Truly We created you from a male and a female, and made you into nations and tribes that you might know each other. Truly the most honored of you in the sight of God is the most God-conscious of you. Truly God is knowing, Aware" (49.13). As Amir Hussain remarks, this passage "does not say that Muslims are better than other people, but that the best people are those who are aware of God."[1]

The Qur'an envisions a world community that is locally diverse but also ultimately unified: all virtuous humans are part of God's community insofar as they submit themselves to God's guidance, to the truth that God provided for them in their own traditions and in their own languages: "Each messenger We have sent has spoken in the language of his own people" (14.4). Although the essential revelation of the Qur'an is universal ("We never sent a messenger before thee save that We revealed to him, saying, 'There is no god but I, so serve me' " [21.25]), this one universal message is always made manifest in a particular culturally specific form. God, who delights in cultural and racial diversity ("Among His other wonders are the creation of the heavens and the earth and the diversity of your tongues and colors"; 30.21), has given each particular historical people the message in its own vernacular—so that the truth is never something alien to a community, never something imposed by one human community upon another (as Ibn Arabi puts it: God has sent "to each and every community an envoy who is one of their kind, not someone different to them."[2]) The message is always there in the tradition of every vernacular.[3] Despite their differing ways, all virtuous believers—all who heed the teachings that God has given them in their own religious tradition and in their own language—will end up returning to God, and all in the end will be saved: "Believers, Jews, Sabaeans and Christians—whoever believes in God and the Last Day and does what is right—shall have nothing to fear or to regret" (5.69). The religious limit that divides "us" from "them"—although it remains in place here on earth as testimony to God's wondrous unlimited creativity—is in the final analysis effaced.

There was in the medieval Islamic exegetical tradition a debate concerning the referent of Qur'an 5.48's li-kull-in ("unto each"; see above: "For

every one of you [*li-kull-in*] We have ordained a law and a way, etc.").[4]
A minority of commentators took "unto each" to mean "unto every
Muslim"; they thus took the verse to mean: "For every Muslim [yet not for
non-Muslims] we have ordained a law and a way." The diversity at stake
here then is *internal* to Islam—a matter of the multiplicity of Islamic sects,
which, according to a famous *hadith* (one of the canonical "Traditions" concerning the sayings and deeds of the Prophet) are said to be seventy-three in
number. The aim of this minority reading of Qur'an 5.48 would then be to
lend scriptural support to the legitimacy of pluralism *within* the Islamic community as a whole. Such a reading would be in accord with the non-canon-
ical *hadith*: "The disagreements of my community are a blessing." Here one
might mention the position of the eminent scholar al-Baghdadi (d. 1037
AD), who maintained that any teachings that fit in the framework of the
seventy-three sects, no matter how "heretical" they may appear in the eyes
of others, have a legitimate place in the Muslim community. He cites an earlier thinker, al-Ka'bi (d. 931 AD), who goes even farther, deeming legitimate
anything taught by anyone who affirms the Prophethood of Muhammad and
the truth of the Prophet's teaching: "When one uses the expression *ummat al-
islam* [the community of Islam], it refers to everyone who affirms the
prophetic character of Muhammad, and the truth of all that he preached, no
matter what one asserts after this declaration."[5] The thrust of this position is
that, *within* the Islamic community, there are no doctrinal limits—that anything taught by a Muslim is by definition authentically "Islamic."

But the majority of medieval exegetes understood the referent of
Qur'an 5.48's "unto each" to include Muslims and non-Muslims alike—so
that the verse is understood not to be directed exclusively to the Muslim
community but rather to a variety of religious communities. In accordance with the commentary of the great historian and exegete al-Tabari
(d. 923 AD)—who showed that taking "unto each" to mean "unto each
Muslim" makes no sense in itself and fails to respect the context of surrounding verses—every major medieval commentator took Qur'an 5.48 to
be God's declaration of ecumenical pluralism. Some of these took the referent of "unto each" to be the so-called People of the Book, a category
that comprised Jews, Christians, and Muslims, but which, as Islamic civilization moved farther east and encountered more peoples in possession of
scriptural traditions, was expanded to include Zoroastrians, Hindus, and
Buddhists. On this reading, the verse teaches that all virtuous individuals
belonging to communities that profess scripture-based religions will in the end
be counted among those in Paradise. An even more "liberal" interpretation
was implied by commentators such as al-Zamakhshari (d. 1144 AD) and
al-Baydawi (d. 1286 AD), for whom the referent of "unto each" is *all
humans*, regardless of their religious identities.[6] The thrust of this

interpretation is that, when it comes to the matter of the afterlife, there are no religious limits dividing cultures or groups of peoples that will be "saved" from those that will be "damned": all virtuous humans will be accorded their place in Paradise.

The Plurality of Paths

Does this recognition of a plurality of right paths work both ways? If the Qur'an mandates that Muslims acknowledge the truth and rectitude of Dante's Christian way, does the *Comedy* in turn insist that Christians acknowledge the legitimacy of non-Christian ways?

Our initial response must be negative, since the *Comedy*'s first twelve lines do indeed give the impression that there is a single right path, one and only one "straight and true way" to the desired destination. But the next two stanzas cast everything in doubt:

> But when I had reached the foot of a hill,
> where the valley ended
> that had pierced my heart with fear,
>
> I looked on high and saw its shoulders clothed
> already with the rays of *the planet*
> *that leads us straight* [*dritto*] *on every path.*
> (*Inf.* I, 13–18)

Doubt is cast on the very idea of *la diritta via*—the idea that one can speak, using the singular, of "*the* straight way," for here Dante calls the sun "the planet that leads us straight *on every path*" (in Ptolemaic cosmology, the sun was considered one of the planets). If the sun is such a guide—if Dante is neither mistaken nor lying—then *any and every path* is potentially a right one. Those guided by the sun are always going the right way, regardless of which way they happen to be going. We learn in line 18, which recalls with its *dritto* the *diritta via* of line 3, that *every* illuminated way is "the straight way."

We ought not gloss over the universalist implications of this verse—perhaps one of the most significant in the entire poem—simply because such implications do not fit our image of a Dante for whom "rectitude" is an accolade that can, in the final analysis, be granted *solely* to the Christian way.

Is there not an intolerable contradiction? How can Dante first speak of "*the* straight and true way," then immediately follow this with talk concerning the inevitable rectitude of every way under the sun?

An attempt to resolve this contradiction must begin with our posing a pair of questions. What is the sun that leads straight on every path? And what are such paths?

Concerning the significance of the "path" (or its synonyms, such as "way" or "road"), we can take as our first guide Saint Augustine. In his *Retractions*, a work written near the end of his life in which he settles any outstanding debts to God, Augustine felt compelled to rectify a statement he had made in an earlier work, *Soliloquies*, in which he had seemed to endorse a rather liberal tolerance for religious diversity:

> Again, my statement, "Union with wisdom is not achieved by a single road," does not sound right, as if there were another way apart from Christ, who said "I am the way." Therefore this offense to religious ears ought to have been avoided. Although that one universal way exists, *there are however other ways* about which we sing in the psalm, "Make known to me your ways, Lord, and teach me your paths."[7]

What is fascinating about this "retraction" is that it seems in the end to retract very little: while insisting that Christianity is "universal," the single religious way that is open for all humans, Augustine still acknowledges that there are other ways and other paths open for some humans. He cites a psalm deliberately to prove that there is a plurality of paths. We witness here the same sort of ambivalence—is there just one or are there many ways?—that we find in the opening verses of Dante's *Comedy*.

Augustine's ambivalent retraction shows that he is still receptive to the philosophical discourse of those of his non-Christian contemporaries for whom tolerance for religious diversity was an urgent and vital issue.

In 364 AD, for instance, the pagan philosopher Themistius addressed the following plea to Jovian, who as the newly-installed emperor was inclined to favor Christianity at the expense of paganism:

> It is not. . .a single road that leads to [God], but there is a road that is barely passable, a broader way, a rough road and a level one. Nevertheless, they all stretch toward that one same haven. Our rivalry and zeal stem from nothing except the fact that all do not walk the same road. If you permit only a single road, you will cut off the others, and you will block off the open space of the contest. . .. Think that the founder of all also takes delight in diversity. He wants the Syrians to be one variety of citizen, the Greeks another variety, and the Egyptians another variety still. Even the Syrians themselves are not homogeneous, but are in fact broken down into small units. Indeed not one single person understands things in exactly the same way as a neighbor, but one in this way and another in that. Why then do we force what cannot be put into practice?[8]

These passages from Augustine and Themistius show us that "path," "way," and "road" were well established metaphorical vehicles meant to signify "a religion"—so that, for instance, the phrase "many paths" means "many religions," and the phrase "every path" means "every religion."

Let us return to the stanza that we are attempting to gloss:

> I looked on high and saw its shoulders
> clothed already with the rays of the planet
> that leads us [*altrui*] straight on every path.

The little word *altrui* deserves some attention. One American translator takes the word to mean "us," whereas another prefers to render it as "men."[9] Yet this word, fairly common in the *Comedy*, is in the majority of instances translated as "others." (In modern Italian *altrui* has become exclusively a possessive, meaning "other people's"; the medieval sense is retained, however, in the modern French *autrui*, "other people.") Why this resistance to the *alterity* that Dante clearly intends to signify? How can the otherness of "others" be glossed over, turned into the sameness of "us" or the supposed universality of "men"? Can we not allow that Dante may have been *altruistic*, may have spoken of the rectitude of *others*? In this case, we need, in order to render the proper sense of this verse, to retrieve Longfellow's translation from the early nineteenth century: "Which leadeth others right by every road."

It seems fairly clear, considering both the traditional significance of the metaphorical phrase "every path" and the usual sense of *altrui*, that the latter part of the stanza in fact speaks of "the rays of the planet that leads *others* right, *those of every religion.*"

And perhaps it is precisely *this*—the idea that rectitude may properly be attributed to humans who are not like us, to those of every religion—that leads to the peace and calm of the following stanza:

> Then was the fear a little quieted that in the lake
> of my heart had lasted through the night
> I passed with so much anguish.
>
> (*Inf.* I, 19–21)

Dante's fear and anguish is assuaged only when he is reassured, by the rays of the sun, that each and every path may potentially be a right one, that those who follow other ways are not lost.

The *Comedy*'s opening, then, seems marked less by an insistence that there is one and only one "true and right way" than by a sense of relief brought about by the thought that—to use Augustine's words—"there are however other ways."

Ibn Arabi

Let us turn for some further illumination concerning the plurality of paths to Ibn Arabi (1165–1240 AD), the Andalusian-born writer, intellectual, and mystic, the Greatest Master, recognized by common consensus as the most profound and influential Islamic thinker of the past 800 years. If it cannot be definitively proven (as Miguel Asín Palacios attempted to do in the early twentieth century) that certain passages from Ibn Arabi are the direct source for Dante's conception of a cosmological journey, neither can it be doubted that both the spirit and the letter of Arabic intellectual culture arrived, through a myriad of channels, to Dante's Italy.

In his massive and brilliant *Meccan Openings*, a work of some 15,000 pages, Ibn Arabi distinguishes between three understandings of "the path."

First, there is a very general sense of "path," according to which all things, including all religions and all human thoughts, are forever on "the right path" (since for Ibn Arabi all things, being diverse manifestations of God's essence, are necessarily true and good): "The path of God is the general path upon which all things walk, and it takes them to God. It includes every divinely revealed religion and every construction of the rational faculty. It takes to God, and embraces both wretched and felicitous."[10]

In his *Bezels of Wisdom*, Ibn Arabi places special emphasis on a verse from the Qur'an's eleventh sura ("Hud"): "No living being is there but He will seize it by its forelock. Surely my Lord is on a straight path" (11:56). Ibn Arabi takes this to mean that God, who is always on the Straight Path, is, as it were, holding and pulling (seizing) by the hair *all of us—all living beings—always*, along with him in his footsteps. God's seizing and guiding all living beings means that it is simply impossible for any of them ever *not* to be walking the straight path: "All things walk on the Straight Path of their Lord and, in this sense, they do not incur the divine Wrath nor are they astray."[11] Ibn Arabi tells us that this particular verse—with its indication that none have gone nor can go astray—is the very foundation of his thinking: "What greater tidings could there be for creation?" This verse amounts to Ibn Arabi's "good tidings"—his Gospel, in a sense. Indeed he tells us that it was only through an encounter with this verse that he became the teacher that he is, that Reality was revealed to him.[12] Since for Ibn Arabi submission to God ("islam") is universal, not something that we can choose to accept or reject, then all humans are necessarily "muslims." From this founding principle follows Ibn Arabi's strident advocacy on behalf of those whom self-proclaimed "pious Muslims" would represent as non-Muslim unbelievers. Characteristically, he defends as truly pious the beliefs and practices of idolaters, pagans, heretics, the damned, and the followers of every imaginable religious path.

Returning to the *Meccan Openings*, we find a second, more narrow sense of "the path"—which refers not just to the way on which God leads all living beings, but also more particularly to the way made manifest by the "religions of the Book"—Judaism, Christianity, Islam, Hinduism, and in fact all religions based on scriptural (as opposed to oral) tradition. Ibn Arabi understands the opening sura's distinction between "blessed" and "misguided" as a distinction between communities to whom the message has been revealed in writing and those to whom it has been revealed only in speech, implying that it is more likely that the latter sort of communities will "lose the way." Hence he interprets the Qur'an's opening prayer as the Muslim community's request for a written scripture, the possession of which will mean that they are to be counted as among those on "the straight path": "Guide us on the straight path, the path of those to whom you are giving, not those with anger upon them, not those who have lost the way" (1:5–7). God is "giving" to those communities to which he grants scriptures. The "blessed" are those peoples who have been given a book. Those "who have lost the way" are not infidels or evil-doers; they are those who do not have a text to which they can turn for guidance. Again, the "straight path" or the "path of blessings" is a broad, pluralistic one—in the sense that it includes all religions with a scriptural tradition.

In a third, most specific sense, "the path" refers solely to Islam, the "Path of Muhammad." Ibn Arabi teaches that Muslims ought to follow this path without hesitation, yet at the same time without denying the rectitude of the other paths. And what marks this path as "the right way" is precisely its "inclusive" quality, its all-embracing acceptance of the other paths as also right in their own ways:

> Among the paths is the path of blessings. It is referred to in God's words, *To every one of you We have appointed a right way and a revealed law* [5:48]. The Muhammadan leader chooses the path of Muhammad and leaves aside the other paths, even though he acknowledges them and has faith in them. However, he does not make himself a servant except through the path of Muhammad, nor does he have his followers make themselves servants except through it. He traces the attributes of all paths back to it, because Muhammad's revealed religion is all-inclusive. Hence the property of all the revealed religions has been transferred to his revealed religion. His revealed religion embraces them, but they do not embrace it.[13]

For Ibn Arabi, the difference between Islam and other religions is that Islam, unlike the others, acknowledges the rectitude of all other ways. And it is only because Islam amounts to the recognition of the legitimacy of all paths that the Muhammadan can with good faith embrace it as the right way:

> The perfect servant, despite his knowledge of this truth [i.e., that "all things walk on the Straight Path"] nevertheless maintains himself, in his outer and limited form, in constant prayer, his face turned toward the Sacred Mosque, believing God to be in that direction when he prays; the Sacred Mosque is, in truth, representative of a facet of the Reality, as in the verse, *Wheresoever you turn, there is the face of God*, and in facing it one is face to face with God in it. However, do not tell yourself that He is in that direction only, but rather maintain both your particular attitude of worship in facing the Sacred Mosque and your more universal attitude of knowledge of the impossibility of confining His face to that particular direction, it being merely one of the many points toward which men turn.
>
> God has made it clear that He is in every direction turned to, each of which represents a particular doctrinal perspective regarding Him. All are in some sense right in their approach; everyone who is right receives his reward, everyone who receives his reward is blessed, and everyone who is blessed is well pleasing to his Lord.[14]

Far from seeing Islam as the "true belief" and other beliefs as "false," Ibn Arabi insists that *all* beliefs are human constructions, "delimitations" of God's unlimited essence: "The creatures are bound to worship only what they believe about the Real, so they worship nothing but a created thing. . . .There are none but idol-worshipers."[15] All religions are idolatry, and every religion is full of error. (Ibn Arabi does not exempt his own religion from this characterization.) In discussing "the diversity of beliefs concerning God, whether among the people of divinely revealed religions or others," Ibn Arabi says: "If God were to take people to account for error, He would take every possessor of a belief to account. Every believer has delimited his Lord with his reason and consideration and has thereby restricted Him. But nothing is worthy of God except nondelimitation. . . . Nevertheless, God pardons everyone."[16]

"Islam" (in the narrow, limited sense), regarded as a fixed set of beliefs, rituals, teachings about God, is for Ibn Arabi not an exhaustively true belief, nor is it the only possible configuration of truth. It is, like other positive belief systems, a "delimitation" or a "specific knotting" of God's infinite and ultimately unknowable diversity. The problem with beliefs, "delimitations" or "knottings," is that they hide or conceal other alternatives, render invisible other potentially beneficial orderings:

> Beware of becoming delimited by a specific knotting and disbelieving in everything else, lest great good escape you. . . .Be in yourself matter for the forms of all beliefs. For God is wider and more tremendous than that He should be constricted by one knotting rather than another.[17]

If there is a single true belief that Ibn Arabi would be willing to endorse and for which he would settle, it is not "Islam"—rather, it is the Muhammadan Path. There is a difference between "Islam"—the historical revealed religion—and the Path of Muhammad. The end of the Muhammadan Path is a "state beyond states," a perfect illumination by which one learns that there is no end to learning, no cessation to the flow of revelations. Or, let us say that Ibn Arabi treats "Islam" as simply another revealed religion (a true but specific knotting), *except insofar* as the essence of Islam is to give guidance preparatory to the illumination received by the Perfect Human Being, the Muhammadan, the one whose knowledge is never complete, never fixed. The only exhaustively and absolutely true belief is the Path of Muhammad; the traveler on this path never comes to a stop at any "station" other than the "station of no station":

> The Muhammadan is not distinguished except by the fact that he has no station specifically. His station is that of no-station, which means the following: if man is dominated by his state, then he is known only by it, is related to it and is determined by it. But the Muhammadan's relationship to the stations is as the relationship of God to the Names—he is not determined by any station that is related to him. On the contrary, in every breath, in every moment, in every state, he is in the form required by that breath, moment, state. His limitation has no temporal continuity. The divine determinations vary at each moment, and so he is variable with their variability.[18]

One may be "dominated by his state," "determined" by his religion. As such, one blocks one's receptivity to other states and forecloses the possibility of variability. The Muhammadan is never "determined by any station," never settles for a delimited, definitive, circumscribed knotting of truth. Always in motion, never static, the Muhammadan Path can never be formulated as a doctrine. If one turns one's Islam into a "station" (a fixed set of beliefs or definitive truths), then one is not following the Straight Way that is the Path of Muhammad.

A central element of Ibn Arabi's effort to debunk self-proclaimed professors of the single truly Islamic doctrine is his hermeneutic approach to "interpretations" of the Qur'an, such as those provided in his massive work *Meccan Openings*. If I am slightly hesitant to call the Qur'anic commentary of the *Meccan Openings* "interpretation," it is because in that work Ibn Arabi deconstructs the distinction between his commentary and the Qur'an itself: the *Meccan Openings* is presented as having been dictated to Ibn Arabi by a certain young man, who himself is a symbol for the Qur'an—which is to say that the text of Ibn Arabi's *Meccan Openings* is nothing other than the transcription of the voice of the Qur'an. For Ibn Arabi, the exegesis or "interpretation" of the Qur'an (a work such as *Meccan Openings*) is an event of revelation of the Qur'an itself. Each instance of authentic reading is the event of a new revelation, as the book continuously augments its significance:

> The servant whose interior perspective is illuminated, the one who is guided *by a light from his Lord* (Qur'an 39.22), obtains, every time he recites a verse [of the Qur'an], a new understanding distinct from the one he had obtained during his previous recitation of the same verse and from the one he will obtain during the next recitation of that verse. God has granted the plea that he addressed to Him in saying *Lord, increase my knowledge!* (Qur'an 20:114). He whose understanding is identical during two successive recitations is the loser. He whose interpretation is new in each recitation is the winner.[19]

To limit oneself to a fixed understanding, to what one already believes, is to lose in the contest of reading. Continual hermeneutic increase, a constant surpassing of the prior limits of exegesis, is essential to the phenomenon of interpreting God's word.

Although Ibn Arabi's hermeneutics insists on the infinity and "limitlessness" of Qur'anic "meaning," it is also based on the principle of scrupulously literal interpretation. He out-does the so-called literalists by showing that what they take to be the "literal" meaning is always already a *selection*, a *limitation*, something culled from a much greater variety of potential literal meanings. His primary hermeneutic principle is this: all readings of a revealed scripture that are grammatically correct *must* be intended by God:

> Any signification of any verse whatsoever of the Word of God—whether it be in the Qur'an, the Torah, the Psalms or any of the others—which is judged admissible by one who knows the language in which this Word is expressed, represents what God intended for the one who interprets it in thus manner.[20]

For Ibn Arabi, no interpretation (so long as it is grammatically possible) ought to be rejected, no matter how scandalous, outrageous, impious, or heretical it may appear, since God, in revealing a verse of scripture, cannot possibly have been ignorant of the whole range of its possible meanings. Much of Ibn Arabi's shocking audacity is rooted in this hermeneutic principle—a principle that justifies his following the letter of the text to its radical extremes.

It is not simply that, for Ibn Arabi, the Qur'an admits of a great diversity of possible meanings. Rather, taking hermeneutic openness to its ultimate limits, Ibn Arabi insists that it is quite simply impossible for anyone ever to offer an erroneous interpretation of anything:

> People like us, who have an overview of all stations and levels, distinguish
> from whence every individual speaks and discourses and recognize that each
> is correct in his own level and makes no errors. Indeed, there is absolutely no
> error in the cosmos.[21]

The reason that there can be no error in the cosmos is that, for Ibn Arabi,
everything, including every breath and every signification, is an instance of
God's self-disclosure (although every such instance is itself always *limited*,
partial). A proposition proffered in human speech is not an attempt (one
that might be judged "true" or "false") to correspond to some external
truth but rather is itself an event of the unveiling of truth. Strictly speaking,
all speech is God's speech, and thus it is impossible to speak falsely about,
for instance, the meaning of the Qur'an: "There is no speaker but God, and
none who causes to speak but God. All that remains is the opening of the
eye of understanding to God's causing to speak in respect to the fact that
He only causes speech that is correct. Every speech in the cosmos derives
either from wisdom or from God's decisive address. So all speech is protected from error or slipping. However, speech has homesteads, loci, and
playing fields within which it has a great expanse to roam. Its playing fields
are so vast that the eyes of insights are unable to perceive their outer
limits."[22]

We can consider, as an example of Ibn Arabi's unorthodox, even
outrageous yet nonetheless literal exegesis, his reading of Qur'an 17.23:
"The Lord has decreed that you worship none but Him." This verse is
probably normally understood to mean that, given that we have some element of choice in determining the object of our worship, we ought to
choose to worship God. If we are, for instance, idolaters, then, following
upon the Lord's decree, we ought to renounce our idolatry and take up
Islam. The conventional understanding of the verse is this: the Lord has
told those who do not worship none but Him that they had better start
worshipping none but him. Ibn Arabi's reading of the verse shows that the
conventional reading diminishes God's power by imagining God's decree
as something that *may or may not be* observed (you may or may not worship
none but him); but for Ibn Arabi what the Lord has decreed *is*. For Ibn
Arabi, the verse *asserts* that it *is* the case that you (no matter who you are
and no matter what you worship) *do* worship none but him. We have no
choice in the matter: no one, not even the idolater, can help but worship
none but God.[23]

Much of Ibn Arabi's exegesis amounts to a defense of those whom puri-
tanical Muslim rigorists might scorn for being "unbelievers," polytheists,

idolaters. Ibn Arabi in fact opens up the hermeneutic playing field of the term "unbeliever" (*kafir*), ascribing to it several senses, including both positive and negative ones. Many of these senses involve a play on the fact that the Arabic word for "unbeliever" (*kafir*) shares the identical root (K-F-R) with the verb "to hide." If you, as an idolater, are an "unbeliever," it is only because you do not know that in worshipping your idol you are worshipping none but God: you are *hiding* from yourself the fact that you are worshipping none but him. Since everything in the cosmos is an instance of God's self-manifestation (more precisely, everything is he/not he: a limited disclosure of God's unlimited essence), polytheism is, strictly speaking, impossible. The "polytheist," for Ibn Arabi, is not someone who worships an object other than God but rather someone who believes that it is possible to worship an object other than God (and, in so believing, admits the possibility of a plurality of gods). The true polytheist is the rigorous monotheist, the one who thinks that there is an essential difference between the idolater's idol and God—and hence thinks that there is something in the cosmos that is not God's self-manifestation, something that escapes or exceeds the Lord's dominion. If for Ibn Arabi the "unbeliever" (*kafir*) is in fact a "believer," so too the best of the believers, the highest of the saints, is also a *kafir*: such saints *hide* their sanctity (in part by not erecting limits between "believers" and "unbelievers" and by not claiming to stand, over against others, on the right side of such limits). And if the best kind of *kafir* (hider, "one who conceals") is the highest of the saints, concealing her or his sanctity, then the worst kind of *kafir* is the one who *hides* from others the *unlimited* extent of God's mercy—the one who, trying in vain to hoard God's mercy for himself and his kind, *conceals* the truth that all humans are believers, that no one is a *kafir*. The worst *kafir*, for Ibn Arabi, is the one who blames others for "unbelief."[24]

Ibn Arabi teaches that the "Path of Muhammad" is nothing other than this utterly open acceptance of all paths—an acceptance the obverse side of which is the recognition that all paths are erroneous. Each of the myriad of diverse beliefs is one manifestation of God's "self-disclosure." The "perfect human being," he or she who has attained the highest understanding, is the one who acknowledges without reservation the truth—and the falsity—of every belief about God. If Ibn Arabi elevates Islam above the other paths, it is because he sees Islam as the only path that does not deny the rectitude of the other paths.

We have seen in Ibn Arabi's *Meccan Openings*, in Augustine's *Retractions*, and in the opening lines of Dante's *Comedy* three instances in which there is posited an apparent contradiction between a single right path and many other legitimate paths. For Augustine, what makes the way of Christ "more right" than the other ways is its "universality"—its status (in Augustine's view) as the single way open to all humans. For Ibn Arabi, what makes the path of Muhammad "more right" is its "inclusive" acknowledgment of the legitimacy of all ways. Is it possible that, for Dante too, "the right path," *la diritta via*, is that which is ever more universal, ever more inclusive of diversity?

The Creed of the Philosophers

We have offered an answer to the latter of our two questions posed above ("What are such paths?"). We now return to the former: "What is the sun that leads straight on every path?"

For Dante, the "sun" is not a general figure for just any kind of enlightenment, nor is it simply figure for religious illumination. Rather, the "sun" represents, specifically, *philosophy* (more specifically, Aristotle's philosophy, Greek rationalism) as the source of a knowledge that may be attained by *all* humans. Hence Dante says to Virgil, "O sun that heals every troubled vision" (*Inf.* XI, 91), just before the latter, in a speech that begins with the word "Philosophy," expounds a doctrine based on an explicit citation of Aristotle's *Physics*—and this just after having explicitly cited Aristotle's *Nichomachean Ethics*. The interjection—"O sun"—is neatly situated right between these two citations of the thinker known to medieval Scholastics simply as "the Philosopher." And in *Paradiso*, in which each of the celestial spheres of the Ptolemaic universe is metaphorically linked with a different human project or endeavor, the Heaven of the Sun, where Dante encounters the souls of two dozen celebrated intellectuals, is linked with Philosophy, presided over as it is by two of the greatest philosophers of thirteenth-century Western Christendom, Aquinas and Bonaventure.

We may now refine our understanding of the passage in question. Fearing that he and others (including all those who are non-Christians) may have strayed from "the right way," Dante is reassured by the thought of *philosophy*'s potential to "lead *others* aright, *those of every religion*." Far from indicating Dante's conversion away from philosophy toward theology, the *Comedy*'s opening attributes to philosophy a profoundly salvific power. Certainly it cannot be the case that the *selva oscura* is, as many have argued, "the dark wood of philosophy," since philosophical illumination, represented by the rays of the sun, is precisely that which leads us and others *out* of the dark wood.

In Dante's era, "philosophy" is not simply a set of themes, not simply a certain group of positions on a variety of metaphysical, physical, and moral issues, nor is it primarily a general name for "wisdom" or "sagacity." Rather, in the Middle Ages, "philosophy" has a special connotation, since it cannot help but imply a certain understanding of religion.

To be a "philosopher" is to be faithful to the universal law of reason. The philosopher is one who, although he may or may not be committed to a specific religion, nonetheless possesses a knowledge that is tantamount to the deepest and authentic understanding of all religions. Philosophers are those elite intellectuals, of various faiths, who have risen above their culturally relative religious laws to see that the truly significant teachings of all such laws are one and the same. These intellectuals, who may have commenced their journeys on any of the various "paths," are all led aright by the illuminating rays of philosophy. These philosophers see the authentic truth of all religions as essentially equivalent to philosophical truth. The medieval philosopher is not the adversary of religion but rather one who accepts the legitimacy of religion without ever accepting the indispensability of any single religion.

In his work known as the *Kuzari*, the great twelfth-century Andalusian Jewish poet and intellectual Judah Halevi strongly opposed this idea of the essential equivalence of all religions. Still, Halevi's portrait of a character called "the philosopher" tells us quite clearly that "philosophy" in the Middle Ages does not mean so much an opposition to but rather a tolerance for all religions. As Y. Tzvi Langermann explains, the dominant trend among Jewish intellectuals in twelfth-century Spain was to view manifest religious differences between peoples of various regions as "accidental" effects of such factors as geography, climate, diet, and the dispositions of the heavenly bodies. Beneath the surface of apparent religious differences, according to these intellectuals, was an "essential" philosophical doctrine that was the authentic core of each religion and was common to all religions:

> One key, unifying feature of the neoplatonism popular among Hispano-Jewish thinkers of the twelfth century is the extension of naturalistic, specifically astrological explanation to the phenomenon of religion as well. In particular, the view was upheld that the spiritual goal of all humanity is the same. The diversity in the observed religious practices, which are undertaken in order to achieve this goal, is, like the diversity in all natural phenomena, due to the locally and temporally varying influences of the stars.

> Judah Halevi's "philosopher" shared in this trend of thought. According to him, the differences between human beings are to be ascribed to "the influences of climate, countries, foods and water, spheres, stars, and constellations." As a principle of natural philosophy, this may seem innocuous, but this is hardly the case. As the philosopher develops his point of view, the devastating consequences for established religious practice emerge quite clearly: "*Be not concerned about the form of your worship of God or the manner of your praying or way of your praising, which speech, which language, which actions. If you wish, make up your own religion. . .or adopt as a religion one of the intellectual*

regimens which the philosophers have set down in their books". . . .Clearly, Judah Halevi is not attacking some fringe element of the Jewish *intelligentsia*; his aim is fixed at what, in his view, is the dominant trend of thought. As it seems to me, the approach that constituted for Judah Halevi *the* philosophical norm, that is to say, that set of beliefs and opinions that makes up the particular "philosophy" that threatened Jewish singularity and, therefore, had to be combatted in the *Kuzari*, is the very tendency towards naturalistic explanation, by means of astrological theory, of the differences among the various faiths. According to this conception, at the heart of all correct faiths one finds the same set of ideas, formulated in the abstract. The different means for coming close to God, the rituals practiced by the major religions, and the law codes and prophetic revelations held sacred by the different faiths are phenomena of a lesser order; all may be ascribed to the natural differences that exist among peoples and climates, all of which can be sufficiently accounted for by astrology. No one faith may be said to enjoy an intrinsic advantage; all are mere instruments, disciplines or regimens, tailored to the varying, astrally determined characteristics of the different peoples.[25]

Dante's notion, in the opening of the *Comedy*, of philosophy (the sun) as that which guarantees the rectitude of every path ("the rays of the planet/that leads others straight on every path") indicates that he had assimilated this understanding of the relation between philosophy and religion: philosophy is not antagonistic to religion, but it *is* antagonistic to the idea that there is one and only one right religion.

Among the best examples of this attitude is the charming philosophical novella *Hayy Ibn Yaqzan* (*'Alive' Son of 'Awake'*), a famous work by the twelfth-century Andalusian Muslim poet and scholar Ibn Tufayl (known in the Latin West as Abubacer). The tale's protagonist, Hayy Ibn Yaqzan, is born on "a certain equatorial island, lying off the coast of India, where human beings come into being without father or mother."[26] As the product of spontaneous generation, Hayy's thoughts and, eventually, his philosophical system develop wholly from his relations with his natural environment (he is raised by a doe, for whom he feels the strongest possible filial love and whose death is the traumatic experience that initiates his philosophical questioning). Hayy's mature and full-blown philosophical system represents the "truth" at which a naturally gifted human mind will autonomously arrive, without the influence or coercion of human family, society and culture. At stake is a thought-experiment meant to answer the question which is nicely formulated by Lenn Goodman, the tale's English translator: "What discoveries would be made by the isolated soul freed from prejudice and unimpeded by dogma and tradition?"[27]

For our purposes, the specifics of Hayy's "naturally" attained philosophy (which, in its highest stage, tends toward mysticism) are unimportant, since the real force of the story has less to do with the positive doctrines of Hayy's thought than with the relations between his thought and that of others. Near the end, we see that the whole novella has been a preparation for the crucial, brief final episodes. Near Hayy's island is "a second island, in which had settled the followers of a certain true religion, based on the teachings of a certain ancient prophet—God's blessings on all such prophets."[28] Among the inhabitants of this second island is a young man named Absal, a devout follower of the island's religion, one who has studied and meditated on its writings so that he has come to see its literal teachings as "symbols, concrete images of things."[29] Seeking solitude conducive to religious contemplation, Absal travels to Hayy's island, thinking it uninhabited. The two soon become fast friends, and in the course of their conversations Hayy teaches Absal his philosophy, while Absal gives Hayy an account of his religion. As a result, Absal comes to see that the "veiled" or "symbolic" meaning of his religion is nothing other than Hayy's philosophy: "Absal had no doubt that all the traditions of his religion about God, His angels, bibles and prophets, Judgement Day, Heaven and Hell were symbolic representations of these things that Hayy Ibn Yaqzan had seen for himself. The eyes of his heart were unclosed. His mind caught fire. Reason and tradition were at one within him. All the paths of exegesis lay open before him. All his old religious puzzlings were solved; all the obscurities, clear."[30]

The "true essence" of Islam (for the identity of the second island's traditional religion is barely disguised) is expressed abstractly, without metaphors, by Hayy's philosophical system. But as the tale comes to an end, and Absal brings Hayy back to Absal's island so that he might teach its inhabitants the truth concerning the scriptures, it is clear that not even those "nearest to intelligence," let alone the masses, will ever accept the philosophical understanding of religious doctrine: "But the moment Hayy rose the slightest bit above the literal or began to portray things against which they were prejudiced, they recoiled in horror from his ideas and closed their minds. . .The more he taught, the more repugnance they felt, despite the fact that these were men who loved the good and sincerely yearned for the Truth. Their inborn infirmity simply would not allow them to seek Him as Hayy did, to grasp the true essence of His being and see Him in His own terms. They wanted to know Him in some human way. In the end Hayy despaired of helping them and gave up his hopes that they would accept his teaching."[31] The tale ends on a pessimistic, or at least quietistic, note. Hayy and Absal return to Hayy's island, reconciled to the fact that philosophy has no role to play in society, which is better left in the hands of traditional religion. Although the "religion of the masses" is not—on the literal level—true, it nonetheless has a positive, utilitarian, policing function: "The sole benefit most people could derive from religion was for this world, in that it helped them lead decent lives without others encroaching on what belonged to them."[32]

Averroes

Ibn Tufayl was himself the mentor of Averroes, the greatest of the Islamic rationalists. In his *The Incoherence of the Incoherence*, a polemical response to the great Sunni theologian al-Ghazali's *The Incoherence of the Philosophers*, Averroes maintains that the "theoretical" or "rational" content of all religious traditions is identical to the content of Aristotle's philosophy. In *his* book al-Ghazali examines twenty philosophical propositions that are suspect in the eyes of Islamic authorities. He concludes that seventeen of these propositions are heretical (and hence those who maintain them ought to be treated in the manner seen fit for heretics, who—given that the tremendous diversity of Islamic doctrines made for a situation in which almost everybody was a "heretic" in someone else's eyes—were often tolerated by Islamic authorities). Three of the philosopher's doctrines, however, are determined by al-Ghazali to be "utterly irreligious" and hence to warrant the putting to death of any Muslim who maintains them. Islam cannot tolerate the teaching of the following tenets which the philosophers have deduced by Aristotelian logic: first, that the world is eternal (not created *ex nihilo* at some point in time); second, that God has no knowledge of particulars; third, that there is no resurrection of the body. Each of these propositions has implications that threaten the very foundation of Islam.

Averroes's critique of al-Ghazali is based on a twofold strategy. For one thing, he shows that the illustrious Islamic neoplatonists al-Farabi and Ibn Sina (Avicenna), from whom al-Ghazali derives his knowledge of Greek rationalism, did not properly understand Aristotle. Al-Ghazali's attack against philosophy does not pertain because he is not attacking the real thing. At the same time he argues that al-Ghazali misreads the Qur'an, finding in it dogmas that are not supported by a judicious reading of the text. The question concerning the eternity of the world is a case in point. Aristotle teaches that matter is eternal and the world (meaning by that the universe of physical material) was not created in time. Al-Ghazali maintains that the creation of matter and the world *ex nihilo* in time is a dogma absolutely fundamental to Islam. Averroes replies that the Qur'an, while certainly presenting God as the creator, at no point says that he creates *ex nihilo*. On the contrary, there are several passages that show God's creating to be his act of shaping and reconfiguring already (and eternally) existing matter. Qur'an 41.10 ("Then He arose to heaven, while it was smoke") implies that heaven was created from something already existing in the form of smoke. Similarly, when the Qur'an says "On the day when the earth shall be changed into other than earth, and the heavens as well" (14.48), it confirms the philosopher's understanding of creation as a transformation of matter, a giving form to raw physical stuff that itself, being eternal, was never created. "He it is who created the heavens and the earth in six days, and His throne was on the water" (11.7) tells the philosopher that some things were already there (the throne and the water) prior to God's creating/configuring the cosmos in its current form.[33]

In his *Decisive Treatise, Determining What the Connection is Between Religion and Philosophy*, Averroes insists that there is no discrepancy between the truths of revealed scripture, properly understood, and the truths of Aristotle's philosophy. The theoretical content of Islamic scripture, like that of the other religious laws (foremost in his mind, of course, are Judaism and Christianity) *is* Aristotle's philosophy: religion, in its authentic teaching concerning the way things really are, is fully compatible with Greek rationalism:

> Now since this Law [i.e. Islam] is true and summons to the study that leads to knowledge of the truth, we the Muslim community know definitively that demonstrative study [i.e., Aristotelian philosophy] does not lead to conclusions conflicting with what is given in the Law; for truth does not oppose truth but accords with it and bears witness to it.[34]

Averroes teaches that (to borrow Dante's metaphor) the "sun" of rational truth shines out from the core of all religious Laws. This universal theoretical content shared by the religions of every people, nation, and community is—again to use Dante's words—what *mena dritto altrui per ogne calle* ("leads others straight on every path").

But Averroes's view does not amount to an indifference to religion nor to the special claims of his own religion. He does not long for the day when everyone will be taught to understand Aristotle. On the contrary he affirms that religion is in the end superior to philosophy. Although religion and philosophy are, as vehicles of theoretical and rational truth, purely equal (since philosophically acute interpreters will see that the truth of religion is identical to the truth of philosophy), nonetheless religion has a "something extra" that philosophy lacks: a practical level that uses moral imperatives and institutes legislation for the sake of peace, justice, and a felicitous social order. Religions prescribe laws and institute practices that are beneficial for the political health of the community. Philosophy, which can only be mastered after great training and by those possessing uncommon intellect, will only ever be understood by a very few, and thus it can never serve as a society's primary practical and ethical guiding discourse. Religion's positive moral and political effects are rarely if ever achieved by philosophy. A prophet (such as Muhammad) performs *two* tasks. Like the philosopher, he presents the truth concerning the way things really are. But at the same time, in his role as "lawgiver," he does something that normally exceeds the philosopher's capacity: he actually inspires human communities to organize themselves in ways conducive to peace and justice. Thus Averroes tells us that, while every prophet is a philosopher (since the theoretical content of every religion is one and the same universal rational truth), not every philosopher is a prophet.[35] The exemplary philosopher should not abandon his religion, should not aim to destroy or demystify the very notion of religion, but rather he should do his best to see that his religion is put to positive social use.[36] (And one might well say that Dante's *Comedy* is precisely this—the putting to positive social use of a religious discourse.)

Averroes not only affirms the value of religion in general, but he also affirms the superiority of Islam.[37] In *The Incoherence of the Incoherence*, he says that one ought to "choose the best religion of his age, although all of them are equally true."[38] But one might ask: if all religions are equally true, how can one of them be deemed superior to others? The answer is that a religion is not deemed better because it is "more true" (in fact the truth-content of all virtuous religions is identical) but rather because, in a given time and place, it *works* better to organize the laws, practices, and ethical attitudes of a community. Since a religion amounts to a universal rational/theoretical truth (common to all religions but accessible only to philosophically acute interpreters) *plus* practical prescriptions (accessible to all members of a community), what makes for distinctions and rankings among religions lies entirely on the practical, "lawgiving" side of things. Some prophets have given laws that are better—that work better—than others (in certain concrete historical situations).

In Averroes's view Islam, with its explicit prescription of regular and collective ritual practices, better organizes its adherents into a peaceful, virtuous, and just civil society than do the other religions of the age.[39] Since the masses do not generally give heed to things that rise higher than the grossly physical or literal, Islam's graphic and concrete depictions of the bodily pains and pleasures, punishments and rewards, of Hell and Heaven are more conducive to social order than are the more "spiritual" depictions of Christianity.[40] But the primary reason for Islam's superiority is its status as the only "inclusive" religious Law, one that with its concern for the welfare of *all* humans aims to unite the diverse nations, races, and ethnicities:

> Because of the universality of the teaching of the Precious Book and the universality of the laws contained in it—by which I mean their liability to promote the happiness of all mankind—this religion is common to all

194   DANTE'S PLURALISM AND RELIGION IN ISLAM

mankind. That is why the Almighty says, "Say, 'Oh people, I am Allah's Messenger to you all.' " [7.157] The Prophet, peace be upon him, has said, "I was sent to the white [literally, "red"] and to the black nations."[41] It appears that the case of religions is similar to that of foods. Just as there are some foods that suit all people (or at least most of them), the same is true of religions. It is for this reason that all religions which have preceded ours were intended specifically for one people rather than another, whereas our religion was intended for all mankind.[42]

According to the early Islamic "occasions" commentary tradition (which offers historical accounts of the events which gave rise to the revelation of specific Quranic verses), Muhammad, upon reentering Mecca as its leader following several years of exile and conflict, asked Bilal, a black African, to call the people to prayer. Several prominent Meccans, newly converted to Islam, were horrified by what was in their eyes a "disgrace." It is the racial prejudice of these Meccans that occasioned the revelation of Qur'an 49.13: "And We made you nations and tribes that you might get to know one another." God wills both diversity and the opportunity it offers to bring people together through encountering differences. In his "farewell address" to Muslims, delivered at Arafat shortly before his death, Muhammad reiterated this principle as one of the fundamental teachings of Islam: "All mankind is from Adam and Eve, an Arab has no superiority over a non-Arab nor a non-Arab has any superiority over an Arab; also a white has no superiority over a black nor a black has any superiority over a white except by piety and good action." And it is this theme of unity through diversity that Averroes singles out as the basis for Islam's preeminence. Islam works better than the other Laws because, by deliberately striving to include "the black and the white," in its purposeful embrace of diversity, it better establishes a model for global peace, unity, and justice.

But, if Islam is intended to unify all of humankind, it does not aim to do so by offering to all one and the same message. Rather, it aims to gain universal assent by offering various levels of discourse suitable for a variety of audiences. The most basic distinction is between those who give their assent to scripture's "apparent" meaning and those who give their assent to its "inner" meaning: "The reason why the Law came down containing both an apparent and an inner meaning," says Averroes, "lies in the diversity of people's natural capacities and the difference of their innate dispositions with regard to assent."[43] Those who respond favorably to the "apparent" (i.e., literal) meaning are the multitudes, for whom the Qur'an's "rhetorical" level of discourse (its imagery and its various persuasive devices) is well suited. Those who are instead attracted by the "inner meaning" are the theologians and the philosophers. The theologians and the philosophers are themselves distinguished by their methods of argument: the theological method is "dialectical," meaning that it constructs syllogistic arguments based upon first premises that are a matter of opinion, belief, hearsay, or authority; the philosophical method is "demonstrative," meaning that it constructs syllogistic arguments based upon first premises that are immediately grasped as true and certain. The result is that theological conclusions are a matter of opinion, while philosophical conclusions are a matter of truth. So we see that Averroes distinguishes between three primary classes of audience:

> Thus the people in relation to the Law fall into three classes.
>
> One class is those who are not people of interpretation at all: these are the rhetorical class. They are the overwhelming multitude, for no man of sound intellect is exempted from this kind of assent.
>
> Another class is the people of dialectical interpretation: these are the dialecticians [i.e., theologians]. . .
>
> Another class is the people of certain interpretation: these are the demonstrative class, by nature and training, that is, the art of philosophy. This interpretation ought not to be expressed to the dialectical class, let alone to the multitude.[44]

In fulfilling its aim to construct a universal community, the Qur'an takes into account this diversity in humankind's hermeneutic capacities. In the same way, the human teacher should always bear in mind that the message must be tailored to suit the audience—a fact that Averroes sees indicated in a saying of one of the Prophet's companions: "Speak to people about what they know. Do you want God and His Prophet to be accused of lying?"[45] Scripture offers something for everyone, but it does not offer any single doctrine that must be acknowledged by everyone:

> We say: the purpose of the Law is to teach true science and right practice. . .But not everyone has the natural ability to take in demonstrations, or even dialectical arguments, let alone demonstrative arguments, which are so hard to learn and need so much time even for those who are qualified to learn them. Therefore, since it is the purpose of the Law simply to teach everyone, the Law has to contain every method of bringing about judgments of assent and every method of forming concepts.[46]

It should be noted that this hermeneutic diversity pertains solely to the Law's theoretical content (what is here called "true science"—assertions concerning the way things really are). The multitudes, who accept literal representations for reality, think that God really does have, for instance, a hand and a throne, and they believe that the Qur'an's depictions of the bodily torments and delights of Hell and Paradise, respectively, amount to accurate information concerning reality. Theologians of one school think that the Qur'an assures them, for instance, that God's will is uncreated, while theologians of a differing school think that it tells them that God's will is created. Philosophers, for their part, find in the Qur'an confirmation of their Aristotelian understanding of reality. Thus, on the theoretical or doctrinal level, there is no possibility for unanimity: "It is not possible for general unanimity to be established about interpretations."[47] Diversity of doctrines concerning reality will never be—and never ought to be— effaced. In its teachings concerning "right practice," however, the Qur'an, demanding no interpretation, calls for unanimity. On the level of practice, all humans are of equal capacity: we can all adhere to laws, do virtuous deeds, perform prescribed rituals, and live in peace with respect for others. Right practice requires no special philosophical or theological acumen.[48]

The "people of interpretation," whether philosophers or theologians, above all ought not try to turn the "people of no interpretation" into inter-preters: "Interpretations ought not be expressed to the multitude."[49] By attempting to present to the masses a philosophized Qur'an that they will either not understand or not accept, the philosopher would cause the mul-titudes either to lose their faith, withdraw assent, and hence stray from right practice, or else to react aggressively against the philosophers ("If divulged to the common people, they would either renounce religion or regard those who divulge such [philosophical] views [e.g., the denial of God's cor-poreality] to them as unbelievers").[50] The theologized Qur'ans of the dialecticians, for their part, plunge the (ideally) unified community into sectarian conflict. In trying to make their particular interpretations into generally held ones, the theologians nearly fatally undermine the very aim of the Law, since rather than to work for peace they instead stand as the instigators of violence:

> From this it will be clear to you that true [i.e. demonstrative, philosophical] interpretations ought not be set down in popular books, let alone false [i.e., dialectical, theological] ones. . . .It was due to interpretations—especially the false ones—and the supposition that such interpretations of the Law ought to be expressed to everyone, that the sects of Islam arose, with the result that each one accused the others of unbelief or heresy. . . .In consequence they threw people into hatred, mutual detestation, and wars, tore the Law to shreds, and completely divided people.[51]

The aim of Islam is the construction of an undivided, yet at the same time diverse, human community. A condition for the undivided community is freedom for a multiplicity of beliefs, interpretations, and understandings— even including the freedom to have no understanding.

But the theologians (whom Averroes regards as the major instigators of violence in the world) fail to recognize that the Law's power is grounded in its hermeneutic openness. They would force people to give assent to one particular understanding of "the way things really are." The theologian's error is mistaking a message that is there in the Qur'an to gain *the theologian's* assent for a universal message that *all* Muslims must embrace or acknowledge. But in Averroes's view the Qur'an does not offer any grounds for deciding theological disputes. The point of Averroes's own exegetical performances is to show that Scripture leaves theological questions in a state of unresolved ambiguity. By refraining from offering unequivocal answers to such questions, the Law is all the better able to gain universal assent. If it were to absolutely exclude certain dialectically possible conclusions, it would fail to appeal to some segments of the theologically inclined. Instead, the Qur'an offers to every sect, and to each of the three main classes of audience, something that is attuned to what they already know and what they wish to find. As Averroes says: "Thus, one must observe the limits which religion has set with respect to the instruction it has proposed for each class of people, and avoid mixing up the. . .kinds of instruction, destroying thereby the religious and the prophetic wisdom [i.e., the Qur'an's discursive power to gain assent]. That is why the Prophet, God's peace be on him, said: 'We, the prophets, have been ordered to put people in their places, and to address them according to their rational capacities.' "[52]

So for Averroes the doctrinal content of the Qur'an is much less important than its discursive power to gain assent from nearly every audience:

> For the natures of men are on different levels with respect to their paths to assent. One of them comes to assent through demonstration; another comes to assent through dialectical arguments, just as firmly as the demonstrative man through demonstration, since his nature does not contain any greater capacity; while another comes to assent through rhetorical arguments, again just as firmly as the demonstrative man through demonstrative arguments.
>
> Thus since this divine Law of ours has summoned people by these methods, assent to it has been extended to everyone. . . .It was for this purpose that the Prophet, peace on him, was sent with a special mission to "the white man and the black man alike." I mean because this Law embraces all the methods of summons to God, the Exalted. This is clearly expressed in the saying of God, the Exalted, "Summon to the way of your Lord by wisdom and good preaching, and debate with them in the most *effective* manner" [16.125].[53]

Citing the same Tradition concerning "the white and the black" that he elsewhere takes to indicate Islam's inclusive embrace of cultural diversity,

Averroes now takes it to indicate as well Islam's openness to hermeneutic diversity: there is room for the interpretation of one reader (figured as the white man) even when it differs from the interpretation of another reader (figured as the black man).

The Qur'an aims to bring all humankind together in universal assent to its *practical* message (peace, justice, law) by providing a diversity of *theoretical/doctrinal* messages and by sanctioning a diversity of methodological approaches—ranging from having no method, to having a faulty method, to having a true method. Primacy lies in the effectiveness rather than the truth of the message. The Aristotelian content is there to attract philosophers to embrace Islam and its prescriptions for right practice. The Law, the goal of which is maximal inclusiveness, shows its strategic efficacy by the fact that it can draw *even* philosophers into the fold of the faithful. Insofar as the Qur'an teaches "true science," this truth is intended to be understood only by a few, and then not to be taught to others. The ultimate end of the Qur'an's power to gain universal assent to a diversity of messages is a nonviolent global community: "God directs all men aright and helps everyone to love him; He unites their hearts in the fear of Him, and removes from them hatred and loathing."[54]

Averroes's rationalism does not aim to destroy anyone else's understanding of the Law. A theologian's interpretation, for instance, is not a delusion; its basis is there in the Qur'an, part of the strategy to gain the theologian's assent. And while Averroes clearly asserts that his own philosopher's understanding is the true one, this is of course exactly the sort of self-assurance that we ought to expect: the Qur'an could not gain Averroes's assent if he thought otherwise.

Averroes's project in his writings on religion and philosophy aims almost literally to "disarm" al-Ghazali, who asserted that, although few in number, there are nonetheless some theoretical doctrines which warrant the death penalty for those who maintain them. Averroes works to lower the stakes in the game of "right interpretation." God does not much mind if the philosopher or the theologian "gets things wrong."[55] He reserves his wrath instead for those who, getting it wrong, are persuaded that they are right and that they must persuade everyone else that they are right.

From *Convivio* to *Comedy*

Before we continue along our path, let us briefly pause to consider how our bearing in mind Averroes's views on philosophical and prophetic discourse may open helpful perspectives for our understanding of Dante.[56]

It is widely recognized that the *Comedy* corrects Dante's *Convivio* in some fashion. The famous *selva oscura* ("dark wood") in which Dante finds himself lost in *Inferno* I is taken to be the overall orientation of his intellectual project when he was writing the *Convivio*. Dante left that book unfinished after coming to see that it was leading him down the "wrong path," and his turning to write the *Comedy* signals his discovery of the "right path." This "conversion" is normally understood as Dante's rejecting "philosophy" and embracing "theology"—a conversion from Aristotelian rationalism to Christian mysticism (see part I).

The problem with the *Convivio* is not that it is philosophical. Rather, the problem is that Dante at that time was attempting to philosophize for "the multitude." The whole aim of the book is to teach Aristotle to those who have neither the natural capacity nor the inclination for philosophy. At the same time, he tries to turn people who may previously simply have enjoyed his lyric poetry for the beauty of its rhetoric and imagery into people who see that the true meaning of that poetry is its philosophical content. On both of these counts—attempting to turn non-philosophers into philosophers and attempting to turn "people of no interpretation" into "people of interpretation"—Dante violates Averroes's principles. He fails to be mindful of the diversity of hermeneutic capacities, and hence he limits his text's power to gain assent.

In the *Convivio*, Dante represents himself as a mediator between philosophers and the ordinary folk. Philosophy is figured as "the bread of angels," while the everyday non-philosophical understanding of things is figured as "the food of sheep." Dante's task is to offer everyone the occasion to share the "bread" heretofore enjoyed only by a happy few:

> Blessed are the few who sit at the table where *the bread of the angels* is eaten, and most unfortunate those who share *the food of sheep*!
>
> . . . . Therefore I (who do not sit at the blessed table, but, having fled the pasture of the common herd, gather up a part of what falls to the feet of those who do sit there, and who know the unfortunate life of those I have left behind, for the sweetness that I taste in what I gather up piece by piece, and moved by compassion, though not forgetting myself) have set aside for those who are unfortunate something that I placed before their eyes some time ago, by which I have increased their desire.[57]

Dante's aim in the *Convivio* is to offer Aristotelian philosophy—"the bread of angels"—to an audience not accustomed or inclined to enjoy such food.

He will do so in the form of a commentary on some of his previously circulated lyric poems. He indicates that these poems have not yet been interpreted correctly, since they have not been seen as possessing philosophical meaning. He proposes to remedy this by interpreting the poems for his audience, providing them with the bread (philosophical content) that they have been lacking:

> By lacking the present *bread* they [i.e., Dante's lyric poems] possessed some degree of obscurity, so that to many their beauty was more pleasing than their goodness. But this *bread* (that is, the present explanation) will be the light that renders visible every shade of their meaning.[58]

Dante is saying that his lyric poems have, beyond the merely literal and rhetorical level, a truth content, and that this truth content, the "bread of angels," is identical to the truth of philosophy. What is Dante doing here if not reading his own lyric poetry in the manner that Averroes reads the Qur'an? Both say that the "apparent" meaning coexists with an "inner" meaning to which philosophers will give their assent. But, contrary to Averroes, Dante thinks that the multitude ought to be made to see this fact—and not only to see it, but to be made to partake of the bread and to enjoy it. The poems will not achieve their full "goodness" unless *everyone* is made to see that they are in harmony with philosophy. In the *Convivio*, Dante thinks that the truth content needs to be made universal. His theory of the value of texts—his notion that one message fits all audiences—lacks the hermeneutic complexity of Averroes's.

Turning to the *Comedy*, we see clearly that Dante rejects this urge to universalize the poem's message. He does so near the beginning of *Paradiso*, using the very phrase "bread of angels," while making a distinction between the diversity of the hermeneutic capacities of various audiences. Whereas in the *Convivio* he aimed to share the bread of angels with everyone, in the *Comedy* it is reserved for the happy few.

Paradiso II opens with Dante's address to the multitude of readers: he in effect tells them *not* to read *Paradiso* because it will exceed their capacity to grasp its meaning:

> O you that are in your little bark,
> eager to hear, following behind
> my ship that singing makes her way,
>
> turn back to see again your shores.
> Do not commit yourselves to the open sea,
> for, if you lost me, you would perhaps remain astray [*smarriti*]
> (*Par.* II, 1–6)

In this *smarriti* ("astray") we hear an echo of the *Comedy*'s opening stanza, in which Dante laments that he had lost the right path ("the straight way was lost [*smarrita*]"). In moving from *Purgatory* to *Paradiso* Dante willingly bids adieu to the multitude of readers, recognizing that the highly theoretical, philosophical, and theological verse of the third canticle is a "surplus" that can only lead the multitude astray from what is for them the right path—the path of right practice. As Averroes says, forcing non-philosophers to engage in a philosophical understanding of scripture will backfire, making them more likely to reject rather than to give assent to the Law. In fact, Averroes says that the philosopher or the theologian who insists on trying to instruct the vulgar masses, on divulging to the multitudes things that he ought keep to himself or circulate only among his peers, causes people to lose the right path and to go astray—and for doing so he is himself to be reckoned as one who "diverges from the right path of religion in these matters [and] has gone astray."[59] Returning to the "right path" does not mean (as Freccero says it does) converting from philosophy to theology. Rather, it means renouncing the idea that all humans must know philosophy. To return to the right path is to learn to keep relatively quiet concerning philosophy, to speak of philosophy to other philosophers but not to the multitudes.

For most readers, the goal of the *Comedy* is located at the summit of Mt. Purgatory. Such readers will have been exposed through rhetorical and literal imagery to examples of vice and virtue, and this is sufficient foundation for their exercise of right practice. (Averroes: "The thoughts of the general public. . .are moved to follow the Scriptures and practice the virtues."[60]) They do not need "theory" or "science" concerning the way things really are. (Averroes's specific point in the passage just cited is that the general public does not need to have a "correct conception of the resurrection"; instead, it is probably best, for them and for society as a whole, if they do not.) The masses do not need truth. But the Dante who opened the *Convivio* by citing Aristotle's famous "all men naturally desire to know" did not himself know that real knowledge is not the natural *telos* of every human existence (Averroes maintains, as we saw in part I, that the faculty for theory only exists in some humans).

The *Convivio* now appears as an attempt to force-feed a theoretical understanding of things to the masses, for *Paradiso* reserves such a feast for a limited intellectual elite:

> You other few who lifted up your neck
> at times for *the bread of angels*,
> on which one here subsists but never becomes sated,
>
> You may indeed commit your vessel
> to the deep brine, holding to my furrow
> ahead of the water that turns smooth again.
>
> (*Par.* II, 10–15)

Now the "bread of angels" is proper fare for only an "other few." *Paradiso* is meant to be read only by aspiring and experienced philosophers and theologians. Dante no longer believes that the world will be saved by a universally cognized discourse of truth. Rather, he recognizes that the assent of most will be gained by rhetoric, while the assent of the few will be gained by truth.

In renouncing the *Convivio* in favor of the *Comedy*, Dante turns from writing as a philosopher to writing as a prophet. A prophetic text, as Averroes tells us, aims to teach everyone. But this universal teaching is accomplished by a diversity of sometimes incompatible doctrines, and by a multileveled discursive strategy. The prophetic text teaches right practice to everyone, reserving its teaching of right theory for an "other few." Such a text operates by employing all registers—philosophical, theological, and literal/rhetorical. This thought may well help us overcome our wrangling over what the *Comedy* "really" is. Is it really meant to be taken as a literal depiction of reality? Is it really theology? Is it really philosophy? Following Averroes, we can affirm that it is really all of these—but it is not so for any one reader. Some audiences will grant their assent to its literal depictions and rhetorical devices; others to its theological doctrines; others to its philosophical tenets. The *Convivio* erred in attempting to teach all humans one and the same set of philosophical doctrines. But what matters about the *Comedy* is not so much its doctrine as its effectiveness to draw humans together in assent to a global community of peace and justice. In both its ultimate goal and its discursive strategies, the *Comedy* is akin to the Qur'an as understood by Averroes.

The Brotherhood of the Pure

The efforts of Andalusians such as Ibn Tufayl and Averroes to show that "reason and tradition are at one"—that all who are guided by the sun of philosophy, regardless of their religions, will find themselves in accord—were by no means unprecedented in the history of Islamic thought. Nearly two centuries earlier a group of Shi'ite thinkers known as the Ikhwan al-Safa ("The Brotherhood of the Pure"), writing in Basra (Iraq) around 1,000 AD, composed the encyclopedia of knowledge known as the *Rasa'il* (*Epistles*). The Ikhwan al-Safa, whose *Epistles* are largely unavailable in any European language, "are as well known to an educated Arab as, say, the names of Descartes, Hegel, and Wittgenstein are to the cultured European."[61] While producing a compendium of treatises on every conceivable scientific and philosophical subject and establishing an Islamic cosmology that would hold sway for the next thousand years, the Brotherhood above all promoted harmony among the world's religions and peoples, driven by the notion that philosophy is not incompatible with the revealed scriptures of Islam (nor with the other revealed religions).

For the Brotherhood, all religious scriptures, indeed all written texts and oral traditions, are legitimate as potential sources of knowledge; all human communities have something valuable to contribute. "Know that," the Brotherhood asserts, "the truth is found in every religion and is current in every tongue. What you should do, however, is to take the best and to transfer yourself to it. Do not ever occupy yourself with imputing defects to the religions of people; rather try to see whether your religion is free from them."[62] As Abu Hayyan al-Tawhidi, a contemporary of the Brotherhood, writes concerning one of their members: "He stands in no definite relation with any one system. He knows how to form his school from all sides. . .If one could but unite Greek philosophy and the religious law of Islam, the perfection of the faith, they the Ikhwan thought, would be reached."[63] And as the modern scholar A.L. Tibawi says: "The Brotherhood of Purity believe that the Truth is one without it being the private work of anyone. God has sent His Spirit to all men, to Christians as to Muslims, to blacks as to whites."[64] In the words of the Brotherhood themselves, the ideal human is of "East Persian derivation, Arabic in faith, of Iraqi, that is, Babylonian, education, a Hebrew in astuteness, a disciple of Christ in conduct, as pious as a Syrian monk, a Greek in the individual sciences, an Indian in the interpretation of all mysteries, but lastly and especially, a Sufi in his whole spiritual life."[65] If priority is given to one's being a Sufi, this is because Sufism is, to a great degree, the very sort of all-embracing acceptance of diversity promoted by the Brotherhood.

Though originating in the East, the writings of the Brotherhood exerted a long-lasting and far-reaching influence in the West. (It has even been averred—though we should not place too much faith in this—that Dante himself was a member of a latter-day chapter of the Ikhwan.[66]) Both the letter and the spirit of the Brotherhood lived on among thirteenth-century Andalusian and Occitanian Jewry. For instance, Ya'aqov ben Makhir, borrowing from the Brotherhood, teaches as do they "the equivalence of all revealed religions" in passages such as this one: "Know that the ambition of the prophets of blessed memory in setting down the divine codes with which they were sent was one and the same correct ambition, even though their teaching (*toratom*) and the customs which they enacted vary with regard to the times of worship, the location of their houses of worship, their calling out and their prayer, just like the aim and desire of all medical doctors is the same, even though their methods of treatment vary."[67] There is, alongside the *Torah*, a plurality of other "*torahs*" suitable to various cultures, peoples, and communities.

For the Brotherhood, human cultural, racial, ethnic, and religious diversity is not a sign of human deficiency but rather is celebrated as the indicator of human nobility. In Epistle 22 ("Concerning the Generation of

Animals and their Species"), which includes a lengthy debate between animalkind and humankind concerning which is to be deemed superior, a man from India bears striking witness to the diversity and unity of humanity. Despite tremendous differences, humans are all one family, all children of the same father:

> "We children of Adam are the most multifarious of animals in numbers, in kind and types and as individuals. Our distinction is our varied experience of the vicissitudes of time and of diverse conditions and situations, the changes and revolutions we have known, the varied goals and the wonders we have seen."
>
> "How so? Explain this," demanded the King.
>
> "The reason is that the inhabited quarter of the earth comprises some nineteen thousand cities, of nations numberless. Among these countless peoples are those of China, India, Sind, Zanj, the Hijaz and the Yemen, Abyssinia, the Nejd, Nubia, Egypt, Sa'id, Alexandria, Cyrenaica, Qayrawan, Tunis, Tangier, Britain, the Canary Islands, Andalusia, Rome, Constantinople, Kalah—Berbers, Miyafarqis, Burjanis, Azerbaijanis, Nisibinis, Armenians, Damascenes, Georgians, Greeks, the folk of the two Diyars, of Iraq and Mahin, Khuzitan and Jebal, those of Khutlan, Badakhshan, Daylaman, Tabaristan, Jurjan, Jilan, Nishapur, Kirman, Kabulistan, Multan, Sijistan, Transoxiana, Jordan, Farghanah, Khwarizm, and the lands of the Khirghiz, Tibetans, and the dwellers in the land of Gog and Magog—not counting the people of villages and hamlets nor the Arabs or Kurds, the nomads of the deserts and wastes, nor the folk of the islands and strands, the forests and moors, all of whom are nations of humans, all of the race of Adam, of diverse colors and tongues, characters and natures, opinions and doctrines, crafts, ways of life and religions, all countless in number save only to God, exalted be He, who created and raised them, provided their sustenance, and knows their inmost essence and the most deep-seated core of their being—'All in a book written plain'."
>
> "The multiplicity of their numbers and the diversity of their situations, the variety and variability of their condition and the marvelous ends they pursue show that they are superior to others, higher than all other sorts of creatures on earth."[68]

Granting dignity and value to each of the diverse multiplicity of human communities, the Brotherhood refuse to set boundaries on their search for knowledge and truth. In fact this absolute openness is the very substance of their creed, as formulated in Epistle 44 ("Creed of the Brotherhood of Purity"), for their creed is

> to shun no science, scorn any book, or to cling fanatically to any single creed. For our own creed encompasses all the others and comprehends all

the sciences generally. This creed is the consideration of all existing things, both sensible and intelligible, from beginning to end, whether hidden or overt, manifest or obscure. . .insofar as they all derive from a single principle, a single cause, a single world, and a single Soul.[69]

Jihad and Crusade

The debate between animals and humans in Epistle 22 includes the Brotherhood's treatment of the question concerning the relation between religion and warfare. The gist of the Brotherhood's position is that coercive violence has nothing to do with religion and everything to do with politics. This amounts to an interpretation of *jihad* as something other than "holy war" as we normally understand the phrase.

The discussion of violence follows from talk concerning which group— animals or humankind—can more rightly be called "unified." A spokesperson for the humans, positing that unity is superior to diversity (in doing so he contradicts the abovementioned Indian, who sees diversity as a sign of superiority), argues that the manifest identity of humankind—the fact that we all share more or less the same physical form and appearance—is a sign that we outrank animals, who come in all shapes and sizes and exhibit every imaginable appearance. The argument is that a group the members of which all look alike is better than a group whose members all look different.

A representative of the animals retorts that human sameness and animal diversity are merely a matter of external physical form. Since the inner spirit outranks the outward form, unity of soul is superior to unity of bodily appearance. On this score, according to the animals, humans are sorely lacking, since human souls are hopelessly at odds with one another. This is proven above all by their contentiousness over matters of faith:

"For among them you find the Jews, the Christians, the Sabaeans, the Magians, polytheists, idolaters, worshippers of the sun and the moon, of the stars and planets, and other things besides. And you will find as well that the adherents of one faith differ in their schools and notions. Such were the doctrines and rival schools which existed among the ancient philosophers. Among the Jews there were the Samaritans, the Ananites and Exilarchs. Among the Christians, the Nestorians, Jacobites, and Melkites. Among the Magians, the Zoroastrians, Zurvanites, Khuramites, Mazdakites, and Manichaeans. There are Brahmans, sun worshippers; and among other sectarians, Buddhists and Disanites. Among the adherents of Islam there are Kharijites, Nasibites, Rafidites, Murji'ites, Qadarites, Jahmites, Mu'tazilites, Ash'arites, Shi'ites, Sunnites, and others whose pretensions and heresy cast doubt upon the faith, not to mention all sort of unbelievers and others whose notions closely resemble those of the factions and sects already mentioned, all of whom give the lie to one another and curse one another.

"But we [animals] are free of all such dissension. We have but one school of thought, one credo—all of us are monotheists, faithful muslims who do not assign God's divinity to any other nor fall into the ways of hypocrisy and crime. We have no doubt or skepticism, nor confusion or perplexity, no straying nor leading others astray. We seek refuge solely in God, our Creator, and Provider, who gives us life and death and whom we praise, sanctify, celebrate, and exalt morning and evening."[70]

Animals are all "muslim" in their instinctive submission to the order of creation. Their unity—hence superiority—is indicated by the homogeneity of their naturally intuited faith. The human spirit, on the contrary, is chaotically shattered by adherence to innumerable complicated and opposing beliefs.

Following this a Persian comes forward to rebut the animals' argument. He responds by taking a page from the animals' playbook, acknowledging that inner unity counts more than outer diversity. But what the animals have failed to see, he says, is that the apparent diversity of human religions pertains only to the external form of faith; the inner content of religions is in fact one and the same:

"Religions, doctrines, sects are only different paths of approach, different means and avenues, but the Goal we seek is one. From whatever quarter we seek to encounter Him, God is there."[71]

Despite the multiplicity of paths, God leads humans right on every path. The right path is whatever path one follows toward the goal.

This celebration of religious pluralism clearly undermines any justification for violence in the name of religion. But it is no less clear, as the King of the *jinn* (who is judging the debate) points out, that people of different faiths persist in killing one another. The Persian responds that violence against others, though it may cloak itself in the guise of religion, is purely a matter of politics, of "kings killing others in seeking dominion" and "the quest for primacy and power in the state":

"Why, then, do they slay one another if all their faiths have the same goal of encounter with God?"

"You are right, your Majesty," said the reflective Persian," this does not arise from faith, for 'there is no compulsion in faith'; rather it comes from the institution of faith, that is from the state. . . .The rule of a realm cannot do without religion, by which its people are to live. And religion cannot do without a ruler to command the people to uphold his institutions out of allegiance or by force. This is the cause of the adherents of different religions slaying one another—the quest for primacy and power in the state. Each desires that all people should follow his own faith or sect and the laws of his own religion. . . .The slaying of selves is an institution in all faiths, creeds, and confessions as well as all earthly dominions. However, the slaying of selves in religion is for the religious aspirant to slay his own self, whereas in the usage of kingdoms it means for the seeker of rule to slay others."

Said the King, "As for kings killing others in seeking dominion, that is plain and clear enough. But that seekers of faith slay themselves—how is that?"

"Let me explain. You are aware, your Majesty, in the faith of Islam, this is clearly and obviously an obligation. For God says, 'Lo, God has purchased of the faithful their substance and selves inasmuch as they shall have Paradise. Let them do battle in behalf of God, let them slay and be slain.' He says further, 'Rejoice in the sale of yourselves you have made.' And, 'God loves those who do battle in His behalf, in ranks like a closely knit structure.' And in the ordinance of the Torah He says, "Turn to your Creator and slay your selves. Your humbling of yourselves is beneficial to you in the eyes of your Creator.' And Christ says in the ordinance of the Gospel, 'Who are my helpers in the service of God?' The disciples answered 'We are God's helpers.' Then Christ said to them, 'Prepare for death and the cross if you wish to aid me, and you shall be with me in the Kingdom of my Heaven with my Father and your Father. Else you are none of mine.' And they were slain but did not forsake the Faith of Christ. . . .On the same pattern the principles and usages of all religions, it will be found, call for the slaying of the self by various forms of worship."[72]

Here the Brotherhood emphasizes the Qur'an's famous "no compulsion" verse ("Let there be no compulsion in religion" [2.256], taking it as a categorical prohibition of violence against others for the sake of religion. It reads in an allegorical key all other verses in the Qur'an that may be taken to contradict or abrogate the "no compulsion" verse. Such verses in its view in fact mandate the "Greater Jihad," the "striving" or "effort" (the primary meanings of the Arabic *jihad*) to improve or reform the self. All religions and all polities have encouraged or instituted killing. But whereas the polity legitimates killing others, religion only legitimates killing the self. And whereas for the state killing is literal and physical, for religion it is figural and moral—the "slaying" of the self. The religious motivation is not to force violent change upon others but rather to force it upon oneself.

In the central cantos of *Paradiso*, Dante dwells upon the Christian equivalent of jihad, "crusade." Although his concerns are not the same as those of the neoplatonic Brotherhood, for whom "slaying the self" involves the individual's overcoming the attractions of the physical world in favor of the spiritual and intellectual world (whereas for Dante it is a matter of a certain violence instigated by European society against itself, the collective political self-reform of Dante's society), there is nonetheless a similar logic at work: in both cases the only violence that is endorsed is self-directed, and that violence is conceived as a "nonviolent" compulsion to change. Dante envisions a "crusade" that precludes literal, physical violence against others.

In these cantos Dante represents his encounter with his great-great-grandfather Cacciaguida, a Florentine who fought against Islam in the Second Crusade (ca. 1147 AD). The encounter takes place in an obviously martial locus, the Sphere of Mars (which appears to Dante even "more red than usual" [*Par.* XIV, 87]), a place upon which entering Dante makes, as he says, "a holocaust to God" (XIV, 89). If the Italian *olocausto* did not yet mean the horror of genocide, it nonetheless did signify a sacrifice in the form of a burning destruction. The crusader Cacciaguida is in the company of other renowned "holy warriors" (Joshua, Charlemagne and Roland, Godfrey of Bouillon, among others), and collectively they appear to Dante in the form of the Cross, insignia of the crusader. All of these details combine to prepare us for what we assume will be a glorification of righteous, holy violence, a defense of the burning martial impulse when its energies are channeled, as with the Crusades, into violence against non-Christians in defense of the faith.

If warfare is undoubtedly the issue at the center of *Paradiso*, it is no less clear that these cantos treat not so much warfare in general as *Dante's* warfare. The *Comedy* is of course a highly personal poem; Dante himself is its hero. But this notion of Dante as "hero" (in the classical, martial sense) is nowhere so impressed upon us as it is in these cantos. For what one must above all bear in mind is that the whole episode of Dante's encounter with his great-great-grandfather in the Sphere of Mars is modeled on Aeneas's encounter with his father Anchises in Book VI of the *Aeneid*. Dante compels us to recognize that he is presenting himself as nothing less than the new Aeneas. Just as that glorious hero was the great founding figure of the Roman Empire, Dante will himself be the great founder of the new global Empire.

Consider, for instance, the "holocaust" which Dante offers to God upon entering the Sphere of Mars. Similarly, Aeneas must offer "holocausts" to the gods in preparation for his descent into Hades in search of his father's shade: "With *holocausts* he Pluto's altar fills; / Sev'n brawny bulls with his own hand he kills."[73] The Sphere of Mars is in a sense Dante's Hades—the place where he will encounter the soul of his deceased ancestor, who will offer him a prophetic glimpse of his heroic future and instill in him the courage to endure unceasing hardship in the pursuit of his destined mission. In the case of Aeneas, this mission—founding a Rome that will "rule mankind, and make the world obey"[74]—depends upon a necessary period of violence, of which the bloody ritual holocausts are the adumbration. Anchises teaches Aeneas that Rome's glory will be founded on its mastery of the arts of warfare. As the sibyl who guides Aeneas into Hades tells him, in what amounts to a synopsis of Rome's history from the time of Aeneas to the time of Augustus: "Wars, horrid wars, I view—a field of blood, / And Tiber rolling with a purple flood."[75] In the same way Dante will be shown that he must accept his calling as a warrior, that the accomplishment of his fated mission is predicated upon his inflicting a certain violence.

The most explicit allusion to book VI of the *Aeneid* comes in the form of a parallel drawn between Cacciaguida and Anchises (and by extension between Dante and Aeneas). Dante's great-great-grandfather darts toward him in a movement of affection that recalls that of Aeneas's father when visited by his son in the underworld:

> With like affection did the shade of Anchises
> stretch forward (if our greatest Muse merits belief),
> when in Elysium he perceived his son.
>
> "*O sanguis meus. . . .*" ["O my flesh and blood. . . ."]
> (*Par.* XV, 25–28)

Cacciaguida's pride and joy in seeing his "blood relative" and his frequent allusions to his genealogical link to Dante are themselves borrowed from the episode of Aeneas's underworld visit with his father; Cacciaguida's *sanguis meus*, addressed here to Dante, is a direct citation of Anchises speech in book VI.[76] These allusions to the *Aeneid* are meant to reinforce our sense of Dante not only as "hero" but specifically as a military one. Like Aeneas, Dante is a virtuous warrior who will employ violence for the sake of a righteous cause.

The central cantos of *Paradiso*, then, do not so much present for Dante's disinterested admiration a collection of famous holy warriors as they present *Dante himself* embracing his role *as a crusader*. He will act as one who "takes up his cross and follows Christ" (XIV, 106). But does this simply mean that Dante will participate, in some fashion, in a religious war, the Christian "reconquest" of the Holy Lands that have been illegitimately occupied by Muslims? Is the structural center of *Paradiso* rightly viewed as Dante's endorsement of the Crusades?

Surprising as it may sound, Paradise is not a place free from error. Dante tells us this at the beginning of Canto XVI, where he indicates that he has been infected with one of Cacciaguida's false values, pride in one's genealogy:

> O our petty nobility of blood!
> If you make folk [*la gente*] glory in you
> here below where our affections languish,
>
> it will nevermore be a marvel to me;
> since there where appetite is not warped,
> I mean in Heaven, I myself gloried in you.
>   (*Par.* XVI, 1–6)

In Paradise Dante is momentarily caught up in Cacciaguida's error, his glorying in the nobility of his own *gente* (from the Latin *gens*, "family, tribe, nation, people"). Cacciaguida's speech is marked by the language of the "family tree":

> "Blessed be Thou, Three and One,
> Who show such favor to my *seed*."
>   (*Par.* XV, 47–48)

> "O my *branch*, in whom I take delight
> only expecting you, I was your *root*."
>   (*Par.* XV, 88–89)

Dante for his part is not immune, for he responds in kind, employing that same arboreal/genealogical metaphor ("O dear *root* of me" [*Par.* XVII, 13]; "Tell me then, dear *stock* from which I spring" [*Par.* XVI, 22]). It is this pride in his *gente* which Dante recognizes, after the fact, as an error.

Cacciaguida is still deluded by a notion of "nobility of blood" that had become outmoded among the intellectuals of Dante's day.[77] This indicates that Cacciaguida's speech is marked by the values of the past, and thus we should take care to read his words with a critical eye. The fact that Cacciaguida is Dante's great-great-grandfather, not his father (as Anchises is Aeneas's father) works to open up a considerable generation gap between the two. Dante calls our attention to Cacciaguida's standing as a figure from a relatively remote past by having him speak Latin not Italian, emphasizing the fact by calling his ancestor's tongue "not this our modern speech" (XVI, 33). Cacciaguida is, in brief, strikingly old-fashioned.

Cacciaguida is most remembered by Dante's readers for his speech praising Florence's "good old days" and condemning its present. It is on the basis of this speech that Dante is frequently regarded as a political reactionary, longing for a return to the past. But such a reading commits a cardinal sin of literary interpretation: mistaking the values of a character in a work for those of the work's author. In fact, Cacciaguida's thinking—the thinking of a fairly distant past—is *not* equivalent to Dante's "modern" thinking. Although perhaps Dante might be comfortable with some of his great-great-grandfather's notions, there are many things in Cacciaguida's idealized picture of the Florentine past that Dante cannot accept:

"Florence, within her ancient circle
from which she still takes tierce and nones,
abode in peace, sober and chaste.

There was no necklace, no coronal,
no embroidered gowns, no girdle
that was more to be looked at than the person.

Not yet did the daughter at her birth
cause fear to the father, for the time and the dowry
did not outrun due measure on this side and that.

Houses empty of family there were none,
nor had Sardanapulus arrived yet
to show what could be done in chamber. . . .

Bellincion Berti have I seen go girt
with leather and bone, and his wife come
from her mirror with unpainted face.

I have seen de' Nerli and del Vecchio
content in unlined skin,
and their wives at the spindle and the distaff. . . .

The one kept watch in minding the cradle,
and, soothing, spoke that speech
which first delights fathers and mothers.

The other, as she drew the threads from the distaff,
would tell her households about the
Trojans, and Fiesole, and Rome. . . .

To so reposeful, to so fair a life
of citizens, to such a trusty community,
To so sweet an abode,

Mary, called on with loud cries,
gave me, and in your ancient Baptistery
I became at once a Christian and Cacciaguida."

(*Par.* XV, 97–135)

(Sardanapulus, "king of Assyria, was notorious in antiquity for his luxury and effeminacy."[78]) In Cacciaguida's eyes, Florence used to be peopled with manly men and natural, virtuous women; now it is filled with women who wear make-up and men who tend toward the queer. Cacciaguida's prudish austerity, his manifest disgust at female grace and sensuous beauty, are greatly at odds with Dante's stilnovist appreciation of all things feminine, and we must surmise that the great-great-grandfather would have been embarrassed by the delicate charm of the *Vita Nuova*. Cacciaguida's horror at the thought of experimental sexuality clashes with the openness of a Dante who in *Inferno* entertains the idea of enjoying himself in a homosexual *ménage à quatre*.[79] His insistence that women be kept "in their place," restricted to the activities of making clothes, watching the children, and telling popular tales in the vernacular (Latin being reserved exclusively for the use of educated men), makes for a world in which the emergence of a Beatrice—past-master, though female, of Latin philosophy and theology— would be unthinkable.[80] When we also consider that his small-town xenophobia and his fear of miscegenation ("The intermingling of people was ever / the beginning of harm to the city"; XVI, 67–68) are opposed to Dante's cosmopolitanism, we must come to picture Dante's great-great-grandfather as a quintessential curmudgeon, a grumpy old man.[81]

If we cannot trust that Cacciaguida simply gives voice to Dante's own values, then we cannot regard his notion of "crusade" as the last word on the subject. For Cacciaguida, whose Christianity is infantile in the sense that it is a status granted him at birth that he never once subjects to doubt ("I became at once a Christian and Cacciaguida"), crusade is a matter of following along in his society's unquestioning disdain for other religions and races:

> "Afterward I followed the Emperor Conrad,
> who girt me with his knighthood [*milizia*],
> so much did I win his favor by good work.
>
> I went, in his train, against the iniquity
> of that Law [i.e., Islam] whose people, through
> fault of the Pastors, usurp your right.
>
> There by that foul race [*gente turpa*]
> I was released from the deceitful world,
> the love of which debases many souls,
>
> and I came from martyrdom to this peace."
>   (*Par.* XV, 139–148)

For Cacciaguida, the old-fashioned crusader, there can be no violence more righteous than that exercised in fighting a foul folk and its bad religion. But this is the crusade of the past—the foil against which Dante will set his crusade of the future.

When Dante is given his marching orders, the means and the object of his new crusade have little in common with the crusade of the past. After sharing with Dante some prophetic insight concerning the hardships of his coming exile, Cacciaguida (who regardless of his past nature shares with all the shades in the afterlife a clear vision of the future) encourages him nonetheless to strike violently against his enemies:

> "A conscience dark,
> either with its own or with another's shame,
> will indeed feel your speech to be harsh.
>
> But nonetheless, all falsehood set aside,
> make manifest all that you have seen;
> and let them scratch where the itch is.
>
> For if at first taste your voice be grievous,
> yet shall it leave thereafter
> vital nourishment when digested.
>
> This cry of yours shall do as does the wind,
> which smites most upon the loftiest summits;
> and this shall be no little cause of honor."
> (*Par.* XVII, 124–135)

Dante will gain honor on the battlefield by "smiting" with his "cry"; it is with the "wind" of his words that he will strike. Aeneas is encouraged in his meeting with Anchises to take up arms; Dante is encouraged in his meeting with Cacciaguida to take up his pen. He will write rather than fight—or, more precisely, he will fight by writing. The *Comedy* will be the weapon that he wields to wage verbal warfare against the "loftiest summits," the great powers of Europe.

If the means by which the crusade of the future is waged—the deployment of the non-violent violence of literature—is markedly different from the crusade of the past, so too is the object of the new crusade. For Dante will aim his attack not against non-European non-Christian others but rather against the very institutional center of Christian Europe—the papacy. The *Comedy* preaches a crusade against the church, against those who hold the office of St. Peter. More precisely, Dante fights for the church against the church, for Peter against Peter. His crusade amounts to a "slaying of the self": Peter must be sacrificed so that Peter may be saved. So we see that in the center of *Paradiso* Dante works to invert the usual logic of holy war: crusade is no longer an externally directed physical violence against the other but rather has become an internally directed verbal violence against the self.[82]

Peter versus Peter

In Canto XXVII of *Paradiso* St. Peter approaches Dante for the second time; this "transmuted" Peter looks and sounds different from the Peter who had examined Dante on articles of faith in Canto XXIV. This Peter has taken on the color of Mars; in appearance he has become "as would

Jupiter if he and Mars / were birds and should exchange plumage"
(XXVII, 14–15). The change from the white of Jupiter to the red of Mars
indicates a reiteration of Dante's mission as a holy warrior. This "martial"
Peter reinforces what Dante had learned in the Sphere of Mars concerning
both the means and the object of his crusade: Dante must use the words of
the *Comedy* to fight the papacy. Peter indicates that the "Peter" whom
humans see ruling the "church" on earth is a fraudulent usurper, an enemy
of God against whom battle in defense of the true church must be waged:

> "If I change color,
> marvel not, for, as I speak,
> you shall see all these change color.
>
> He who on earth usurps my place,
> my place, my place, which in the
> sight of the Son of God is vacant,
>
> has made my burial-ground a sewer
> of blood and of stench, so that the Perverse One
> who fell from here above takes comfort there below. . . ."
>
> Then his words continued,
> in a voice so altered from itself
> that his looks were not more changed,
>
> "The spouse of Christ [i.e., the church] was not nurtured
> on my blood and that of Linus and of Cletus,
> to be employed for the gain of gold;
>
> but for gain of this happy life [i.e., Heaven]
> Sixtus and Pius and Calixtus and Urban
> shed their blood after much weeping.
>
> It was not our purpose that one part of the
> Christian people should sit on the right
> of our successors, and one part on the left. . . .
>
> Rapacious wolves in shepherd's garb
> are seen from here above in all the pastures:
> O defense of God, why do you yet lie still?
>
> Cahorsines and Gascons make ready
> to drink our blood. O good beginning
> to what vile ending must you fall!
>
> But the high Providence, which with
> Scipio defended for Rome the glory of the world,
> will succor speedily, as I conceive.
>
> And you, my son, who, because of your mortal weight
> will again return below, open your mouth
> and do not hide what I hide not."
>
> (*Par.* XXVII, 19–66)

Peter here calls upon Dante to play a leading role in the defense of the faith against its enemies. But these are not some imagined external enemies threatening from some distant land; rather, the chief enemies of the faith are its recognized chiefs, the popes. The "threat of terror" comes from within Christendom itself: those Cahorsines and Gascons who are "making ready to drink our blood" are Pope John XXII, who hailed from Cahors in Occitania and became pope in 1316 (he was thus the current pope when Dante wrote these lines), and his immediate predecessor, Pope Clement V, who hailed from Gascony. From its "good beginning" in Peter himself, the church has come to a "vile ending" in Peter's self-proclaimed but bogus successors.

Dante does not appear to recognize the legitimacy of any popes since Sylvester I, who bears a terrible burden of guilt for accepting the Donation of Constantine (ca. 314 AD), the point in history after which the boundary separating church and state became blurred.[83] The popes here praised by Peter (Linus, Cletus, Sixtus, Pius, Calixtus, Urban) are all early popes (from the first three centuries AD). And, in recent times, it is Satan himself ("the Perverse One / who fell from here above") who has found refuge and comfort by usurping and perverting the papacy. Dante's mission as a *jihadist* in defense of the faith is to fight the Great Satan, the Whore of Babylon—the official Catholic Church that has ruled illegitimately for the past thousand years. The *Comedy* is a weapon that will help restore the early church, whose sole role was to serve as a spiritual example that might guide humans toward Heaven; it will do so by destroying the church as a temporal institution claiming political and legal authority here on earth.

In his treatise *On Kingly and Papal Power* (ca. 1302), John of Paris, although on the whole siding with the kings in their effort to argue that political authority belongs first of all to them and not to the popes, nonetheless sees himself as steering a middle way between two extremes. On the one hand are champions of the church such as Giles of Rome, who had argued in *On Ecclesiastical Power* (ca. 1301) that the pope has complete "power and jurisdiction in all areas of human life."[84] Their error is, John says, their assertion that "the Pope, in so far as he occupies the place of Christ on earth, has dominion over the temporal goods of princes and barons, as well as cognizance of, and jurisdiction over, them."[85] On the other hand are those (whom we recognize as Spiritual Franciscans and various sects of "heretics") who "argue that the prelates of the church of God, the successors of the apostles, should not have any dominion over temporal riches."[86] Between these two extremes (that the church rightly owns everything and that the church rightly owns nothing), John presents a compromise: the church may rightly possess dominion and jurisdiction over those temporal things that have been granted it by the state or by individual benefactors.

My point here is not to elucidate Dante's position on the church's right to the possession of temporal things—although it can be shown to be close if not identical to that of the heretics and the Spiritual Franciscans (Dante refers to Sylvester I, the first post-Donation—and hence fraudulent—pope, as "the first rich father,"[87] and Peter here indicates that his satanic pseudo-successors have "employed" the church "for the gain of gold"). Rather, it is to suggest that Dante's critique of the church was hardly distinguishable, in its main outlines, from that of those whom the church called "heretics." Even a strident proponent of the power of the state such as John of Paris does not hesitate to categorize a position such as Dante's as extreme, an "error":

> The error of the Waldenses consisted in saying that dominion in temporal matters was inconsistent with the successors of the Apostles, that is, the Pope and the ecclesiastical prelates, and that they were not allowed to possess temporal riches. Hence, they say, the church of God and the successors of the apostles and the true prelates of the church of God lasted only until Sylvester [i.e., 314 AD], at which time, in virtue of a donation made to the church by the Emperor Constantine, the Roman church began, which, according to them, is no longer the church of God. The church of God, they say, has already disappeared, except to the extent to which it is continued in them or has been restored by them.[88]

The *Comedy* teaches, explicitly, almost everything that John here categorizes as "the error of the Waldenses." Yet Dante is not a card-carrying Waldensian, for certainly he would not have identified himself as a follower of Peter Waldo.[89] Nonetheless, as did Waldensians and other like-minded heretical groups, Dante considers the church of his day—indeed the church since the time of Sylvester—as profoundly corrupt and illegitimate. For Dante, the Roman Church is not the church of God.

One way that Dante is not Waldensian is that he has no sense of belonging to the authentic cult of the true church. For Dante the true church is not a small group set off from all others, not a select few humans who alone constitute the ranks of the truly faithful. Rather, the true church is the whole community (which for Dante is always thought in global terms, as the entirety of humankind).

For the term "church" is ambiguous. It can signify the physical building, the temple where people gather to worship; it can signify the official clerical institution charged with administering religious practice; and it can signify the whole community of the faithful. These various senses of the term are spelled out by Dante's intellectual partner Marsilius of Padua in his *Defensor pacis* (*Defender of the Peace*), a work that aims to locate authority in the whole body of the community rather than in the official clerical institution:

> Among the Latins, this word [*ecclesia*, "church"] according to colloquial and familiar usage means, in one of its senses, a temple or house in which the believers worship together and most frequently invoke God. . . .

Again, in another sense, and especially among the moderns, this word "church" means those ministers, priests or bishops and deacons, who minister in or preside over the metropolitan or principal church. This usage was long since brought about by the church of the city of Rome, whose ministers and overseers are the Roman pope and his cardinals. Through custom they have brought it about that they are called the "church," and that one says the "church" has done or received something when it is these men who have done or received or otherwise ordained something.

But the word "church" has also another meaning which is the truest and the most fitting one of all, according to the first imposition of the word and the intention of these first imposers, even though this meaning is not so familiar nor in accord with modern usage. According to this signification, the "church" means the whole body of the faithful who believe in and invoke the name of Christ, and all the parts of this whole body in any community, even the household. And this was the first imposition of this term and the sense in which it was customarily used among the apostles and in the primitive church. . . .And therefore all the Christian faithful, both priests and non-priests, are and should be called churchmen according to this truest and most proper signification, because Christ purchased and redeemed *all men* with his blood. . . .Thus, then, the blood of Christ was not shed for the apostles alone; therefore it was not they alone who were purchased by him, nor consequently their successors in office, the priests or ministers of the temple, alone; therefore it is not they alone who are the "church" which Christ purchased with his blood. . . .But now Christ delivered himself up not for the apostles alone or their successors in office, the bishops or priests and deacons, but rather for *the whole of humankind*. Therefore it is not they alone or their congregation who are the bride of Christ, although a certain congregation of them, abusing the word in order to advance fraudulently their own temporal well-being to the detriment of others, calls itself exclusively the bride of Christ.[90]

For Marsilius, the "church" properly means the whole community, and it is this community which has the right to judge its clergy—not vice versa. Marsilius retrieves what he takes to be the ancient Greek sense of "church":

Let us say that this term "church" [*ecclesia*] is a word used by the Greeks, signifying among them, in those writings which have come down to us, an assembly of people contained under one regime. Aristotle used it in this sense when he said, in the *Politics*, Book II, chapter 10: "All men share in the ecclesia."[91]

The "church" of a given political unit or regime is every human who dwells within the boundaries of that regime. Now, since Dante's political vision admits of but a single regime, the global Monarchy, there can be for

Dante but a single "church" in this sense, a "church" to which all humans necessarily belong. It is in this sense that Dante will wage his crusade for the "church" against the "church." He will defend the global community against the Church of Rome that has helped tear that community apart.

The papacy's greatest offense in Dante's eyes is its misappropriation of the right to *judge*—a right that, where temporal (secular) matters are concerned, properly belongs to the state and, where matters of eternal salvation are concerned, properly belongs to Christ. The Church of Rome, with no legitimate authority to do so, presumes to determine who counts as the "good" and the "bad," the "saved" and the "damned." But this act of dividing the community into winners and losers, insiders and outsiders, was not the aim designated by God for the primitive apostolic (pre-Donation) church, as Peter tells Dante in the passage cited above:

> It was not our purpose that one part [*parte*] of the
> Christian people should sit on the right
> of our successors, and one part [*parte*] on the left.

The primitive church's purpose was to work toward universal salvation. The church of Dante's day thrives on damnation, wielding power through the mechanism of division. It is significant that Peter calls this a division into "parts," since the same word functions in Dante's Italian to signify "parties" in the political sense. The church now plays "party politics" on a multiplicity of levels. It "saves" members of the Guelph party and "damns" members of the Ghibelline party. It proclaims its political supporters to be "good" Christians and its opponents to be "bad" ones, "heretics." On a broader scale, it divides the globe itself into "parties"—pronouncing that Christians as a whole are "on the right" and non-Christians as a whole are "on the left." This separation into "parties" of what ought to be one whole undivided "church" (global community) is for Dante the most satanic aspect of the pseudo-church's wicked legacy.

At stake here is the question of *judgment*. For the notion of separating people into those who sit on the right (the saved) and those who sit on the left (the damned) is an allusion to the Gospel of Matthew, in which Christ offers the following prophetic vision of Judgment Day:

> "When the Son of Man comes in his glory, and all the angels with him, then he will sit on the throne of his glory. All the nations [*ethne*] will be gathered before him, and *he will separate people one from another as a shepherd separates the sheep from the goats, and he will put the sheep at his right hand and the goats at the left*. Then the king will say to those at his right hand, 'Come, you that are blessed by my Father, inherit the kingdom prepared for you from the

foundation of the world; for I was hungry and you gave me food, I was thirsty and you gave me something to drink, I was a stranger and you welcomed me, I was naked and you gave me clothing, I was sick and you took care of me, I was in prison and you visited me.' Then the righteous will answer him, 'Lord, when was it that we saw you hungry and gave you food, or thirsty and gave you something to drink? And when was it that we saw you a stranger and welcomed you, or naked and gave you clothing? And when was it that we saw you sick or in prison and visited you?' And the king will answer them, 'Truly I tell you, just as you did it to one of the least of these who are members of my family, you did it to me.' Then he will say to those who are at his left hand, 'You that are accursed, depart from me into the eternal fire prepared for the devil and his angels; for I was hungry and you gave me no food, I was thirsty and you gave me nothing to drink, I was a stranger and you did not welcome me, naked and you did not give me clothing, sick and in prison and you did not visit me.' Then they will answer, 'Lord, when was it that we saw you naked or sick or in prison, and did not take care of you?' Then he will answer them, 'Truly I tell you, just as you did not do it to one of the least of these, you did not do it to me.' And these will go away into eternal punishment, but the righteous into eternal life." (Matt. 25.31–46)

Who are those that will be gathered before Christ on Judgment Day? It is possible to reply that they are all the Christians from all the nations (*ethne*) of the world, the multi-ethnic and international Christian community that will have been produced by the global missionary project preached at the end of the Gospel of Matthew. In this case the judgment represented here—the sheep on the right hand and the goats on the left—will be Christ's separating good from bad Christians. But this is not the only possible, and not the most compelling, reading. For the text literally says simply that this judgment will pertain to *all the nations*; it does not say that Christ will first pre-select from amongst all the nations only those individuals who are Christians. This is a *universal* judgment, one to which all people will be subject. Indeed those who do not know themselves as or call themselves Christians (those who would say to Christ, "When have I ever seen you?") yet who nonetheless practice Christian charity are looked upon with special favor; they seem to be ignorant concerning Christ, having no idea that they have been serving him, no sense that they are his intimates, yet still they lead lives marked by acts of kindness to others. Salvation for them is not all a function of their holding the "right belief." Rather, it is entirely a matter of their ethical practice, defined as an elemental and universally accessible life of charity. Good people, from no matter what nation or ethnicity, shall be numbered among those who sit on the right hand; bad people from no matter what nation or ethnicity shall sit on the left.

Papal judgment is a perversion of Christ's judgment. Christ, first having gathered before him all of the earth's various politically divided units (nations, communities), then effaces all boundaries except that eternal division that will separate the saved from the damned. Since for Christ good and evil are measured by a standard of basic charity and kindness applicable to all humans, both of the two eternal groupings will be populated with people from every nation (*ethnos*). Every political unit, every community, has its sheep and its goats. When it comes time to pass judgment Christ does not consider polity, party, or nation. For the (post-Donation) pope, on the other hand, the political unit is the very basis for judgment. A Waldensian or a Cathar is automatically damned for being a member of such a group. A Ghibelline is necessarily a goat, while a Guelph is quite likely a sheep. A European is, barring some anomaly, destined to sit on the right hand, while odds are high that an Arab will wind up on the left. The pope first checks one's party credentials, then passes judgment, designating as "good Christian people" those who are politically allied with the papacy. Christ sees good and bad individuals in all communities; the pope designates communities *as such* as either good or bad.

Marsilius argues that the pope has absolutely no legal authority to penalize heretics or others deemed "non-Christian." Insofar as heretics and unbelievers *as such* do sin, they sin against divine not human law. Since only Christ has legal authority to administer divine law, the papal division of the Christian community into sheep (the orthodox faithful) and goats (heretics) is an illegitimate usurpation of Christ's authority. (To understand the following passage one needs to know that Marsilius distinguishes between various senses of the word "judge." In what is here called the "third sense," the "judge" means "the ruler who has the authority to judge concerning the just and beneficial in accordance with the laws or customs, and to command and execute through coercive force the sentences made by him." This is the *legal* sense of the word. In what is here called "the first sense," "judge" means "anyone who discerns or knows. . . . In this sense, the geometer is a judge, and judges concerning figures and their attributes; and the physician judges concerning the healthy and the sick, and the prudent man concerning what should be done and what should be avoided, and the house builder concerning how to build houses."[92] This is a more general sense, according to which to "judge" is to express a fact or a well-grounded opinion or to propose a wise course of action). Marsilius asserts that in matters of divine law, only Christ is a "judge" in "the third sense"; that is, the legal right to "command and execute through coercive force" belongs to Christ alone. The clergy can rightly judge in "the first sense" by offering for our consideration their knowledge or well-grounded opinions concerning divine law, but they cannot in any instance assume the legal right to punish any human for transgressing that law:

> But now let us say, in accordance with our previous conclusions, that any
> person who sins against divine law must be judged, corrected, and punished
> according to that law. But there are two judges according to it. One is a
> judge in the third sense, having coercive power to punish transgressors of this
> law; and this judge is Christ alone. . . .But Christ willed and decreed that all
> transgressors of this law should be coercively judged and punished in the
> future world only, not in this one. . . .There is another judge according to
> this law, namely the priest or bishop, but he is not a judge in the third sense,
> and may not correct any transgressor of divine law in this world and punish
> him by coercive force. . . .However, the priest is a judge in the first sense of
> the word, and he has to teach, exhort, censure, and rebuke sinners or trans-
> gressors of divine law, and frighten them by a judgment of the future inflic-
> tion of damnation and punishment upon them in the world to come by the
> coercive judge, Christ. . . .Since, then, the heretic, the schismatic, or any
> other infidel is a transgressor of divine law, if he persists in this crime he will
> be punished by that judge to whom it pertains to correct transgressors of
> divine law as such, when he will exercise his judicial authority. But this
> judge is Christ, who will judge the living, the dead, and the dying, but in the
> future world, not in this one. For he has mercifully allowed sinners to have
> the opportunity of becoming deserving and penitent up to the very time
> when they finally pass from this world at death. But the other judge, namely,
> the pastor, bishop or priest, must teach and exhort man in the present life,
> must censure and rebuke the sinner and frighten him by a judgment or pre-
> diction of future glory or eternal damnation; but he must not coerce, as is
> plain from the previous chapter.[93]

Marsilius completely undermines the legitimacy of inquisition. Although
religious authorities can impart their knowledge, offer their opinions, and
use rhetorical means of persuasion concerning salvation and the afterlife,
they have no jurisdiction over religious beliefs and practices in this life.

Marsilius is optimistic concerning the purposes and rationale of human
law. Communities on the whole have established their laws for good
reason. If the law of a community allows for the coexistence of diverse religious beliefs and practices, then no religious authority is entitled to upset
this status quo. Since in Marsilius's view it is manifestly the case that the
mainstream of European law does not legislate against persons on the basis
of their religious beliefs and practices, the Church of Rome has no right to
interfere by legislating against, for instance, Jews and heretics:

> Now if human law were to prohibit heretics or other infidels from dwelling
> in the region, and yet such a person were found there, he must be corrected
> in this world as a transgressor of human law, and the penalty fixed by that law

for such transgression must by inflicted upon him by the judge who is the guardian of human law by the authority of the legislator. . . .But if human law did not prohibit the heretic or other infidel from dwelling among the faithful in the same province, *as heretics and Jews are now permitted to do by human laws even in these times of Christian peoples, rulers, and pontiffs,* then I say that no one is allowed to judge or coerce a heretic or other infidel by any penalty in property or in person for the status of the present life. And the general reason for this is as follows: no one is punished in this world for sinning against theoretic or practical disciplines precisely as such, however much he may sin against them, but only for sinning against a command of human law.[94]

Any religious theory or practice not prohibited by human law is to be tolerated. Insofar as Jews and heretics do not violate the laws of the society in which they dwell, they are completely free to hold whatever belief and to perform whatever rites they please.

Among the first of the "saved" souls (*spiriti eletti*, "elect spirits"; *Purg.* III, 73) whom Dante meets at the foot of Mt. Purgatory is Manfred, son of the Emperor Frederick II, who more than anyone else formulated a theory of the Empire based on the principle that the state should have total dominion in temporal affairs, the church none.[95] For our present purposes it is enough to know that Manfred, who fought for the Ghibelline cause against the papacy until his death at the battle of Benevento in 1266, was excommunicated as a heretic by Pope Alexander IV in 1258. The papacy proclaimed its conflict with Manfred to be a crusade, a holy war (Manfred was not only a heretic but, like his father, freely associated with Muslims and displayed his affection for Islamic civilization).

Dante's aim in this episode of *Purgatory*, which presents as "saved" and as a member of the community of the faithful the very one whom the church proclaims a "damned" excommunicant, is to disarm the papacy's principal weapon, its authority to "judge," in the coercive and juridical sense, concerning matters of faith. For we learn from Manfred that the sentence imposed upon him by popes was irrelevant to the ultimate destiny of his eternal soul. Though the church, on the order of Pope Clement IV, had his bones scattered beyond the confines of papal territory as befitting a heretic with no hope of salvation, nonetheless Manfred ends up among the eternally blessed:

"After I had my body pierced
by two mortal stabs, I gave myself
weeping to Him who pardons willingly.

Horrible were my sins,
but the Infinite Goodness has such wide arms
that It receives all who turn to It.

If Cosenza's pastor, who was then
sent by Clement to hunt me down,
had well read that page in God,

The bones of my body would yet be
at the bridge-head near Benevento,
under the guard of the heavy cairn.

Now the rain washes them and the wind stirs
them, beyond the kingdom, hard by the Verde,
where he transported them with tapers quenched.

By curse of theirs [i.e, excommunication] none is so lost
that the Eternal Love cannot return,
so long as hope keeps aught of green."

(*Purg.* III, 118–135)

Excommunication is a punishment executed by the church against those, such as heretics, who transgress divine law. But just as Marsilius insists that religious authorities do not have the jurisdiction to punish transgressions of divine law, so Dante shows that excommunication is in effect an empty proclamation. The breadth and extent, the inclusiveness, of God's salvation is far greater than the church purports it to be. Dante thus deprives the papacy of one of its chief tools of terror. Dante gives the church's political opponents—who learn from Manfred's example that they need not fear that in resisting the papacy they are risking the salvation of their souls—the courage to fight. A doctrine of potentially universal salvation, according to which, as Manfred says, God's Infinite Goodness "receives all who turn to It" (in which case salvation is not mediated or administered by the church), is part and parcel of Dante's dismantling the ideological machinery of papal power.

Dante's choice of Manfred to signify the nullity of excommunication and the limitations of papal judgment was by no means arbitrary. For Manfred himself authored a manifesto in which he marshaled arguments against the legitimacy of the Donation of Constantine (several of which Dante drew upon in composing his *Monarchy*).[96] Manfred insists on the state's complete autonomy from the church, which in his view ought to have no dominion over temporal possessions and no authority in the realm of *ius humanum*, human law.

In transporting Manfred's excommunicated remains "beyond the king-dom," outside the boundaries of papal territory, the church demonstrates that it equates the regime of the saved with an earthly polity, mistaking the inhabitants of an earthly kingdom for the inhabitants of the kingdom of Heaven. But we have seen in the Gospel of Matthew that there can be no such thing as a sanctified polity: Christ in his judgment ignores political boundaries, saving and damning people from every *ethnos*.

Cathars and Universal Salvation

In the twelfth century, the Cathar "heresy" (if I hesitate to use the word, it is because in their own eyes, of course, the Cathars were by no means heretics; they normally called themselves the "good people" or the "Christians"; the name "Cathar," referring to *catharsis*, "purification," was a designation used by the Church of Rome more than by the Cathars themselves) rose to a great degree of popularity in Occitania and Catalonia (and to a lesser degree in Lombardy). Catharism was a form a dualism somewhat akin to the Manicheism that flourished in the age of St. Augustine. It had migrated to the West from Bosnia and Bulgaria. For the Cathars there are two eternal principles, Good and Evil (whereas for Catholic orthodoxy, as formulated by Augustine, Evil is "nothing," non-being). Good is associated with light, life, spirituality, the soul; Evil with darkness, death, materiality, the body. According to Cathar doctrine, all human souls partake of the Good; they are all particles of light, of pure spirit, that have been "captured" by Evil and imprisoned on earth in physical bodies. But in the end all will be saved, all will return to the Good whence they derive. Catharism was, in the words of René Weis, "a dissident faith, with, at its doctrinal core, gentleness and the promise of universal redemption."[97]

The Cathar community distinguished between those who were "Hearers" (the great majority, who continued to lead ordinary lives while they "heard" and were taught Cathar doctrine) and the "Perfect" (those who had received the *consolamentum*—the rite indicating that one had been sufficiently purified, made "perfect," prepared to return to the immaterial realm of the Good). Humans who happen to die before having received the *consolamentum* are not consigned to eternal damnation; rather, they are reincarnated, either as animal or human, until eventually they "get it right" through incarnation as a "good Christian" and finally, a "Perfect." Though Catharism insisted on the evil of the flesh and of life on earth, only the relatively few "Perfect" led ascetic lives, practicing vegetarianism and refraining from all sexual contact.

Though the Cathar "Perfect" may have at any one time only numbered in the hundreds and those who would have considered themselves "Hearers" may have never amounted to more than several thousand, the Cathar influence on Occitan society was very strong—so much so that Catharism and Occitania became, in the eyes of the Church of Rome, identified. This was not merely papal mythmaking. Most noble families in Occitania had a member or two who was either a Cathar "Hearer" or "Perfect," and those who did not still offered protection to Cathars in times of persecution. Though Occitans on the whole remained "orthodox"

Christians, most nonetheless extended their sympathy and support to the Cathars. This was in part due to the relative independence (from Rome) of the official "church" in Occitania: its bishops were more likely to owe allegiance to and share common financial interests with the local aristocracy (since they themselves were members of those noble families; indeed bishoprics and their revenues were routinely part of a family's inherited possessions). Although this configuration of economic interest was common to all of Latin Christendom, the conflict between the local bishops and the central authority of Rome was particularly intense in Occitania. When the papacy set out to eliminate Catharism it was at the same time establishing itself as a centralized power, wresting control (and revenues) away from the local Occitan nobles. For these nobles, defending Catharism and resisting the political and economic intrusion of the Church of Rome were two sides of the same coin.

The success of Catharism in Occitania posed a tremendous threat to the papacy. In 1209, Pope Innocent III preached a crusade—known as the Albigensian Crusade, a name referring to the town of Albi, near Toulouse, which was known to be a heretic stronghold—against Cathar Occitania. The aristocratic warrior class from France (who were relatively more willing to cede control over church property to the papacy) was engaged to stamp out the Cathar heresy; in exchange they were given the right to possess conquered Occitan territories. Over the course of the next several decades, not without meeting resistance, the French managed to subdue Occitania, eventually annexing to the French crown the lands that we now know as "the South of France." Were it not for the Albigensian Crusade, it is likely that there would today be a nation called Occitania and a national Occitan language.

The popularity of Catharism, a religion that denied the value of the flesh and abhorred worldly luxury and physical pleasure, is at first glance a bit puzzling. Occitania, after all, was by no means predisposed toward asceticism. It was marked by a rich and vibrant material life, relatively urban and cosmopolitan, and was the birthplace of the elegant and sophisticated literary culture of the troubadour poets who did so much to shape future notions of romantic love. Why did Occitania embrace a dualism that seems to run counter to the overall secularism of its culture? What did Catharism offer to Occitans?

The answer is that it offered various modes of hope and comfort to various constituencies. There were certainly many ordinary people who were "turned off" by the manifest corruption and decadence of the official Catholic clergy. For them, the simple, chaste, and gentle (Catharism prohibited all killing; for the "Perfect" this applied even to the killing of animals) lives of the Cathar "Perfect" presented an attractive alternative.

This is the usual explanation for the rise of Catharism, and indeed the papacy seems to have accepted this view, since it promoted the establishment of the Mendicant Orders (Franciscans and Dominicans) as a way to co-opt the moral high-ground displayed by the "Perfect," in the hope of returning Occitans back to the fold of the orthodox faithful by appealing to their admiration for simplicity, humility, and voluntary poverty. Catharism's fundamental message of tolerance (all human souls belong to the Good and are destined to return there) also appealed to Occitans, who were comfortable in their cohabitation with minorities (there were significant Jewish communities and less sizeable Muslim communities in Occitania). Minorities themselves were comforted to know that living in "Cathardom" meant that they dwelled amidst a fundamentally tolerant majority. For the rich and powerful, Catharism offered a theological doctrine upon which to ground resistance to the authority of the Church of Rome: since all souls will be saved, one's eternal soul is immune from the threat posed by papal judgment. In sum, Cathar teachings galvanized resistance, giving hope and comfort to all those who, in the eyes and decrees of the church, were not on the "right path." For Catharism, with its doctrine of universal salvation, *everyone*, every human soul, is necessarily on the "right path"—the path of return to the source of the light that is the true reality of all humans. All in the end will reach the same goal, the Good; some, more trapped and darkened by materiality than others, will take longer to get there. Even the most wicked of popes, the most violent of persecutors of the "good people," will get there in the end—perhaps among the last to return, but return they will. Thus Catharism loves and forgives its worst enemies.[98]

The Cathars rejected the Old Testament as a fraud, since they could not accept that the good God would be responsible for creating a physical cosmos, a realm of darkness, death, materiality. On the other hand, they accepted the authenticity of the Gospels. Their cornerstone text was the Gospel of John; the rite of *consolamentum* included the recitation of its first chapter. As Forrester Roberts remarks, "the Cathar 'parfaits' or priests dismissed the Old Testament as a mistaken portrayal of a vindictive and cruel god prone to tribal prejudice rather than radiating universal love. They particularly embraced the concept of the Lord as revealed by St. John and carried his testament with them wherever they went."[99]

Whatever may have been the original intentions of the author of the Gospel of John, his text lends itself quite well to appropriation by a Cathar interpretation. For this is above all else the gospel of "light" ("While you have the light, believe in the light, so that you may become children of light"; John 12.36) and of universal salvation ("And I, when I am lifted up from the earth, will draw *all people* to myself"; John 12.32; emphasis added).

Light and darkness figure prominently in the opening passage, the words recited for the *consolamentum*, as does a denial that humans are "of blood. . .or flesh":

> In the beginning was the Word, and the Word was with God, and the Word was God. He was in the beginning with God. All things came into being through him, and without him not one thing came into being. What has come into being through him was life, and the life was the light of all people. The light shines in the darkness, and the darkness did not overcome it.
>
> There was a man sent from God, whose name was John. He came as a witness to testify to the light, so that all might believe through him. He himself was not the light, but he came to testify to the light. The true light, which enlightens everyone, was coming into the world.
>
> He was in the world, and the world came into being through him; yet the world did not know him. He came to what was his own, and his own people did not accept him. But to all who received him, who believed in his name, he gave power to become children of God, who were born, not of blood or of the will of the flesh or of the will of man, but of God. (John 1.1–13)

One can readily imagine the appeal of these words to those who, whether "heretics," minorities, or political opponents, were told by the church that their souls were damned to eternal darkness. For John announces that the light "enlightens *everyone*" and is "the light of *all* people." The message is optimistic: "darkness did not overcome" the light. All human souls, all of which are light, remain light, not having been touched in their essence by their exile in the realm of Evil. No matter how much the light of the human soul is entangled in materiality, imprisoned by the body and held captive by the physical world, darkness can never overcome the light. Eternal damnation makes no sense from the Cathar perspective.

In 1309, as Dante was composing *Inferno*, the Cathar Perfect Pierre Authié, a leading figure of the Cathar "renaissance" that had arisen in Lombardy, Occitania, and Catalonia, was arrested and tried by the Inquisition; he was sentenced to death and burnt at the stake the following year. The inquisitorial register records that he told his accusers that people were faced with a choice between the church

> which flees and forgives, and the other which fetters and flays: the former holds to the *straight path* of the apostles, and does not lie and deceive; the latter is the Church of Rome.[100]

The Cathar way is presented as the way of "forgiveness," of those who flee punishment and coercive judgment even while they forgive their persecutors.

But what is most significant about this remark for our purposes is the insight it offers concerning the sense of the "straight path," the *diritta via* of *Inferno*'s opening stanza:

> In the middle of the journey of our life,
> I came to myself in a dark wood,
> for *the straight way* [*la diritta via*] was lost.

The project of a return to the "straight path" announced here can hardly be, as it is so often said to be, Dante's return to Catholic "orthodoxy." For the phrase was just as likely to signify to Dante's contemporaries the path followed by the primitive apostolic church. This church, as St. Peter tells Dante in the verses that we considered above, did not occupy itself with separating the community into "orthodox" and "heretical," into sheep and goats. Its purpose was not to judge who was and who was not a true Christian worthy of salvation.

We are accustomed to reading *la diritta via* as an element of autobiography, referring it to some manner in which Dante himself had strayed from the right way. We read the *Comedy*'s opening as if Dante is saying, "I lost the right path; now I shall work to regain it." Perhaps—we speculate—Dante has been living a sinful life that he will now rectify through a devotion to virtue. Or perhaps he has placed too much trust in philosophy, in natural reason; now he will return to the straight way by acknowledging that faith in Christian revelation is necessary for salvation. Or perhaps he has been too entangled in the "dark wood" of partisan politics; now he will give himself over to religion. In each case we are assuming that it is *Dante* who has lost the way.

But in fact Dante does not say "I had lost the straight way." He says, rather, that "the straight way was lost." The journey in question is not Dante's own personal journey but instead the "journey of *our* life," and what is at stake here is not a personal but a collective error. If we, collectively, have lost our way, it is because the straight way has been lost. If we, the "church" (as the whole community of humankind), have lost our way, it is because we have forgotten the straight path of the apostles. To return to *la diritta via* is decidedly not to return to the embrace of the church (the "orthodox" Church of Rome).[101] If Dante counsels a return to "Christianity," this is by no means a return that would be looked upon with favor by the official religious authorities of Dante's day.

The "straight way" does not simply mean "Christianity" in a generic sense, for there were in Dante's day competing versions of Christianity. If the *Comedy*, as its opening stanza indicates, is in some sense about Dante's regaining the "straight way," this is not a movement from being an infidel to a Christian but rather from a wrong Christianity to a right one.

Turmeda

Dante opens the *Comedy* by implying that he had turned away from, then, fortunately, regained the right path. The theological school of Dante criticism says that this means he had turned away from Catholic orthodoxy, from the Catholic Church, then returned. But in Dante's eyes, the Catholic Church of his day was nothing less than "the Whore of Babylon"—the very opposite of the right path.[102] Finding *la diritta via*, the authentic, primitive apostolic path, may very well demand a turning away from the Catholic Church.

This is precisely what it demanded of the fourteenth-century Catalan poet Anselm Turmeda, a Franciscan writer and scholar of some prominence in Europe who, following a long period of study in Bologna (the famous university town where Dante, several decades earlier, had also studied), emerged in Tunisia with a new name, Abdallah al-Taryuman. (We should note that Turmeda's best known work in his native Catalan, *The Dispute of the Ass*, is a debate concerning the relative superiority of humans and animals, adapted from a text discussed above—the Ihkwan al-Safa's *Case of the Animals versus Man Before the King of the Jinn*).

What is perhaps most fascinating about Turmeda's autobiographical account (written ca. 1385) of his conversion is that it represents the impulse to Islam as welling up from within the heart of Europe. For it is none other than a venerable old Catholic priest in Bologna who teaches Turmeda that Islam is the "straight way," the authentic way of Christ and his apostles, a way that the Catholic Church has abandoned.

The event of Turmeda's conversion is of such intrinsic interest that it deserves to be cited at length. The focal point is the question concerning the identity of the mysterious Paraclete, the "Advocate" or "Helper" who Christ, in the Gospel of John, says will be sent by God to humankind some time following Christ's death to remind us of Christ's message: " 'I have said these things to you while I am still with you. But the Advocate, the Holy Spirit, whom the Father will send in my name, will teach you everything, and remind you of all that I have said to you. Peace I leave with you; my peace I give to you' " (John 14.25–27; see also John 14:15; 15:26; 16:7–15). The revered old priest privately teaches Turmeda that the Paraclete is none other than Muhammad:

> I later traveled to the city of Bologna in the land of Lombardy. . . .There is a church there with an old priest who was of very high rank, by the name of Nicolo Martello. His status among them in knowledge, observance, and asceticism was very high. He was peerless in these characteristics in his time among all the people of Christendom. Questions, particularly those concerning religion, would be brought to him from distant regions from kings

and others, accompanied by great gifts which was the point of the matter for they wished to acquire his blessings by doing this. When their gifts were accepted, they deemed themselves greatly honored. With this priest I studied the principles and the details of the Christian religion. . . .

I studied with him there and served him, as I have recounted above, for ten years. Then one day he unexpectedly took ill and did not attend his seminar. The students of his class waited for him and passed the time discussing various problems of knowledge. Eventually, their discussion turned to the words of God Almighty as expressed by the Prophet Jesus (upon whom be peace!): "There will come after me a prophet whose name shall be the Paraclete," and they began to discuss the identity of this prophet: Which was he among the Prophets? Each one spoke according to his own knowledge and understanding. Their discussion was lengthy and they debated a great deal, but they left without having reached any conclusion regarding this matter.

I went to the residence of the teacher of the aforementioned class, and he asked me, "What studying did you do today while I was absent?" So I told him of the disagreement among the students concerning the identity of the Paraclete. I reported that so-and-so had answered thus, and so-and-so had answered in this manner, and thus I narrated to him all of their answers. Then he asked me, "And how did you answer?" "I responded with the answer given by such-and-such a religious scholar in his exegesis of the Gospels." He said to me, "Well, that was a good try and you did get close; but so-and-so is mistaken and so-and-so almost got it right, but the truth is not any of these, because the explanation of this holy name is known only by scholars of extraordinary learning, and as of yet, you [students] have achieved only a small amount of knowledge." So I rushed forward to kiss his feet and said to him, "Master, you know that I have come to you from a far-off land and have served you now for ten years. During this time I have received from you an amount of knowledge which I cannot reckon, but could you find it possible, out of your great beneficence, to supplement this with knowledge of this holy name?" The priest then began to weep and said to me, "My son, God knows that you are very dear to me because of your service and devotion to me. Knowledge of this holy name is indeed a great benefit, but I fear that if this knowledge were revealed to you that the Christian masses would kill you immediately." I said to him, "Master, by God Almighty, by the Truth of the Gospels and He Who brought them, I shall never speak of anything you confide to me in secret except at your command!"

Then he said to me, "My son, when you first came to me I asked you about your country: whether it was close to the Muslims and whether your countries raid each other, in order to determine what aversion you might have for Islam. Know, then, my son, that the Paraclete is one of the names of our Prophet Muhammad (may God bless and preserve him!), to whom was revealed the Fourth Book which is mentioned by Daniel (upon whom be peace!) who says that this book shall be revealed, its religion shall be the

True Religion, and its followers the True Community mentioned in the Gospels." I responded, "But, Master, what then do you say of the religion of the Christians?" He replied, "My son, *if the Christians had persisted in the original religion of Jesus, they would indeed belong to the religion of God, for the religion of Jesus and all of the Prophets is that of God.*" "But what then is one to do in this matter?" I asked. He said, "My son, enter into the religion of Islam!" I asked, "Does whoever enter Islam achieve salvation?" He responded, "Yes, he is saved in this world and in the Hereafter." I said to him, "Master, an intelligent man chooses for himself the very best of what he knows, so if you know that the religion of Islam is superior, what then keeps you from it?" He said, "My son, God Almighty only revealed to me the truth of what I have disclosed to you about the superiority of Islam and the holiness of the Prophet of Islam in my old age and after the decrepitude of my body— (There is, however, no excuse for him, for the proof of God is clear to all!)— but if God had guided me to this while I was still your age, I would have left everything and entered the True Religion. Love of the material world is at the heart of all sins. You can see my status among the Christians, the dignity I am accorded, the wealth, the honor, and my reputation in this world. If I were to demonstrate any leanings toward the religion of Islam, the masses would kill me at the earliest possible opportunity. Even if I were able to save myself from them and make my way to the Muslims and say to them, 'I have come to you to become a Muslim,' they would say to me, 'You have done yourself a great benefit by entering into the True Religion, but you do not bestow upon us any favor with your entrance into a religion by which you have saved yourself from the punishment of God.' I would remain among them a poor old man, ninety years of age, where I don't understand their language and they do not know my worth, and I would end up dying of starvation. So *I remain, thank God, of the religion of Jesus and of Him who brought it. God knows this of me.*"

So I said to him, "Master, are you indicating to me that I should go to the lands of the Muslims and enter into their religion?" He responded, "If you are intelligent and seek salvation, then rush to do this, thereby gaining for yourself both this world and the next! But, my son, this is a matter which no one is here to witness and which you must conceal to the utmost of your ability, for if any of it were to become known, the masses would kill you instantly, and I would not be able to help you. Nor would it help you to trace this back to me, for I would deny it, and my word about you would be believed, but your statements against me would not be believed. I am innocent of your blood should you utter a word of this."[103]

We cannot say for certain whether or not the most revered of Catholic educators in Bologna was secretly teaching to his favorite students the harmony of Islam and the "original religion of Jesus." Turmeda may well have made this up out of whole cloth. But we can say that, in Turmeda's eyes at least, Islam and "the religion of Jesus" and "the religion of God" are all one and the same. In turning to Islam, he does not turn away from Christianity but rather returns to it. For Turmeda, "the straight way was lost" so long as he remained a Catholic. For him, to regain *la diritta via* is to regain the path that is at once truly Christian and Islamic.[104]

Peire Cardenal

Dante was an enthusiastic reader and scholar of the Occitan troubadour poets, as we can gather from the *De Vulgari Eloquentia*, where he treats them at length, citing a great many passages from individual works. Among the towering figures of the late troubadour period was Peire Cardenal (ca. 1180–ca. 1272), one of literary history's greatest cranks, past-master of the no-holds-barred vitriolic rant.

What was Peire most often cranky about? Although the targets of his scorn are several, such that he displays at times a generalized misanthropy ("I sing for myself alone,/since no one understands my language / . . . .What do I care if such crass men don't/heed my song, for they're all swine"[105]), Peire's primary gripe is against the Church of Rome and its hypocritical representatives. He lived a long life, witnessing the Albigensian Crusade and its aftermath, the destruction of Occitan culture. His songs send out a belated cry of resistance to the narrow-minded persecutorial power that ruined the relative openness of Occitan society.

The ambience that had been destroyed was one that, as Charles Camproux remarks, permitted peaceful contestation and diversity of belief, accepting "as entirely natural that Catholics coexisted with Cathars and Waldensians, just as it had accepted coexistence with Jews and Muslims." (And we might agree with Camproux in seeing the following verses by Peire as displaying the effects of the Occitan embrace of diversity: "I want to have the speech [i.e., linguistic/rhetorical skill] of a Muslim/and the faith and Law of a Christian/and the subtlety [i.e., reasoning skill] of a pagan/and the audacity of a Tartar").[106]

Peire interests us here, specifically, for a poem that he wrote that calls into question the very notion of "judgment." Peire's typical audacity reaches new heights, for his interlocutor in this poem is none other than God, whom he chastises for condemning some humans to Hell while saving others. The poem contrasts the tragic and shameful role that Saint Peter is now constrained to play—discriminating between good and bad, sheep and goats—with the hope of universal redemption announced by Saint John ("And I, when I am lifted up from the earth, will draw *all people* to myself"; John 12.32). It is a diatribe, in the name of inclusion, against a church that has become nothing if not exclusionary. Peire imagines himself on Judgment Day making a case before God and his court for the abolition of judgment:

> I want to begin an unusual poem
> that I shall perform on the day of judgment
> to him who made me and formed me from nothing.
> If he intends to accuse me of anything
> and tries to put me in Hell,
> I shall tell him, "Lord, mercy, let it not be,
> for I have tormented the wicked world all my years,
> so protect me, please, from the torturers."
>
> I shall make all his court marvel
> when they hear my plea,
> for I say he commits a wrong toward his own
> if He intends to destroy them and send them to Hell;
> for he who loses what he could win
> by rights has lack instead of abundance,
> so he should be kind and generous
> in appointing his dying souls as retainers.
>
> You should never refuse your gate,
> for *Saint Peter* takes great shame by that,
> who is the gatekeeper; but let every soul
> enter smiling that wants to enter there,
> for no court is ever quite perfect
> if one man weeps while the other laughs;
> so even though you are a sovereign and powerful king,
> if you don't open to us, a complaint will be made to you.
>
> You ought to disinherit the devils,
> and you would get more souls and get them more often,
> and the disinheritance would please everybody;
> and you could pardon yourself yourself.
> (For all of me he would destroy them all,
> since they all know he could absolve himself.)
> Fair Lord God, please disinherit
> the envious and vexatious enemies!
>
> I do not wish to despair of you,
> rather I have in you my good hope
> that you will help me at my death,
> which is why you must save my soul and my body.
> So I shall offer you an attractive choice:
> either I return to where I started on the first day,
> or you pardon me for my wrongs—
> since I would not have committed them, if I had not been born first.
>
> If I have harm here and had it in Hell,
> By my faith, it would be a wrong and a sin;
> For I can surely reproach you

That for one good thing, I have a thousand times more bad.

For mercy I beg you, lady Saint Mary,
To be a good guide for us with your son
So that he will take the father and the children
And put them where *Saint John* is.[107]

On Judgment Day, Peire will herald the end of judgment. God is severely taken to task; rather than separating humankind into the "laughing" and the "weeping," He ought instead never refuse His gate, "but let every soul/enter smiling that wants to enter there." Peire's "protect me, please, from the torturers" indicates that this is a manifesto against Inquisition, a plea on behalf of all the minority and opposition groups of Occitania—Jews, Muslims, Cathars, Waldensians, Spiritual Franciscans, etc. We recognize that in talking to "God" Peire is talking to the deity as envisioned and represented by the Church of Rome—a harsh unforgiving deity who would countenance persecution and damnation. The poem aims to replace this "God" with a God more akin to the Good of the Cathars, to the Infinite Goodness which with open arms receives Manfred and "all who turn toward It." The Church of Rome has turned Peter into "Peter," a perverse remnant of himself: now he holds closed the gate that ought to swing wide open.

Peire was not a Cathar (insofar as we can identify his theological stance, he is most properly regarded as an associate of the Spiritual Franciscans).[108] But he nonetheless borrows from the Cathars their special reverence for John, author of the gospel of universal redemption. The poem is in fact structured on *an opposition between Peter and John*—between a church that "fetters and flays" and one that "forgives"; between an exclusionary and an inclusive vision of the community that is to be reckoned as belonging to the "church"; between the fraudulent Church of Rome and the true church of the true God, the church of those gathered up by John.

It will be helpful to bear in mind this distinction between Peter and John. We have seen that Turmeda's confidence in a Christian alternative to the Church of Rome, his confidence in a "religion of God" that is nothing other than the path of Jesus and of Muhammad, is grounded in his reading of the Gospel of John. We have seen that the Cathars regarded that same gospel as the authoritative formulation of their doctrine of universal salvation. This contrast between "Peter" and "John" reappears as a sort of *leitmotiv* in the discourse of Dante's age concerning Christian challenges to Catholic orthodoxy.

Dante Judges the Pope

If Peire dares judge God's judgment, in *Inferno* Dante dares judge the self-appointed judges, the popes. As will be discussed, he reserves for the post-Donation popes a special place in Hell, and when visiting there he, a layman, assumes the role of a clergyman hearing the pope's confession. Dante presents himself as a "churchman"—that is, a representative of the lay community as a whole—endowed with the right to pass judgment on the clergy. In doing so he turns on its head the claim of papal supporters such as Giles of Rome, who had asserted in *On Ecclesiastical Power* (ca. 1301) that "clerics, who are not subject to earthly power, are in a more perfect state than laymen."[109]

This is pointedly ironic given that the one pope whom Dante held in contempt more than any other, his arch-enemy Boniface VIII, proclaimed in his Papal Bull *Unam Sanctam* (promulgated Nov. 18, 1302) that the pope can rightly judge all humans but can himself be judged by none. Boniface, who held the papal office from 1294 until his death in 1303, was the current pope during the time of Dante's fictional journey, which is represented as having taken place in 1300. The *selva oscura* of the *Comedy*'s opening is in part to be understood as the "dark wood" of Boniface's papacy, in which the most extreme imaginable deviation from *la diritta via*, the straight path of the apostles, had become a reality.

For Boniface's *Unam Sanctam* proclaims that the pope is the absolute and singular authority over all things and all people, in matters both religious and secular. It is probably the high-water mark of hierocratic thinking in the medieval West. Boniface asserts that temporal power (the state) is inferior, subordinate, and subject to spiritual power (the church); moreover, he insists that no one can gain eternal salvation without the mediation of the papacy and its priestly agents:

> Hence we must recognize the more clearly that spiritual power surpasses in dignity and in nobility any temporal power whatever, as spiritual things surpass the temporal. . . . For with truth as our witness, it belongs to spiritual power to establish the terrestrial power and to pass judgment if it has not been good. Thus is accomplished the prophecy of Jeremias concerning the Church and the ecclesiastical power: "Behold to-day I have placed you over nations, and over kingdoms' and the rest." Therefore, if the terrestrial power err, it will be judged by the spiritual power; but if a minor spiritual power err, it will be judged by a superior spiritual power; but *if the highest power of all* [i.e, the pope] *err, it can be judged only by God, and not by man*, according to the testimony of the Apostle: "The spiritual man judgeth of all things and he himself is judged by no man" [1 Cor 2:15]. . . . Furthermore, we declare, we proclaim, we define that it is absolutely necessary for salvation that every human creature be subject to the Roman Pontiff.[110]

Boniface's conception of papal judgment as absolute and as legitimately coercive and juridical concerning things both human and divine stands in stark contrast to Marsilius of Padua's restriction of that judgment (which is for Marsilius always only judgment in "the first sense," the sharing of knowledge or discernment) to the realm of things divine.

The *Comedy* strongly implies that most all of the post-Donation popes are among the eternally damned, since one will search in vain to find more than a very few in Purgatory or Paradise. This means that we cannot accept the argument of Catholic apologists who would tell us that Dante revered the papal office in itself, although he may have acknowledged that there were from time to time unfit and corrupt holders of that office. In fact he insists that the office itself was nearly fatally corrupted with the Donation in 314 AD. Or, more precisely, if the authentic uncorrupted papal office—which Dante does revere (as he tells us in *Inf.* XIX, 101)—still exists, it has remained for the large part empty since the time of Sylvester, as Peter tells Dante in the passage from *Paradiso* that we examined above ("He who on earth usurps my place, / my place, my place, which in the Sight/of the Son of God is vacant"). Dante rejects the notion that the papal office as conceived by the Church of Rome is good in itself, for he calls for the radical reform of that office, such that the future papacy will have no possessions, no property, and no power. If it is true that Dante voices respect for "the Church," we need to avoid confusing this with respect for the actual Catholic Church of his day. The church that Dante respects, and of which all humans are members, is a wholly different church than the church that "fetters and flays" and that ruled Christendom in Dante's age.

Dante encounters the post-Donation popes in the third pouch of the eighth circle of Hell, a space designated for simonists (those who buy or sell church offices or privileges). He comes upon a landscape of stone, punctuated by a number of deep round tubes:

> Upon the sides and the bottom I saw
> the livid stone [*pietra*] full of holes,
> all of one size and each was round
>   (*Inf.* XIX, 13–15)

The stony landscape is a physical pun on the name *Pietro*, Peter, whom Christ called the "rock" upon which would be founded the church. But this is a rock "full of holes," indicating the church's current state of corrupt fragility—not to mention its status as "partial" or incomplete.

Dante sees protruding from each of the holes the feet (the soles of which are covered with flames) and legs of a simonist; the rest of the body is submerged. The upside-down disposition of the simonists' bodies is a further allusion to Peter, who is said in the Acts of the Apostles to have been martyred by crucifixion with his head toward the ground and his feet toward the sky.

THE RIGHT PATH (DANTE'S UNIVERSALISM)   237

Dante pauses over one of the tubes and addresses its occupant. We learn that this is Pope Nicholas III (who held the office from 1277 to 1280). Apparently this particular tube is reserved for popes, the other tubes being designated for the holders of other church offices that have been rendered corrupt by simony since the time of the Donation. With great derisive humor Dante has Nicholas mistake him for Boniface VIII, Dante's arch-enemy. Assuming as a matter of course that Hell is Boniface's eternal destiny (although surprised to see him there already in 1300, three years before the appointed time of his death), Nicholas thinks that Boniface has died and is approaching to take his place planted head-down in the papal orifice. Dante addresses Nicholas thus:

> "O wretched soul, whoever you are that,
> planted like a stake, have your upper part down under!"
> I began, "speak if you can."
>
> *I was standing there like the friar who confesses*
> *the perfidious assassin* who, after he is fixed,
> recalls him in order to delay his death;
>
> And he cried, "Are you already standing there,
> are you already standing there, Boniface?
> by several years the writ has lied to me.
>
> Are you so quickly sated with those gains
> for which you did not fear to take by guile
> the beautiful lady, and then to do her outrage?"
>
> *(Inf. XIX, 46–57)*

Boniface was still alive at the time of the *Comedy*'s fictional journey (although not at the time its composition), so Dante could not show his nemesis in Hell without violating the contract of historical verisimilitude that he tries more or less to respect. But he does just as much by announcing Boniface's future arrival there.

Dante is standing above Nicholas III "like the friar who confesses / the perfidious assassin." The tables have been turned: the pope, who according to the dogma of *Unam Sanctam* judges all men but is himself judged by none, is here represented as subject to a higher authority that has been assumed by Dante himself. The authority that in the view of the papacy can only belong to the clergy has been shifted to the layman. Dante is every bit as entitled to be called a man of the "church" as are the officially recognized ecclesiastical authorities.

That the whole scene is to be taken as one of Dante's "judgment" is indicated by a line from the canto's opening verses, "Now must I sound the trumpet for you!" (XIX, 5). As Singleton comments, "town criers sounded a trumpet to announce their reading of judicial sentences in public; the word here may also suggest the sounding of the angel's trumpet on the Day of Judgment."[111] This allusion to the issue of judgment is reiterated in the words with which Dante surrounds the extended denunciation of the papacy that he delivers as he stands over Nicholas III (XIX, 90–117): he prefaces his remarks by saying, "I do not know if I was overbold, / but I answered him in this strain [metro]" (XIX, 88–89); and he concludes by saying, "and while I sung these notes to him" (XIX, 118). Dante's denunciation is figured as a musical performance, with language meant to bring to mind the notions of musical "measure" and "meter" (metro). The operative scriptural text is Matthew 7.1–2: "Judge not, that ye be not judged. For with what judgment ye judge, ye shall be judged: and with what measure ye mete, it shall be measured [metietur] to you again." Dante metes out justice to the pope, answering the punitive papacy "measure for measure," affirming that Nicholas has been "justly punished" (ben punito XIX, 97).

With these details Dante helps us see that, even while the canto aims to denounce ecclesiastical corruption in general, it aims more specifically to reject the theory of the pope's absolute power to judge promulgated by Boniface VIII in Unam Sanctam. Like Marsilius of Padua, Dante insists that religious authorities have no role to play in matters concerning judgment here on earth. It is the people who rightly hold the power to judge the papacy, not vice versa.

Dante learns from Nicholas III that he is not the only pope to occupy the tube. Each time a simonist pope dies, he is shot down into Hell, where he crashes headfirst into the feet of his predecessor, tamping him down further into the tube and compacting the collection of mashed popes trapped below:

> "Beneath my head are the others
> that preceded me in simony,
> mashed down through the fissures of the rock.
>
> I shall be thrust down there in my turn
> when he comes for whom I mistook you
> when I put my sudden question.
>
> But longer already is the time that
> I have cooked my feet and stood inverted thus
> than he shall stay planted with glowing feet,
>
> For after him shall come a lawless shepherd
> from the west, of uglier deeds,
> one fit to cover both him and me."
>
> (Inf. XIX, 73–84)

This punishment—one pope after another being jammed into the tube, each for a time occupying the "seat" at the tube's opening—parodies the notion of a papal "chain of succession." And, significantly, it is toward this tube that Beatrice's final thoughts in *Paradiso* are directed, for the very last words that she speaks in the *Comedy* amount to another insult cast at Peter's current pseudo-successors. She tells Dante that first Boniface VIII, then Clement V (1305–1314) will be thrust and crammed into the papal orifice:

> "But not for long shall God then suffer him [i.e., Clement V]
> in the holy office; for he shall be thrust down
> Where Simon Magus is for his deserts,
>
> And shall make him of Alagna [i.e., Boniface VIII] go deeper still."
> (*Par.* XXX, 145–148)

Beatrice's final speech-act is this acerbic depiction of the arch-villain Boniface VIII's being "stuffed" in the "Unholy See" that awaits the simonist popes. For those readers who may have been awaiting an ultimate theological revelation in Beatrice's closing utterance this may seem anticlimactic. But it indicates the extent to which *Paradiso*, which can be said to offer a transcendent and supernatural perspective on reality, is always at the same time at the service of Dante's earthly political concerns.

If in *Inferno* XIX, Dante represents the real popes of his age as justly punished with eternal damnation, in *Purgatory* IX he presents an ideal image of the papacy, as it was before the Donation of Constantine and as it shall be consequent to the restoration of the Global Empire.[112] There Dante and Virgil pass from "antepurgatory"—the lower slopes of the mountain—up a cliff to where they now stand at the gate of Purgatory proper. The gate to Purgatory proper is St. Peter's gate, as we will soon learn:

> I saw a gate, with three steps beneath
> for going up to it, of different colors,
> and a warder who as yet spoke not a word.
>
> And as I looked more and more intently
> I saw that he was seated upon the topmost step,
> and in his face he was such that I endured it not.
>
> In his hand he had a sword [*una spada*], naked,
> which so reflected the rays on us,
> that often in vain I directed my eyes upon it.
> (*Purg.* IX, 76–84)

This "warder" or gatekeeper of St. Peter's gate, with his simple clothing the color of "ashes, or earth that is dug out dry" (*Purg.* IX, 115), represents the pope as he should be, as he will be after the establishment of Monarchy: without possessions and property and without power in the temporal sphere.[113] The "salvation policy" of such a pope will be guided by the principle of inclusion rather than exclusion (speaking of the keys to Heaven he says: "From Peter I hold them, and he told me to err / rather in opening than in keeping shut" (*Purg.* IX, 127–128). Most significantly, this ideal pope holds in his hand *one* sword (*una spada*), not two, for the church had traditionally claimed to hold both temporal and spiritual power, figured by its holding two swords. In *Unam Sanctam*, for instance, Boniface VIII had said this: "We are informed by the texts of the gospels that in this Church and in its power are two swords; namely, the spiritual and the temporal. For when the Apostles say: 'Behold, here are two swords' [Lk. 22:38] that is to say, in the Church, since the Apostles were speaking, the Lord did not reply that there were too many, but sufficient." But in *Monarchy* Dante forcefully denies that the two swords mentioned in Luke have anything to do with a doctrine of temporal and spiritual power.[114] Here in *Purgatory*, the ideal papacy's *one* sword signifies that its authority as Christ's vicar is restricted solely to the sphere of spiritual things.

The Spiritual Franciscans

Probably the most influential late medieval dissidents, in terms of their direct impact on Dante, were the "radical" or "extremist" Franciscans known as the Spirituals. Dante had very close ties to certain important Spirituals—so close that it is not beyond question to consider him among their number. We have seen in part I that in his youth Dante studied at the Cathedral School of Santa Croce in Florence, where the major Spiritual intellectual Pier Olivi was a preeminent presence. Many of the *Comedy*'s most strident views are consonant with the Spirituals' central teachings—particularly the notion of the present-day Church of Rome as the Great Whore of Babylon, "the *carnalis meretrix*, the synagogue of Satan which will be destroyed in the third status, as the Jewish Synagogue in the second, whereas the *ecclesia spiritualis* will reign until the end of the world."[115] Fundamental to both the *Comedy* and the Spirituals is the prophetic or apocalyptic vision (generally indebted to the twelfth-century Calabrian visionary Joachim of Fiore's Trinitarian view of history as marked by three ages, corresponding to the Father, Son, and Holy Spirit; see part I) of a new historical age in which the church, and indeed global society as a whole, would be radically transformed for the better. Dante's enigmatic prophecies—the *Veltro* of *Inferno* I, the 515 (which for Dante functions as the antitype of Revelation's 666) of *Purg.* XXXIII—and the apocalyptic pageantry that predominates at the end of *Purgatory* would not have seemed unfamiliar to the Spirituals, who placed special emphasis on John's Apocalypse. We can also see Dante's support for the cause of the Spirituals in the identity of the very first historical figure whom he encounters on the margins of

Hell—Pope Celestine V, a saintly hermit, hailed by the Spirituals as the Angelic Pope, he whose papacy would signal the age of the *ecclesia spiritualis* but who dashed these great hopes when he abdicated the papal office after just five months. Dante's manifest disgust at Celestine for his "great refusal" (his cowardly failure to take part in the struggle to reform the corrupt church) indicates that Dante, too, had placed a great deal of hope in him. One can also point to various popular verses of Spiritual provenance, written in the decades following Dante's death, that share Dante's hope for Empire and his penchant for expressing this hope in the framework of Joachimism. One of these Imperialist-Joachite poems ends by citing a line from Dante, "e vero frutto verrà dopo 'l *fiore*" ("and good fruit shall come after the flower"; *Par.* XXVII, 148). This poem's mid-fourteenth-century author understood Dante's *fiore* as an unmistakable reference to Joachim of Fiore.[116]

But what is pertinent for our purposes is the Spiritual Franciscans' relatively positive attitude toward "infidels" in general and Muslims in particular. If in some cases, such as for Olivi himself, this means the Christianization of the globe (although a Christianization for which St. Francis is the exemplar), in other cases what is envisioned is a post-Christian "religion of the Spirit." And, in any case, the envisioned global ecumenicalism is not predicated on an increased world domination by the Western powers-that-be. It is, rather, the aftermath of the destruction of those powers.

Saint Francis of Assisi is usually thought of as one who, troubled by the church's ever-increasing devotion to wealth and luxury, preached the return to the simple life of poverty practiced by Christ and the apostles. This is certainly true, and indeed much of the effort of the Spirituals was directed toward reforming the Franciscan order, which in their view had deviated from Francis's rule of poverty. But, as Giulio Basetti Sani has shown, Francis's project to reform the lives of the clergy was part of a more fundamental project: the evangelization of Muslims. This evangelization would be accomplished not by force, not by dispute, not by logic or dialectic or even rhetoric, but only by example. Only models of Christ-like practice—humility, compassion, pacifism, love—will bring about the global conversion to Christianity. Francis's project of clerical reform is the first step in providing the non-Christian world proper examples of Christian life.

The primary characteristic of those who imitate Christ is nonviolence, even to the point of suffering martyrdom. Hence Francis desired to journey to the lands of the "Saracens," not to preach the Gospel there but in a sense to embody it, ultimately by meeting his death there. He did not go to the Holy Lands to kill but rather to be killed. The conversion of non-Christians to Christianity will come about, not through a deployment nor even a display of strength, but only through *a display of weakness*.

Of course the missionary project of converting "infidels" is unpalatable to us, for it is, in our eyes, a kind of intolerant religious imperialism, motivated by the assumption that the salvation of non-Christian souls depends on their becoming Christian. But in passing judgment on Francis's project we ought to consider its historical context. This was the age of Crusades, the mobilization of European material force to take, through violence, possession of Jerusalem and the Holy Lands. In 1215 Francis, in the days just prior to the Fourth Lateran Council, pleaded with Pope Innocent III, begging him not to proclaim a new crusade. His pleas were to no avail, however, as the centerpiece of the major decree of that council was a detailed set of legislation compelling Christendom to wage total war against Islam. Francis's whole life project, including even the establishment of his mendicant order with its vow of poverty, was directed toward providing a non-violent alternative to the Crusades. As Sani says:

> Francis understood that Christ's victory had not been accomplished by the sword and by violence, such as the violence that had been perpetrated against His own sacred Person. . . .Francis could not understand why his contemporary Christians. . .were afraid of Islam. "Love your enemies, do good to those who hate you" was a commandment that they should put in practice with respect to Muslims. The Crusades had appealed, in the name of Christ, to physical force to combat physical force. People thought that by blessing swords (which were shaped like crosses) and by decorating shields, helmets, and breastplates with the image of the Cross, they had changed the nature of killing. Saint Bernard proclaimed that killing a Muslim in the name of Christ was not a "homicide" but a "malicide." For Saint Francis, on the other hand, it was the murder of a "brother" for whom Christ had spilled His blood, even if the Muslim did not yet understand this divine love.[117]

Francis was utterly opposed to the notion that the leaders of Christendom had the right or the duty to take political possession of the Holy Lands. Drawing upon a passage from the New Testament ("For the Lord's sake accept the authority of every human institution, whether of the emperor as supreme, or of governors, as sent by him to punish those who do wrong and to praise those who do right" [1 Peter 2.13–14]), Francis taught his followers that, when finding themselves in Islamic territories, they ought to humbly submit to the authority of Muslim rulers and respect their right, as God-given, to rule over their own lands.[118] This submission to the governing Islamic authorities would itself be a major element of the imitation of Christ.

Saint Francis was, as Sani remarks, interested not only in the salvation of Christian souls "but especially those of the 'Saracens,' to whom it was his duty to bring words of peace, with the aim of the universal reconciliation of brothers."[119] And a key point here is that he was interested in the welfare of Muslims' souls, *not in their land*.

Sani offers an intriguing suggestion concerning the extraordinary fact that, in the summer of 1216, Francis convinced Pope Honorious III (who had just been elected that July) to proclaim that a plenary indulgence would be granted to all pilgrims to the little chapel of Portiuncula, a few miles from Assisi, the place where Francis had founded his Order of Friars Minor. A plenary indulgence exempts one from all temporal punishment (time spent in Purgatory) for all sins that one has ever committed up to that point in one's life. This was extraordinary, since a plenary indulgence was among the rarest of privileges, normally reserved for very special purposes and very special places—such as the Holy Sepulcher in Jerusalem or St. Peter's in Rome. Most notably, a plenary indulgence had been granted the previous year, by decree of the Fourth Lateran Council, to those who would fund and/or participate in the Fifth Crusade, which, with the aim of conquering Jerusalem, was scheduled to commence from Brindisi on June 1, 1217. The effect of Francis's gaining for his little chapel in Umbria the privileges normally associated with pilgrimage or crusade to Jerusalem was potentially profound—although this possibility was perhaps unnoticed by Honorious III. For Francis, in offering an alternative way to gain a plenary indulgence, had in effect devalued one of the major "payoffs" that the church offered as an enticement to crusaders. In a subtle fashion, Francis was telling warriors and pilgrims to turn their backs on the so-called Holy Land. And Francis was telling them that the "land" on which they should focus their desire should be a simple, insignificant, unremarkable village near Assisi. Thus they would come to see that what matters is not the land that one covets but the welfare of one's soul. Setting up his native territory as the prime focus of pilgrimage was for Francis an act of "re-orientation": shifting the "Orient" from Palestine to Italy. (Dante seems to have understood this "re-orientation," for in *Paradiso* XI he has Aquinas say the following about Francis's native town of Assisi [which was usually called "Ascesi" in Dante's Tuscan]: "Therefore let him who talks of this place / not say 'Ascesi,' which would be to speak short, / but 'Orient,' if he would name it rightly"; *Par.* XI, 52–54). By making the "Orient" more a state of mind than a specific place, or, insofar as it is a place, making that place moveable and in one's own backyard, Francis aims to cure Europe of its obsessive desire to gain possession of the physical territory that we now call the Middle East. For Francis, the entire earth is sacred (as his famous ecological manifesto, the "Canticle of the Sun," so joyfully expresses) but no particular land is especially "holy." Following the "re-Orientation" proposed by Francis, those who would still insist on fighting for control of Jerusalem would be exposed as participants in an enterprise that was nothing more than an attempted land-grab.[120]

If we can fault Francis for thinking that his mission was to turn Muslims into Christians, we can also acknowledge that his attitude of love, respect, and compassion for and humble submission to Muslims sowed the seeds of a "post-Christian," universalist ecumenicalism that later emerged as one possible development of the Spiritual Franciscan tradition.

The Spiritual Franciscans (like many such appellations, this name is a convenient label for a variety of disparate movements and tendencies) are defined by their following Joachim of Fiore in looking forward to a third age of human history, the Age of the Spirit, an age that would develop from but to some degree surpass the previous two ages (the Age of the Father, the religion of which is Judaism, and the age of the Son, the religion of which is Christianity). Joachim divided the history of revelation into three rather than two periods. For Joachim, there was not simply an Old Law (centered around the writings of Moses) and a New Law (centered around the Gospels concerning Christ); rather, taking the historical logic of the Trinity more seriously than does orthodox Catholicism, Joachim prophesied a future dispensation that one might call a "New New Law." The Spiritual Franciscans' freely adopting this Joachite scheme is what makes them "Spirituals." What makes them "Franciscans" is their maintaining that this Age of the Spirit is inaugurated or adumbrated by, or in some sense associated with, Saint Francis of Assisi. In its more radical formulations, the doctrine of some Spirituals amounted to a "de-centering" of Christ: He was no longer the be-all and end-all, the center of history, the last word in matters concerning salvation.

This notion of a coming new, post-Christian dispensation that would surpass the present order of things was of course received by the church as a great danger, and is the reason why certain Spirituals were pursued by the Inquisition and deemed to be heretics. The "moderate" Spirituals, as Marjorie Reeves explains, tried to protect themselves by insisting that the Age of the Spirit was at the same time the age of Christ's Second Coming, to be followed by his Third Coming at the end of time:

> Their models might be drawn from the past, but their belief was that the life of the future would far exceed the past. It was not so much a recapturing of the life of the first Apostles that they expected as the creating of the life of new apostles. It was this claim, which so easily passed into arrogance, which most shocked and offended the orthodox. Again and again in Inquisitorial proceedings the claim to greater perfection than Christ and the Apostles was a major accusation against them. Thus the most unpalatable part of the Joachimist view was the claim that the future could transcend the past. . . .Perhaps it was an

instinctive avoidance of the extreme consequences of this logic that led Spiritual Franciscans to try to combine faith in the future with a special devotion to the Person of Christ, and to find the focus of this combination in the life of St. Francis. The leap forward into the future was made possible by Joachim's doctrine of the Third Age, with its more abundant outpouring of the Spirit. Yet among the Spiritual Franciscans particularly there was a great emphasis on conformity to the life of Christ. The faith of these groups seems more directly Christocentric than that of Joachim. But still the role of Francis is not simply that of imitating the earthly life of Christ as closely as possible: it is to be conformed to Christ in order that at the opening of the Third Age Francis might stand as Christ had stood at the crossing from the First into the Second. The fusion of their own emphasis upon Christ with Joachim's on the Spirit is best seen in their concept of the three Advents of Christ, with Francis embodying the Second, and the orthodox Second Advent becoming the Third at end of history.[121]

As seen in part I, the notion of Christ's Second Coming as marking, not the end of time and the Last Judgment, but rather the inauguration of a lengthy period of peace on earth in which the church would be "spiritual" rather than "carnal," is a key element of the Olivi-inspired Spiritual teachings to which Dante was exposed in his youth as a student at Santa Croce.

Dante's apocalyptic scenario, alluded to throughout the *Comedy* and formally presented in *Purgatory* XXXII and XXXIII, follows Olivi's in a key respect: as David Burr says, Olivi envisions that "continued decay of the church will lead to rule by a pseudopope who, with the aid of secular authority, will support a carnal version of Christianity."[122] This notion of a malignant alliance of the papacy and a secular ruler is based on Revelation's reference to "the great whore who is seated on many waters, with whom the kings of the earth have committed fornication" (Rev. 17.1–2). The notion was appealing to Dante, for the chief opponents of empire were the "national" rulers (especially the French kings) and the popes, who, each having their own reasons to resist subjecting themselves to a higher political authority, joined together in common cause against the claims of the emperor. In *Purgatory* XXXII Dante represents the papacy as an "ungirt harlot" fornicating with a "giant," representing the kings of France:

> Secure, like a fortress on a high mountain,
> there appeared to me an ungirt harlot,
> sitting upon it, with eyes quick to rove around.

> And, as if in order that she should not be taken from him,
> I saw standing at her side a giant,
> and they kissed each other again and again.
>
> (*Purg.* XXXII, 148–153)

For Dante, this alliance of pseudo-pope and secular king will, sometime in the near future, be defeated by the global Monarch, represented somewhat enigmatically as a "Five Hundred, Ten, and Five":

> "For I see surely, and therefore I tell of it,
> stars already close at hand, secure from all check
> and hindrance, that shall bring us a time
>
> wherein a Five Hundred, Ten, and Five
> sent by God, shall slay the thievish woman [i.e., the papacy]
> with that giant [i.e, the French royalty] who sins with her."
> (*Purg.* XXXIII, 40–45)

It is less important to identify a precise historical referent for this 515 than to recognize that, as a version of the 666 of Revelation, it functions to show that in this part of *Purgatory*, Dante is writing his version of John's Apocalypse. And, like Apocalypse for the Spirituals, who, as Burr remarks, envisioned a scenario that was "apocalyptic without being notably eschatological," Apocalypse for Dante does not mean "last things," the end of time, the termination of human history on earth, but, rather, it means a fundamental amelioration of life on earth.[123] The outcome of Apocalypse for Dante will be, to use Olivi's words from his commentary on Apocalypse, that "a certain new world or new church will then seem to have been formed, the old having been rejected, just as in Christ's first advent a new church was formed, the synagogue having been rejected."[124]

For Olivi, as for many of the Spirituals, the new church that will be formed after Apocalypse will be a universal Christian Church—that is, there will be a universal conversion of all peoples of all faiths to Christianity. This universal conversion, as Burr says,

> will be shaped by opposition to evangelical renewal within the church. Just as the apostles, seeing the hostility they aroused within Judaism, directed their missionary efforts primarily at the Gentiles and only secondarily at the Jews, so the spiritual men [i.e., the Spiritual Franciscans]. . . .seeing the same opposition within the Latin church, will turn to the Greeks, Muslims, Mongols, and Jews. . . .Olivi draws a parallel between the transition from synagogue to church in the first century and the transition under way in his own. One possible result of universal conversion is that the capital of Christendom may migrate from Rome to Jerusalem. Olivi is not insistent on the matter, since he sees no clear indication of it in Scripture, yet the idea obviously makes sense to him. Why? There is reason to suspect that he sees it at least partly as a judgment on Rome, but that is not what he actually says. Instead he evokes the ebb and flow of Christian history. The apostles preached first to the Jews, then turned to the Gentiles after the Jews rejected

them. Spiritual preachers of the third age, rejected by leaders of the carnal Western church, will turn to the Greeks, Muslims, Tartars, and finally Jews. . . .Moreover, in an age of universal conversion, moving the capital to Jerusalem would reflect geographical realities. Olivi suggests that the [Age of the Spirit] will see a *sublimissimus cultus Christi* on Mount Zion. "Nor would it be surprising if the place of our redemption should be exalted over all other places at that time, especially in view of the fact that the highest rulers of the world will find that place more suitable for the conversion and later the governance of the whole world, since it is the geographical center of the habitable world." Thus the shift to Jerusalem would imply not merely a return to the original center of Christianity, but the progressive advance of conversion. Rome was a convenient capital in the second age, when Christianity was essentially a Mediterranean and northern European phenomenon; in the third age of universal conversion, however, as the geographical center of Christianity shifts east, it would be sensible for the capital to follow it, settling in Jerusalem, which—Olivi might note, pointing to a contemporary *mappa mundi*—is the geographical center of the world.[125]

Olivi's suggestion of a global Christianity centered in Jerusalem is not a plan for Western religious imperialism. In fact Olivi's notion of moving the church from Rome to Jerusalem is a matter of disassociating Christianity from Euro-ethnocentrism. If for Olivi the post-Apocalyptic world will be entirely "Christian," this will not result from the Westernization of the world but rather from the Orientalization of Christianity. If the Christian Church shifts its center to Jerusalem, it will not be in the aftermath of a successful Crusade, by means of which the Church of Rome and its secular European allies will have taken up power in the Orient. This cannot possibly be the scenario, for the Church of Rome and the secular powers of Europe will have been destroyed. The Christianization of Jerusalem will not be a matter of the present Church's coming to even greater power but rather of its passing away. Olivi and his followers imagine the third church not as the Church of Rome become a universal, global power but as a church marked by what we have called the *weakness* of Francis: "As for the 'third church,' they saw this mainly in terms of the *viri spirituales*, the true sons of Francis who would constitute it in poverty, humility, and gentleness on the ruin of all other churches."[126]

One of the recurring themes of some Spirituals is that few or virtually none of those who presently call themselves Christians will survive the apocalyptic shift to the Age of the Spirit. If the third church will continue to be called "Christian," this is because at the heart of all religions is a genuine Christian content, which will be carried over into the new age, while the external formal, institutional, and ecclesiastical trappings of the various particular religions will be jettisoned. Of those who now call themselves

Christians, only the Spirituals themselves will enjoy the new world order of the future. But they will not be alone; rather, they will be joined by new Christians, a world community of the virtuous culled from among those who in the present, pre-Apocalyptic world are called Muslims, Jews, Tartars, etc. As Dominique Urvoy explains, the missionary project of the Spirituals is not a matter on converting infidels to Christianity in its current form, not merely a matter of increasing the membership rolls of the Church of Rome; instead it involves a transformation of Christianity itself:

> This conversion is never envisioned as the passage from one religion to another, but as access to the "genuine" religion, the one that "distills the truth" from that religion of which one only rejects the external ecclesiastical aspects. The idea can take the shape of a genuine Christianity which is nourished by the inner substance of the other religions. Thus the Majorcan Bartolomé Jancessius, in the middle of the fourteenth century. . .thought that during the time of the coming of the Antichrist Christians would be so perverted that they would never be able to convert. The Church [in the Age of the Spirit] would thus of necessity be constituted by Jews, Muslims, and pagans who would become Christians after the death of the Antichrist. But more generally, the idea was that the new religion would be the "religion of God," without any more precise details.[127]

In trying to understand what was intended by the notion of an *ecclesia spiritualis*, we should bear in mind that, to the medieval mind, this would necessarily connote the distinction between the "letter" and the "spirit." For the Spirituals, the notion of "the church" is to be understood "spiritually" (i.e., metaphorically) not "literally." Those persons who *literally* belong to the Christian Church (such as the pope, the cardinals, and the clergy; the congregation of pious worshippers and donors; professed believers, etc.) are not necessarily the real members of the church. Conversely, the *real* church may well include multitudes who are not, literally speaking, "Christians." *Literally* speaking, the new "religion of God" will not be a church. It will be, rather, the idea or notion of a universally accessible "Church of God"—a church with neither walls nor institutions.

The idea of a religion whose content is the inner substance of the various other specific religions is, as we saw near the beginning of part II, one of the fundamental ideas of Islam. Urvoy sees the Franciscan Turmeda's conversion to Islam in this light: it was less about rejecting one set of doctrines for an alternate set, but rather was motivated by his rejecting all purely institutional or formal aspects of religion. Turmeda's "adoption of Islam was due solely to the fact that this religion is a 'community' structured by rites but without any hierarchy or ecclesiastical authority that could rigidify it."[128] Urvoy, who speaks of Islam as "a silent, indirectly influential partner" in the development of the resistance discourses of the dissident Christian minorities of Europe, is suggesting that the "religion of the Spirit" of the Third Age was, for some Spirituals, Islam, or an Islamicized version of Christianity—that some Spirituals saw in Islam their own ideal of a "religion without a church."[129] An interesting case is that of the mid-fifteenth-century Franciscan Fray Alfonso de Mella, an accused heretic who was forced to take refuge in the Muslim territory of the southern Iberian Peninsula. Muslims, says Fray Alfonso, "believe in one sole true God, creator of the heavens and the earth, Whom they worship with great faith, fear, humility, reverence, and devotion, and Whom they honor with their words and deeds. And may it please heaven that those who call themselves Christians would fear Him, adore Him, and honor Him with as much reverence and fear."[130] Moreover, since Muslims believe in Christ and greatly honor him, we must recognize that God is not the God of Christians but the God of "all those who believe in Him with rectitude and who accomplish His commandments through appropriate deeds."[131] An interesting counter-case is Dante's contemporary and fellow Florentine, Riccoldo da Monte Croce, a Dominican friar from the church of Santa Maria Novella. Riccoldo's *Liber Peregrinationis* combines an account of the several months that he spent in Baghdad (*ad interiora*, as he says, "in the heart" of Muslim territory) in 1291 with praise of Muslims (who, says Riccoldo, are notable for "their application to study, their devotion in prayer, their compassion toward the poor, their veneration for the name of God, the prophets, and holy places, their moral seriousness, their affability toward strangers, and their fellowship and love for one another") and vehement scorn for Islam (which he attacks on the grounds that it is "liberal, confused, obscure, mendacious, irrational, and violent").[132] In calling Islam overly "liberal" (*larga*), Riccoldo means that the way to salvation as conceived in Islam is too wide open, not sufficiently narrow: "[Their Law] is liberal. . .[and] contrary to the rule of the greatest, most sublime philosopher, Christ, who said 'Narrow is the way that leads to life, etc.' For them there is nothing necessary for salvation other than saying, 'There is no God but God and Muhammad is the messenger of God.' For Saracens generally maintain that whoever says this single phrase will be saved. . . .Thus their Law is broad [*larga*], and the devil cleverly provided it: for those who do not want to take the narrow way [*viam strictam*] to ascend to beatitude, he prepared the broad way [*viam largam*] to lead them to Gehenna [i.e., Hell]."[133] For Riccoldo, Christianity's "narrowness" recommends in its favor, while Islam's "liberality" recommends against it: Islam's tendency in the direction of universal salvation proves that it is wrong, since the truth is that salvation is difficult to attain, and reserved only for a few—and only for Christians.

Salvation, for some of the Spirituals, was by no means a possibility reserved exclusively for Christians. This was most often taught by those on the radical margins, by popular movements the members of which were not Franciscans but who believed Olivi's teachings and were as likely to be women as men. Among the remarkable Spirituals was the Occitan woman Na Prous Boneta de Montpellier. As Reeves describes it,

> her confession of 1325 shows a strange, ill-assorted mixture of Catharism and Joachimism, but its chief emphasis is on the new era of history just beginning. To usher this in, the Holy Spirit must be incarnate, undergo passion and death, and rise again. This second Crucifixion was being accomplished in the condemnation of Olivi's works and the persecution of Prous herself. For she had been chosen to be the abode of the Trinity and the giver of the Holy Spirit to the world. Whoever believed the writings of Olivi and the words of Prous would be baptized with the Holy Spirit.[134]

Responding to the Inquisition in 1326 as she was about to be burned to death (just a few years after Dante's death), Na Prous openly proclaimed that "Christian, Hebrew, and Saracen [i.e., Muslim] men and women, no matter what state they are in, will all be saved—provided that they believe in the operation of the Holy Spirit."[135] One might suggest that these words were offered not without reference to some well-known events of just a few years before: in 1320 several thousand "shepherds" (*pastouroux* or *pastorelli*) from Northern France, stirred up into a frenzy of hate against the Muslims of Andalusia, set out on "the Shepherd's Crusade" to reclaim Iberia for Christendom; along the way, as they passed through Na Prous's region of Occitania, and then into Catalonia and Aragon, they slaughtered hundreds of Jews.

A few decades earlier, a Milanese noblewoman named Guglielma (d. 1282) became noteworthy for her remarkable feminist variation of the Spiritual teaching. Following her death, her sect developed through the work of her disciples, a woman named Manfreda (cousin of Matteo Visconti, the head of Milan's ruling dynasty) and a man named Andreas Saramita, both of whom were burned by the Inquisition in 1300:

> The main tenets of Manfreda and Saramita were quite unambiguous: they declared that, as the Word had been incarnate in a Man, so the Holy Spirit had become incarnate in a woman, Gugielma. She, too, would rise from the dead, ascend into heaven in the sight of her disciples, and send upon them the Holy Spirit as tongues of flame. Once more the extreme implication is worked out: all authority has now departed from the existing ecclesiastical hierarchy and Boniface VIII is no true pope. Once more the new spiritual roles are allotted, this time to women, for Manfreda will be the new pope

and her cardinals will be women. She will baptize Jews, Saracens, and all other infidels, entering into peaceable possession of the Holy See.[136]

Again, there is the notion here that "the new pope," the papacy such as it will be in the Age of the Spirit, will work to include rather than to exclude: its task will be to welcome as "insiders" all those whom the Church of Rome has persecuted as "outsiders."

Pentecost and the Eternal Gospel

The Spirituals are not so named simply because they urge a more "spiritual" (ascetic) life than do other more worldly members of the Catholic clergy (or other more worldly members of the Franciscan order), but rather because they tend to shift the center of revelatory gravity away from Christ and on to the Spirit.

What does it mean to substitute, as Na Prous does, belief in the Spirit for belief in Christ as the prerequisite to salvation? What is the essential signification of the Spirit?

The Spirit, in the medieval tradition, is inseparable from the question of cultural diversity that is at the core of Na Prous's proclamation. For the Spirit is above all else associated with the miraculous interlinguistic and intercultural communication that took place, according to the Acts of the Apostles, when all the apostles had come together to celebrate the festival of Pentecost:

> When the day of Pentecost had come, they were all together in one place. And suddenly from heaven there came a sound like the rush of a violent wind, and it filled the entire house where they were sitting. Divided tongues, as of fire, appeared among them, and a tongue rested on each of them. All of them were filled with the Holy Spirit and began to speak in other languages, as the Spirit gave them ability. Now, there were devout Jews from every nation under heaven living in Jerusalem. And at this sound the crowd gathered and was bewildered, because each one heard them speaking in the native language of each. Amazed and astonished, they asked, "Are not all these who are speaking Galileans? And how is it that we hear, each of us, in our own native language? Parthians, Medes, Elamites, and residents of Mesopotamia, Judea and Cappadocia, Pontus and Asia, Phrygia and Pamphylia, Egypt and the parts of Libya belonging to Cyrene, and visitors from Rome, both Jews and proselytes, Cretans and Arabs—in our own languages we hear them speaking about God's deeds of power." All were amazed and perplexed, saying to one another, "What does this mean?" (Acts 2.1–2.12)

This lengthy enumeration of geographical communities and place-names emphasizes the notions of linguistic, ethnic and cultural diversity that, for medievals, are always among the Holy Spirit's primary connotations. Above all, the Spirit bridges the gap between self and other, between "us" and "them." The Spirit grants the self the gift of "otherness": the power to speak to others, but also to speak *as* an other, to put oneself in another's place.

The miracle of Pentecost is founded on the idea that the Word is not the exclusive property of any one linguistic or ethnic community. As Alexandre Leupin says: "Turning back to the Pentecost, we see that the faithful are surprised not only by the miracle of speaking a language that one does not know; it is also a matter of the miracle's effect: the notion of a sacred language is destroyed, as all hierarchy of languages dissolves. Every language is capable of revelation, not just Hebrew alone."[137] It is this very sort of anti-ethnocentrism, this de-emphasis on the absolute necessity of "one's own" (one's own religion, language, nation, gender, social status) that resounds in Na Prous's words, which one might take as a manifesto of the Spiritual movement. We are saved by a "belief in the Spirit"—which is to say by our belief in the salvation of others.

The Spirituals are most frequently presented as one faction in a dispute, internal to the Franciscan order, concerning the degree to which clergy ought to follow Francis's rule of poverty. This is undoubtedly correct, but a more essential project envisioned by at least some of the most radical among them was a revision of the very notion of "the church"—nothing less than the invention of a new religion. But regardless of their actual project, what matters for us are the conceptions of that project with which Dante would have been familiar.

One of these conceptions involved the founding of a "post-Christian" religion of the Spirit. This project, hardly clandestine, in fact attracted a great deal of attention. Jean de Meun's *Romance of the Rose*, the most popular literary work of the late Middle Ages (a work which Dante himself rendered into Italian, under the title *Il Fiore*), indicates that the conflict between Spirituals and the orthodox church was no minor skirmish, but rather a major, apocalyptic ideological struggle. Jean tells us about the ubiquity of talk in and around the University of Paris from the 1250s through the 1270s concerning the Spirituals' *new* New Testament, a work known as the *Eternal Gospel*. One of Jean's characters, False Seeming, delivers what appears to be an attack against the Spirituals and the book that had caused such a stir (given that False Seeming is an avowed liar—"I am a perjurer. . . .But the deception is so complete that it is very difficult to recognize"—it is hard to determine Jean de Meun's own position concerning the radical movement):

> "Had it not been for the vigilance of the University, which keeps the key of Christendom, everything would have been thrown into turmoil when, with

evil intent, in the year of Our Lord 1255 (and no man living will contradict me) there was released as a model for imitation, and this is true, a book written by the devil, the *Eternal Gospel*, which, according to the title, was transmitted by the Holy Spirit, for so it is called; it deserves to be burned. There was not a man nor a woman in Paris, in the square in front of Notre-Dame, who could not have had it to copy if he had wanted. He would have found there many outrageous comparisons such as this: just as the sun in the great excellence of its light and heat surpasses the moon, which is much dimmer and darker, just as the kernel surpasses the nutshell, I tell you truly upon my soul—and do not imagine that I am making fun of you—that in the same way this gospel surpasses those written by the four evangelists of Jesus Christ under their own names. A great many such comparisons would have been found there, which I forbear to mention. . . .Thus it is written in the book whose words convey the following meaning: *as long as Peter is lord, John cannot show his power.* I have given you the shell of the meaning which hides the real intention; now I will explain the kernel to you. Peter signifies the Pope and includes the secular clergy, who will keep the Law of Christ, guarding and defending it against all who would obstruct it; John stands for the friars, who will say that the only tenable Law is the *Eternal Gospel*, sent by the Holy Spirit to set men on *the right path.*"[138]

The gist of the Spirituals' endeavor, in the extreme form manifest as the *Eternal Gospel*, is the prophecy of a new religion (which is at the same time an old one, for this message is, after all, "eternal") that will surpass Christianity, of a church the cornerstone of which would be John, not Peter, and the law of which would be that of the Spirit, not of Christ.[139]

We have already seen what is meant by the substitution of the Spirit for Christ. But what is the significance of John's supplanting Peter as the apostolic foundation of the new church? What would be the essential spirit of a church of John, a church of the spirit?

The title *Eternal Gospel* refers to a passage in Revelation, the author of which is "John" (considered in the Middle Ages identical to the author of the Gospel of John, but recognized by modern scholars as having been someone else). Among the multitude of prophetic visions revealed to John is the following (in which some Spirituals claimed to recognize the foundation of their post-Christian religion):

> Then I saw another angel flying in midheaven, with an *eternal gospel* to proclaim to those who live on the earth—*to every nation and tribe and language and people.* He said in a loud voice, "Fear God and give him glory, for *the hour of his judgment has come*; and *worship him who made heaven and earth, the sea and the springs of water.*" (Rev. 14.6–7)

The most general reason why the Spirituals embraced John is Revelation's tremendous emphasis on apocalyptic, momentous change: these radicals preferred, in opposition to the "rock" of stability and permanence that is "Peter," the tumultuous winds and fires of change associated with "John." But this specific passage, with its mention of the *Eternal Gospel*, signified much more to the Spirituals than simply a general notion of apocalypse. For it repeats what is probably Revelation's primary leitmotiv: "to every nation and tribe and language and people." (In Revelation 5.9 we read about "saints from every tribe and language and people and nation"; in Revelation 7.9 we read that "there was a great multitude that no one could count, from every nation, from all tribes and peoples and languages"; Revelation 10.11 tells us that the book is indeed centered on this theme: "Then they said to me, 'You must prophesy again about many peoples and nations and languages and kings'.")

In an era in which the official Catholic Church operated by excluding otherness, denigrating cultural diversity, and promoting fear of ethnic and religious difference, the Spirituals saw in this *Eternal Gospel* an alternative way—an embrace of diversity. They do not interpret the imperative to preach to "every nation and tribe and language and people" as endorsing a religious imperialism by which "Peter" shall conquer the world. Rather, they see "John" as refusing to promote an "us" versus "them," "good" versus "evil," "true" versus "false" mentality. In thirteenth-century Europe, when the official church's ideological pay-off to its adherents resided in its offer of the prestige of being "better than" non-Christians (morally superior, exclusively eligible for eternal salvation, loved and aided by God, closer to truth), the project of opening up a gospel for others signifies an attempt to break down this attitude of arrogant superiority. The Spirituals understood John to be saying that truth is not the exclusive property of one culture, of one religion.

According to the narrative in Revelation, the *sum total* of the message of the *Eternal Gospel* is this: "Fear God and give him glory, for the hour of his judgment has come; and worship him who made heaven and earth, the sea and the springs of water." The *Eternal Gospel*, then, makes no mention of Christ. Rather, it tells us to focus on the God of the initial verses of Genesis, on God as creator of the physical cosmos—thereby shifting emphasis away from any particular (culturally specific) prophets.

Also significant is the *temporality* of the *Eternal Gospel* that is revealed in Revelation 14.7. Presumably, an "eternal" gospel is one valid at all times and in all places, meant to appeal to audiences both from centuries ago and centuries into the future. But among the crucial contents of this eternal gospel is an insistence on its absolute "present-ness": "the hour of his judgment has come." The *Eternal Gospel*, being eternal, is not exclusively bound up with any particular historical time; yet, paradoxically, the very message of this gospel is, "now is the time." Thus, any and every audience of the *Eternal*

Gospel, from no matter what time, is necessarily situated by that gospel at the very center of time. The all-important hour is always "here and now"—no matter when the *Eternal Gospel* happens to be revealed to an audience.

Since any and every time turns out to be the center of time, the *Eternal Gospel* teaches that there is no single historical event (other than the "now") that is "more central" than others. The "hour of judgment" is not a particular moment in chronological history, in relation to which all other historical events are peripheral. Rather, *the* momentous event in history is always *now*, everywhere. A corollary of the *Eternal Gospel* is the denial of the historical centrality and preeminence of the Christ-event.

This may help explain the astonishing fact that Dante sets the events of the *Comedy*, not so much in the chronological middle of his own lifespan, but rather at the very chronological center of human history. For in *Paradiso* Dante provides us with information concerning the age of the universe and the chronology of human existence which, although probably striking some readers as irrelevant trivia, is in fact part of a coherent system of "clues" meant to direct us to one conclusion: 1300 AD, the year in which Dante found himself in a dark wood and subsequently undertook his voyage through Hell, Purgatory and Heaven, is *the very center of historical time*—that is, 1300 AD is 6500 years after the creation of Adam and 6500 years before the end of the world.[140] Once we have learned this, the *Comedy*'s famous opening line ("Nel *mezzo* del cammin di nostra vita" ["In the *middle* of the journey of our life"]) appears in a new light. Here, "our life" means the chronological history of the human species on earth from its beginning to its end. The *Comedy*'s opening line means: *in the center of historical time*. Dante takes literally and to its extreme the prescription of classical poetics according to which the epic poem must begin *in media res*. For Dante's epic literally begins "in the middle" (with its first words, *Nel mezzo*), and the "thing" in the middle of which it begins is nothing other than the entire history of human life on earth.

Dante's placing himself at the very center, thereby making claims for the absolute centrality of his own life, time and place, is not an arrogant assertion that he is history's singular central event. Instead it is meant to signify that one is always, in relation to the agency of truth and salvation, situated at the very center. This is why Dante marginalizes Christ, replacing him with Beatrice, who is Dante's own personal agent of salvation. Salvation comes from the here-and-now of Dante's own life, not from some other life in a distant time and place. By insisting that his own time and place are as close as can be to the center of truth, Dante refuses a hierarchy according to which some times and places (e.g., Jerusalem at the time of Christ's death) are more central than others. By de-centering the Christ-event, Dante affirms the potential centrality of any and every culture.

It is in Dante's conversation with Adam in *Paradiso* XXVI where we learn for certain that the "present time" narrated by the *Comedy*—1300 AD—is the chronological midpoint of human history. Significantly, this same conversation tells us that no human languages are more natural, closer to truth, than any others. Just as there has been no "fall" in the import of one's own historical time (the present time is not less significant than some more truly and fully significant past), neither has there been a "linguistic fall" after which language is less worthy than it had once been.

For Dante learns from Adam that human language has been a matter of "usage" (convention) from the very beginning, that Babel did *not* mark a fall from a single natural to a multitude of conventional languages:

> "The language that I spoke was long extinct
> before that unaccomplishable task
> entered the minds of Nimrod's followers;
>
> no product of the human mind can last
> eternally for, as all things in Nature,
> man's inclination varies with the stars.
>
> That man should speak is only natural,
> but how he speaks, in this way or in that,
> Nature allows you to do as you please.
>
> Till I descended to the pains of Hell,
> *I* was He called on earth That Highest Good
> Who swathes me in the brilliance of His bliss;
>
> And then He was called *El*: for man's
> customs, like the leaves upon the branch,
> change as they fall and others take their place."
>
> (*Par.* XXVI, 124–138)

Here the *Comedy* teaches a linguistic doctrine in radical contrast to a more-than-thousand-year-old medieval tradition that had maintained that, were it not for Babel, all of humankind would continue to speak Adam's language, the language "natural" to humans—Hebrew. Dante himself had ascribed to this tradition in his *De Vulgaria Eloquentia*, in which special status is attributed to Hebrew, "the language of grace":

> I say that a certain form of speech was created by God along with the first soul. . . .And this form would be used by all the tongues of those who speak had it not been dissipated by the sin of human presumption, as will be shown below.
>
> In this form of speech Adam spoke; in this form of speech all his posterity spoke up to the time of the building of the tower of Babel, which is interpreted,

the tower of confusion; this form of speech was inherited by the sons of Heber, who are called Hebrews after him. In them alone it remained after the confusion, so that our Redeemer, who was born out of them insofar as he was human, could enjoy the language, not of confusion, but of grace. The Hebrew language, therefore, was that formed by the lips of the first speaker.[141]

Virtually everything taught by Dante in the *De Vulgari Eloquentia* on the issue of humankind's original language is shown by Adam to be just plain wrong. First, we should note that in *Paradiso* XXVI, Adam does not indicate that his language was Hebrew, nor does he give his language any specific cultural identity; it is simply called "the language that I spoke." As an effect of this vague nonidentification, no particular human community can trace its own language back to a supposed locus of primacy and authenticity.

We know that Adam's original language was *not* Hebrew, since he tells us that he called God "I," whereas it was only later that God was called "El." This "El," Dante had told us in the *De Vulgari Eloquentia*, is the Hebrew name for God and was the first word ever spoken by the first human speaker ("I do not hesitate to affirm what occurs immediately to any man in his right mind, that what the voice of the first speaker first sounded was the word for 'God,' which is to say 'El' ").[142] But here Dante learns that what he had once supposed to be the "original" and "natural" name for God, "El," was in fact at best a secondary and belated, entirely conventional, human invention. The Hebrew language, which Dante and the medieval tradition had deemed natural, primary, original—and thus more capable than any other of serving as a vehicle for the expression of God's thoughts—had been preceded, at the very least, by the unknown and unnamed "language that Adam spoke."

Whatever may have been Adam's language, it was not God-given but was the production of his own invention. Adam's original naming was an *ad placitum* imposition of conventional signifiers—since, as he says, when it comes to using this or that set of signifiers, "Nature allows you to do as you please." Absent is any notion that Adam's primal language somehow named truth better than other languages might possibly have done—and this despite the fact that his name for God, "I," seems designed to seduce us into cratylism, the notion that some names, through a natural bond with what they signify, reveal the very essences of things. It is tempting to think that the name *I*, with its connotations of unity, simplicity, primacy, and integrity, is a more "natural" name for God, more revelatory of God's essence, than is the name *El*. But Adam is very insistent that his name for God was an arbitrary signifier imposed *ad placitum*: even the most apparently natural name is in fact entirely conventional. And there never was any possibility that, were it not for Babel, Adam's language would have endured, immutable and imperishable: clearly refuting Dante's *De Vulgari Eloquentia*, Adam says that his language, no less mutable and ephemeral than any other, was entirely "extinct" well before Babel.

Anti-Ethnocentrism

Dante's aim in revising his linguistic doctrines in *Paradiso* XXVI is not to attack Hebrew. Rather, it is to undermine the very idea of a privileged or preeminent language, to expose as an illusion the idea that there is a language intrinsically closer to truth than others. The capacity to bear truth is neither restricted to far away or ancient languages nor is it in any way the exclusive property of one's own language. One's own language is every bit as authoritative as the language of others (this is why Dante is not ashamed to write the *Comedy*, which aims to be a work of world-historical import, in his own Florentine language). Yet this confidence in "one's own" goes hand-in-hand with a respect for the revelatory potential of the languages of others. The lesson that Adam teaches is *Spiritual*—that is to say Pentecostal—promoting the idea that the Word does not belong exclusively to any one linguistic or ethnic community. One might recall Leupin's remarks concerning Pentecost that I cited above: "The notion of a sacred language is destroyed, as all hierarchy of languages dissolves. Every language is capable of revelation, not just Hebrew alone."

In *Paradiso* XXIX, in the course of a speech treating a variety of matters, Beatrice sharply rebukes those preachers who use rhetoric to twist or distort the Gospel for their own purposes. The example given by Beatrice not only criticizes the sophistical use of scriptures; more specifically, it condemns those whose rhetoric serves ethnocentric purposes:

> "Some say that during Christ's Passion the moon
> reversed its course intruding on the sun
> whose light, then, could not reach as far as earth—
>
> Such preachers lie! For that light hid itself,
> so this eclipse took place for the Spaniards
> and the Indians, as well as for the Jews.
>
> Fables like these are shouted right and left,
> pouring from the pulpits—more in just one year
> than all the Lapi and Bindi found in Florence!
>
> So *the poor sheep*, who know no better, come
> from *pasture* fed on air—the fact that they
> are ignorant does not excuse their guilt."
>
> (*Par.* XXIX, 97–108)

Beatrice is saying that the darkness that, according to the Gospel, cloaked the "whole earth" during the three hours of Christ's Passion—from around noon until around three o'clock—could not have been caused, as are ordinary solar eclipses, by the moon's passing between the earth and the sun. For an ordinary solar eclipse would have caused darkness at different time periods in different geographical zones—following the progressive course of the moon's shadow across the earth's surface—rather than all at once during the same three hour period the world over. Beatrice, who is nothing if not a scientist, explains the only physically possible explanation for a global yet simultaneous solar eclipse: somehow the sun's rays withdrew themselves ("that light hid itself"), failing to shine toward earth for a three hour period. The resulting darkness was simultaneously experienced by all of the inhabited earth, from its western to its eastern limits (Spain and India, respectively) and throughout the space encompassed within these limits.

If Beatrice chastises rhetorician-preachers who claim that the eclipse in question was caused by the moon's blocking the sun's rays, it is not simply for their scientific inaccuracy. Rather, she recognizes the ethnocentric basis of their error: if it were a matter of the moon's blocking the sun's rays, then at a given time (the commencement of Christ's Passion) the eclipse would have darkened only a relatively limited geographical area. There would have been a "privileged circle" (the moon's shadow) of darkness somewhere on the earth, delimiting the boundaries of a specially chosen place and people. From the point of view of these preachers and their gullible audiences, the import of Christ's Passion was directed exclusively toward a particular geographical place, signifying that Christ's message was meant for a particular people, from whose perspective this benefit was granted to "us" not to "them." In the erroneous view of these preachers, the surface of the earth has a cultural and religious "central point," and the moon must have aligned itself between this central point and the sun, causing a solar eclipse at the moment of Christ's Passion. If Dante refers here to the Lapi and Bindi, common Florentine names that connote something akin to "regular Joes," he is suggesting that an ignorant, vulgar, popular mentality is particularly susceptible to the lure of ethnocentric pseudo-science. Given that Dante may not have finished writing *Paradiso* until as late as 1321, one might even suggest—but I would not insist on this point—that the fourth of these stanzas, with its reference to the "poor sheep" coming from "pasture" fed on air, alludes to the "Shepherd's Crusade" of 1320, in which thousands of bumpkins from Northern France, riled up by hate speech, journeyed to Spain to slaughter Muslims and Jews.

But the Lapi and Bindi, and the ignorant shepherd crusaders, are deceived, since the whole point of this extraordinary eclipse, the culmination of the Gospel, is that *the earth has no cultural center:* as Beatrice says, "this eclipse took place for the Spaniards/and the Indians, as well as for the Jews." (Since according to the geography of Dante's day, the extreme west of the inhabited world was Spain and the extreme east the Ganges, Beatrice means to indicate that the eclipse was an event equally pertinent to all peoples of the earth.) The target of Dante's critique here is the idea that illumination is directed to *us* and to *us* alone—to us Christians, who may like to think of ourselves as the real inheritors of the Jewish covenant with God, representing the cultural center of the inhabited world. But in truth, as we have seen above, in our analysis of *Inferno* I, lines 17–18 ("the rays of the planet that leads *others straight, those of every religion*"), the sun is specially endowed to enlighten not just us but especially others. Beatrice exposes the gap between current Eurocentric Christian teachings and the authentic Christian message of universalism.

Salvation

In a famous passage in *Paradiso* the deepest implications of which seem generally to be left unexplored, Dante presents "salvation" as a possibility that is open *not* solely to Christians. But before attempting to understand this passage, let us first briefly consider the apparently orthodox presentation of the issue of salvation as presented in Dante's conception of Limbo.

I say "apparently" because, from our modern perspective, the point of Dante's Limbo appears to be the assertion that pagans such as Virgil or Plato and non-Christians such as Saladin and Averroes (who, in moral terms, may be every bit as good as Christians) cannot be "saved" because they do not hold the right beliefs concerning God and Christ. To us, Dante's Limbo seems to be an instance of medieval narrowness, a matter of *excluding* whole categories of humans from the ranks of the blessed.

In fact, with regard to the orthodox medieval Catholic doctrine of Limbo, Dante's representation of the concept in *Inferno* IV is highly heterodox, marking a major movement in the direction of *inclusion*, an extension of, so to speak, "citizenship" to those who until then traditionally had been treated as outsiders. According to the orthodox doctrine, Limbo (so named for its location on the *limbus*, the "border" or "edge" of Hell) was divided into two sectors, in accordance with the two categories of persons whose souls would be transported there after the death of their bodies. There was, first, a *limbus patrum* ("Limbo of the Fathers"). This was the holding station for the souls of "the Hebrew righteous"—virtuous Jews (both men and women) who lived before the time of Christ. All such Jews were eventually saved; they did not go directly to Heaven, however, but were obliged to abide in Limbo until the Harrowing of Hell—that event when, between his death and resurrection, Christ ventured into Hell and liberated the Hebrew righteous, transporting them to their rightful places in Heaven. (According to some accounts, there were also a certain few just pagans in the Limbo of the Fathers.) After the Harrowing of Hell there are no longer ever any "fathers" (adults) in Limbo.[143] The other sector of Limbo is the *limbus puerorum* ("Limbo of the Children"), the eternal dwelling place of the souls of children who, having died unbaptized, are stained by original sin. Their punishment, according to most accounts, is not physical torment but rather the deprival of felicity, of the beatific vision of God.

According to the orthodox doctrine, then, the only souls inhabiting Limbo at the time of Dante's journey would be those of children who die unbaptized. But, while briefly mentioning the children, Dante instead presents an unprecedented account of what we might call "the Limbo of the non-Christians"—a Limbo populated by pagans such as Cicero, Hector, and Homer and by Muslims such as Avicenna, Saladin, and Averroes. Dante's account of Limbo opens wide the narrow confines that had been placed around it by Catholic orthodoxy. As Manlio Pastore Stocchi says: "Dante concedes [the condition of being unstained by any guilt] to classical antiquity. . .and to the non-Christian world in infinitely greater and more trusting measure than medieval thought was accustomed to do."[144]

Dante's opening Limbo to non-Hebrew ancients and to non-Christian moderns, if it does not amount to an assertion that such humans might be saved, nonetheless does adumbrate the possibility of their salvation—a possibility that is, if only obliquely, affirmed in Dante's treatment of the question in *Paradiso*.

In *Paradiso* XIX, having been transported to the sphere of Jupiter, Dante converses with a collectivity of souls who appear in the shape of a giant eagle. This eagle's role is to represent and to speak of justice. Addressing the eagle, Dante refers to a certain question concerning God's justice—a question clearly of crucial significance, a more-than-nagging question that Dante says has long haunted him:

> "You know my eagerness to hear you speak,
> you also know the nature of the question
> whose answer I have hungered for so long."
> (*Par.* XIX, 31–33)

Several verses later the eagle returns to this question "concerning which you [Dante] were so plagued with doubts" (line 69). The difficulty for Dante is not so much his ascertaining the answer to the question—since that answer is clearly provided by Catholic dogma—but rather his accepting the unwanted implications of that dogmatic answer. The answer is so unpalatable that it plagues him with doubts concerning the very legitimacy of Christianity.

At issue is nothing other than the very question that still prevents many from respecting Christianity's claims concerning salvation. How can a just

262 DANTE'S PLURALISM AND RELIGION IN ISLAM

God deny salvation to non-Christians? What about those perfectly "good" humans who just happen to have been born on the other side of the earth, with never an inkling of the Christian creed? The eagle, who can read Dante's thoughts, formulates the question thus:

> "For you would say: 'Consider that man born
> along the Indus where you will not find
> a soul who speaks or reads or writes of Christ,
>
> and all of his desires, all his acts
> are good, as far as human reason sees;
> not ever having sinned in deed or word,
>
> he dies unbaptized, dies without the faith.
> What is this justice that condemns his soul?
> What is his guilt if he does not believe?' "
> (*Par.* XIX, 70–78)

This question haunted Dante for so long because the simple and undeniable answer offered by his native creed—only Christians are saved—gave rise to grave doubts concerning the legitimacy of that creed. How can God's denial of salvation to a perfectly virtuous Hindu, for instance, possibly be construed as being consonant with "justice"?

One aspect of the eagle's response is to insist that "justice" is not some objective or external standard that might stand apart from God and to which God's actions, to be deemed "just," must conform. Rather, whatever God wills and however God acts is necessarily "just." God is not compelled to perform a certain set of "good deeds" while being constrained from performing a certain set of "bad" ones. Instead, whatever deeds God (who is the Good) performs are by definition "good":

> "The Primal Will, which of Itself is good,
> never moves from Itself, the Good Supreme.
>
> Only that which accords with It is just.
> It is not drawn to any created good,
> but sending forth its rays creates that good.
> (*Par.* XIX, 86–90)

God is never "pulled" or "drawn" toward something outside of God—not even toward an objective standard of right and wrong. The eagle's understanding of God's ethics—an issue that had been debated fully in Arabic philosophy and theology—are quite in keeping with the positions that had been made famous by the great Islamic theologian al-Ghazali. As Oliver Leaman remarks, "the very notion of God being compelled to behave in a certain way is repugnant to Ghazali."[145]

But more important than the explicit doctrinal content of the eagle's response to Dante's nagging question is its tone of indignation. The eagle scolds Dante for even thinking that humans might ever understand God's justice:

> "Now who are you to sit in judgment's seat
> and pass on things a thousand miles away,
> when you can hardly see beyond your nose?"
> (*Par.* XIX, 79–81)

> Circling, it sang, then spoke: "Even as my notes
> are too high for your mind to comprehend,
> so is Eternal Judgment for mankind."
> (*Par.* XIX, 97–99)

If the eagle had stopped here, it would be hard not to conclude that he answers Dante's doubts with purely dogmatic assurance. Faced with the apparent injustice of God's allowing for the salvation of but a small portion of humanity, one must simply answer: Such a thing is unfathomable, so let us just accept it and let it be. Let us be thankful that God has favored us and not them. We know that we may be saved and that they may not be, although we can never see why this is just.

But the eagle does not stop here. For as its discourse continues into Canto XX, it becomes clear that its indignation is aimed primarily not at those seeking to answer the question that has haunted Dante, but rather at those claiming to know who are the saved and who are the damned:

> "You men who live on earth, be slow to judge,
> for even we who see God face to face
> still do not know the list of His elect."
> (*Par.* XX, 133–35)

With this admonition the eagle reiterates what the soul of Aquinas had already told Dante in *Paradiso* XIII—that one should refrain from claiming to know how God will judge others:

> "Nor should one be too quick to trust his judgment;
> be not like him who walks his field and counts
> the ears of corn before the time is ripe,
>
> for I have seen brier all winter long
> showing its tough and prickly stem
> eventually produce a lovely rose,

and I have seen a ship sail straight and swift
over the sea through all its course, and then
about to enter the harbor, sink.

No Mr. or Miss Know-it-All should think,
when they see one man steal and one give alms
that they are seeing them through God's own eyes,

for one may yet rise up, the other fall."

                    (*Par.* XIII, 130–42)

God's justice is inscrutable not because we cannot fathom why Christians are eligible for salvation and non-Christians are not, but rather because we have no grounds for claiming to know who will be saved. Taken together, the eagle's and Aquinas's denials that humans can ever know who is in Heaven or Hell amount to a tremendously ironic indictment of the "literal truthful-ness" or "objective accuracy" of the *Comedy*.[146] Dante quite consciously acknowledges that a mortal ought not pass judgment on who might populate the infernal or celestial realms. To claim otherwise would be to act in the manner of the very sort of Mr. Know-it-All whom Aquinas here condemns.

But there is something of a difference between Aquinas's and the eagle's admonitions. Aquinas clearly seems to be talking about ostensibly "good" and "bad" members of the selfsame Christian community—for instance, the "pious donor" and the "thief." He is saying that Christians of ill-repute, such as the thief, may end up in Heaven, while well-reputed ones, such as the pious donor, may end up in Hell. There is nothing in Aquinas's words suggesting that his remarks pertain to the fate (or plight) of non-Christians. Aquinas is reminding Dante that the possibility of salvation is always open even to apparently wicked members of a Christian community.

The eagle, however, is without a doubt teaching Dante that the possi-bility of salvation is open even to non-Christians, even to those who live in times and places remote from Christendom and outside the biblical (Hebraic-Christian) community. For it uses the case of Ripheus the Trojan as its prime example showing why "men who live on earth" ought to "be slow to judge." Ripheus, a very minor character in Virgil's *Aeneid*, is one of the Trojans who dies in battle during the sack of Troy. But he is not simply another Trojan; rather, Virgil describes him as "the most just of all the Trojans, and keenest for what was right." Yet, Virgil says, the gods have no regard for Ripheus's great merit: "the gods' vision was otherwise" (*Aeneid* 2.426–28). That is to say, the gods sanction—or at least do not prevent—Ripheus's death and defeat, his ultimately amounting to nothing, despite his status as the most virtuous and just among his people.

There is a great deal of playful irony in Dante's placing Ripheus in Heaven—irony aimed in Virgil's direction. Virgil's entire poem glorifies

Aeneas, yet, according to the *Comedy*, "God's vision was otherwise"—which is to say that Aeneas is not among the saved. Instead the *Comedy* glorifies Ripheus, one whom Virgil deems barely worthy of mention. In effect, Dante "corrects" Virgil's own erroneous vision: Virgil thinks that Ripheus is not divinely blessed; Dante says otherwise. And the most striking irony is that Virgil himself, apparently excluded from Heaven, is "outdone" by one of his own minor characters.

Ripheus is the exemplary "virtuous pagan." Neither Christian nor Jew, he stands outside the fold of the "chosen people" to whom God has granted the possibility of salvation. Yet here he is, most certainly, in Heaven—a fact by which the eagle means to startle us into being "slow to judge" concerning who belongs among the chosen: "Who in your erring world would have believed/that Ripheus of Troy was here?" (*Par.* XX, 67–68).

But the question of how God's saving the just Ripheus may be deemed "just" still remains. Why is Ripheus in Heaven, while any number of equally virtuous pagans—Aeneas, Virgil, those who *Inferno* tells us dwell in Limbo, not to mention the perfectly just Hindu whom Dante has asked about—are not? Where is the justice in singling out one, or a few (the eagle also tells us that the pagan emperor Trajan is among the saved; Cato, as seen in part I, is another pagan who will end up in Heaven), virtuous pagans for salvation, yet omitting from those ranks a vast number of equally deserving ones?

The answer provided by the eagle falls squarely within the boundaries of orthodox Catholic doctrine. Ripheus, through God's grace, was granted a prospective vision of Christ's redeeming mankind, even though that redemption was still several centuries in the future. Ripheus was a believer, did have faith in Christ, even though he lived in pre-Christian times:

> The other soul [i.e., Ripheus], by means of grace that wells
> up from a spring so deep that no man's eye
> has ever plumbed the bottom of its source,
>
> devoted all his love to righteousness,
> and God, with grace on grace, opened his eyes
> to our redemption and he saw the light,
>
> and he believed in this; from that time on
> he could not bear the stench of pagan creed,
> and reproved the perverse peoples [*genti perverse*] for it.
> (*Par.* XX, 118–26)

Ripheus, the eagle says, was a Christian living in a non-Christian (and pre-Christian) community. The dogma remains intact: only Christians may be saved. And Ripheus is an exceptional, extraordinary individual: a solitary Christian in the midst of "perverse peoples" who profess a stinking creed. The non-Christian community *as such* remains completely deprived of the possibility of salvation. Only by setting himself apart from and in opposition to his non-Christian community does Ripheus manifest the grace that allows for his salvation. Here the eagle's orthodox teaching reinforces a view according to which there are inherently perverse ("them") and inherently righteous ("us") peoples.

I call this view "orthodox" because it is for all intents and purposes identical to Augustine's authoritative solution to the problem of the virtuous heathen. For Augustine, God's "chosen people" include two groups: the Jews who lived before the Christian era, and Christians since. These two peoples in fact merge as one people united by biblical tradition: Jews before the Christian era were "Christians" insofar as their scriptures centered around and foretold the coming of Christ; since then Christians are "the real Jews" insofar as Christ is the *telos* and fulfillment of the Jewish scriptures. (Jews who persist in being Jews in the Christian era forfeit the status of belonging to the "chosen people"—they are no longer real Jews.) But Augustine allows that there may be exceptional individuals, a certain few "foreigners" whom God's grace admits into the ranks of the chosen ones. In the *City of God* Augustine's example of such a "foreigner" is Job, who, although he lived before the Christian era yet was not a Jew, most assuredly has been awarded citizenship in Heaven:

> There is nothing far-fetched in the belief that among other peoples besides the Jews there existed men to whom this mystery was revealed, and who were compelled to go on to proclaim what they knew. . . .And I do not imagine that the Jews dare to maintain that no one has ever belonged to God apart from the Israelites. . . .The Jews cannot deny that in other nations also there have been some men who belonged not by earthly but by heavenly fellowship to the company of the true Israelites, the citizens of the country that is above. In fact, if the Jews deny this, they are very easily proved wrong by the example of Job, that holy and amazing man. He was neither a native of Israel nor a proselyte (that is, a newly admitted member of the people of Israel). He traced his descent from the race of Edom; he was born in Edom; he died there. And such is the praise accorded him in inspired utterances that no man of his period is put on the same level as far as righteousness and devotion are concerned. . . .I have no doubt that it was the design of God's providence that from this one instance we should know that there could also be those among other nations who lived by God's standards and were pleasing to God, as belonging to the spiritual Jerusalem. But it must not be believed that this was granted to anyone unless he had received a divine revelation of "the one mediator between God and men, the man Christ Jesus" [1 Tim. 2, 5].[147]

Augustine's doctrine is essentially the same as the eagle's: special individuals who are born and live "among other peoples"—outside the Judeo-Christian community—may well be saved, provided that God, through his grace, grants them a divine revelation of Christ. The possibility of salvation is open to exceptional individuals if and only if they become Christians in non-Christian communities. Job is an exception to the rule dictating that those of his race—"the race of Edom"—are unqualified to be citizens of the country that is above. The non-Jewish community of Edomites *as such* remains alien to "the spiritual Jerusalem"; the Edomites remain, as the eagle would put it, a perverse people professing a stinking creed.

It appears that the eagle has responded to Dante's troubling question. The answer is essentially equivalent to that provided by Augustine in *City of God*. But Dante had surely read *City of God* time and again. If the Augustinian reply had not satisfied him in the past, why should it satisfy him now?

The eagle appears to speak with the voice of orthodoxy, of "Peter." Yet is it really "Peter" for whom the eagle speaks, or is it perhaps for another? (Recall that, for the Spirituals, "Peter" signifies the papacy and the official Catholic Church, while "John" signifies the coming era of the Spirit, which will be marked by the unity of those of "every nation and tribe and language and people.")

The eagle *appears* with the voice of "Peter." Yet, in its appearance, the eagle is clearly none other than "John." I say this, first, because the "flying eagle" is the traditional medieval iconographical symbol for John; secondly, because Dante reminds us of this iconography a few cantos later, calling John "Christ's eagle" (*Par.* XXVI, 53); thirdly and most tellingly, because just as it is about to speak on the very issue of the possible salvation of non-Christians, Dante calls the eagle, in unmistakable Pentecostal terms, "the blazing flames of the Holy Spirit":

> Those blazing flames of the Holy Spirit
> stopped still, and then still in that ensign shape [i.e., of an eagle]
> which had brought Rome the reverence of the world,
>
> it began again: "And to this realm
> none ever rose who did not believe in Christ,
> either before or after he was nailed to the tree."
>
> (*Par.* XIX, 100–105)

An eagle, appearing as the blazing flames of the Holy Spirit—nothing could more loudly proclaim that this speaker is "John"—and not just any "John," but "John" as evangelist of the new Age of the Spirit, the era of inclusive religious pluralism and tolerance longed for by the Spirituals.

In the stanzas that follow, we see that the eagle—which we have just said speaks in the orthodox voice of "Peter"—does also and at the same

time speak in the voice of "John." Seeming to maintain that "none ever
rose who did not believe in Christ," the eagle also indicates, in language
not completely veiled, that the heavenly ranks will be filled with plenty of
non-European, non-Christians:

> "And to this realm [i.e., Heaven]
> none ever rose who did not believe in Christ,
> either before or after he was nailed to the tree.
>
> But listen here [*Ma vedi*]! Many cry 'Christ, Christ!'
> who, at the Judgment, will be far less near [*prope*]
> to Him than he who does not know Christ;
>
> And the Ethiopian will condemn such Christians
> when the two companies shall be separated,
> the one forever rich, and the other poor.
>
> What may the Persians say to your [European] kings,
> when they see that volume open
> in which are recorded all their dispraises?"
>
> (*Par.* XIX, 103–114)

The *Ma vedi* ("But look!," "Listen here!") is important: it is a forceful indication that the notion expressed in the preceding stanza (only believers in
Christ go to Heaven) is not so simple, that it needs to be qualified, rendered
more complex. And, in saying that many apparent Christians (those who
cry "Christ," "Christ") will be "less near" to him at the Last Judgment than
many who "do not know Christ," the eagle uses, as the word for "near,"
the Latin word *prope* (the only Latin word in the eagle's rather long discourse). If Dante has the eagle use Latin here, when he could just as easily
had it use an Italian word for "near," it is because he wishes for us to linger
a bit over the word's connotations. The Latin *prope*, meaning "near," calls
to mind the related Latin words *proprius*, meaning "one's own," "special,"
"peculiar," "particular" and *proprie*, meaning "exclusively," "particularly,"
"peculiarly." Christians who cry "Christ," "Christ" think that they are
near, and particularly, peculiarly, or exclusively near, to Christ. They think
of Christ as their own *property*, as *properly* theirs, in a way that would
exclude the possibility that he could also belong to Ethiopians (black
Africans) and Persians (Iranians).

   There follows a lengthy catalogue of wicked European rulers and their
foul deeds—an insistence that the corrupt potentates of Christendom will
go to Hell. As for whether good Ethiopians and Persians will be among the
ranks of the "forever rich" in Heaven, this passage remains (intentionally)
ambiguous. Dante does not explicitly say that they will be saved (saying so
would have been manifest heresy), but neither does he deny it. When the
"two companies shall be separated" into "the one forever rich, and the

other poor," it is obvious that the wicked European Christians will be in the latter company. But to which company will virtuous black Africans and Iranians belong? These stanzas *suggest* that they will be separated from the bad Christians—hence that they will be among the "forever rich."[148]

There is no sense here that these Ethiopians and Persians who will end up in Heaven are rare, extraordinary individuals who have been granted special grace to know and believe in Christ. Unlike Ripheus (as described by the eagle speaking as "Peter"), these non-Christians do not gain entrance to Heaven after deeming their own religious traditions to be "stinking creeds" and their own races (*genti*) "perverse." On the contrary, here it is not a matter of unusual individuals who set themselves apart from their communities but rather of large collective groupings: the unnamed "Ethiopian" as representing all good Ethiopians; "the Persians" as representing all good Persians. Here, *non-Christian communities as such* are by no means excluded.

The "volume" referred to in line 113, which will be open and in which the Persians will see written all the "dispraises" of the wicked European kings, is one of the books that will be displayed at the time of the Last Judgment, according to Revelation 20 (a text which, as mentioned above, was thought in the Middle Ages to have been authored by the same "John" who wrote the Gospel). This allusion to John's apocalyptic vision suggests that Dante is indeed quietly affirming the salvation of non-Christians. For the judgment in Revelation is universal, pertaining to all humans from all places and cultures (recall that the phrase "every tribe and language and people and nation" [Rev. 5.9] is the recurring *leitmotiv* of Revelation), and is based on *deeds* and *actions* ("works") not on *beliefs* ("faith"):

> Then I saw a great white throne and the one who sat on it; the earth and the heaven fled from his presence, and no place was found for them. And I saw the dead, great and small, standing before the throne, and books were opened. Also another book was opened, the book of life. And *the dead were judged according to their works*, as recorded in the books. And the sea gave up the dead that were in it, Death and Hades gave up the dead that were in them, and *all were judged according to what they had done*. (Rev. 20.11–15; emphasis added)

According to Revelation, all humans will be judged *according to their works*, not according to whether or not they know or believe in Christ. With this allusion to Revelation 20, Dante attributes to the eagle, which elsewhere in his discourse speaks in the orthodox voice of "Peter," the potentially heterodox voice of "John." For Revelation 20 is a significant site of resistance to the church's official position on salvation, which was based above all on Paul's teaching that we are saved by *faith* (belief) not by *works* (deeds).

Paul, for instance, says the following: "For by grace you have been saved through faith, and this is not your own doing; it is the gift of God—not the result of works, so that no one may boast" (Ephesians 2.8–9). Revelation to some degree diminishes the importance, for purposes of one's salvation, of one's *Christian* identity; it is the same text, as we saw above, which proclaims, as the Eternal Gospel, a pure and simple monotheism ("Fear God and give him glory, for the hour of his judgment has come; and worship him who made heaven and earth, the sea and the springs of water" [Rev. 14.7]). At the Last Judgment, in John's account, all are judged according to virtue and vice, not according to creed.

But the eagle says that none has ever gone to Heaven who did not believe in Christ. Salvation *is* a matter of belief. Does this not contradict the possibility that there are plenty of non-Christians—for instance, multitudes of virtuous Iranians—in Heaven?

The eagle says that one can "believe in Christ / either *before or after* He was nailed to the tree." From a doctrinal perspective, this is again ambiguous. Perhaps it is simply stating the orthodox position that, as it explains elsewhere, God grants to certain pre-Christian individuals a prospective belief in Christ— and such pre-Christian believers are *literally* Christians, that is, they literally do believe in Christ. Or perhaps there is a way to "believe in Christ" that is not merely literal. Perhaps there is a metaphorical (or, as it would be termed in the Middle Ages, a *spiritual*) sense of the phrase "belief in Christ." There can be a "belief in Christ" before there is Christianity, before there is a Christian creed. The eagle appears to be saying that one can "believe in Christ" without literally being called a Christian. Those who cry "Christ, Christ" are, literally speaking, believers in Christ, but they are not necessarily real believers (and certainly their status as literal believers does nothing to protect them from eternal damnation); conversely, those who do not know Christ, like the Hindu who never "speaks. . .of Christ" (XIX, 72), may be, through their actions, for all intents and purposes real believers. To truly believe is to put into practice, and hence the dead *are judged according to their works.*

If we are saved by the Gospel, and if some are saved before the time of Christ, there is, somehow, a Gospel before as well as after Christ. One might call this, with its *before and after*, an Eternal Gospel. At any rate, Dante opens up a very significant distinction between a literal and a spiritual sense of "believing in Christ," such that one "who does not know [*non conosce*] Christ" (XIX, 108) can nonetheless "believe in Christ," although without literally being familiar with Him. This distinction has been nicely expressed by Martin Heidegger in his essay "The Word of Nietzsche":

> Nietzsche does not consider the Christian life that existed once for a short time before the writing down of the Gospels and before the missionary

propaganda of Paul to belong to Christendom. Christendom for Nietzsche is the historical, world-political phenomenon of the Church and its claim to power within the shaping of Western humanity and its modern culture. Christendom in this sense and the Christianity of New Testament faith are not the same. Even a non-Christian life can affirm Christendom and use it as a means of power, just as, conversely, a Christian life does not necessarily require Christendom. Therefore, a confrontation with Christendom is absolutely not in any way an attack against what is Christian.[149]

Dante plainly attacks Christendom, not what is Christian. The wicked European rulers chastised in the stanzas that follow the passage we have been considering exemplify "non-Christian lives that affirm Christendom and use it as a means of power." The Ethiopian and the Persians, the "man born / along the Indus," are evidence that "a Christian life does not necessarily require Christendom."

Dante's Aquinas opens up the possibility of salvation to the "outsiders" of Christendom—thieves and other such disreputable persons. The eagle, following Augustine and presenting the orthodox position of the Roman Church (which in the Middle Ages was personified as "Peter") opens up salvation to a certain happy few non-Christians individuals who have been granted special grace. But the eagle also speaks in another voice, the voice of "John," offering a message, consonant with that of the Eternal Gospel and the more radical (post-Christian) Spirituals, in which salvation, based on deeds rather than creed, is a possibility generally available to Christians and non-Christians alike, including to those *genti* situated completely outside the boundaries of Christendom.

The double-voiced eagle is a double for Dante, who himself speaks in a double manner. In part I we saw that Dante speaks as a philosopher while also speaking as a theologian, and that he sustains this double register throughout the *Comedy* (in other words, there is no pivotal place in the poem in which theology supplants philosophy once and for all). Here we see that, when speaking as a theologian, Dante speaks both as an orthodox and as a heterodox one (we can construct a coherent reading supporting Dante's orthodoxy and an equally coherent reading supporting his heterodoxy). The most basic reason for this doublespeak is the reality of persecution. As Paul Alexis Ladame remarks, Dante, "considering himself to be more valuable to humanity alive than dead, knows that he has to be prudent, to camouflage his thought, to encode his messages."[150] But there is also another chief reason for the "inclusiveness" of Dante's discourse: he aims to write a prophetic text, a revelation—a discourse that will gain the assent, and thus ideally shape the practice, of all readers, orthodox and heterodox, Christian and non-Christian.

Peter and John

In *Paradiso* XXIII, Dante reaches the Heaven of the Fixed Stars, the outer-most sphere of the created universe. Before he can proceed from there to the two remaining "higher levels" of the cosmos (the sphere of the primum mobile and the Empyrean, a "place" beyond space and time where the blessed souls dwell eternally and where Dante will enjoy, in the poem's final episode, a vision of God), he must first pass an examination on the three theological virtues, faith, hope, and love. (On the level of the poem's theological allegory, the meaning is clear: our salvation depends on our possessing not just the four cardinal or moral virtues, but also the three the-ological virtues; see part I for discussion of the four cardinal virtues). This examination, which occupies three cantos (XXIV–XXVI), is administered by Christ's three chief apostles, Peter, James, and John. Whatever else is at stake in this part of *Paradiso*, one thing is clear: Dante has arranged things so that we can witness his encounter, first, with "Peter," and then (following an intermediate phase—with James—that serves to situate the first and third as two contrasting poles) with "John."

As Marjorie Reeves points out in her comprehensive history of the Joachimite–Spiritual Franciscan tradition, and as we have seen above, "Peter" and "John" were well established symbols for the opposition between the present social order ruled by the papacy and a future social order in which the papacy would be transformed or, more often, surpassed and rendered obsolete: "Joachim. . .uses the figure of the transition from the 'church' or the 'life' designated in Peter to that designated in John in such a way as to lead to the conclusion that something in the [present-day] *status* really does pass away, leaving the life in John alone to endure to the end. This is the most damaging point in relation to his orthodoxy, all the more so because St. Peter in some passages clearly stands for the Papacy. . .Thus his statements on. . .the life symbolized in Peter are always set in juxtaposition to the life represented by John."[151]

This episode is literally an examination, as Dante finds himself in the position of one who holds the Bachelor's degree hoping to join the ranks of those who hold the Master's degree. Our sense that this amounts to Dante's "orals"—his fulfillment of the final requirements for a higher degree—is especially strong as he prepares to respond to Peter's line of questioning concerning faith:

> Even as the bachelor arms himself—and does not
> speak until the master propounds the question—
> in order to adduce the proof, not to decide it,
>
> so, while she [i.e., Beatrice] was speaking, I was arming myself

with every reason, to be ready
for such a *questioner* [i.e., Peter] and for such a profession.

"Speak, good Christian, and declare yourself:
Faith, what is it?"

(Par. XXIV, 46–53)

Notable here is the discourse of conflict, of violence, of self-defense: Dante has to "arm himself" because there is some sense in which he is under attack. Peter, who must confirm his expectation that Dante will answer as a "good Christian," is represented as the guardian of orthodoxy. In the portrait of Peter offered here, the language of (military, institutional) power predominates: he is, in Dante's eyes, the "high primipilus" *(alto primipilo;* XXIV, 59)—the chief centurion, one of the highest ranking officers of the Roman army—and a "baron" (XXIV, 115), that is, an aristocratic military leader. This should cause us to wonder, since we know that Dante's ideal papacy is entirely without power—and, above all else, without coercive power. Is it possible that this is not Peter but rather "Peter," the one whom the real Peter, a few cantos later (as we saw above), calls "he who on earth usurps my place,/my place, my place" *(Par.* XXVII, 22–23)?[152]

Those of us who have withstood the ordeal of an academic oral examination know that one must be prepared with a supply of "ready answers," some of which may but others of which may not correspond to one's own deeply held beliefs. We do not always tell the examiners what we really think; there are times when it is expedient to say what they expect or wish to hear. This is precisely the state of mind that Dante represents as his when facing Peter's questioning: he acts as someone for whom what matters most is not telling the truth but passing the exam.

Dante must show that he is a "good Christian" to one whose powerful presence intimidates and who is called, in line 51, a "questioner." The Italian word translated "questioner" here is *querente,* a word derived from the Latin *quaerere,* "to seek," "to search for," "to inquire," "to investigate," "to interrogate." The name "inquisition" comes from the verb *inquirere,* that is, *in* + *quaerere.* The inquisitor is one who seeks, searches, investigates, interrogates—a questioner, a *querente.* But the inquisitor is not just any questioner; he is a questioner who serves and is served by a powerful coercive apparatus of enforcement. The inquisitor is a sort of primipilus, a baron among questioners.

When considering Dante's "profession of faith," the creed that he formulates for Peter in *Paradiso* XXIV, we need to bear in mind that we are hearing *what Dante would say if he were facing the Inquisition.*

To Peter's question ("Faith, what is it?"), Dante replies with a verbatim citation of St. Paul (Heb. 11.1): "Faith is the substance of things hoped for / and the evidence of things not seen" (*Par.* XXIV, 64–65). This is one of the "ready answers" with which Dante had armed himself. It requires no thinking on Dante's part, only the retrieval of some memorized phrases.

Once Dante assures Peter that he knows the definition of faith, and that he himself has faith (which is described as a coin in one's purse, as if faith is the currency with which one buys one's way into Heaven; *Par.* XXIV, 84–85), Peter asks how his faith came to him. Dante replies that it was through revelation, through his reading the Bible:

> And I said: "The plenteous rain
> of the Holy Spirit, which is poured
> over the old and over the new parchments [i.e., testaments]
>
> is a syllogism that has proved it to me
> so acutely, that, in comparison with this,
> every *demonstration* seems obtuse to me."
>
> (*Par.* XXIV, 91–96)

Here Dante indicates the primacy of revelation to philosophical reasoning (syllogism, demonstration). Recall that Averroes refers to philosophers as "the demonstrative class" and to the philosopher as "the man of demonstration." Here Dante, in a way that runs counter to the whole thrust of the Arabo-Islamic rationalist tradition, indicates that there is a wide epistemological gap between reason and faith, and he unequivocally asserts the superiority of the latter. But this assertion (which no doubt contradicts the gist of what I argue in part I) is not to be taken as Dante's deeply held view. It is nothing more than what he would say to the Grand Inquisitor.

Peter, pleased by what he hears, grants Dante his *nihil obstat*: "I approve," he says, since Dante has spoken as he "should" (*Par.* XXIV, 120–21). Peter then asks Dante for a formal profession of his creed; Dante obliges, addressing Peter as the Holy Father (*O santo padre*; XXIV, 124)— that is, as the pope. In listening to Dante's creed, we are hearing what he would say were he being questioned by, say, Boniface VIII.

Dante's exoteric creed—that formulation of his faith that he would not hesitate to proclaim in the public forum of a papal inquisition—has two parts. The first part is a basic profession of monotheism:

> I began, "you would have me declare here
> the form of my ready belief,
> and also you have asked the cause of it.
>
> And I reply: I believe in one God,
> sole and eternal, who, unmoved, moves
> all the heavens with love and with desire,
>
> And for this belief I have not only proofs

physical and metaphysical, but it is given to me
also in the truth that rains down hence

through Moses and the Prophets and the Psalms,
through the Gospel and through you [i.e., the apostles] who wrote
when the fiery Spirit made you holy."

                                    (*Par.* XXIV, 127–138)

This is a general monotheism, such that it would offend neither Jew, nor Christian, nor Muslim. The one elemental truth ("one God") has been made manifest through the vehicle of a plurality of prophets, in various times and places. Moreover, here Dante presents the relation between philosophy ("proofs / physical and metaphysical") and revelation ("the truth that rains down") as a relation between equals, a relation of concordance and harmony. This could well be the philosopher's creed.

But elemental monotheism does not suffice to please the papacy. There is nothing particularly Christian about Dante's creed thus far, so he has to complete it with the second part—his profession of faith in the Trinity:

"And I believe in three Eternal Persons, and these
I believe to be one essence, so one and so threefold
so that *are* and *is* [i.e., the singular or the plural] both describe it.

Concerning this profound divine condition [i.e., the Trinity]
of which I speak, the teachings of the Gospel,
in many places, sets the seal upon my mind."

                                    (*Par.* XXIV, 139–144)

In this case, the sole basis for Dante's belief is revelation—and, specifically Christian revelation ("the teachings of the Gospel"). Philosophy has been surpassed, superceded. It is no longer a "separate but equal" path to the truth. Christians know, through faith, something that non-Christian monotheists and philosophers cannot possibly know. And this special knowledge is what qualifies them for salvation—a salvation that is exclusively theirs. And now Dante has passed his first exam. Now Peter/the pope is quick to congratulate Dante for saying those things that he ought to say. Dante has passed this test only by setting himself among those who set themselves apart, those who qualify by their faith in the Trinity for a salvation that will include them and exclude all other humans.

As the canto and this test come to an end, Dante reiterates the power relation—a relation of master and servant—that has determined the rules for Dante's response. And Dante makes it clear, by saying it twice (the second occasion coinciding with the final verse of the canto and thus sounding even more emphatic) that his performance in professing his creed has been all about pleasing Peter:

> Even as the *master* who listens *to that which pleases him*,
> then embraces his *servant*, rejoicing
> in the news, as soon as he is silent;
>
> So, singing benedictions on me,
> the apostolic light [i.e., Peter] at whose bidding I had spoken
> encircled me three times when
>
> I was silent: *I so pleased him by my speech!*
> (Par. XXIV, 148–154)

Dante, like a good degree candidate, says what it takes to pass his orals. And, with an ironic wink at some of his readers, he indicates that the exam may have brought more pleasure to the examiner than to anyone else involved.

Let us turn now to Canto XXVI to consider the third of the three tests, Dante's final exam, on the topic of Love, administered by John. If Dante professed to Peter his exoteric creed, here he shall profess his esoteric creed.

I have called Dante's dialogue with John the "final exam," and this is in a sense true, since it is here where he answers the third of the three sets of questions concerning the three theological virtues. On the other hand, in this canto there is much less of the atmosphere of "pressure" and intimidation that marked Dante's encounter with Peter. There are none of the bureaucratic trappings telling us that an examination is in progress, such as Peter's formal indication that he has granted his "approval." In fact, Dante is never "graded" on this test, and the examiner, John, fades completely from view somewhere in the middle of Dante's discourse on love. Dante is no longer speaking just to please the members of his examining committee. He is now speaking in his own voice.

Dante begins by saying that he loves *lo ben*, "the good" (more precisely, "the good which satisfies this court"—i.e., the good that makes for the felicity of the eternally blessed). And he says that loving the good is the entirety of his "scripture": "The good which satisfies this court / is Alpha and Omega of all the scripture / which Love reads to me" (*Par.* XXIV, 16–18). Any single particular scripture—the Bible, for instance—is transcended, in the sense that it is rendered superfluous, for there is only one ethical imperative: to love the good. And we should bear in mind here that this doctrine of loving *lo ben*, the good, was at the heart of Virgil's philosophical teaching in *Purgatory* XVII, the *Comedy*'s centermost canto (see part I). There Virgil teaches that we ought above all love "the good / essence [*buona essenza*], the fruit and root of every good [*ben*]" (*Purg.* XVII, 134–135).

John tells Dante to go into more detail, asking him first where he learned to conceive of love as love of the good. Dante replies that he gained his understanding of love from *both* philosophy *and* religion: "By philosophic arguments / and by authority that descends from here, / such love must needs imprint itself on me" (*Par.* XXIV, 25–26). Here there is no sense (as there was in the second part of the creed that Dante professed to Peter) of philosophy's subordinate or inferior position with respect to Christian revelation. The notion of the equality, concordance, and harmony of philosophy and religion, which was dismissed in Dante's exam with Peter, is here restored. Moreover, once reinstated, this notion is never again dismissed: throughout the exam with John, there is a repeated emphasis that the view of love presented here can be acquired *either* through philosophy *or* through revelation. The notion of the subordination of reason to Christian faith, of the inferiority of philosophy to the Gospels (a notion that has served as the basis of the mainstream of American Dante criticism for the past four decades), is affirmed by Dante in Canto XXIV only as a ruse by which to fool an inquisitorial Church of Rome. It is not his real creed, which is instead the creed of the philosophers, expressed here in Canto XXVI in his dialogue with John.

Dante continues by saying that the more one understands something to be good, the more one will love it. Ultimately, our love will be directed at that which we understand to be the highest of all goods, the source of all goods ("that Essence wherein is such supremacy, / that whatsoever good be found outside of It / is nothing but a beam of Its radiance"; XXVI, 31–33). Notice that Dante is still speaking as a philosopher: he calls the highest good "that Essence [*essenza*]," using the same term by which Virgil named the highest good in *Purgatory* XVII. This is one of those philosopher's names for God, such as Being, or the One, or the Good, which are, as al-Farabi says (see part I), alternate ways to name the same thing named by names such as Allah.

How did Dante come to learn the truth concerning the Highest Good? He came to it through philosophy, he says, but also through the Hebrew Scriptures and the Gospels:

> "Such a truth makes plain [*sterne*] to my intellect
> he [i.e., Aristotle] who *demonstrates* the first love
> of all the eternal substances.
>
> The voice of the veracious Author makes it plain [*sternel*]
> where, speaking of Himself, He says to Moses,
> 'I will make you see all goodness.'
>
> You also make it plain to me [*sternilmi*] in the beginning
> of your sublime heralding [i.e., the Gospel of John], which *more than
> any other* heralding declares below the mystery of this place on high."
>
> (*Par.* XXVI, 37–45)

The same verb (*sternere*, from the Latin meaning "to spread out," "to unfold") is used for the teaching provided by Aristotle, Moses, and John, who all teach the same truth. This repetition of one and the same verb is meant to emphasize the equivalence, the interchangeability, of the truth-content of philosophy and various revealed religions. This notion, that the "people of demonstration" will find the truth (which is the truth expressed by Aristotle) in all of the revealed scriptures, is pure Averroes.

But if Dante's esoteric creed transcends the need for any single particular scripture, there is still one particular scripture of which he is especially fond—the Gospel of John. Recall that this text, with its inclusive message of universal salvation ("And I, when I am lifted up from the earth, will draw *all people* to myself"; John 12.32) was the favorite of the various dissident communities which the Church of Rome intimidated with threats of exclusion. The Cathars, for instance, carried a copy of the Gospel of John with them wherever they went as they taught that all human souls are good, light, life. Their rite of *consolamentum* included the recitation of the first chapter of John—the very scriptural passage which Dante here says reveals the truth of Heaven "more than / any other":

> In the beginning was the Word, and the Word was with God, and the Word was God. He was in the beginning with God. All things came into being through him, and without him not one thing came into being. What has come into being through him was life, and *the life was the light of all people.* The light shines in the darkness, and the darkness did not overcome it. (John 1.1–5; emphasis added)

Recall, as well, that the proponents of the Eternal Gospel were dedicated especially to John, teaching that, as Jean de Meun phrased it in the *Romance of the Rose*, "as long as Peter is lord, John cannot show his power." Recall that the Occitan poet Peire Cardenal, an affiliate of the Spiritual Franciscans, structures his complaint against God's damning some humans to Hell around the opposition between a disgraced Peter and the future promise represented by John.

As Canto XXVI continues, John asks Dante if his love is directed toward anything else besides the Essence, the Highest Good. Dante, indicating to the reader that he understood the direction in which "the Eagle of Christ," John, "wanted to lead my profession" (*Par.* XXVI, 54), replies that he does not only love God alone, but rather that his love for the Highest Good makes him also love all creatures inasmuch as they are good:

> "The leaves [*fronde*] with which is enleaved [*s'infronda*] all the garden
> of the Eternal Gardener I love in measure

of the good that is borne to them from Him."

As soon as I was silent a most sweet song
resounded through the heaven, and my lady
sang with the rest, "Holy, Holy, Holy."
> (*Par.* XXVI, 64–69)

All of the plants of God's garden are good, and Dante loves them all in a measure appropriate to their goodness.

These turn out to be the final words of Dante's oral exam, which is apparently over. John has faded out of the scene, and there is an immediate "fade in" of Adam. In keeping with the vegetal metaphor that was introduced by Dante's saying that his love is not solely for God but also for all of the "leaves" of God's garden (and Adam's presence here makes us think of this garden as Eden, the created world, and hence of Dante's love as love for all creatures), Dante, in describing the manner in which he was, as we say, "blown away" by Adam's appearance, compares himself to a tree branch blown by the wind:

As the bough [*fronda*] which bends its top
at passing of the wind, and then uplifts itself
by its own virtue which raises it,

So did I, in amazement, while she [i.e., Beatrice] was speaking,
and then a desire to speak, wherewith I was burning,
gave me assurance again.

And I began: "O *fruit* [i.e., Adam] that were alone
produced mature, O ancient father
of whom every bride is daughter and daughter-in-law,

as devoutly as I can, I implore you
that you speak to me."
> (*Par.* XXVI, 85–95)

Dante describes himself as a *fronda*, a word similar to that he used for the leaves [*fronde*] that "enleave" [*s'infronda*] God's garden. Adam is himself also described botanically, as a "fruit." We are meant to see that Dante's loving all of the vegetation of God's garden, is, specifically, his loving all humankind. For John, loving God alone does not suffice; such love must also include universal love for humanity. (This is something different than Saint Augustine's *caritas* [love], which he defines as "love of God carried as far as contempt of self." *Caritas*, for John, must not be carried as far as contempt for the human. Dante, who loves all the "fronds" of the garden, himself one of those "fronds," must naturally love himself. Humanity must, in an appropriate measure, love itself. But this is not the self-love of egotism. It is, rather, the self-love of humanism, such as discussed in part I.)

In reply to John's question whether he loves anything other than the Highest Good, Dante replies that he loves all humans. The examiner fades from our view, the heavens rejoice, and the poem progresses to its next episode, Dante's conversation with Adam.

But this next episode grows naturally from Dante's discourse on love, for the very first words that he addresses to Adam emphasize the genealogical unity of all humans—all of whom belong to the same family ("O ancient father / of whom every bride is daughter and daughter-in-law"). Despite the manifest diversity of human "tribes and languages and peoples and nations," all humans, by virtue of their common ancestry in Adam, belong to the same *gens*. (Recall that in the Ikhwan al-Safa's Epistle 22, a man from India prefaces his enumeration of humankind's multifarious ethnic diversity by pointing out our common genealogy: "We children of Adam.") One can no longer speak, as the imposter "Peter" would in denying salvation to those dwelling beyond the limits of Christendom, of "perverse races (*genti*) and their stinking creeds." John's message of universal salvation surpasses the narrow, exclusionary doctrine of Peter.

There is a truly definitive difference between the reaction to, the accolades received for, the exam answers presided over by Peter and John. As we have seen, John has already faded from the scene before Dante finishes speaking. It is not John who commends Dante's discourse but rather the heaven itself, which resounds with song:

"The leaves with which is enleaved all the garden
of the Eternal Gardener I love in measure
of the good that is borne to them from Him."

As soon as I was silent [*sì com 'io tacqui*] a most sweet song [*canto*]
resounded through the heaven, and my lady
sang with the rest, "Holy, Holy, Holy."

(*Par.* XXVI, 64–69)

Dante's reply to John's question on love pleases the heavenly hosts. His reply to Peter's question on faith pleases Peter. Looking back to the passage describing Peter's reaction in Canto XXIV, we see that Dante intends us to compare it with the passage describing the heaven's reaction in Canto XXVI: both passages contain the identical phrase *sì com'io tacqui* and a form of the verb *cantare*:

Even as the master who listens to that which pleases him,
then embraces his servant, rejoicing
in the news, as soon as he is silent;

So, singing [*cantando*] benedictions on me
as soon as I was silent [*sì com'io tacqui*], the apostolic light [i.e., Peter]

at whose bidding I had spoken encircled me
three times: I so pleased him by my speech!

(*Par.* XXIV, 148–54)

In the case of the exam on faith, there is only one singer who sings his
pleasure at Dante's reply: Peter is isolated in his egotism. In the case of the
exam on love, everyone collectively (including the ego-less John, whose
voice blends into the chorus) sings their pleasure. We have already seen this
distinction, when discussing Casella's song and the psalm "In exitu Israel de
Aegypto," between a song sung by a solitary individual and a song sung by
a multitude (see part I). *Paradiso* tells us that there is something narrow and
selfish about "faith" as it is conceived by the church. The official doctrine
of faith is here transcended by the universality of love.

We can conclude by recalling that this contrast between Peter and John
is absolutely central to the dissident tradition of radical opposition to
Catholic orthodoxy. Consider (bearing in mind that "glory," *gloria*, means
"fame," "renown," "honor," not without connotations of pride and van-
ity) these words from Joachim of Fiore's *Expositio in Apocalypsim*, a commentary on John's Revelation: "The great Peter is the Prince of Apostles
and the prelate of the entire Church; but O how happy is John. . . .The
former is greater in glory; the latter is happier in love."[153]

In part I we saw that knowledge of the uniquely Christian articles of
faith—the Trinity and the Incarnation—is by no means a prerequisite for
the attainment of earthly happiness. If Christianity does excel the other
religions, it does so only in providing true belief concerning the highest
object of theory—God. But since such belief is neither necessary nor useful
as a ground for practice, Christian faith adds nothing to humankind's
first ultimate goal that is not equally available in other religions and in
philosophy.

Part I thus showed that for Dante the Christian faith is "accidental" but
not essential for our first ultimate goal, the construction of the ideal global
polity. But the possibility remained that for Dante the Christian faith is
essential to the attainment of our second ultimate goal, eternal happiness in
the afterlife. Here in part II we have seen that even in this respect
Christianity is not absolutely indispensable. The *Comedy* teaches that love
is higher than faith and that no single faith has a monopoly on love.

NOTES

Introduction: A *Comedy* for Non-Christians

1. George Holmes, "*Monarchia* and Dante's Attitude to the Popes," in *Dante and Governance*, ed. John Woodhouse (Oxford: Oxford University Press, 1997), p. 46.

2. For this point and a brief account of the reception of *Monarchy*, see Anthony K. Cassell, "Monarchy," in *The Dante Encyclopedia*, ed. Richard Lansing (New York: Garland Publishing, Inc., 2000), pp. 618–623.

3. The consequences of positing the virtual identity of Dante and Aquinas, a strategy of neo-Thomism, are still with us today, manifest in the "theological" reading of Dante that has dominated mainstream American Dante criticism since about 1960 (see below, note 6). The great historian of medieval philosophy Etienne Gilson, emphasizing the substantial difference between Dante and Aquinas, considers Dante's *Monarchy* "one of the gravest dangers that have ever threatened" the Thomistic universe (*Dante the Philosopher* [New York: Sheed & Ward, 1949], p. 201). On the question of the relation between church and state, for instance, "the essential thing is. . .for us to notice the profound gulf that separates the actual nature of the problem propounded by Dante from the apparently similar problem in St. Thomas Aquinas to which it is often compared" (Gilson, *Dante the Philosopher*, p. 179). Another truly eminent medievalist, Ernst H. Kantorowicz, has also insisted on the dissimilarity of Dante and Aquinas, as well as on Dante's radical novelty: "Dante. . .was anything but a Thomist although he used the works of Aquinas constantly. . . .The difficulty with Dante is that he, who reproduced the general knowledge of his age on every page, gave every theorem which he reproduced a slant so new and so surprising that the evidence proving his dependency on other writings serves mainly to underscore the novelty of his own approach and his own solutions." (*The King's Two Bodies: A Study in Mediaeval Political Theology* [Princeton: Princeton University Press, 1957], pp. 451–452.)

4. Father John A. Zahm, as described by Christian Dupont in his "Collecting Dante in America: Lessons from Library History," *Access* no. 81 (Fall 2002), pp. 10–11.

5. For a well-informed recent account of that ideological struggle, see Gilberto Sacerdoti, *Sacrificio e sovranità: Teologia e politica nell'Europa di Shakespeare e Bruno* (Torino: Einaudi, 2002). Sacerdoti shows the seminal role played by

Dante and, before him, Arabo-Islamic rationalism (al-Farabi, Averroes, and Maimonides) in the secularization of the European political order.

6. In broad outline, American Dante criticism since 1960 has been dominated by theological/Christianizing readings. Of course there have been numerous important exceptions—perhaps most notably Joan Ferrante's *The Political Vision of the "Divine Comedy"* (Princeton: Princeton University Press, 1984) and John A. Scott's *Dante's Political Purgatory* (Philadelphia: University of Pennsylvania Press, 1996). But the major authorities in American Dante scholarship—Charles Singleton, John Freccero (whose widely influential approach to the *Comedy* I discuss at the beginning of part I), Robert Hollander—despite variations and differences in approach, all read the poem theologically. Collectively, they have trained more than a generation of American scholars to do the same, so that the hyper-theologizing of Dante shows little sign of waning. They all view the crucial relation between Virgil and Beatrice as marked by the subordination of the former to the latter. But what makes Dante different from Aquinas is precisely his refusal to subordinate those things represented by Virgil (philosophy, secularism, practical reason, ethics, virtue, politics, the earth, the community, the common good, nature, innate wisdom, peace on earth, etc.) to those things represented by Beatrice (theology, faith, theoretical reason, metaphysics, knowledge, heaven, the eternal salvation of the individual soul, grace, revealed wisdom, peace in heaven, etc.). Dante insists that these two spheres of concern are of equal priority; he even strongly suggests that (in the final analysis—*if* one were absolutely forced to choose between two sets of values that are in fact intertwined and both essential) Virgil outranks Beatrice. But the main "theologizing" stream of American Dante criticism has spun out endless variations on a single theme: Beatrice outranks Virgil, which is another way to say that the message of the *Comedy* is: "Thou shalt be Christian!" Hollander's remark, "Poor Virgil!"—indicating that Christians are supposed to feel a sort of self-complacent sense of sorrow that the great pagan poet was not blessed to have been Christian—may be taken as the motto of the "theologizing" school of American Dante criticism. (For this "Poor Virgil!" see p. 637 of *Purgatorio*, trans. Jean Hollander and Robert Hollander [New York; Doubleday, 2003].)

7. Benedetto Croce, *The Poetry of Dante*, trans. Douglas Ainslie (Mamaroneck, NY: Paul P. Appel, 1971), p. vi.

8. Ibid., p. 2.

9. Teodolinda Barolini, *The Undivine Comedy: Detheologizing Dante* (Princeton: Princeton University Press, 1992), pp. 16–17.

10. Ibid., pp. 11, 13.

11. Ibid., p. 17.

12. Ibid., p. 20.

13. Dante, *Monarchy* 1.4.2–4. Translation from *Monarchy*, trans. and ed. Prue Shaw (Cambridge: Cambridge University Press, 1996), pp. 8–9, emphasis added.

14. Marsilius of Padua, *Defensor pacis* 1.1.5. Translation from Marsilius of Padua, *The Defender of Peace (The Defensor Pacis)*, trans. Alan Gewirth (New York: Harper & Row, 1967), p. 6.

15. Saint Augustine, *On Christian Doctrine* 1.36, trans. D.W. Robertson (Indianapolis: Bobbs-Merrill, 1958). For a good account of the recognition of the importance of "reception" in the hermeneutics of late antiquity and the Middle Ages, see Pier Cesare Bori, *L'interpretazione infinita: l'ermeneutica cristiana antica e le sue trasformazioni* (Bologna: Il Mulino, 1987).

16. On the Statius episode in particular, and Dante's hermeneutics in general, see William Franke, *Dante's Interpretive Journey* (Chicago: University of Chicago Press, 1996).

17. *Purgatory* XXII, 70–72. Trans. Charles S. Singleton, *The Divine Comedy: Purgatorio, Part 1: "Text"* (Princeton: Princeton University Press, 1973). Unless otherwise noted, all translations of the *Comedy* will be from Singleton's edition, slightly modified when necessary. Italicized emphasis of Dante's text is added, except in cases where it indicates a Latin phrase in the original.

18. This point is made by Ernest L. Fortin in his *Dissidence et philosophie au moyen âge: Dante et ses antécédents* (Montreal: Bellarmin, 1980), p 138. My understanding of the Statius episode, as well as my general sense of Dante's "skepticism," is partly indebted to Fortin's very valuable book, which has recently been issued in English as *Dissent and Philosophy in the Middle Ages: Dante and His Precursors* (Lanham, MD: Rowman and Littlefield, 2002).

19. Dante, "Epistle VII." See John A. Scott, "Henry VII of Luxembourg," in *The Dante Encyclopedia*, ed. Richard Lansing (New York: Garland Publishing, Inc., 2000), pp. 479–481.

20. See Gewirth's introduction to Marsilius of Padua, *The Defender of Peace*, pp. liv–lix. Dante is a dualist or "separatist" on the issue of church and state, while Marsilius, reversing the logic of the papacy, nonetheless supports, like the papacy, a monist absolutism. Dante imagines a state entirely free from church control and, in turn, a church entirely free from state control. Dante's ideal church has absolutely no possessions, no property, no power (above all, no power to coerce). But it is free to teach its doctrines and to offer humankind spiritual guidance. For Marsilius, both "church" and "state" really mean "the people" (the entire community), and it is "the people" who, through their proper representatives, themselves rule all aspects of this single "state-church," one aspect of which is its official religious institutions. But while this monistic state-church ("the people") can and ought to regulate and legislate in matters concerning the doctrines and practices of official ecclesiastical institutions (so as to ensure that those doctrines and practices are conducive to the highest goal of peace or civil tranquility), it cannot however coerce the religious beliefs and practices of laymen in any way whatsoever: individuals enjoy complete religious liberty, while the state's religious institutions are restricted by the will of "the people."

21. Ibid., p. xix.

22. Ibid., p. xlvi.

23. Averroes, *The Decisive Treatise, Determining What the Connection is Between Religion and Philosophy*, in Ralph Lerner and Muhsin Mahdi, eds., *Medieval Political Philosophy* (Ithaca: Cornell University Press, 1972), p. 181. Averroes

is the name by which the great Islamic rationalist Ibn Rushd (1126–1198 AD) was known in the Latin West. The chief jurisprudent of Cordoba in Muslim Spain, Averroes also served as physician to the caliph. He was often referred to in the Latin West as "the Commentator" for his voluminous explanations of almost the whole corpus of Aristotle (who, for his part, was known as "the Philosopher"), which had previously been almost entirely unknown in Europe. In the *Comedy* Dante honors Averroes by placing him in Limbo, alongside such intellectual luminaries as Aristotle, Socrates, and Plato. It is not much of an exaggeration to say that the whole edifice of Scholastic philosophy is built on the accomplishments of Averroes.

24. Marsilius of Padua, *Defensor pacis* 1.1.1; trans. Gewirth, pp. 3–4.
25. For a somewhat detailed discussion of this phrase from the *Epistle to Cangrande*, see below, part I. Some scholars have questioned the Epistle's authenticity. It is fair to say that the question remains unresolved, although probably the majority accept that Dante wrote the letter—which, as Albert Russell Ascoli points out in his excellent treatment of the various issues surrounding this text ("Epistle to Cangrande," in *The Dante Encyclopedia*, ed. Lansing, pp. 348–352), is really more a treatise in literary criticism than it is a "letter" in the normal sense. Barolini (*The Undivine Comedy*, p. 10) accepts the Epistle's authenticity and, more importantly, suggests that the letter is relevant to our understanding of the *Comedy* whether or not it was authored by Dante.
26. *Epistle to Cangrande* 7. Translation from *The Literary Criticism of Dante Alighieri*, trans. and ed. Robert S. Haller (Lincoln: University of Nebraska Press, 1973), p. 99.
27. *Defensor pacis*, trans. Gewirth, p. 20
28. *Defensor pacis* 1.5.11; trans. Gewirth, pp. 19–20, emphasis added.
29. Thus Zygmunt G. Baranski, who excels in showing Dante's sophisticated semiotic and metafictional experimentalism, refuses to allow that Dante is anything but an orthodox medieval Catholic: "Nevertheless, it is crucial to recognize that Dante's literary experimentalism never transgresses the limits of theological propriety. He manages to accomplish his task in the *Comedy* within an ideological structure whose orthodoxy is its best defense." (*Dante e i segni: Saggi per una storia intellettuale di Dante Alighieri* [Naples: Liguori Editore, 2000], p. 126, trans. mine.)
30. *Epistle to Cangrande* 8; trans. Haller p. 99, emphasis added.
31. Al-Ghazali, *Deliverance from Error*. Trans. from Arthur Hyman and James J. Walsh, eds., *Philosophy in the Middle Ages*, 2nd ed. (Indianapolis: Hackett Publishing Co., 1973), p. 273.
32. Cited in *Defensor pacis*, trans. Gewirth, p. xlviii.
33. Cited in Kantorowicz, *The King's Two Bodies*, pp. 98–99.
34. Ibid., p. 10.
35. Valerio Lucchesi, "Politics and Theology in *Inferno* X," in Woodhouse, ed., *Dante and Governance*, p. 96. The great Islamic philosopher al-Farabi, whose treatment of the relation between religion and philosophy is, I argue in part I, fundamental for our understanding of the *Comedy*, presents a similar, if more cynical, opinion on the socio-political origin of religion (an opinion

which is *not* to be taken as al-Farabi's own view; rather, he is describing the view of "the ancients"): "To believe that, when men. . .give up many of the cherished goods of this world. . .they will be rewarded and compensated with wonderful goods which they attain after death; and that, if they. . .prefer the goods of this life, they will be punished for it after their death and requited with terrible evils which will befall them in the world-to-come—all these attitudes are kinds of tricks and ruses used by people against people; for they are tricks and contrivances found out by men who are too weak to gain these goods by force, in tough and open fight, and are ruses used by those who lack the strength to fight openly and forcefully with their body and their weapons." Al-Farabi, *Principles of the Views of the Citizens of the Perfect State* 18.12; trans. Richard Walzer, *Al-Farabi on the Perfect State* (Oxford: Oxford University Press, 1985), p. 305.

36. "Condemnation of 219 Propositions," trans. Ernest L. Fortin and Peter D. O'Neill, in Lerner and Mahdi, *Medieval Political Philosophy*, pp. 335–354.

37. Jean-Baptiste Brenet's recent study of Jean de Jandun, *Transferts du sujet: La noétique d'Averroès selon Jean de Jandun* (Paris: J. Vrin, 2003), offers an excellent introduction to the Averroism of Dante's generation. Jean de Jandun, who was an "arch-Averroist" in the sense that, for him, Averroes' writings are authoritative truth, fled to Nuremberg with Marsilius following the papal condemnation of *Defensor pacis* in 1326.

38. Eugène Aroux, *Dante: hérétique, révolutionnaire et socialiste* (Paris, Jules Renouard, 1854).

39. For Dante as a Hindu, see Maria Soresina, *Le segrete cose: Dante tra induismo ed eresie medievali* (Bergamo: Moretti Honegger, 2002). For Dante as a Templar, see Paul Alexis Ladame's fascinating "novelized" account of Dante's life and works, *Dante: Prophète d'un monde uni* (Paris: Jacques Grancher, 1996). Exercising broad poetic license—imagining, for instance, conservations between Dante and some of his like-minded contemporaries such as Ramon Llull and Meister Eckhart—Ladame's is not meant to be taken as documentary biography. In my view he does manage, as well as anyone, to capture the essential spirit of Dante's thinking. For Dante as a Kabbalist, see Mark Jay Mirsky's *Dante, Eros, & Kabbalah* (Syracuse, NY: Syracuse University Press, 2003).

40. Adriano Lanza, *Dante all'inferno* (Rome: Tre Editori, 1999).

41. Ladame, *Dante*, p. 146, trans. mine.

42. Petrarch, *Seniles* II,1. Francesco Petrarca, *Le senili*, ed. Guido Martellotti (Torino: Einaudi, 1976), pp. 23–27, trans. mine.

43. Ugo Dotti, *Pétrarque* (Paris: Editions Fayard, 1991) p. 361, trans. mine. Originally published as *Vita di Petrarca* (Rome: Laterza, 1987).

44. Ibid., p. 301.

45. Petrarch, *Canzoniere* 28, lines 46–60. Translation from *Petrarch's Lyric Poems: The Rime sparse and Other Lyrics*, trans. and ed. Robert M. Durling (Cambridge, Mass: Harvard University Press, 1976), p. 77.

46. Lauro Martines, *Power and Imagination: City-States in Renaissance Italy* (New York: Alfred A. Knopf, 1979), pp. 35–38.

47. In general terms, the "Guelphs" were those factions (or city-states) who, in defending their autonomy and independence from the emperor, supported the pope's authority in central-north Italy, while the "Ghibellines" supported the emperor's. For more details, see the entries "Ghibellines" and "Guelfs" in *The Dante Encyclopedia*, ed. Lansing.

48. Mirsky, *Dante, Eros, & Kabbalah*, p. 76, calls Dante's political project "fascist."

49. *Monarchy* 1.1.5; trans. Shaw, p. 4.

50. Gilson, *Dante the Philosopher*, pp. 176–177.

51. "As far as hereditary nobility is concerned, we find that each of the three regions into which the world is divided [i.e. Asia, Europe, Africa] made him [i.e., Aeneas] noble, both through his ancestors and through his wives. For *Asia* did so through his more immediate forebears, such as Assaracus and the others who ruled over Phrygia, a region of Asia. . . .*Europe* did so with his most ancient forebear, i.e. Dardanus; *Africa* did so with his most ancient female forebear Electra, daughter of King Atlas of great renown. . . .That Atlas came from Africa is confirmed by the mountain there which bears his name." *Monarchy* 2.3.9–13; trans. Shaw, p. 35; emphasis added.

52. Kantorowicz, *The King's Two Bodies*, p. 457.

53. *Unam Sanctam*, http://www.fordham.edu/halsall/source/b8-unam.html.

54. Ibid.

55. *Monarchy* 3.14.7; trans. Shaw, p. 89.

56. Gilson, *Dante the Philosopher*, p. 164.

57. Ibid., p. 199.

58. Ibid., p. 196.

59. Kantorowicz, *The King's Two Bodies*, p. 454.

60. Gewirth, p. xlviii.

61. Kantorowicz, *The King's Two Bodies*, pp. 463–464.

62. Gilson, *Dante the Philosopher*, p. 201.

63. *Monarchy* 1.3.1; 1.3.4; trans. Shaw, pp. 5–6.

64. Ibid. 1.3.6–7; trans. Shaw, pp. 6–7, emphasis added.

65. Ibid. 1.3.7; trans. Shaw, p. 7.

66. Gilson, *Dante the Philosopher*, p. 170.

67. Avempace, *The Regime of the Solitary*, trans. Lawrence Berman, in Lerner and Mahdi, *Medieval Political Philosophy*, p. 132.

68. *Monarchy* 1.3.4; trans. Shaw, p. 6.

69. Ibid. 1.3.7–9; trans. Shaw, p. 7.

70. Ibid. 1.1.1; trans. Shaw, p. 3.

71. Ibid. 1.14.6; trans. Shaw, p. 24.

72. Gilson, *Dante the Philosopher*, p. 168.

73. Emmanuel Levinas, "Revelation in the Jewish Tradition," in *The Levinas Reader*, ed. Seán Hand (Oxford: Blackwell Publishers, 1989), p. 195.

74. *Defensor pacis* 1.11.3; trans. Gewirth, pp. 39–40, emphasis added.

75. *Monarchy* 1.4.1; trans. Shaw, p. 8.

76. Gilson, *Dante the Philosopher*, p. 171.

77. Ian Richard Netton, *Muslim Neoplatonists: An Introduction to the Thought of the Brethren of Purity (Ikhwan al-Safa)* (London: RoutledgeCurzon, 2002), p. 7.

78. Cited in Majid Fakhry, *A History of Islamic Philosophy*, 2nd ed. (New York: Columbia University Press, 1983), p. 166.

79. Jacqueline Luquet-Juillet, in *Occitanie Terre de fatalité*, vol. 3: "Troubadours et Spiritualité" (Paris: Editions Dervy, 2000), p. 159, claims that "it has often been asserted that [Dante] was a member of the Brotherhood of the Pure."

80. Cited in Seyyed Hossein Nasr, *An Introduction to Islamic Cosmological Doctrines* (Albany: SUNY Press, 1993), p. 30.

81. Roger Bacon, *Opus tertium* 14; cited in Gilson, *Dante the Philosopher*, p. 206; emphasis added.

82. Gilson, *Dante the Philosopher*, p. 206.

83. Roger Bacon, *Opus Maius*: "Moral Philosophy" 1.1. Trans. Richard McKeon, Donald McCarthy, and Ernest L. Fortin, in Lerner and Mahdi, *Medieval Political Philosophy*, pp. 360–401.

84. Ibid. 3.5 and 3.6; p. 375.

85. Ibid. 3.6; pp. 375–376.

86. Dante, *Convivio* 2.8. Trans. Richard H. Lansing, *Dante's Il Convivio/The Banquet* (New York: Taylor and Francis, 1990).

87. Kantorowicz, *The King's Two Bodies*, pp. 464–465.

88. Miguel Asín Palacios, *La escatología musulmana en la Divina Comedia*, 2nd ed., (Madrid-Granada: Las Escuelas de Estudios Árabes de Madrid Y Granada, 1943), p. 399, trans. mine.

89. Ibid., p. 398.

90. Ibid., pp. 420–421.

91. See Stephen Hirtenstein, *The Unlimited Mercifier: The Spiritual Life and Thought of Ibn Arabi* (Oxford: Anqa Publishing, 1999).

92. Khaled Abou El Fadl, "The Ugly Modern and the Modern Ugly: Reclaiming the Beautiful in Islam," in *Progressive Muslims: On Justice, Gender, and Pluralism*, ed. Omid Safi (Oxford: Oneworld Publications, 2003), p. 42.

93. See Lawrence V. Berman, "Maimonides the Disciple of Alfarabi," *Israel Oriental Studies* 4 (1974), pp. 154–178.

94. Averroes, *The Incoherence of the Incoherence*; cited in Majid Fakhry, *Averroes (Ibn Rushd): His Life, Works, and Influence* (Oxford: Oneworld Publications, 2001), p. 24.

95. Exemplary of this aspect of Sufism is the following anecdote recounted by Rumi (cited in *The Way of the Sufi*, ed. Idries Shah [New York: Penguin, 1974], p. 111):

> Four people were given a piece of money.
> The first was a Persian. He said: "I will buy with this some *angur.*"
> The second was an Arab. He said: "No, because *I* want *inab.*"
> The third was a Turk. He said: "I do not want *inab*, I want *uzum.*"
> The fourth was a Greek. He said: "I want *stafil.*"

Because they did not know what lay behind the names of things, these four started to fight. They had information but no knowledge.

One man of wisdom present could have reconciled them all, saying: 'I can fulfill the needs of all of you, with one and the same piece of money. If you honestly give me your trust, your one coin will become as four; and four at odds will become one united.'

Such a man would know that each in his own language wanted the same thing, grapes.

96. Cited in William C. Chittick, *Imaginal Worlds: Ibn al-Arabi and the Problem of Religious Diversity* (Albany: SUNY Press, 1994), p. 154.

97. Ibid., pp. 159–160.

98. Ibid., p. 140.

99. Ibid., p. 160.

100. In *Convivio* 2.8.8, Dante terms the denial of the immortality of a part of the human soul not "false" or "incorrect" but rather "most foolish" (*stoltissima*), "most vile" (*vilissima*), and "most harmful" (*dannosissima*): regardless of its truth or falsity, such a denial, by undermining the citizenry's conviction that their actions will be subject to rewards and punishments in the afterlife, harms the social order.

101. Averroes, *Faith and Reason in Islam*, trans. Ibrahim Najjar (Oxford: Oneworld, 2001), p. 123.

102. Ibid., p. 121, emphasis added.

103. Ibid., p. 125.

104. Ibid., p. 126

105. In *The Decisive Treatise* (p. 176), Averroes characterizes as an "unbeliever" anyone "who thinks that there is no happiness or misery in the next life, and that the only purpose of this teaching is that men should be safeguarded from each other in their bodily and sensible lives, that it is but a practical device, and that man has no other goal than his sensible existence." Averroes, then, clearly insists that religion is not *solely* a matter of social utility, that there is a "next life" or afterlife. But he does not say *what* this "next life" is, and this statement is not equivalent to an insistence on the immortality of the individual human soul.

106. Averroes, *Faith and Reason in Islam*, p. 126.

107. *The Epistle on the Possibility of Conjunction with the Active Intellect by Ibn Rushd with the Commentary of Moses Narboni*, ed. Kalman P. Bland (New York: The Jewish Theological Seminary of America, 1982), p. 111, emphasis added.

108. Ibid., 103, emphasis added.

109. Ibid., p. 108.

110. Ibid.

111. Ibid., p. 5.

112. Ibid., p. 109.

113. Ibid., pp. 104–105.

114. Ibid., pp. 6–7.

115. Cited in Sacerdoti, *Sacrificio e sovranità*, pp. 295–296.

116. Ibid., pp. 297–298.

117. See Singleton, *The Divine Comedy: Inferno*, Part 2: "Commentary," p. 503. For an exhaustive bibliography of scholarship on legends concerning Muhammad that circulated in medieval Europe, see Yvan G. Lepage's edition of Alexandre Du Pont's *Le Roman de Mahomet* (Louvain-Paris: Peeters, 1996), pp. 170–172. Still authoritative on this question is Alessandro d'Ancona's "La leggenda di Maometto in Occidente," *Studi di critica e storia letteraria* 2 (1912), pp. 165–308.

118. I have treated Brunetto Latini's "violence against nature" and its relation to Dante's political vision in an essay entitled "Sodomy, Diversity, Cosmopolitanism: Dante and the Limits of the *Polis*" (forthcoming).

119. See Aquinas, *Summa Theologica* Pt. I–II Q. 39 Art. 1.

Part I   Virgil's Happiness (Dante, Al-Farabi, Philosophy)

1. John Freccero, *Dante: The Poetics of Conversion* (Cambridge, Mass.: Harvard University Press, 1986), pp. 1–28.

2. In his chapter on *Inferno*'s first canto (cited above), Freccero does not explicitly mention the *Convivio*; but it is clear from his later remarks (pp. 187–194) on Dante's "philosophical pride" that he regards the *Convivio* as the prime instance of such pride.

3. "And being thence admonished to return to myself, I entered even into my inward self, *Thou being my Guide*: and able I was, for *Thou wert become my Helper*. And I entered and beheld with the eye of my soul the Light Unchangeable." Augustine, *Confessions* 7.10. Cited in Freccero, *Poetics of Conversion*, p. 9.

4. Ibid.

5. Freccero's basic point—that the *Comedy* marks Dante's turn from philosophy to theology—has a very long history and is sanctioned by a century or more of exegesis. See, for instance, Luigi Pietrobono, *Il poema sacro: saggio d'una interpretazione generale della Divina Commedia*, 2 vol. (Bologna: Zanichelli, 1915). Pietrobono also sees the *Comedy* as Dante's return to theology and mysticism following a dead-end "detour" into rationalist philosophy. Freccero's exegesis is also rooted in the works of the great Italian Dante scholar Bruno Nardi; see, among others, Nardi's *Dal "Convivio" alla "Commedia" (Sei saggi danteschi)* (Rome: Istituto Storico Italiano per il Medio Evo, 1960) and his *Saggi di filosofia dantesca* (Milan: Società Editrice Dante Alighieri, 1930). Nardi, who more than anyone else has demonstrated that Dante draws freely from the Islamic intellectual tradition, is also more than anyone else responsible for viewing the *Comedy* as Dante's act of repentance following the overly audacious formulations of the *Convivio* and, especially, *Monarchy*. Nardi is firmly of the opinion that the *Comedy*'s basic allegory means to subordinate Virgil (reason, philosophy) to Beatrice (faith, theology). One should also mention here that Freccero's interpreting the Virgil

of *Inferno* I as an allegory for "theology" or "religion" is highly idiosyncratic, since Virgil is normally understood as an allegory for natural reason or philosophy.

6. Freccero, *Poetics of Conversion*, p. 9.

7. Augustine, *City of God* 15.4. Translation from *City of God*, trans. Henry Bettenson (New York: Penguin Classics, 1984), p. 599.

8. Ibid.

9. As Ugo Dotti says: "From Purgatory and on up what matters to [Dante] is the apprehension of the celestial order of things, as a paradigm on which to model historical reality on earth. . . .In this always accelerating movement toward the summit, we should not see a mystical ascent or an itinerary of the soul toward God but rather a progressive discovery of that ordered heavenly realm which. . .represents the supreme example of a possible (indeed obligatory) happiness of life down here on earth." (*La Divina Commedia e la città dell'uomo* [Rome: Donzelli, 1998], pp. 122–123, trans. mine.)

10. Dotti, *La Divina Commedia*, pp. 19–20; p. 22.

11. Augustine, *City of God* 19.6; trans. Bettenson, p. 858.

12. On Olivi's influence on Dante's education at Santa Croce, see Sergio Cristaldi, *Dante di fronte al gioachismo: Dalla "Vita Nova" alla "Monarchia"* (Rome: Salvatore Sciascia, 2000), esp. chap. 2. As Raoul Manselli says: "Olivi's spiritualism indelibly marked one who was then a lively and impetuous young Florentine, Dante Alighieri. The memory of Olivi and the veneration of which he was the object at Santa Croce endured for more than a century" ("L'idéal du spirituel selon Pierre Jean-Olivi," *Cahiers de Fanjeaux* 10 [1975], pp. 121; trans. mine).

13. Augustine, *De Genesi contra Manichaeos* 1.23.35–41; *City of God* 22.30. On Olivi's and Dante's revision of Augustine's historical scheme, see Cristaldi, *Dante di fronte*, pp. 203–206.

14. Cristaldi, *Dante di fronte*, pp. 173–174, trans. mine.

15. In *Paradiso* XXVI Adam tells Dante that, having lived for 930 years on earth, he spent the next 4302 years in Limbo, and then ascended to Heaven in 33 AD when Christ died and harrowed Hell. This means that Adam (if his existence were measured in earthly time) would have been 5232 years old in 33 AD; this in turn means that "now," 1300 AD, marks 6499 years since the creation of Adam. In *Paradiso* IX, Cunizza tells Dante that "this centennial year" (i.e., 1300 AD, the year proclaimed by the papacy as a "jubilee" year) will be "fived" (i.e., multiplied by five) before the world comes to an end; $1300 \times 5 = 6500$, the number of years before the Last Judgment and the end of time. For this particular insight as well as for general views concerning Dante's radical opposition to the church, his relation to Islamic political philosophy, and the possibility of reading Dante as a "non-Christian," I am indebted to Ernest L. Fortin, *Dissidence et philosophie au moyen âge: Dante et ses antécédents* (Montreal: Bellarmin, 1980). Fortin deciphers the chronology of the poem's time-scheme on pp. 153ff. Fortin's

book has recently been issued in English as *Dissent and Philosophy in the Middle Ages: Dante and His Precursors* (Lanham, MD: Rowman and Littlefield, 2002).

16. David Burr, *The Spiritual Franciscans: From Protest to Persecution in the Century After Saint Francis* (University Park, PA: The Pennsylvania State University, 2001), pp. 310–311.

17. Dante, *Epistle to Cangrande* 15. Trans. Robert S. Haller, *Literary Criticism of Dante Alighieri* (Lincoln: University of Nebraska Press, 1973), pp. 101–102.

18. *Monarchy* 3.16.7; Translation from *Monarchy*, trans. and ed. Prue Shaw (Cambridge: Cambridge University Press, 1996), p. 92.

19. Augustine, *City of God* 14.25; trans. Bettenson, p. 590.

20. Franco Ferrucci, *Le due mani di Dio: Il cristianesimo e Dante* (Rome: Fazi, 1999), pp. 112–113; trans. mine; emphasis added.

21. Thomas Sheehan, *The First Coming: How the Kingdom of God Became Christianity* (New York: Random House, 1986), pp. 61–62.

22. Dotti, *La Divina Commedia*, pp. 122–123.

23. Elaine Pagels, *Adam, Eve, and the Serpent* (New York: Random House, 1988), pp. 80–81.

24. Ibid., p. 81.

25. Antonio Piromalli, *Gioacchino da Fiore e Dante* (Soveria Manelli: Rubbettino, 1984), p. 51.

26. *Aeneid* 2.564ff, trans. John Dryden.

27. Ibid. 2.707ff; trans. Dryden.

28. Augustine, *City of God* 19.5; trans. Bettenson, pp. 858–859.

29. On the "paganism" of Dante's Christianity, see Ferrucci, *Le due mani di Dio*.

30. Aristotle, *Nichomachean Ethics* 1.2 1094b7–10; trans. W.D. Ross, revised by J.O. Urmson, in *The Complete Works of Aristotle*, vol. 2, ed. Jonathan Barnes (Princeton: Princeton University Press, 1984), p. 1730.

31. Remigio dei Girolami, *De bono communi*. Cited in M.S. Kempshall, *The Common Good in Late Medieval Political Thought* (New York: Oxford University Press, 1999), p. 295. My understanding of Remigio is indebted to Kempshall's two excellent chapters on his thought. See also Charles T. Davis, "An Early Florentine Political Theorist: Fra Remigio de' Girolami," in his *Dante's Italy and Other Essays* (Philadelphia: University of Pennsylvania Press, 1984), pp. 198–223.

32. *De bono communi*. Cited in Ernst H. Kantorowicz, *The King's Two Bodies: A Study in Mediaeval Political Theology* (Princeton: Princeton University Press, 1957), p. 479.

33. *De bono communi*. Cited in John A. Scott, *Dante's Political Purgatory* (Philadephia: University of Pennsylvania Press, 1996), p. 13.

34. Kempshall, *Common Good*, p. 305.

35. Ibid., p. 300.

36. Kantorowicz, *The King's Two Bodies*, p. 478.

37. Ibid.

38. Kempshall, *Common Good*, p. 309.

39. Kempshall, *Common Good*, p. 312; emphasis added.

40. *De Bono Communi*. Cited in Francesco Bruni, *La città divisa: Le parti e il bene comune da Dante a Guicciardini* (Bologna: Mulino, 2003); trans. mine.

41. Kempshall, *Common Good*, pp. 295–296.

42. Ibid., p. 301.

43. Ibid., pp. 301 and 303.

44. Ibid., p. 306.

45. For this view, see Robert Hollander, "*Purgatorio* II: The New Song and the Old," *Lectura Dantis* 6 (1990), pp. 28–45.

46. Teodolinda Barolini, *The Undivine Comedy: Detheologizing Dante* (Princeton: Princeton University Press, 1992), p. 107.

47. Amilcare Iannucci, "Casella's Song and Tuning of the Soul," *Thought: A Review of Culture and Ideas* 65 (1990), p. 43. See also, among many others, Robert Hollander, "Cato's Rebuke and Dante's *scoglio*," *Italica* 52 (1975), pp. 348–363; Teodolinda Barolini, "Casella's Song," in *Modern Critical Interpretations: Dante's 'Divine Comedy'*, ed. Harold Bloom (New York: Chelsea House, 1987), pp. 151–158.

48. Freccero, *Poetics of Conversion*, p. 189.

49. Ibid., p. 190; emphasis added.

50. On the tension in late medieval European literature between individual and collective subjectivity, see my *The Death of the Troubadour: The Late Medieval Resistance to the Renaissance* (Philadelphia: University of Pennsylvania Press, 1994).

51. Dante, *Convivio* 3. Ed. Piero Cudini (Milan: Aldo Garzanti, 1980), p. 137, trans. mine; emphasis added.

52. Ronald L. Martinez, "Cato of Utica," in *The Dante Encyclopedia*, ed. Richard Lansing (New York: Garland Publishing, 2000), pp. 146–149.

53. Scott, *Dante's Political Purgatory*, pp. 73–74.

54. See Joan Ferrante, *The Political Vision of the 'Divine Comedy'* (Princeton: Princeton University Press, 1984).

55. *Monarchy* 2.7.2–3; trans. Shaw, p. 48.

56. Richard Hazelton, "The Christianization of 'Cato': The *Disticha Catonis* in the Light of Late Medieval Commentaries," *Medieval Studies* 19 (1957), 157–173; cited in Scott, *Dante's Political Purgatory*, pp. 77–78. Scott follows Hazelton and many others in seeing Dante's Cato as a Christian—after all, if he were not, how else could he be saved? Scott tells us that Cato must have been "granted the grace of implicit faith." I am arguing, on the other hand, that only a truly non-Christian Cato suits Dante's overall purpose in *Purgatory*.

57. St. Thomas Aquinas, *Summa Theologica* Pt. I–II Q. 62 Art. 1. Translated by the Fathers of the English Dominican Province (New York: Benzinger Brothers, 1947), p. 851.

58. Kempshall, *Common Good*, p. 289.

59. Enzo Noè Girardi, "Al centro del Purgatorio: il tema del libero arbitrio," in Alessandro Ghisalberti, ed., *Il pensiero filosofico e teologico di Dante Alighieri* (Milan: Vita e Pensiero, 2001), p. 27.

60. Scott, *Dante's Political Purgatory*, p. 189. My understanding of the significance of *Purgatory*'s Earthly Paradise is indebted to Scott, esp. p. 64 and pp. 66–67.

61. *Monarchy* 3.16.5–6; trans. Shaw, p. 92; emphasis added.

62. Aquinas, *Summa Theologica* Pt. I–II Q. 3 Art. 5, trans. p. 599.

63. Etienne Gilson, *Dante the Philosopher* (New York: Sheed & Ward, 1949), pp. 192–193: "These *duo ultima* [two ultimate goals]. . .have a strange sound to ears accustomed to the language of St. Thomas Aquinas. One of the principal theses of the latter's *De regimine principium* is, on the contrary, that man has but one final goal: the eternal beatitude to which he is summoned by God and which he can attain only through that Church without which there is no salvation. That precisely is the reason why the princes of this world are subject to the Pope, as to Jesus Christ Himself, Whose vicar he is. The connection between the two pairs of theses is here fully apparent, as is the irreducible character of their opposition. Dante maintains that man has two final goals; if both are final, neither can be subordinate to the other; if they cannot be graduated, neither can the two authorities that preside over each of these two orders. St. Thomas certainly does not deny that natural man has a natural goal to seek and attain in this life. Rather ought it be said that, of all the theologians of the Middle Ages, none did more than he to establish this thesis. It is inseparable from his differentiation between nature and grace, which pervades his work like a principle infinitely productive of unity in the sphere of life. On the other hand, differentiation between the orders is accompanied by unity in the Thomistic doctrine only because here differentiation between the orders entails their gradation. Consequently St. Thomas never admitted that man's natural goal in this life was man's final goal in this life, for man experiences this life only with a view to the after-life, and his goal in this life is to be sought only with a view to the goal of the after-life. With an utter inflexibility that excludes in advance Dante's thesis considered in its proper form, St. Thomas declares that the final goal of the body of society is not to live in accordance with virtue, but, through a virtuous life, to come to the enjoyment of God."

64. *Monarchy* 3.4.2–3; trans. Shaw, p. 69.

65. Ibid. 3.16.7–9; trans. Shaw, p. 92; emphasis added.

66. Ibid. 3.14.7; trans. Shaw, p. 89.

67. Ibid. 1.14.5–7; trans. Shaw, pp. 24–25.

68. Marsilius of Padua, *Defensor pacis* 1.10.3. Translation from Marsilius of Padua, *The Defender of Peace* (*The Defensor Pacis*), trans. Alan Gewirth (New York: Harper & Row, 1967), p. 35.

69. According to Y. Tzvi Langermann ["Some Astrological Themes in the Thought of Abraham ibn Ezra," in *Rabbi Abraham Ibn Ezra: Studies in the Writings of a Twelfth-Century Jewish Polymath*, ed. Isadore Twersky and Jay M. Harris (Cambridge: Harvard University Press, 1993), p. 70], it was common among Jewish and Muslim philosophers of twelfth-century Andalusia to teach that "the different means for coming close to God, the rituals practiced by the major religions, and the law codes and prophetic revelations held sacred by the different faiths are phenomena of a lesser order; all may

be ascribed to the natural differences that exist among peoples and climates, all of which can be sufficiently accounted for by astrology."

70. One should emphasize that Virgil's reasoning concerns *actions*. Aristotle says in *Nicomachean Ethics*, Book 6, as we shall see later in part I, that practical wisdom is a matter of deliberating good and bad concerning *actions*. Virgil is not simply "philosophy" or "natural reason" in general; he is, specifically, *practical philosophy*, the aim of which is judging what ought to be done in the sphere of human actions.

71. Ferrucci, *Le due mani di Dio*, p. 105.

72. Ibid., pp. 106–107.

73. Ibid., p. 105

74. Ibid., p. 108

75. *Book of Religion* 5, in *Alfarabi, The Political Writings: "Selected Aphorisms" and Other Texts*, trans. Charles E. Butterworth (Ithaca: Cornell University Press, 2001), p. 97.

76. *Convivio* 2.8.9. For the full passage, see above, introduction, note 86.

77. Al-Farabi, *Principles of the Views of the Citizens of the Perfect State* 17.2; trans. Richard Walzer, *Al-Farabi on the Perfect State* (Oxford: Oxford University Press, 1985), pp. 279–281; emphasis added. Hereafter, this text will be referred to as *The Perfect State*.

78. Al-Farabi, *The Political Regime*, trans. Fauzi M. Najjar, in Ralph Lerner and Muhsin Mahdi, eds., *Medieval Political Philosophy* (Ithaca: Cornell University Press, 1972), p. 41; emphasis added.

79. Ibid.

80. Al-Farabi, *The Attainment of Happiness*, trans. Muhsin Mahdi, in Lerner and Mahdi, pp. 79–80.

81. Ibid., p. 78

82. Al-Farabi, *The Perfect State* 15.11; trans. Walzer, p. 247.

83. Averroes, *The Incoherence of the Incoherence*, cited in Majid Fakhry, *Averroes (Ibn Rushd): His Life, Works, and Influence* (Oxford: Oneworld Publications, 2001), p. 94.

84. Al-Farabi, *The Attainment of Happiness*, p. 77.

85. The issue of Dante's debt to Islamic philosophy, particularly in the domain of cosmology, has recently been treated by Carmela Baffioni, "Aspetti delle cosmologie islamiche in Dante," in Ghisalberti, ed., *Il pensiero filosofico*, pp. 103–122. Baffioni cites Massimo Campanini's assertion, in his edition of al-Farabi's *Perfect State* (Al-Farabi, *La città virtuosa*, ed. and trans. M. Campanini [Milan: 1996], p. 304), that Dante's cosmology "certainly must have been inspired by the Arab philosophers." For a brief but excellent treatment of the question, see Paul A. Cantor, "The Uncanonical Dante: *The Divine Comedy* and Islamic Philosophy," *Philosophy and Literature* 20.1 (1996), pp. 138–153.

86. Roger Arnaldez, *Averroès, un rationaliste en Islam* (Paris: Editions Balland, 1998), pp. 86–88, trans. mine; emphasis added.

87. In *The Decisive Treatise* Averroes refers to those relatively few humans endowed with the speculative (theoretical) faculty as the "elect." If Virgil is not one of "God's elect," this signifies, on the level of the *Comedy's*

philosophical allegory, that he, like all humans, has been endowed with the practical faculty and, like most humans, not with the theoretical faculty.

88. Al-Farabi, *The Attainment of Happiness*, trans. Mahdi, p. 76.
89. Al-Farabi, *The Perfect State* 15.19; trans. Walzer, p. 259, emphasis added.
90. Ibid. 15.15–20; trans. Walzer, pp. 253–259.
91. Ibid. 19.1–4; trans. Walzer, pp. 315–317.
92. Ibid. 19.7; trans. Walzer, p. 323.
93. Al-Farabi, *The Political Regime*, trans. Najjar, p. 53.
94. Al-Farabi, *The Perfect State*, trans. Walzer, pp. 455–456.
95. Gnosticism, of which the Catharism that was widespread in the southern parts of Western Europe in the twelfth through the fourteen centuries is one manifestation, teaches that there are two conflicting principles: a "Good" of light and spirit versus an "Evil" of darkness and body. Hence, salvation depends on our escaping the physical body and the material world.
96. Miriam Galston, *Politics and Excellence: The Political Philosophy of Alfarabi* (Princeton: Princeton University Press, 1990), p. 59. As Galston points out, Ibn Bajja acknowledges that in his commentary on the *Nicomachean Ethics* (a text that has not survived), al-Farabi does claim that there is no afterlife; but Ibn Bajja says that this is merely al-Farabi's rendition of what Aristotle's text says, not his own belief on the matter. Shlomo Pines tells us the following concerning the reception of al-Farabi's notorious commentary on the *Ethics* in the Muslim West: "Many of the most famous Spanish philosophers of the twelfth century were provoked into criticizing or explaining away certain uncompromising opinions expressed in this work. According to Ibn Tufayl, al-Farabi sets forth in this commentary the view that happiness exists in this life and this world and, after this assertion, makes a statement according to which 'everything else that is spoken of is nothing but drivel and old wives' tales.' Ibn Bajja, for his part, in an as yet unpublished text defends al-Farabi against the charge that in his commentary he professed the opinion that there is no afterlife, that there is no happiness but political happiness, that the only existence is that known to the senses, and that all assertions concerning a different kind of existence are old wives' tales." (Moses Maimonides, *The Guide of the Perplexed*, ed. and trans. Shlomo Pines [Chicago: University of Chicago Press, 1963], p. lxxx.) The passage from Ibn Tufayl (whom I discuss below, in part II) is this: "Those of Farabi's books that have reached us are for the most part on logic, and those on philosophy are full of doubts. In *The Ideal Religion* he affirms that the souls of the wicked live on forever in infinite torments after death. But in his *Civil Politics* he says plainly that they dissolve into nothing and that only the perfected souls of the good achieve immortality. Finally in his commentary on Aristotle's *Ethics*, discussing human happiness, he says that it exists only in this life, and on the heels of that has words to the effect that all other claims are senseless ravings and old wives' tales. This makes mankind at large despair of God's mercy. It puts the wicked on the same level with the good, for it makes nothingness the ultimate destiny of us all. This is an unspeakable lapse, an unforgivable fall. This on top of his mis-belief, openly

avowed, that prophecy belongs properly to the imagination, and his preference of philosophy to revelation—and many more failings which I pass
over" (Lenn E. Goodman, *Ibn Tufayl's Hayy Ibn Yaqzan* [Los Angeles: gee
tee bee, 1996], p. 100).

97. "Condemnation of 219 Propositions," trans. Ernest L. Fortin and Peter
    D. O'Neill, in Lerner and Mahdi, p. 351.
98. Al-Farabi, *The Perfect State* 16.7; trans. Walzer, p. 273.
99. Ibid. 16.9; trans. Walzer, p. 275.
100. See Ferrante, *The Political Vision of the 'Divine Comedy'*.
101. Al-Farabi, *The Perfect State*, Walzer, p. 468.
102. Since Marco Lombard's denial of original sin is theologically heterodox,
    the theological school of Dante exegetes must deny that his position on
    this issue is consonant with Dante's. Rocco Montano's scandalized reac-
    tion against Marco Lombard (in Montano, *Storia della poesia di Dante*
    [Naples, 1962]), as paraphrased by Girardi ("Al centro del Purgatorio,"
    p. 35), is telling, not only in reference to this particular point, but as a fur-
    ther example of that trend which has dominated Dante criticism since
    1960 (in America more than in Italy), according to which the *Comedy* is
    Dante's return to Catholic orthodoxy: "Montano [argues that] by the time
    he began to write the *Comedy* Dante was an orthodox Catholic, convinced
    that the Church had authority over all of human reality, thus even over
    the State; Marco on the other hand is still marked by paganism, a layper-
    son, a Ghibelline [i.e., a supporter of the emperor against the pope],
    entirely ignorant of theology, who dreams of the bygone days of Frederick II.
    Dante knows that man is the child of sin and that his freedom depends on
    grace; Marco however believes that human nature is not corrupt, and he
    ignores the Christian doctrine of the *infirmitas peccati*."
103. Charles S. Singleton, "The Poet's Number at the Center," *Modern
    Language Notes* 80 (1965), pp. 1–10.
104. Augustine, *City of God* 22.30; trans. Bettenson, p. 1089.
105. Ibid.
106. Ibid.
107. Al-Farabi, *The Political Regime*, trans. Najjar, p. 38.
108. Ibid.
109. Al-Farabi, *The Perfect State* 15.2; trans. Walzer, 229.
110. Ibid. 15.11; trans. Walzer, p. 247.
111. Ibid. 15.3; trans. Walzer, p. 231.
112. Al-Farabi, *The Political Regime*, trans. Najjar, p. 32.
113. See Al-Farabi, *The Political Regime*, pp. 32–33, for al-Farabi's fairly lengthy
    treatment of the "natural causes of the differences between nations." Since
    al-Farabi's "absolutely perfect human societies" are by definition multina-
    tional, and since nations are by nature different, it follows that internal
    difference is an essential quality of the perfect society.
114. Al-Farabi, *The Attainment of Happiness*, trans. Mahdi, p. 63.
115. Ibid., p. 70.

116. Ibid., p. 73; emphasis added.

117. Al-Farabi, *The Perfect State* 15.19; trans. Walzer, p. 259; emphasis added.

118. Al-Farabi, *Selected Aphorisms* 35; trans. Butterworth, p. 29; emphasis added.

119. Ibid. 38; trans. Butterworth, p. 31; emphasis added.

120. Al-Farabi, *The Perfect State* 17.1; trans. Walzer, p. 277.

121. Ibid., trans. Walzer, p. 277.

122. Ibid., trans. Walzer, p. 279.

123. *Book of Religion* 5; trans. Butterworth, p. 97.

124. Al-Farabi, *The Attainment of Happiness*; trans. Mahdi, p. 79.

125. Walzer, p. 476.

126. Ibid., p. 477.

127. Ibid., pp. 479 and 441.

128. Amilcare A. Iannucci, "Philosophy," in Lansing, ed., *The Dante Encyclopedia*, pp. 692–696.

129. *Monarchy* 1.4; trans. Shaw, pp. 8–9.

130. Gilson, *Dante the Philosopher*, p. 174; emphasis added.

131. See above, introduction, note 6.

132. *The Epistle on the Possibility of Conjunction with the Active Intellect by Ibn Rushd with the Commentary of Moses Narboni*, ed. Kalman P. Bland (New York: The Jewish Theological Seminary of America), p. 109.

133. The notion that, whatever she may be, Beatrice is *not* philosophy, has become a commonplace in American Dante criticism. For example, Alison Cornish asserts that "in the *Commedia*, the beloved Beatrice of the poet's adolescence will return triumphant, supplanting philosophy on the mental itinerary toward God" (*Reading Dante's Stars* [New Haven: Yale University Press, 2000], p. 12). My point here is not to criticize Cornish's excellent book, but to suggest that the theological reading of the *Comedy* is now so pervasive that its tenets appear "natural" even to our most sophisticated critics. In the present book I am arguing that, on one level of the poem's primary allegory, Beatrice in fact *is* philosophy; more precisely, that she is one branch of philosophy—theoretical science.

134. Trans. George F. Hourani, in Lerner and Mahdi, p. 179.

135. I do not mean to ignore that copious amount of ethical and practical discourse in *Paradiso*, presented by the various souls whom Dante meets. There is plenty of political teaching in the poem's final canticle; in fact, it is in a sense nothing but politics. But what I mean is that Beatrice's assigned role in *Paradiso* is to give Dante knowledge concerning the objects of theory.

136. Al-Farabi, *The Perfect State* 17.1; trans. Walzer, p. 279.

137. For the notion that Statius offers a Christian theory of the soul, see Singleton, *Purgatorio, Vol. 2: Commentary*, pp. 607–608. But even if Statius's discourse is a combination of philosophy and theology (although certainly there is much more of the former than the latter), what really makes it out of place here is not its theology but the fact that its object is theoretical.

138. Al-Farabi, *The Perfect State* 17.1; trans. Walzer, pp. 677–679.
139. Hava Tirosh-Samuelson, "Introduction, Judaism and the Natural World," in Hava Tirosh-Samuelson, ed., *Judaism and Ecology: Created World and Revealed Word* (Cambridge, Mass: Harvard University Press, 2002), p. xxxv.
140. *Convivio* 2.14. Cited in Gilson, *Dante the Philosopher*, p. 105.
141. Gilson, *Dante the Philosopher*, pp. 105–106.
142. *Epistle to Cangrande* 16; trans. Haller, p. 102.
143. Aristotle, *Metaphysics* II.1.20: "For the end of theoretical knowledge is truth, while that of practical knowledge is action." Trans. from Barnes, vol. 2, p. 1570.
144. *Monarchy* 1.2.4–6; trans. Shaw, p. 5; emphasis added.
145. Ibid. 1.2.4; 1.4.6; trans. Shaw, pp. 5 and p. 9.
146. For a good, succinct account of the critical reception of the Ulysses episode, see Teodolinda Barolini, "Ulysses," in *The Dante Encyclopedia*, ed. Lansing, pp. 842–847.
147. Barolini, "Ulysses," p. 847.
148. There are several textual links between the Ulysses episode and the first canto of *Inferno*—a fact that Dante seems to be calling to our attention when, near the end of *Inferno* XXVI, he refers to the front part of Ulysses' sinking ship as *il primo canto* (which means "the forepart" but also "the first canto").
149. As Scott (*Dante's Political Purgatory*, pp. 75–76) says, the Cato–Ulysses relation is "one of the basic antitheses in the Comedy—an opposition possibly sparked off by Seneca's assertion that 'in Cato the immortal gods had given to us a truer example of the wise man than earlier ages had in Ulysses and Hercules.' "
150. Lucan, *The Civil War* IX, 551–563. Translation from Lucan, *The Civil War*, trans. J.D. Duff (Cambridge, Mass.: Harvard University Press, 1928), p. 547; emphasis added.
151. Lucan, *The Civil War* IX, 564–586; trans. Duff, pp. 547–549; emphasis added.
152. On Maimonides's place in the Islamic philosophical tradition, see See Lawrence V. Berman, "Maimonides the Disciple of Alfarabi," *Israel Oriental Studies* 4 (1974), pp. 154–178.
153. Moses Maimonides, *The Guide of the Perplexed*, ed. and trans. Shlomo Pines (Chicago: University of Chicago Press, 1963), p. lxxviii.
154. Al-Farabi, "Selected Aphorisms" 35; trans. Butterworth, p. 29.
155. Al-Farabi, "Selected Aphorisms" 36; trans. Butterworth, pp. 29–30.
156. Maimonides, *The Guide of the Perplexed* 1.2; trans. Pines, p. 23.
157. Maimonides, *The Guide of the Perplexed* 1.2; trans. Pines, pp. 23–24.
158. Ibid.
159. Ibid., pp. 24–25.
160. Ibid., p. 25.
161. Stefano Tardini, "*Endoxa* and Communities: Grounding Enthymematic Arguments," http://www.ils.com.unisi.ch/paper_Lugano2002.pdf

162. Cited in Scott, *Dante's Political Purgatory*, p. 74.

163. Maimonides, *The Guide of the Perplexed* 1.2; trans. Pines, pp. 25.

164. Marvin Fox, *Interpreting Maimonides* (Chicago: University of Chicago Press, 1990), p. 188.

165. As Leo Strauss says in "How to Begin to Study *The Guide of the Perplexed*" (the Introductory Essay to Pines's edition of *The Guide of the Perplexed*), the *Guide* is a book "sealed with many seals" (Pines, p. xiii).

166. Fox, *Interpreting Maimonides*, p. 189.

167. Ibid.

168. Ibid., pp. 180–181.

169. Aristotle, *Nichomachean Ethics* 6.5 1140a30–1140b5; in Barnes, p. 1800.

170. Aristotle, *Nicomachean Ethics* 1.3 1095a5. This translation, from Charles Trinkaus, *The Poet as Philosopher: Petrarch and the Formation of Renaissance Consciousness* (New Haven: Yale University Press, 1979), p. 108, is a slight embellishment of Aristotle's Greek, which says, more succinctly: "since the aim is not knowledge but action [*praxis*]."

171. Aristotle, near beginning of *Nicomachean Ethics* (in the same passage cited in the previous note), refers to the subject matter of his treatise as "political science." In the Aristotelian tradition, "ethics" and "political science" were regarded as two facets of the same field. The difference, insofar as there is one, is this: ethics deals with discerning the good and bad in individual actions, political science the good and bad in collective actions. Since Dante tends to view the individual in terms of the collective, for our purposes "ethics" and "politics" are virtually synonymous.

172. For an excellent treatment of "prudence," see Daniel Mark Nelson, *The Priority of Prudence: Virtue and Natural Law in Thomas Aquinas and the Implications for Modern Ethics* (University Park, PA: Pennsylvania State University Press, 1992). As Nelson says (p. 80), prudence "enables our rational activities of deliberation and choosing to be done well. Thomas [Aquinas] describes it as an application of 'right reason to action'. . .and as 'wisdom about human affairs'. . . .Its concerns are essentially practical. Although one can speak about a prudent natural or social scientist (insofar as the scientist is a prudent individual) prudence is concerned with contingent rather than necessary truths. In the realm of action, the means to ends are not predetermined by the natures of things." We should also note that Dante specifies that the particular prudence that Solomon possesses is "kingly prudence"; this is what (the real) Aquinas called "political" or "regnative" prudence, which, Aquinas says, "regards not only the private good of the individual, but also the common good of the multitude" (cited in Nelson, p. 83).

173. Aristotle, *Nicomachean Ethics* 6.7 1141b 2–3.

174. Ibid. 6.7 1141b 3–7.

175. Cited in Georg Weiland, "Happiness: the perfection of man," in *The Cambridge History of Later Medieval Philosophy*, ed. Norman Kretzmann, Anthony Kenny, Jan Pinborg (Cambridge: Cambridge University Press, 1982), p. 685.

176. Gilson, *Dante the Philosopher*, p. 188.
177. See above, introduction, note 32.
178. Maimonides, *The Guide of the Perplexed* 3.32; trans. Pines, p. 525.
179. Ibid.
180. Ibid., pp. 525–526.
181. Sacerdoti, *Sacrificio e sovranità*, p. 235.
182. Maimonides, *The Guide of the Perplexed* 3.32; trans. Pines, p. 526.
183. Ibid., pp. 526–527.
184. Ibid., p. 526.
185. Ibid., p. 527.
186. Sacerdoti, *Sacrificio e sovranità*, p. 231.
187. Ibid., p. 237.
188. Shlomo Pines, "Dieu et l'être selon Maïmonide: Exégèse d'Exode 3,14 et doctrine connexe," in *Celui qui est: interprétations juives et chrétiennes d'Exode 3,14*, ed. Alain de Libera et Emilie Zum Brunn (Paris: Editions du Cerf, 1986), p. 23; trans. mine.
189. Maimonides, *The Guide of the Perplexed* 1.59; trans. Pines, p. 139.
190. Ibid., p. 143.
191. Pines, "Dieu et l'être selon Maïmonide," pp. 23–24: "The only certain science, in the framework of which, since we cannot know His essence, we can know God's 'actions' (which is the term Maimonides uses to designate natural processes), is terrestrial physics. It seems that Maimonides, through his complete rejection of all metaphysics, considered marking the limits of human reason to be one of philosophy's principal tasks."
192. Maimonides, *The Guide of the Perplexed* 3.32; trans. Pines, p. 527.

Part II The Right Path (Dante's Universalism)

1. Amir Hussain, "Muslims, Pluralism, and Interfaith Dialogue," in *Progressive Muslims: On Justice, Gender, and Pluralism*, ed. Omid Safi (Oxford: Oneworld Publications, 2003), p. 255.
2. Ibn Arabi, *Meccan Openings* III:83; cited in Stephen Hirtenstein, *The Unlimited Mercifier: The Spiritual Life and Thought of Ibn Arabi* (Oxford: Anqa Publishing, 1999), p. 63.
3. As William Chittick says, in his *Imaginal Worlds: Ibn al-Arabi and the Problem of Religious Diversity* (Albany: SUNY Press, 1994), p. 124: "The Koran declares that the essential message of every prophet is the same, while the details of each message is unique. Hence the universality of religious truth is an article of Islamic faith. It is true that many Muslims believe that the universality of guidance pertains only to pre-Koranic times, but others disagree; there is no 'orthodox' interpretation that Muslims must accept."
4. My discussion of the exegesis of *li-kull-in* is based on Issa J. Boullata, "Fa-stabiqu 'l-khayrat: A Qur'anic Principle of Interfaith Relations," in Yvonne Y Haddad and Wadi Z. Haddad, eds., *Christian–Muslim Encounters* (Gainesville: University Press of Florida, 1995), pp. 43–53.

5. Cited in Sarah Stroumsa, *Freethinkers of Medieval Islam: Ibn al-Rawandi, Abu Bakr al-Razi, and Their Impact on Islamic Thought* (Leiden: Brill, 1999), p. 3.

6. Boullata, "Fa-stabiqu 'l-khayrat," pp. 47–48. As Stroumsa remarks (*Freethinkers of Medieval Islam*, p. 6), in al-Zamakhshari's view, "a person was labeled a [heretic] not when he abandoned one religion for the sake of another, but only when he adopted a system which deviated from all religions."

7. Saint Augustine, *Retractions* 1.4.3; emphasis added. Cited in John Vanderspoel, "The Background to Augustine's Denial of Religious Plurality," in *Grace, Politics, and Desire: Essays on Augustine*, ed. H.A. Meynell (Alberta: University of Calgary Press, 1990), p. 179.

8. Cited in Vanderspoel, "Background to Augustine's Denial," pp. 186–187.

9. I am referring to, respectively, the translations by Robert Durling and Charles Singleton.

10. Ibn Arabi, *Meccan Openings* III 410.24. Cited in Chittick, *Imaginal Worlds*, p. 145 (Chittick treats Ibn Arabi's three understandings of "the path" on pp. 145–146).

11. Ibn Arabi, *The Bezels of Wisdom*, trans. R.W.J. Austin (Mahwah, NJ: Paulist Press, 1980), p. 130.

12. Ibid., pp. 133–134.

13. *Meccan Openings* III 410.21; Chittick, *Imaginal Worlds*, pp. 145–146. Ibn Arabi expressly insists that the revelation given to Muhammad does not "abrogate" or render null and void the previous revelations: "We have been required in our all-inclusive religion to have faith in the truth of all the messengers and all the revealed religions. They are not rendered null by abrogation—that is the opinion of the ignorant" (III 153.12; Chittick, *Imaginal Worlds*, p. 125).

14. Ibn Arabi, *Bezels of Wisdom*, pp. 137–138.

15. *Meccan Openings* IV 386.17; Chittick, *Imaginal Worlds*, p. 150.

16. Ibid. III 309.30; Chittick, *Imaginal Worlds*, p. 153.

17. Cited in Chittick, *Imaginal Worlds*, p. 176.

18. Meccan Openings IV 76; cited in Stephen Hirtenstein, *The Unlimited Mercifier: The Spiritual Life and Thought of Ibn Arabi* (Oxford: Anqa Publishing, 1999), p. 133.

19. Cited in Michel Chodkiewicz, *Un océan sans rivage: Ibn Arabi, le Livre, et la Loi* (Paris: Seuil, 1992), p. 47, trans. mine.

20. Ibid., pp. 51–52.

21. *Meccan Openings* II 541.23. Chittick, *Imaginal Worlds*, p. 140.

22. Ibid. III 541.1. Chittick, *Imaginal Worlds*, p. 140.

23. See Chodkiewicz, *Un océan sans rivage*, p. 62.

24. See Ibn Arabi, *Bezels of Wisdom*, p. 134.

25. Y. Tzvi Langermann, "Some Astrological Themes in the Thought of Abraham ibn Ezra," in *Rabbi Abraham Ibn Ezra: Studies in the Writings of a Twelfth-Century Jewish Polymath*, ed. Isadore Twersky and Jay M. Harris (Cambridge: Harvard University Press, 1993), pp. 68–70.

26. Lenn E. Goodman, *Ibn Tufayl's Hayy Ibn Yaqzan* (Los Angeles: gee tee bee, 4th ed. 1996).
27. Ibid., p. xii.
28. Ibid., p. 156.
29. Ibid.
30. Ibid., p. 160.
31. Ibid., p. 163.
32. Ibid., p. 164.
33. Averroes uses these particular examples in both the *Incoherence of the Incoherence* and the *Decisive Treatise*. See Majid Fakhry, *Averroes (Ibn Rushd): His Life, Works, and Influence* (Oxford: Oneworld Publications, 2001), p. 19.
34. Averroes, *The Decisive Treatise, Determining What the Connection is Between Religion and Philosophy*, in Ralph Lerner and Muhsin Mahdi, eds., *Medieval Political Philosophy* (Ithaca: Cornell University Press, 1972), p. 169.
35. See Fakhry, *Averroes*, pp. 93–94.
36. As W. Montgomery Watt remarks, Averroes "does not believe that the philosopher should withdraw from active life or eschew popular religion, but that he 'should choose the best religion of his period'; it is assumed that this is 'the one in which he has been brought up'. . . .Because of the importance of religion for the life of the state the philosopher must accept its formulations and explain them. A religion of pure reason Averroes thinks inferior to the revealed religions when philosophically understood. All this shows that he has a full understanding of the place of religion in society and polity, and also in the early training even of the philosopher." W. Montgomery Watt, *Islamic Philosophy and Theology* (Edinburgh: Edinburgh University Press, 1985), p. 118.
37. As Averroes says in his treatise *Exposition of Religious Arguments*: "If the Precious Book [i.e., the Qur'an] is contemplated with all the laws, which are useful both for knowledge and actions conducive to happiness it contains, and then compared with what all other religions and Scriptures contain, they would be found to infinitely surpass them all in this respect." The treatise is translated as Averroes, *Faith and Reason in Islam*, trans. Ibrahim Najjar (Oxford: Oneworld, 2001), p. 103.
38. Cited in Fakhry, *Averroes*, p. 24.
39. Ibid.
40. Ibid., pp. 24–25.
41. The racial distinction that we name "white/black" was named in Arabic "red/black"; that is, the Arabs called themselves "red" people, and they distinguished their skin color from that of the "black" people of sub-Saharan Africa.
42. Averroes, *Faith and Reason*, pp. 103–104.
43. Averroes, *The Decisive Treatise*, p. 170.
44. Ibid., p. 181.
45. Ibid., p. 171.
46. Ibid., p. 179.

47. Ibid., p. 172.

48. Ibid., pp. 171–172: "Unanimity on theoretical matters is never determined with certainty, as it can be on practical matters. . . .So how can it possibly be conceived that a unanimous agreement can have been handed down to us about a single theoretical question, when we know definitely that not a single period has been without scholars who held that there are things in the Law whose true meaning should not be learned by all people? The truth is different in practical matters: everyone holds that the truth about these should be disclosed to all people alike."

49. Ibid., p. 181.

50. Averroes, *Faith and Reason*, p. 76.

51. Averroes, *Decisive Treatise*, p. 183.

52. Averroes, *Faith and Reason*, p. 77.

53. Averroes, *Decisive Treatise*, p. 169; emphasis added.

54. Ibid., p. 185.

55. Thus, Averroes insists that erroneous interpretation will still be rewarded by God: "It seems that those who disagree on the interpretation of these diffi-cult questions earn merit if they are right and will be excused by God if they are in error. . . .This is why the Prophet, peace on him, said, 'If the judge after exerting his mind makes a right decision, he will have a double reward; and if he makes a wrong decision, he will still have a single reward' " (*Decisive Treatise*, p. 175).

56. I have previously argued that Dante's theory of interpretation as suggested in the *Vita Nuova* is in some ways comparable to Averroes's hermeneutics. See my "Dante's Averroistic Hermeneutics (On 'Meaning' in the *Vita Nuova*)," *Dante Studies* 112 (1994), pp. 133–159.

57. *Convivio* 1.1.2–3. Trans. Richard H. Lansing, *Dante's Il Convivio/The Banquet* (New York: Taylor and Francis, 1990).

58. Ibid. 1.1.4; trans. Lansing.

59. Averroes, *Faith and Reason*, p. 76.

60. Ibid., p. 126.

61. Ian Richard Netton, *Muslim Neoplatonists: An Introduction to the Thought of the Brethren of Purity (Ikhwan al-Safa)* (London: RoutledgeCurzon, 2002), pp. ix.

62. *Epistles* III, 501.

63. Cited in Sayyed Hossein Nasr, *An Introduction to Islamic Cosmological Doctrines* (Albany: State University of New York Press, 1993), p. 26.

64. Cited in Nasr, *An Introduction*, p. 32.

65. Ibid., p. 31.

66. See above, introduction, note 79.

67. Cited in Langermann, "Some Astrological Themes," p. 73.

68. *The Case of the Animals versus Man Before the King of the Jinn*, trans. Lenn E. Goodman (Boston: Twayne, 1978), p. 196.

69. Cited in Majid Fakhry, *A History of Islamic Philosophy*, 2nd ed. (New York: Columbia University Press, 1983), p. 166.

70. *The Case of the Animals versus Man*, pp. 193–194.

71. *The Case of the Animals versus Man*, p. 194.

72. Ibid., pp. 194–196.

73. *Aeneid* 6.251–52. Trans. John Dryden; emphasis added.

74. Ibid. 6.851; trans. Dryden.

75. Ibid. 6.86.

76. Ibid. 6.835.

77. The "nobility of blood" is debunked earlier in the *Comedy*, in *Purgatory*'s "Valley of the Princes" episode. The troubadour poet Sordello, the poets of the *dolce stil nuovo*, and Dante himself in the *Convivio* had all rejected the concept of genealogical nobility. I treat this in detail in my essay "Sodomy, Diversity, Cosmopolitanism: Dante and the Limits of the *Polis*" (forthcoming).

78. C.H. Grandgent, cited in Singleton, *The Divine Comedy: Paradiso*, vol. 2 ("Commentary"), p. 261.

79. *Inferno* XVI, pp. 46–48.

80. On the "feminist" aspects of Dante's Beatrice, see Joan Ferrante's pamphlet, *Dante's Beatrice: Priest of an Androgynous God* (Pegasus Press, 1992).

81. Dante's most notable formulation of a cosmopolitanism that wholly contradicts Cacciaguida's xenophobia is this passage from the *De Vulgari Eloquentia*: "For whoever is so beneath contempt in his reasoning as to believe the place of his birth to be the most delightful under the sun attributes the same preeminence as well to his own vernacular, that is, his mother tongue, against all others, and consequently believes that his own native language was the same as Adam's. *I, on the other hand, have the world as my native land* as a fish has the sea; and although I drank from the Arno before I had teeth, and although I have loved Florence so much that I have suffered exile unjustly for my love, I support the shoulders of my judgment on reason rather than on sense impressions. And even if there exists no place in the world more in accord with my delight or with the repose of my senses than Florence, in reading over the volumes of the poets and of other writers in which the world is described totally and in its parts, and in considering within myself the situations of the various places in the world and their arrangements in relation to either pole and to the equator, I have decided and firmly believe that there are many regions as well as cities both more noble and more delightful than Tuscany and Florence where I was born and a citizen, and that there are many nations and peoples who use a language more delightful and useful than the Latins." (*De Vulgari Eloquentia* 1.6.2–3. Trans. Robert S. Haller, *Literary Criticism of Dante Alighieri* [Lincoln; University of Nebrask Press, 1973], trans. Haller, pp. 8–9; emphasis added.)

82. For a good argument that Dante's "crusade" is "aimed against Western structural and individual corruption," see Brenda Deen Schildgen, *Dante and the Orient* (Urbana and Chicago: University of Illinois Press, 2002), chap. 3.

83. According to legend, the Roman Emperor Constantine (288–337 AD), having been cured of leprosy by Pope Sylvester I, in turn gave the papacy temporal authority over the western half of the empire. This entry of the church into the practice of statecraft is, for Dante, history's single most disastrous event.

84. The phrase is from Lerner and Mahdi's preface to their selection from Giles of Rome's treatise in their *Medieval Political Philosophy*, p. 392.
85. John of Paris, *On Kingly and Papal Power*, in Lerner and Mahdi, p. 404.
86. Ibid.
87. *Inf.* XIX, 115–17: "Ah, Constantine, of how much ill was mother,/not your conversion, but that dowry/which the first rich Father took from you!"
88. Lerner and Mahdi, pp. 403–404.
89. The Waldensians or the "Poor," following the teachings of their founder, Peter Waldo (d. ca. 1217 AD), a rich merchant of Lyon who gave up all of his possessions, believed that they were the remnant of the true Apostolic Church, such as it was before the Donation of Constantine—without property and without temporal power.
90. Marsilius of Padua, *Defensor pacis* 2.2.3. Translation from Marsilius of Padua, *The Defender of Peace (The Defensor Pacis)*, trans. Alan Gewirth (New York: Harper & Row, 1967), pp. 103–104; emphasis added.
91. Ibid. 2.2.2; trans. Gewirth, p. 102.
92. Ibid. 2.2.8; pp. 107–108.
93. Ibid. 2.10.2; p. 174.
94. Ibid. 2.10.3; p. 175; emphasis added.
95. On Frederick II's political writings, see Sergio Cristaldi, *Dante di fronte al gioachismo: Dalla "Vita Nova" alla "Monarchia"* (Rome: Salvatore Sciascia, 2000), pp. 235ff.
96. See Cristaldi, *Dante di fronte*, p. 246.
97. Rene Weis, *The Yellow Cross: The Story of the Last Cathars' Rebellion Against the Inquisition 1290–1329* (New York: Vintage Books, 2002), p. xxi.
98. Weis, *Yellow Cross*, p. xxi: "Like Christ they intended to forgive those who persecute them."
99. Forrester Roberts, *The Cathar Eclipse* (Forrester Roberts, 2003).
100. Cited in Weis, *Yellow Cross*, p. xxiv.
101. There is much significance in the fact that Dante sets his journey in 1300, the year proclaimed by Boniface VIII as a "Jubilee," in which the faithful from throughout Christendom were encouraged to make a pilgrimage to Rome, a journey that would be beneficial for the salvation of their souls. In contrast to this, Dante undertakes his own journey, an extra-ecclesiastical journey, not to Rome but directly to God. That is, for Dante the "way" to God does not pass through the Church of Rome. As Baldassare Labanca remarked in 1901, Dante "wanted to place in opposition to the Catholic pilgrimage to Rome the Christian pilgrimage toward God, Who is the only true dispenser of indulgences and grace through the mediation of Christ." Cited in Gregorio Piaia, "Un dibattito su Dante e il Giubileo agli albori del Novecento," in Alessandro Ghisalberti, ed., *Il pensiero filosofico e teologico di Dante Alighieri* (Milan: Vita e Pensiero, 2001), p. 229.
102. For the Church of Rome as the Whore of Babylon, see the references below, note 115.

103. The text of Turmeda's autobiography is from Dwight F. Reynolds, *Interpreting the Self: Autobiography in the Arabic Literary Tradition* (Berkeley: University of California Press, 2001), pp. 196–199; emphasis added.

104. For more on Turmeda, see Lourdes Maria Alvarez, "Anselm Turmeda: The Visionary Humanism of a Muslim Convert and Catalan Prophet," in *The Foreigner in the Middle Ages*, ed. Albrecht Classen (New York: Routledge, 2002), pp. 172–191.

105. Anthony Bonner, *Songs of the Troubadours* (New York: Schocken Books, 1972), p. 199.

106. Charles Camproux, "Présence de Peire Cardenal," in *Annales de l'Institut d'Etudes Occitanes* (1970), pp. 17–18.

107. Peire Cardenal, "In sirventes novel voill comensar," trans. William Paden, *An Introduction to Old Occitan* (New York: Modern Language Association of America, 1998), pp. 551–552; emphasis added.

108. On Peire Cardenal's affinities for the Spiritual Franciscans, see Charles Camproux, "La mentalité 'Spirituelle' chez Peire Cardenal, in *Cahiers de Fanjeaux* 10 (1975).

109. Lerner and Mahdi, *Medieval Political Philosophy*, p. 397.

110. *Unam Sanctam*, http://www.fordham.edu/halsall/source/b8-unam.html; emphasis added.

111. Singleton, *Inferno, Vol. 2:* Commentary, p. 330.

112. See Peter Armour, *The Door of Purgatory: A Study of Multiple Symbolism in Dante's "Purgatorio"* (Oxford: Oxford University Press, 1983).

113. See John A. Scott, *Dante's Political Purgatory* (Philadelphia: University of Pennsylvania Press, 1996), p. 138.

114. See *Monarchy* 3.9; Shaw, pp. 77ff.

115. Marjorie Reeves, *The Influence of Prophecy in the Later Middle Ages: A Study in Joachimism* (Notre Dame: University of Notre Dame Press, 1969), p. 69. For Dante's representation of the Church of Rome as the Whore of Babylon, see *Inf.* XIX, 106–108 and *Purg.* XXXII, 142ff.

116. Cited in Reeves, *The Influence of Prophecy*, p. 217. The passage from which this line comes, the closing stanzas of *Par.* XXVII, is interesting for the light it can shed on the meaning of *Inferno* I's *diritta via* ("straight way"). Beatrice is explaining that the problem with human society is "that on earth there is no one to govern/wherefore the human family thus goes astray [*svïa*]" (lines 140–141). The deviation from the right way (*via*) does not at all mean Dante's alienation from Christianity; and the return to the right way would not be a return to religion but rather the return of government by a secular emperor.

117. Giulio Basetti Sani, *L'Islam et St. François d'Assise: La mission prophétique pour le dialogue* (Paris: Editions Publisud, 1987), pp. 71–72.

118. See Sani, *L'Islam et St. François d'Assise*, p. 96.

119. Sani, *L'Islam et St. François d'Assise*, p. 74.

120. See Sani, *L'Islam et St. François d'Assise*, pp. 107ff.

121. Reeves, *The Influence of Prophecy*, pp. 291–292.

122. David Burr, *The Spiritual Franciscans: From Protest to Persecution in the Century After Saint Francis* (University Park, PA: Pennsylvania State University Press, 2001), p. 76.

123. Burr, *The Spiritual Franciscans*, p. 310.

124. Pier Olivi, *Commentary on Apocalypse*; cited in Burr, *The Spiritual Franciscans*, p. 78.

125. Burr, *The Spiritual Franciscans*, p. 87–88.

126. Reeves, *The Influence of Prophecy*, p. 411.

127. Dominique Urvoy, *Penser L'Islam: Les Présupposés Islamiques de l'Art de Lull* (Paris: J. Vrin, 1980), p. 131.

128. Ibid., p. 132.

129. Ibid., p. 133.

130. Ibid., p. 134.

131. Ibid.

132. Riccold de Monte Croce, *Pérégrination en Terre Sainte et au Proche Orient*, ed. René Kappler (Paris: Honoré Champion, 1997), pp. 158 and 172.

133. Ibid. pp. 172–174.

134. Reeves, *The Influence of Prophecy*, p. 248.

135. Cited in Urvoy, *Penser L'Islam*, p. 121.

136. Reeves, *The Influence of Prophecy*, p. 249.

137. Alexandre Leupin, *La Passion des Idoles 1: Foi et pouvoir dans la Bible et la "Chanson de Roland"* (Paris: L'Harmattan, 2000), p. 125, trans. mine.

138. Guillaume de Lorris and Jean de Meun, *The Romance of the Rose*, trans. Frances Horgan (Oxford: Oxford University Press, 1994), pp. 182–183.

139. See Reeves, *The Influence of Prophecy*, for numerous examples of the Joachite distinction between Peter and John.

140. For references to the calculation of this chronology, see above, part I, note 15.

141. *De vulgari eloquentia* 1.6.4–6. Trans. from *Literary Criticism of Dante Alighieri*, trans. Robert S. Haller (Lincoln: University of Nebraska Press, 1973), p. 9.

142. *De vulgari eloquentia* 1.4.4; trans. Haller, p. 6.

143. As Amilcare Iannucci says in his informative account of the doctrine of Limbo (in *The Dante Encyclopedia*, ed. Richard Lansing [New York: Garland Publishing, Inc., 2000, pp. 565–569), "there is no scholastic thinker who proposes that any adults are to be found in the *limbus patrum* after the Harrowing of Hell." While Iannucci's account provides the materials for an understanding of Dante's revision of Limbo, I strongly disagree with his conclusion that this revision aims to show "the tragic limits of pagan civilization." This is another instance of the insistence on a "tragic Virgil" that I have criticized in part I.

144. Manlio Pastore Stocchi, "A Melancholy Elysium," in *Lectura Dantis: Inferno*, eds. Allen Mandelbaum, Anthony Oldcorn, Charles Ross (Berkley: University of California Press, 1998), p. 55.

145. Oliver Leaman, *An Introduction to Medieval Islamic Philosophy* (Cambridge: Cambridge University Press, 1985), p. 131.

146. For this point and for a significant treatment on the issue of the salvation of virtuous pagans in the *Comedy*, see Mowbray Allen, "Does Dante Hope for Virgil's Salvation?" *MLN* 104 (1989), pp. 193–205.

147. Augustine, *City of God* 18.47. Translation from *City of God*, trans. Henry Bettenson (New York: Penguin Classics, 1984), p. 829.

148. For an excellent treatment of this passage and of Dante's position on the question of the salvation of non-Christians, see Schildgen, *Dante and the Orient*, chap. 4. Schildgen offers a different, but no less useful, perspective on Dante's understanding of salvation in her "Dante's Utopian Political Vision, the Roman Empire, and the Salvation of Pagans," *Annali d'Italianistica* 19 (2001), pp. 51–69. In this article she argues that those pagans whom Dante "saves" all share his optimistic political vision in some manner.

149. Martin Heidegger, "The Word of Nietzsche," in *The Question Concerning Technology and Other Essays*, trans. William Lovitt (New York: Harper & Row, 1977), pp. 63–64.

150. Paul Alexis Ladame, *Dante: Prophète d'un monde uni* (Paris: Jacques Grancher, 1996), p. 14.

151. Reeves, *The Influence of Prophecy*, p. 131.

152. As mentioned above, when Dante encounters Peter in *Paradiso* XXVII (after the exam with Peter, which is three cantos before), he is much altered in both voice and appearance ("his words continued/in a voice so altered from itself/that his looks were not more changed"; *Par.* XXVII, 37–39). This is clearly a "different" Peter. But is it in fact also *another* Peter—the real Peter, as opposed to the imposter "Peter" who examined Dante on faith in *Par.* XXIV? For the suggestion that "Peter" (the examiner) is a figure for Dante's arch-enemy, Boniface VIII, see Ernest L. Fortin, *Dissidence et philosophie au moyen âge: Dante et ses antécédents* (Montreal: Bellarmin, 1980), p. 148ff.

153. Reeves, *The Influence of Prophecy*, pp. 395–396.

WORKS CITED

Abou El Fadl, Khaled. "The Ugly Modern and the Modern Ugly: Reclaiming the Beautiful in Islam." In *Progressive Muslims: On Justice, Gender, and Pluralism*, ed. Omid Safi. Oxford: Oneworld Publications, 2003.

Alexandre du Pont. *Le Roman de Mahomet*. Ed. Yvan G. Lepage. Louvain-Paris: Peeters, 1996.

Alighieri, Dante. *Convivio*. Ed. Piero Cudini. Milan: Aldo Garzanti, 1980.

———. *Dante's Il Convivio/The Banquet*. Trans. Richard H. Lansing. New York: Taylor and Francis, 1990.

———. *The Divine Comedy*. Trans. Charles S. Singleton. Princeton: Princeton University Press, 1973.

———. *Epistle to Cangrande*. In *The Literary Criticism of Dante Alighieri*. Ed. and trans. Robert S. Haller. Lincoln: University of Nebraska Press, 1973.

———. *Monarchy*. Ed. And trans. Prue Shaw. Cambridge: Cambridge University Press, 1996.

———. *Purgatorio*. Trans. Jean Hollander and Robert Hollander. New York: Doubleday, 2003.

———. *De Vulgari Eloquentia*. In *The Literary Criticism of Dante Alighieri*. Ed. and trans. Robert S. Haller. Lincoln: University of Nebraska Press, 1973.

Allen, Mowbray. "Does Dante Hope for Virgil's Salvation?" *MLN* 104 (1989): 193–205.

Alvarez, Lourdes Maria. "Anselm Turmeda: The Visionary Humanism of a Muslim Convert and Catalan Prophet." In *The Foreigner in the Middle Ages*, ed. Albrecht Classen. New York: Routledge, 2002.

Aquinas, Thomas. *Summa Theologica*. Trans. the Fathers of the English Dominican Province. New York: Benzinger Brothers, 1947.

Aristotle. *The Complete Works of Aristotle*. Ed. Jonathan Barnes. Princeton: Princeton University Press, 1984.

Armour, Peter. *The Door of Purgatory: A Study of Multiple Symbolism in Dante's "Purgatorio."* Oxford: Oxford University Press, 1983.

Arnaldez, Roger. *Averroès, un rationaliste en Islam*. Paris: Editions Balland, 1998.

Aroux, Eugène. *Dante: hérétique, révolutionnaire et socialiste*. Paris: Jules Renouard, 1854.

Ascoli, Albert Russell. "Epistle to Cangrande." In *The Dante Encyclopedia*, ed. Richard Lansing. New York: Garland Publishing, Inc., 2000.

Augustine. *City of God*. Trans. Henry Bettenson. New York: Penguin Classics, 1984.

———. *On Christian Doctrine*. Trans. D.W. Robertson. Indianapolis: Bobbs-Merrill, 1958.

Avempace, *The Regime of the Solitary*. In *Medieval Political Philosophy*, ed. Ralph Lerner and Muhsin Mahdi. Ithaca: Cornell University Press, 1972.

Averroes. *The Decisive Treatise, Determining What the Connection is Between Religion and Philosophy*. Trans. George F. Hourani. In *Medieval Political Philosophy*, ed. Ralph Lerner and Muhsin Mahdi. Ithaca: Cornell University Press, 1972.

———. *The Epistle on the Possibility of Conjunction with the Active Intellect by Ibn Rushd with the Commentary of Moses Narboni*. Ed. Kalman P. Bland. New York: The Jewish Theological Seminary of America, 1982.

———. *Faith and Reason in Islam*. Trans. Ibrahim Najjar. Oxford: Oneworld, 2001.

Bacon, Roger. *Opus Maius*. In *Medieval Political Philosophy*, ed. Ralph Lerner and Muhsin Mahdi. Ithaca: Cornell University Press, 1972.

Baffioni, Carmela. "Aspetti delle cosmologie islamiche in Dante." In *Il pensiero filosofico e teologico di Dante Alighieri*, ed. Alessandro Ghisalberti. Milan: Vita e Pensiero, 2001.

Baranski, Zygmunt G. *Dante e i segni: Saggi per una storia intellettuale di Dante Alighieri*. Naples: Liguori Editore, 2000.

Barolini, Teodolinda. "Casella's Song." In *Modern Critical Interpretations: Dante's 'Divine Comedy,'* ed. Harold Bloom. New York: Chelsea House, 1987.

———. *The Undivine Comedy: Detheologizing Dante*. Princeton: Princeton University Press, 1992.

———. "Ulysses." In *The Dante Encyclopedia*, ed. Richard Lansing. New York: Garland Publishing, Inc., 2000.

Berman, Lawrence V. "Maimonides the Disciple of Alfarabi." *Israel Oriental Studies* 4 (1974): 154–178.

Bonner, Anthony. *Songs of the Troubadours*. New York: Schocken Books, 1972.

Bori, Pier Cesare. *L'interpretazione infinita: l'ermeneutica cristiana antica e le sue trasformazioni*. Bologna: Il Mulino, 1987.

Boullata, Issa J. "Fa-stabiqu 'l-khayrat: A Qur'anic Principle of Interfaith Relations." In *Christian–Muslim Encounters*, ed. Yvonne Y Haddad and Wadi Z. Haddad. Gainesville: University Press of Florida, 1995.

Brenet, Jean-Baptiste. *Transferts du sujet: La noétique d'Averroès selon Jean de Jandun*. Paris: J. Vrin, 2003.

Bruni, Francesco. *La città divisa: Le parti e il bene comune da Dante a Guicciardini*. Bologna: Mulino, 2003.

Burr, David. *The Spiritual Franciscans: From Protest to Persecution in the Century After Saint Francis*. University Park, PA: The Pennsylvania State University, 2001.

Camproux, Charles. "La mentalité 'Spirituelle' chez Pier Cardenal." *Cahiers de Fanjeaux* 10 (1975).

———. "Présence de Peire Cardenal." In *Annales de l'Institut d'Etudes Occitanes* 1970.

Cantor, Paul A. "The Uncanonical Dante: *The Divine Comedy* and Islamic Philosophy." *Philosophy and Literature* 20.1 (1996): 138–153.

Cassell, Anthony K. "Monarchy." In *The Dante Encyclopedia*, ed. Richard Lansing. New York: Garland Publishing, Inc., 2000.

Chittick, William C. *Imaginal Worlds: Ibn al-Arabi and the Problem of Religious Diversity*. Albany: SUNY Press, 1994.

Chodkiewicz, Michel. *Un océan sans rivage: Ibn Arabi, le Livre, et la Loi*. Paris: Seuil, 1992.

Cornish, Alison. *Reading Dante's Stars*. New Haven: Yale University Press, 2000.

Cristaldi, Sergio. *Dante di fronte al gioachismo: Dalla "Vita Nova" alla "Monarchia"*. Rome: Salvatore Sciascia, 2000.

Croce, Benedetto. *The Poetry of Dante*. Trans. Douglas Ainslie. Mamaroneck, NY: Paul P. Appel, 1971.

d'Ancona, Alessandro. "La leggenda di Maometto in Occidente." *Studi di critica e storia letteraria* 2 (1912): 165–308.

Davis, Charles T. *Dante's Italy and Other Essays*. Philadelphia: University of Pennsylvania Press, 1984.

Dotti, Ugo. *La Divina Commedia e la città dell'uomo*. Rome: Donzelli, 1998.

———. *Pétrarque*. Paris: Editions Fayard, 1991.

Dupont, Christian. "Collecting Dante in America: Lessons from Library History." *Access* 81 (Fall 2002).

Fakhry, Majid. *Averroes (Ibn Rushd): His Life, Works, and Influence*. Oxford: Oneworld Publications, 2001.

———. *A History of Islamic Philosophy*, 2nd ed. New York: Columbia University Press, 1983.

Farabi, al-. *Al-Farabi on the Perfect State*. Trans. Richard Walzer. Oxford: Oxford University Press, 1985.

———. *The Attainment of Happiness*. Trans. Muhsin Mahdi. In *Medieval Political Philosophy*, ed. Ralph Lerner and Muhsin Mahdi. Ithaca: Cornell University Press, 1972.

———. *The Political Regime*. Trans. Fauzi M. Najjar. In *Medieval Political Philosophy*, ed. Ralph Lerner and Muhsin Mahdi. Ithaca: Cornell University Press, 1972.

———. *Alfarabi, The Political Writings: "Selected Aphorisms" and Other Texts*. Trans. Charles E. Butterworth. Ithaca: Cornell University Press, 2001.

Ferrante, Joan. *Dante's Beatrice: Priest of an Androgynous God* (Pegasus Press, 1992).

———. *The Political Vision of the "Divine Comedy"*. Princeton: Princeton University Press, 1984.

Ferrucci, Franco. *Le due mani di Dio: Il cristianesimo e Dante*. Rome: Fazi, 1999.

Fortin, Ernest L. *Dissidence et philosophie au moyen âge: Dante et ses antécédents*. Montreal: Bellarmin, 1980.

———. *Dissent and Philosophy in the Middle Ages: Dante and His Precursors*. Lanham, MD: Rowman and Littlefield, 2002.

Fox, Marvin. *Interpreting Maimonides*. Chicago: University of Chicago Press, 1990.

Franke, William. *Dante's Interpretive Journey*. Chicago: University of Chicago Press, 1996.

Freccero, John. *Dante: The Poetics of Conversion*. Cambridge, Mass.: Harvard University Press, 1986.

Galston, Miriam. *Politics and Excellence: The Political Philosophy of Alfarabi*. Princeton: Princeton University Press, 1990.

Ghazali, al-. *Deliverance from Error*. In *Philosophy in the Middle Ages*, ed. Arthur Hyman and James J. Walsh. Indianapolis: Hackett Publishing Co., 1973.

Gilson, Etienne. *Dante the Philosopher*. New York: Sheed & Ward, 1949.

Girardi, Enzo Noè. "Al centro del Purgatorio: il tema del libero arbitrio." In *Il pensiero filosofico e teologico di Dante Alighieri*, ed. Alessandro Ghisalberti. Milan: Vita e Pensiero, 2001.

Guillaume de Lorris and Jean de Meun. *The Romance of the Rose*. Trans. Frances Horgan. Oxford: Oxford University Press, 1994.

Hazelton, Richard, "The Christianization of 'Cato': The *Disticha Catonis* in the Light of Late Medieval Commentaries." *Medieval Studies* 19 (1957): 157–173.

Heidegger, Martin. *The Question Concerning Technology and Other Essays*. Trans. William Lovitt. New York: Harper & Row, 1977.

Hirtenstein, Stephen. *The Unlimited Mercifier: The Spiritual Life and Thought of Ibn Arabi*. Oxford: Anqa Publishing, 1999.

Hollander, Robert. "Cato's Rebuke and Dante's *scoglio*." *Italica* 52 (1975): 348–363.

———. "*Purgatorio* II: The New Song and the Old." *Lectura Dantis* 6 (1990): 28–45.

Holmes, George. "*Monarchia* and Dante's Attitude to the Popes." In *Dante and Governance*, ed. John Woodhouse. Oxford: Oxford University Press, 1997.

Hussain, Amir. "Muslims, Pluralism, and Interfaith Dialogue." In *Progressive Muslims: On Justice, Gender, and Pluralism*, ed. Omid Safi. Oxford: Oneworld Publications, 2003.

Iannucci, Amilcare. "Casella's Song and Tuning of the Soul." *Thought: A Review of Culture and Ideas* 65 (1990): 27–46.

———. "Limbo." In *The Dante Encyclopedia*, ed. Richard Lansing. New York: Garland Publishing, Inc., 2000.

———. "Philosophy." In *The Dante Encyclopedia*, ed. Richard Lansing. New York: Garland Publishing, Inc., 2000.

Ibn Arabi. *The Bezels of Wisdom*. Trans. R.W.J. Austin. Mahwah, NJ: Paulist Press, 1980.

Ibn Tufayl. *Ibn Tufayl's Hayy Ibn Yaqzan*. Trans. Lenn E. Goodman. Los Angeles: gee tee bee, 1996.

Ikhwan al-Safa. *The Case of the Animals versus Man Before the King of the Jinn*. Trans. Lenn E. Goodman. Boston: Twayne, 1978.

John of Paris. *On Kingly and Papal Power*. In *Medieval Political Philosophy*, ed. Ralph Lerner and Muhsin Mahdi. Ithaca: Cornell University Press, 1972.

Kantorowicz, Ernst H. *The King's Two Bodies: A Study in Mediaeval Political Theology*. Princeton: Princeton University Press, 1957.

Kempshall, M.S. *The Common Good in Late Medieval Political Thought*. New York: Oxford University Press, 1999.

Ladame, Paul Alexis. *Dante: Prophète d'un monde uni*. Paris: Jacques Grancher, 1996.

Langermann, Y. Tzvi. "Some Astrological Themes in the Thought of Abraham ibn Ezra." In *Rabbi Abraham Ibn Ezra: Studies in the Writings of a Twelfth-Century*

Jewish Polymath, ed. Isadore Twersky and Jay M. Harris. Cambridge: Harvard University Press, 1993.

Lanza, Adriano. *Dante all'inferno*. Rome: Tre Editori, 1999.

Leaman, Oliver. *An Introduction to Medieval Islamic Philosophy*. Cambridge: Cambridge University Press, 1985.

Leupin, Alexandre. *La Passion des Idoles 1: Foi et pouvoir dans la Bible et la "Chanson de Roland."* Paris: L'Harmattan, 2000.

Levinas, Emmanuel. "Revelation in the Jewish Tradition." In *The Levinas Reader*, ed. Seán Hand. Oxford: Blackwell Publishers, 1989.

Lucan. *The Civil War*. Trans. J.D.Duff. Cambridge, Mass.: Harvard University Press, 1928.

Lucchesi, Valerio. "Politics and Theology in *Inferno* X." In *Dante and Governance*, ed. John Woodhouse. Oxford: Oxford University Press, 1997.

Luquet-Juillet, Jacqueline. *Occitanie Terre de fatalité*, vol. 3: "Troubadours et Spiritualité." Paris: Editions Dervy, 2000.

Maimonides, Moses. *The Guide of the Perplexed*. Ed. and trans. Shlomo Pines. Chicago: University of Chicago Press, 1963.

Manselli, Raoul. "L'idéal du spirituel selon Pierre Jean-Olivi." *Cahiers de Fanjeaux* 10 (1975): 99–126.

Marsilius of Padua. *The Defender of Peace (The Defensor Pacis)*. Trans. Alan Gewirth. New York: Harper & Row, 1967.

Martines, Lauro. *Power and Imagination: City-States in Renaissance Italy*. New York: Alfred A. Knopf, 1979.

Martinez, Ronald L. "Cato of Utica." In *The Dante Encyclopedia*, ed. Richard Lansing. New York: Garland Publishing, Inc., 2000.

Mirsky, Mark Jay. *Dante, Eros, & Kabbalah*. Syracuse, NY: Syracuse University Press, 2003.

Nardi, Bruno. *Dal "Convivio" alla "Commedia" (Sei saggi danteschi)*. Rome: Istituto Storico Italiano per il Medio Evo, 1960.

———. *Saggi di filosofia dantesca*. Milan: Società Editrice Dante Alighieri, 1930.

Nasr, Seyyed Hossein. *An Introduction to Islamic Cosmological Doctrines*. Albany: SUNY Press, 1993.

Nelson, Daniel Mark. *The Priority of Prudence: Virtue and Natural Law in Thomas Aquinas and the Implications for Modern Ethics*. University Park, PA: Pennsylvania State University Press, 1992.

Netton, Ian Richard. *Muslim Neoplatonists: An Introduction to the Thought of the Brethren of Purity (Ikhwan al-Safa)*. London: RoutledgeCurzon, 2002.

Paden, William. *An Introduction to Old Occitan*. New York: Modern Language Association of America, 1998.

Pagels, Elaine. *Adam, Eve, and the Serpent*. New York: Random House, 1988.

Palacios, Miguel Asín. *La escatología musulmana en la Divina Comedia*, 2nd ed. Madrid-Granada: Las Escuelas de Estudios Árabes de Madrid Y Granada, 1943.

Petrarca, Francesco. *Petrarch's Lyric Poems: The Rime sparse and Other Lyrics*. Ed. and trans. Robert M. Durling. Cambridge, Mass.: Harvard University Press, 1976.

———. *Le senili*. Ed. Guido Martellotti. Torino: Einaudi, 1976.

Piaia, Gregorio. "Un dibattito su Dante e il Giubileo agli albori del Novecento." In *Il pensiero filosofico e teologico di Dante Alighieri*, ed. Alessandro Ghisalberti. Milan: Vita e Pensiero, 2001.

Pietrobono, Luigi. *Il poema sacro: saggio d'una interpretazione generale della Divina Commedia*. Bologna: Zanichelli, 1915.

Pines, Shlomo. "Dieu et l'être selon Maïmonide: Exégèse d'Exode 3,14 et doctrine connexe." In *Celui qui est: interprétations juives et chrétiennes d'Exode 3,14*, ed. Alain de Libera et Emilie Zum Brunn. Paris: Editions du Cerf, 1986.

Piromalli, Antonio. *Gioacchino da Fiore e Dante*. Soveria Manelli: Rubbettino, 1984.

Reeves, Marjorie. *The Influence of Prophecy in the Later Middle Ages: A Study in Joachimism*. Notre Dame: University of Notre Dame Press, 1969.

Reynolds, Dwight F. *Interpreting the Self: Autobiography in the Arabic Literary Tradition*. Berkeley: University of California Press, 2001.

Riccoldo da Monte Croce. *Pérégrination en Terre Sainte et au Proche Orient*. Ed. René Kappler. Paris: Honoré Champion, 1997.

Roberts, Forrester. *The Cathar Eclipse*. Forrester Roberts, 2003.

Sacerdoti, Gilberto. *Sacrificio e sovranità: Teologia e politica nell'Europa di Shakespeare e Bruno*. Torino: Einaudi, 2002.

Sani, Giulio Basetti. *L'Islam et St. François d'Assise: La mission prophétique pour le dialogue*. Paris: Editions Publisud, 1987.

Schildgen, Brenda Deen. *Dante and the Orient*. Urbana and Chicago: University of Illinois Press, 2002.

———. "Dante's Utopian Political Vision, the Roman Empire, and the Salvation of Pagans." *Annali d'Italianistica* 19 (2001): 51–69.

Scott, John A. *Dante's Political Purgatory*. Philadelphia: University of Pennsylvania Press, 1996.

———. "Henry VII of Luxembourg." In *The Dante Encyclopedia*, ed. Richard Lansing. New York: Garland Publishing, Inc., 2000.

Shah, Idries, ed. *The Way of the Sufi*. New York: Penguin, 1974.

Sheehan, Thomas. *The First Coming: How the Kingdom of God Became Christianity*. New York: Random House, 1986.

Singleton, Charles S. "The Poet's Number at the Center." *Modern Language Notes* 80 (1965): 1–10.

Soresina, Maria. *Le segrete cose: Dante tra induismo ed eresie medievali*. Bergamo: Moretti Honegger, 2002.

Stocchi, Manlio Pastore. "A Melancholy Elysium." In *Lectura Dantis: Inferno*, ed. Allen Mandelbaum, Anthony Oldcorn, and Charles Ross. Berkley: University of California Press, 1998.

Stone, Gregory B. "Dante's Averroistic Hermeneutics (On 'Meaning' in the *Vita Nuova*)." *Dante Studies* 112 (1994): 133–159.

———. *The Death of the Troubadour: The Late Medieval Resistance to the Renaissance*. Philadelphia: University of Pennsylvania Press, 1994.

Stroumsa, Sarah. *Freethinkers of Medieval Islam: Ibn al-Rawandi, Abu Bakr al-Razi, and Their Impact on Islamic Thought*. Leiden: Brill, 1999.

Tempier, Etienne. "Condemnation of 219 Propositions." In *Medieval Political Philosophy*, ed. Ralph Lerner and Muhsin Mahdi. Ithaca: Cornell University Press, 1972.

Tirosh-Samuelson, Hava. "Introduction, Judaism and the Natural World." In *Judaism and Ecology: Created World and Revealed Word*, ed. Hava Tirosh-Samuelson. Cambridge, Mass.: Harvard University Press, 2002.

Trinkaus, Charles. *The Poet as Philosopher: Petrarch and the Formation of Renaissance Consciousness*. New Haven: Yale University Press, 1979.

Urvoy, Dominique. *Penser L'Islam: Les Présupposés Islamiques de l'Art de Lull*. Paris: J. Vrin, 1980.

Vanderspoel, John. "The Background to Augustine's Denial of Religious Plurality." In *Grace, Politics, and Desire: Essays on Augustine*. Ed. H.A. Meynell. Alberta: University of Calgary Press, 1990.

Watt, W. Montgomery. *Islamic Philosophy and Theology*. Edinburgh: Edinburgh University Press, 1985.

Weiland, Georg. "Happiness: the perfection of man." In *The Cambridge History of Later Medieval Philosophy*, ed. Norman Kretzmann, Anthony Kenny, Jan Pinborg. Cambridge: Cambridge University Press, 1982.

Weis, Rene. *The Yellow Cross: The Story of the Last Cathars' Rebellion Against the Inquisition 1290–1329*. New York: Vintage Books, 2002.

INDEX

PQ 4394 .S76 2006

Stone, Gregory B., 1961-

Dante's pluralism and the
 Islamic philosophy of

GAYLORD S